HUNG LIU

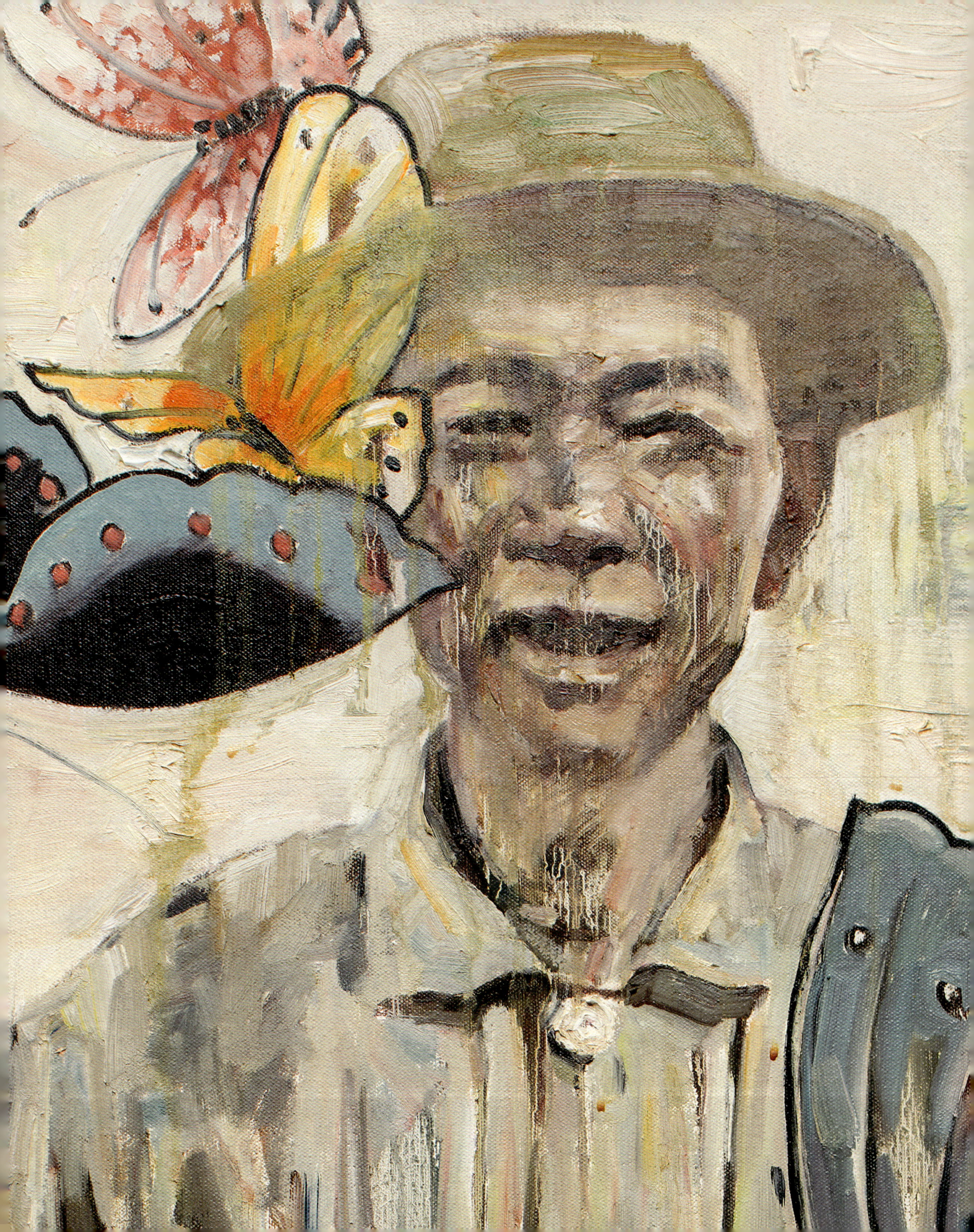

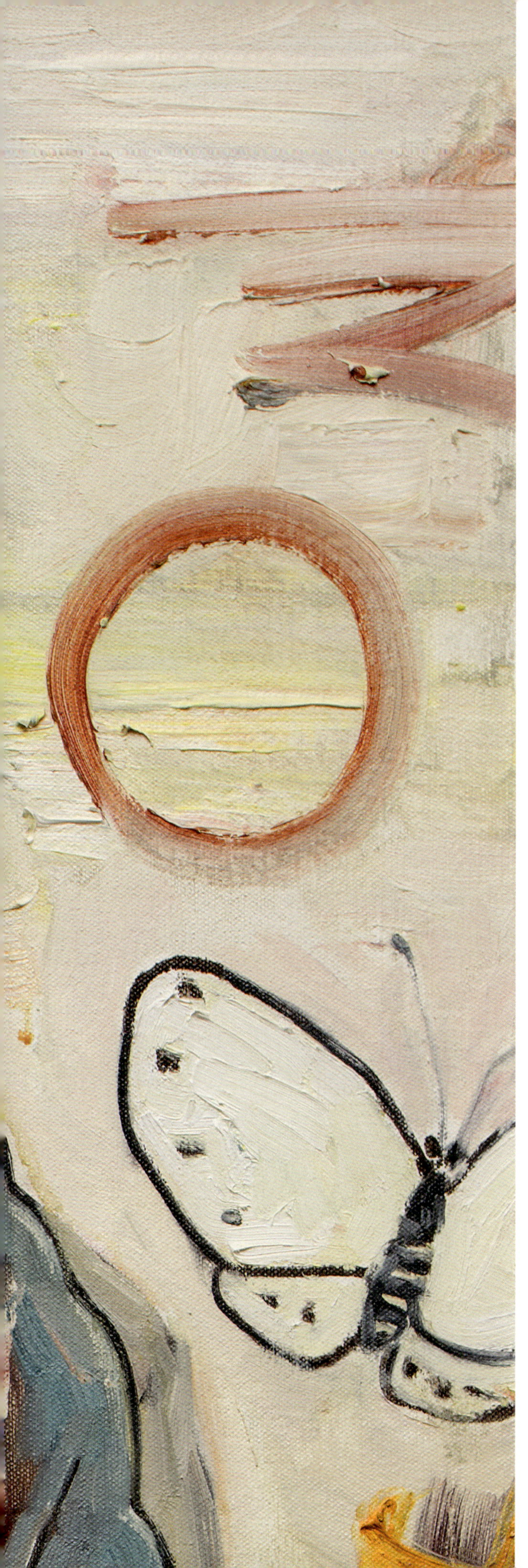

HUNG LIU

PORTRAITS OF PROMISED LANDS

Dorothy Moss

With Nancy Lim, Lucy R. Lippard,
Elizabeth Partridge, and Philip Tinari

National Portrait Gallery,
Smithsonian Institution, Washington, D.C.
in association with
Yale University Press, New Haven and London

Published to accompany the exhibition *Hung Liu: Portraits of Promised Lands* at the National Portrait Gallery, Smithsonian Institution, Washington, D.C. (August 27, 2021–May 29, 2022).

National
Portrait
Gallery

Smithsonian

The Plates sections of this volume represent the exhibition checklist as of February 2021.

yalebooks.com/art

Designed by Rita Jules, Miko McGinty Inc.
Cover designed by Rita Jules, Miko McGinty Inc.
Set in Atlas Grotesk and FS Neruda type by Tina Henderson
Printed in Italy by Verona Libri

Library of Congress Control Number: 2020945366
ISBN 978-0-300-25744-1

A catalogue record for this book is available from the British Library.

This paper meets the requirements of ANSI/NISO Z 39.48-1992 (Permanence of Paper)
10 9 8 7 6 5 4 3 2 1

Cover illustrations: (front) *Strange Fruit: Comfort Women* (detail of cat. 30); (back) *Cotton Picker* (detail of cat. 46)

Frontispiece: *Chinese in Idaho, Portrait IV* (detail of cat. 42)

Page vi: *Chinese in Idaho, Portrait II* (detail of cat. 41); 4–5: *Father's Day* (detail of cat. 22); 24–25: Hung Liu painting in the countryside, c. 1972–75 (detail); 70–71: *Mission Girls 20* (detail of cat. 39); 88–89: *Cotton Picker* (detail of cat. 46); 108–9: *Avant-Garde* (detail of cat. 20); 170–71: *Mission Girls 14* (detail of cat. 36); 206: *Madonna* (detail of cat. 26)

CONTENTS

Donors — 1

Director's Foreword — 2
  Kim Sajet

Interface: Hung Liu's Family Portraits and Their Afterlives — 5
  Dorothy Moss

Picturing the Cultural Revolution: Hung Liu's Early Work — 25
  Nancy Lim

Plates: Part I — 37

Hung Liu: China Trade — 71
  Lucy R. Lippard

Deeply Familiar: Hung Liu and Dorothea Lange — 89
  Elizabeth Partridge

Hung Liu: Passer-by — 109
  Philip Tinari

Plates: Part II — 123

Artists' Reflections — 171
  Enrique Chagoya
  Judy Chicago
  Mel Chin
  Yu Hong
  Martin Mull
  Amy Sherald
  Stephanie Syjuco
  Lava Thomas
  Carrie Mae Weems
  Liu Xiaodong

Chronology — 183
  Jeff Kelley

Selected References — 207
Acknowledgments — 210
Index — 212
Illustration Credits — 218

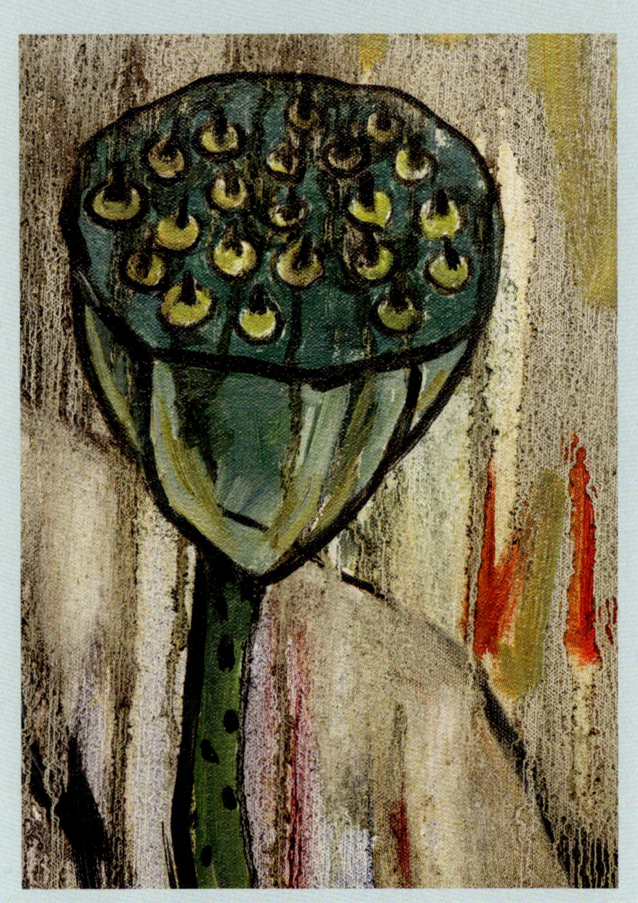

The story of America as a destination for the homeless and hungry of the world is not only a myth. It is a story of desperation, of sadness, of uncertainty, of leaving your home. It is also a story of courage, of sacrifice, of determination, and—more than anything—of hope.

—Hung Liu, Women's March speech, 2017

DONORS

Hung Liu: Portraits of Promised Lands has been made possible through the generous support of the following donors:

Anonymous
Fred M. Levin, the Shenson Foundation, in memory of
     Nancy Livingston Levin and Ben and A. Jess Shenson
E. Rhodes and Leona B. Carpenter Foundation
Haynes and Boone Foundation, Purvi and Bill Albers,
     Susan and David McCombs
Roselyne Chroman Swig
Frances Stevenson Tyler
Covington & Burling
Lorrie and Richard Greene
Koret Foundation
Rena Bransten Gallery
Turner Carroll Gallery, Santa Fe, NM
Nancy Hoffman Gallery
Mr. Charles Ziegler and Ms. Conan Putnam
Mr. Walter Maciel

This project received Federal support from the Asian Pacific American Initiatives Pool, administered by the Smithsonian Asian Pacific American Center, and support from the Smithsonian American Women's History Initiative. Additional support was provided by the American Portrait Gala endowment.

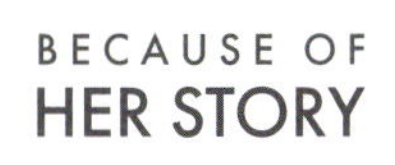

Smithsonian

http://womenshistory.si.edu/donors

DIRECTOR'S FOREWORD

As we have seen at length, [the] past was real, but it is lost or at least displaced, only to be reinstated as the referent of language, the relic or trace of the real. —Linda Hutcheon

Portraiture is powerful. It can also be dangerous. Unlike spoken words and written texts, its language is universal, crossing cultures and ideologies. Totalitarian regimes know this. It's why there is an easily identifiable genre of "supreme leader" portraiture that is always deployed first during any regime change. It is also why families like Hung Liu's hid or destroyed their photographic past in order to survive. As historians know all too well, so much of recorded history is the result of cobbling together the fragments of what is left behind—that which has been saved by design, chance, or accident. The past, as the theorist Linda Hutcheon notes, is both a prize for those whose histories are saved and a shadow of those lost and displaced.

Hung Liu, as Dorothy Moss asserts in her essay, is an artist who has made it her life's work to ensure not only that the memories of people are kept but also that they are treated as subjects—people who don't just warrant our attention but *claim* it. Based upon photographs that have an inherent veracity, Liu's sitters convey a strong sense of agency; they are neither emotionally distant nor clichés.

Lucy R. Lippard observes that the people Liu chooses to represent are individuals who have stood their ground in the face of adversity. In many ways, Liu's portraits can be compared with those made by the German printer and sculptor Käthe Kollwitz at the turn of the twentieth century. Kollwitz's works were often made in black and white and may at first seem to have little in common with Liu's paintings, but both artists present defiant laborers, people who stand as a testament to the resiliency of the human spirit. As the scholar Linda Nochlin notes in her final book, *Misère,* Kollwitz's *portraits* "as a whole constituted powerful, and at the same time, aesthetically sophisticated calls to action in the contemporary public of [her] day."

The National Portrait Gallery is proud to have organized this exhibition. Now is a time for cultural organizations to join artists in taking a stand, not just against a history of racism and discrimination of migrant communities but also in relation to *how* we think about and record history. And we must always be cognizant of whom we look to for inspiration. Now is the time for the portraits of those who have held economic and political power in the past to face a reckoning with those who have worked—and continue to work—to create a more equitable and inclusive future. Now is also the time to support artists who serve as harbingers of a new future where the power of portraiture is still dangerous, but in a good way.

I would like to take this moment to thank Hung Liu for her bravery, honesty, and generosity in allowing us to show her work, and Dorothy Moss, the National Portrait Gallery's curator of painting and sculpture, for conceiving and executing *Hung Liu: Portraits of Promised Lands* with such dedication and care. I also extend thanks to Jeff Kelley, Nancy Hoffman, Rena Bransten, and Tonya Turner Carroll for their insights and support.

To the Smithsonian American Women's History Initiative, and the Smithsonian Asian Pacific American Center for helping to fund the exhibition, we are so appreciative. Similarly, deepest appreciation is extended to an anonymous donor; Fred M. Levin, the Shenson Foundation, in memory of Nancy Livingston Levin and Ben and A. Jess Shenson; and the many friends and supporters who helped make this exhibition possible.

Kim Sajet
Director, National Portrait Gallery

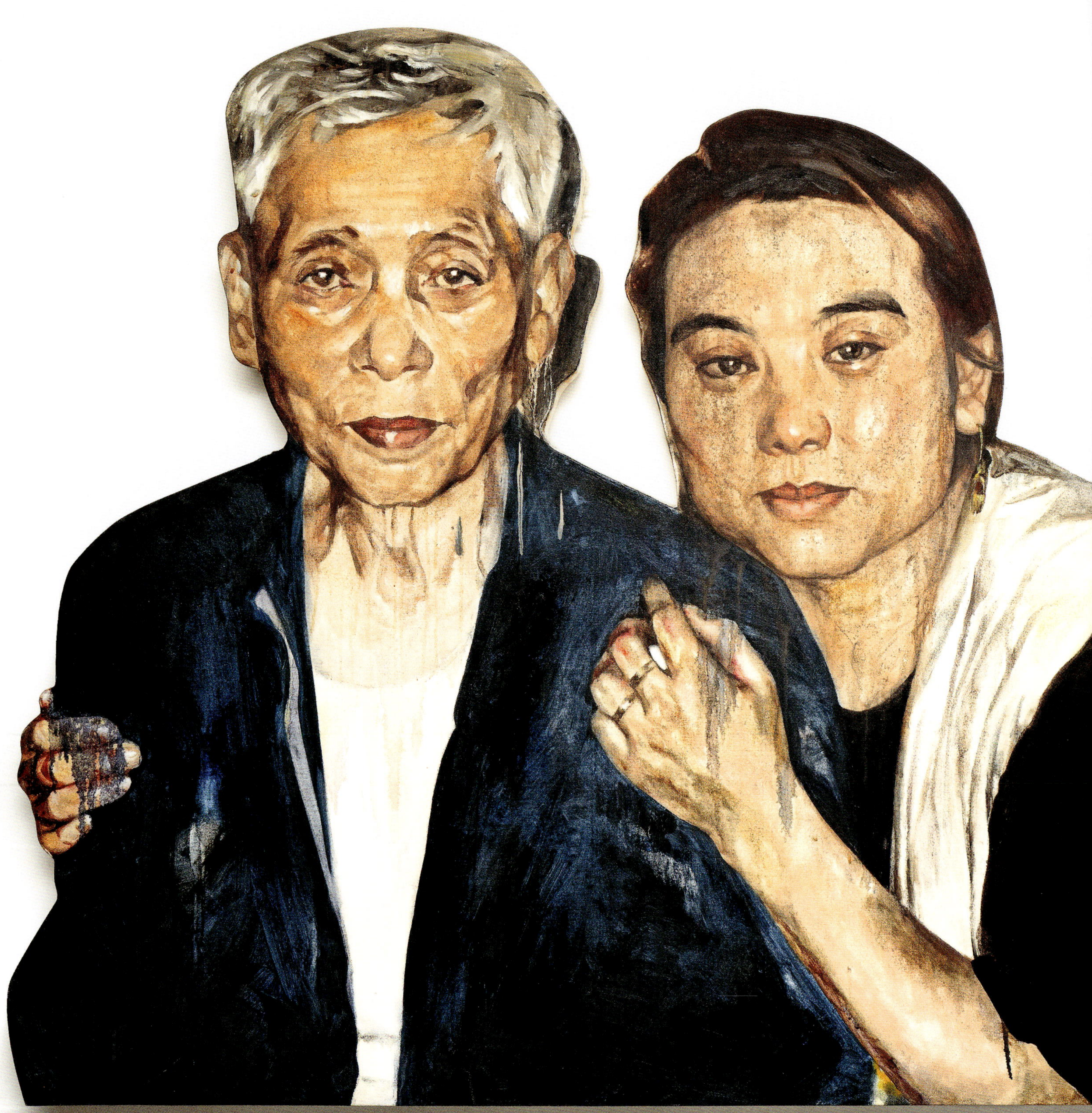

DOROTHY MOSS

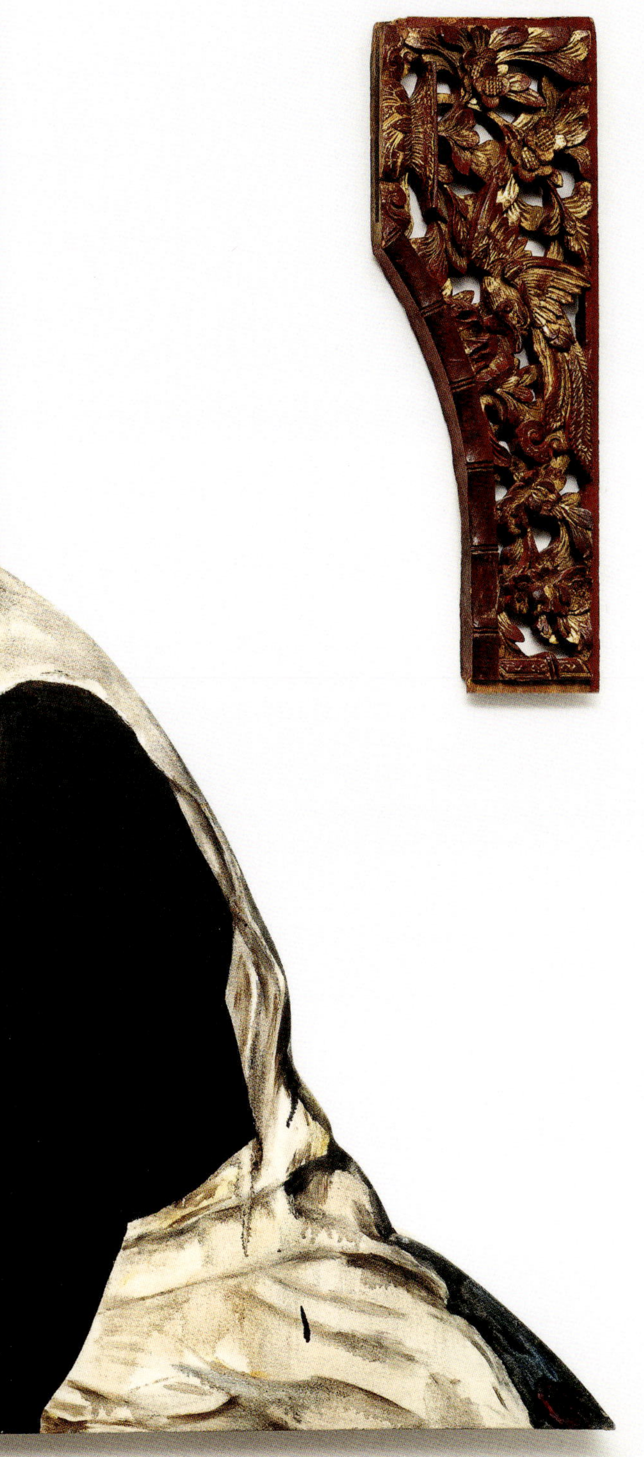

INTERFACE

Hung Liu's Family Portraits and Their Afterlives

Things of the spirit stay with us much longer than things of the flesh. —Hung Liu

My mother—I suppose she was more Westernized—felt I should have my photograph taken every year as a memento. . . . And it's because of this connection that there's always been this special link between me and photographs. It's linked to my family history. —Hung Liu

In the late 1960s, Hung Liu (born 1948) sought to protect her family by setting fire to most of the photographs of her youth and burning her diaries. She was not alone. During the Cultural Revolution (1966–76), many people in China destroyed their personal records out of fear. Liu's family, among countless others, felt compelled to erase their past so as not to leave a trace of their earlier, more privileged lives. "My mother burned a lot of family photographs because she was married to an officer, and photographs of my grandparents didn't look like we were working class," Liu recalled. Because Liu's family was educated and her mother and her mother's father were teachers, they were seen as a threat to the government. Simply having photographic portraits made in a studio setting signaled one's status: "Peasants could not afford food; how could they have photographs? There was a picture of Grandfather at his death, but it was taken by the Red Guards. . . . You couldn't keep anything personal. It was dangerous. That is why I am so interested in old photographs. They are rare. It is not like today."[1]

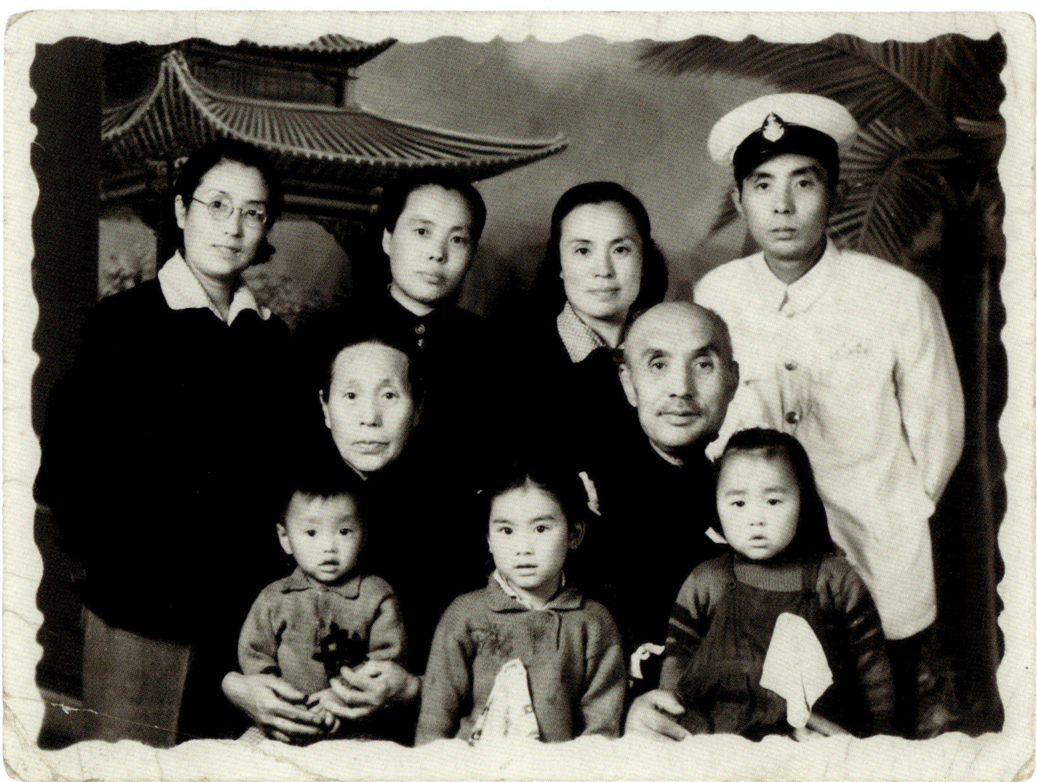

Fig. 1. Hung Liu with family, 1953.

Hung Liu's maternal grandfather, Liu Weihua, was a scholar of the monasteries of Qianshan until he died in 1962, four years before the start of the Cultural Revolution. When Red Guards broke into the family's home in Changchun, they searched for anything that would be considered anti-proletarian.[2] Even family photographs featuring a loved one who had passed away could be used against someone—to criticize, even to arrest, if necessary. The few family photographs that Liu carries with her today exist because her mother, Liu Zongguang, had the foresight to remove them from the family albums, which were subsequently burned (figs. 1, 2).

Liu remembers her mother's concerted efforts to document the family in annual trips to a photographer's studio. This ritual, begun in 1949, started after the Communists had taken over China, and shortly after Liu's father, Xia Peng, had been sent to prison. Liu was only an infant when her father was detained for having served as a captain in the Kuomintang (Nationalist Army) and would not see him again for nearly fifty years. The studio portraits are therefore piercing reminders of his absence, yet they also signify the journey of a close, resilient, and proud family. Liu protects them among her most cherished possessions, never neglecting the memories of her loved ones. Their images are embedded in her life's work.

The family photographs that Liu keeps with her have survived through the years and have consistently served as the foundation for her approach to portraiture. The images predominantly feature women: the artist's mother, Liu Zongguang, a middle-school teacher;

  Dorothy Moss

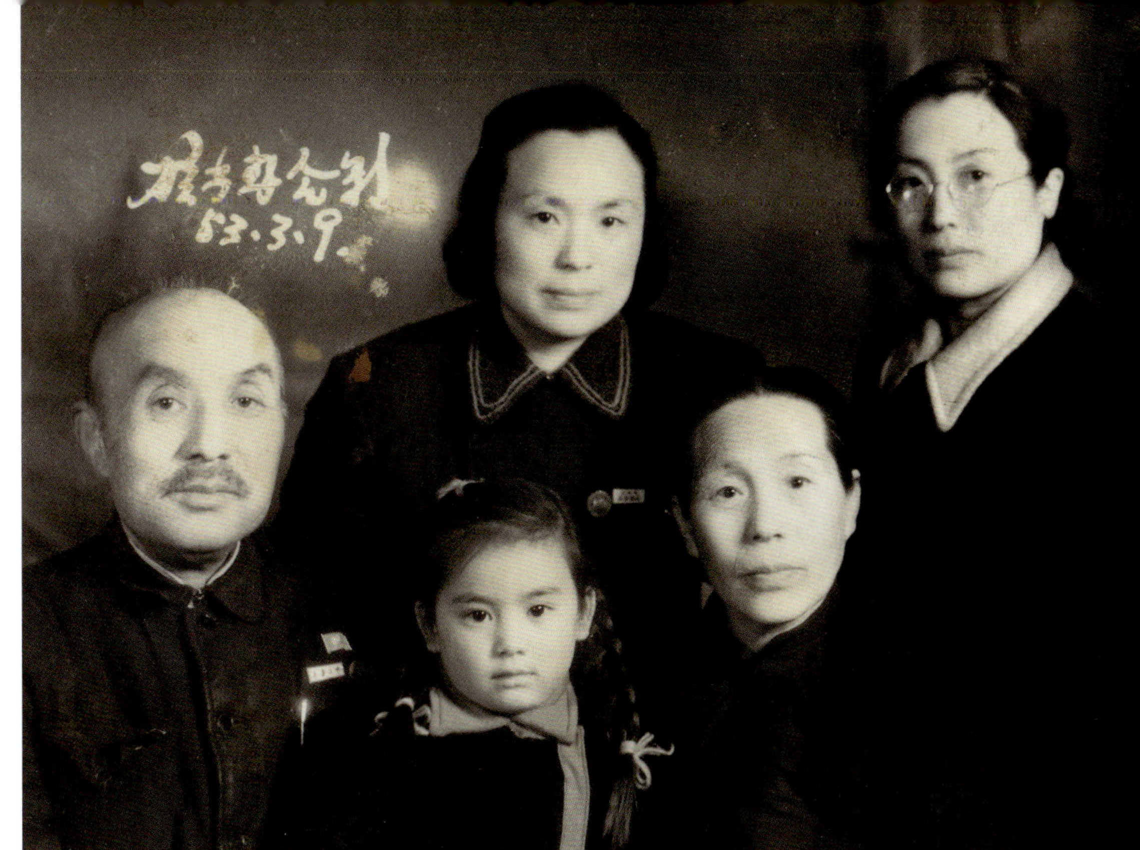

Fig. 2. Clockwise from left: Liu's grandfather Liu Weihua; her mother, Liu Zongguang; her aunt Liu Zongyu; her grandmother Wang Jushou; and young Liu (five years old), 1953.

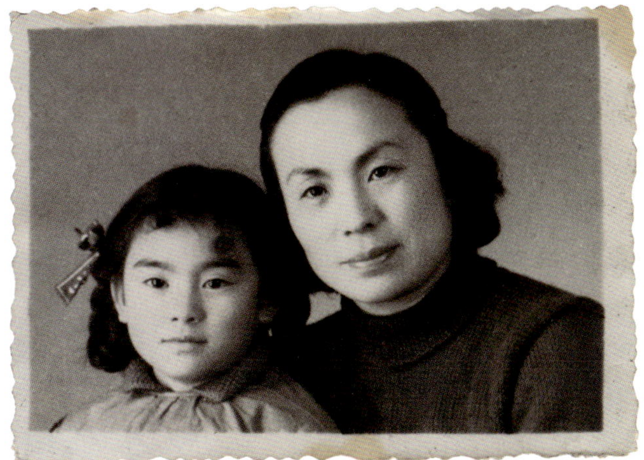

Fig. 3. Hung Liu with her mother, Liu Zongguang, 1954.

her aunt Liu Zongyu (who later in 1966 had her head shaved in public for joining the Nationalist Army); and her grandmother Wang Jushou. The one man who consistently shows up is her grandfather Liu Weihua. Sometimes, Liu's young cousins from other cities are present, as well as her oldest aunt, Daiyi Liu Zongyu; her second aunt, Eryi Liu Zongshi; and her uncle Liu Zongtian, who was in the Chinese Communist Navy, or People's Liberation Army Navy. Sometimes, Liu appears in close-ups with her mother (fig. 3).

In nearly every one of these pictures, the individuals look determined and strong, traits that are often made visible through self-possessed expressions. The subjects' faces act as templates, or maps, revealing the close intergenerational bloodlines of Liu's upbringing. These are the faces that she draws on in her broader conceptualization of portraiture, where the specific and individual interface with the archetypal and universal. "In terms of which face is going to be used as the subject and how to make the image into a portrait, there comes the artist," she has acknowledged.[3]

Liu is not alone when she turns to family portraits and other archives to bring meaning to her art. But her work has been ground-breaking since the mid-1980s, when she began translating photographs into paintings with the direct purpose of repositing the subject of portraiture—reframing history by carefully considering whom she portrays. Others have followed her in this pioneering effort, including highly influential younger contemporary portrait artists who use family photographs—both snapshots and studio portraits—as source

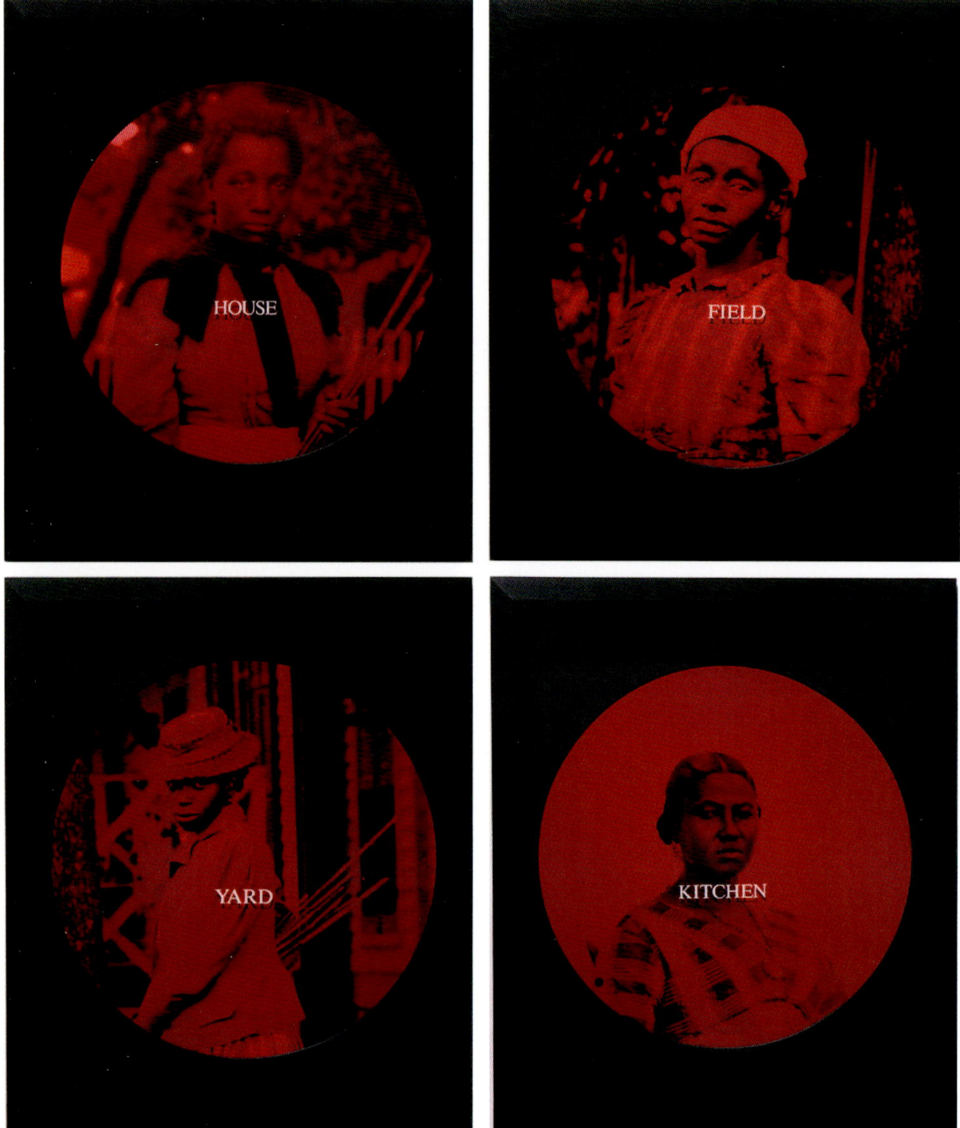

Fig. 4. Carrie Mae Weems (b. 1953)
House, Field, Yard, and *Kitchen,* from the series *From Here I Saw What Happened and I Cried,* 1995–96
Chromogenic prints with sandblasted text on glass, each: 23⅞ × 19¹⁵⁄₁₆ in. (60.7 × 50.7 cm)
The Museum of Modern Art, New York. Gift on behalf of the Friends of Education of the Museum of Modern Art

material. She is also in the company of Carrie Mae Weems, who places historical photographs and family imagery in her conceptual portraits, and Kerry James Marshall, who incorporates historical imagery into large-scale paintings that critique the artistic canon and shed light onto missing narratives in our nation's museums (figs. 4, 5).

Liu's ideas about identity and portraiture are firmly grounded in the notion that the more specific a face, the more universal it is. Often relying on faded, tattered black-and-white prints, she translates the faces of familiar and anonymous people alike into dynamic, colorful, and layered figures in oil and linseed drips, activating a sense of transformation and, eventually, kinship with the viewer, across time and place (figs. 6, 7). The subjects exist in her mind and vision as one people, and therein lies Liu's deep sense of empathy. She has described her concept in the following way: "When we talk about

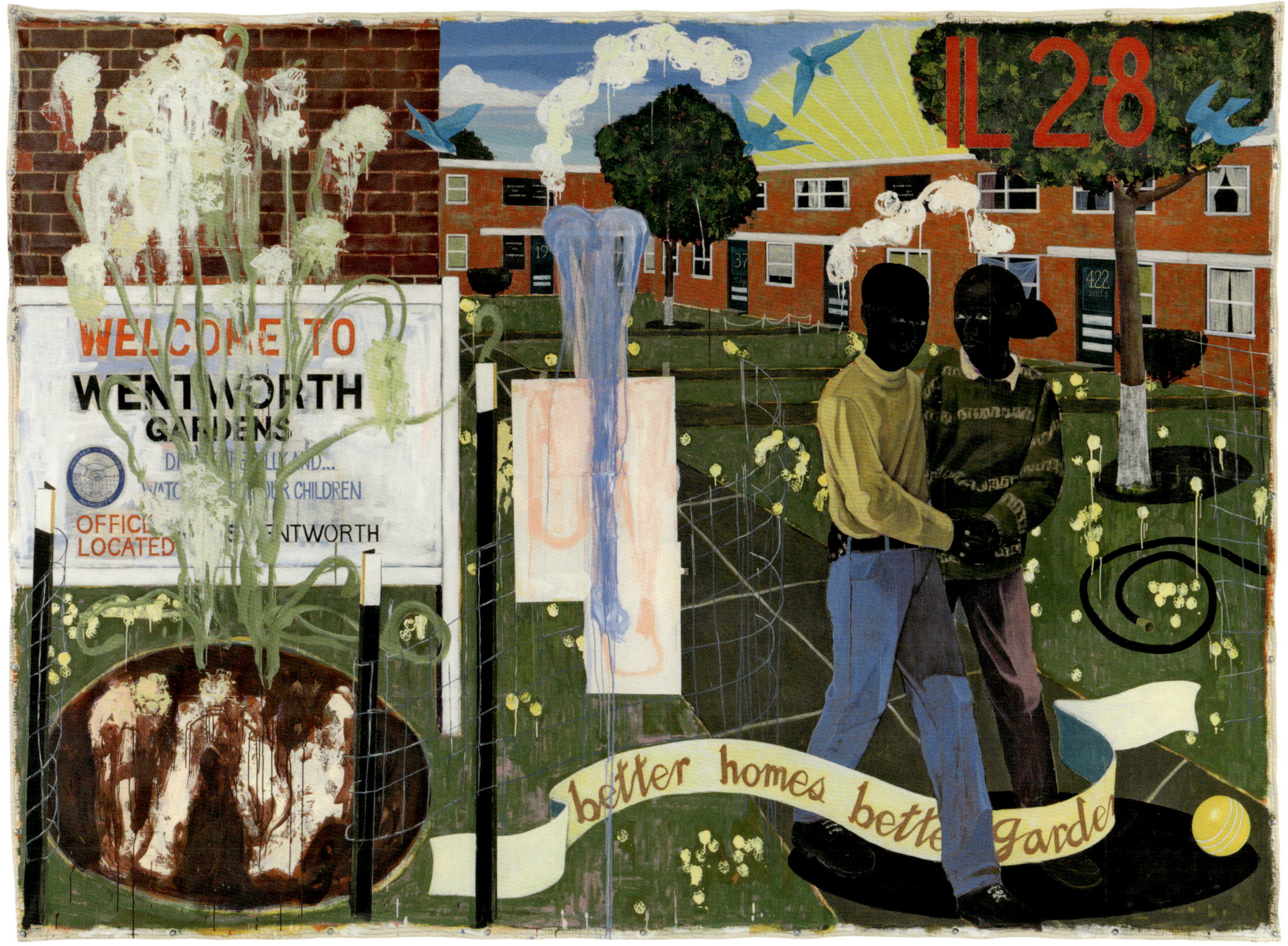

Fig. 5. Kerry James Marshall (b. 1955)
Better Homes, Better Gardens, 1994
Acrylic paint and paper collage on canvas, 100 × 142 in.
(254 × 360.7 cm)
Denver Art Museum. Funds from Polly and Mark Addison, the
Alliance for Contemporary Art, Caroline Morgan, and Colorado
Contemporary Collectors: Suzanne Farver, Linda and Ken
Heller, Jan and Frederick Mayer, Beverly and Bernard Rosen,
Annalee and Wagner Schorr, and anonymous donors

portraiture, that's a transformation from a real face to an art form.
I believe only a specific face with its unique visage can be turned into
a portrait—the more particular, the more universal. There's no generic
human face to represent any of us."[4]

The faces and characteristics of those who raised Liu form the
foundation for her contributions to the broader art historical genre
of portraiture. Hers is a humanistic, activist, and, ultimately, hopeful
means of making visible those who are at risk of being unseen and
forgotten, those in her family and in all of our families. Additionally,
the empathic worldview she developed as a youth guides her practice.
She carries these memories with honor; they are both joyful and
tragic, and they include distinct colors and sensory details that she
highlights in her brushstrokes.

Liu's art conveys the longing for those who are missing, particularly her father, whose absence reverberates in the textured surfaces that she creates through diluting oil paint with generous

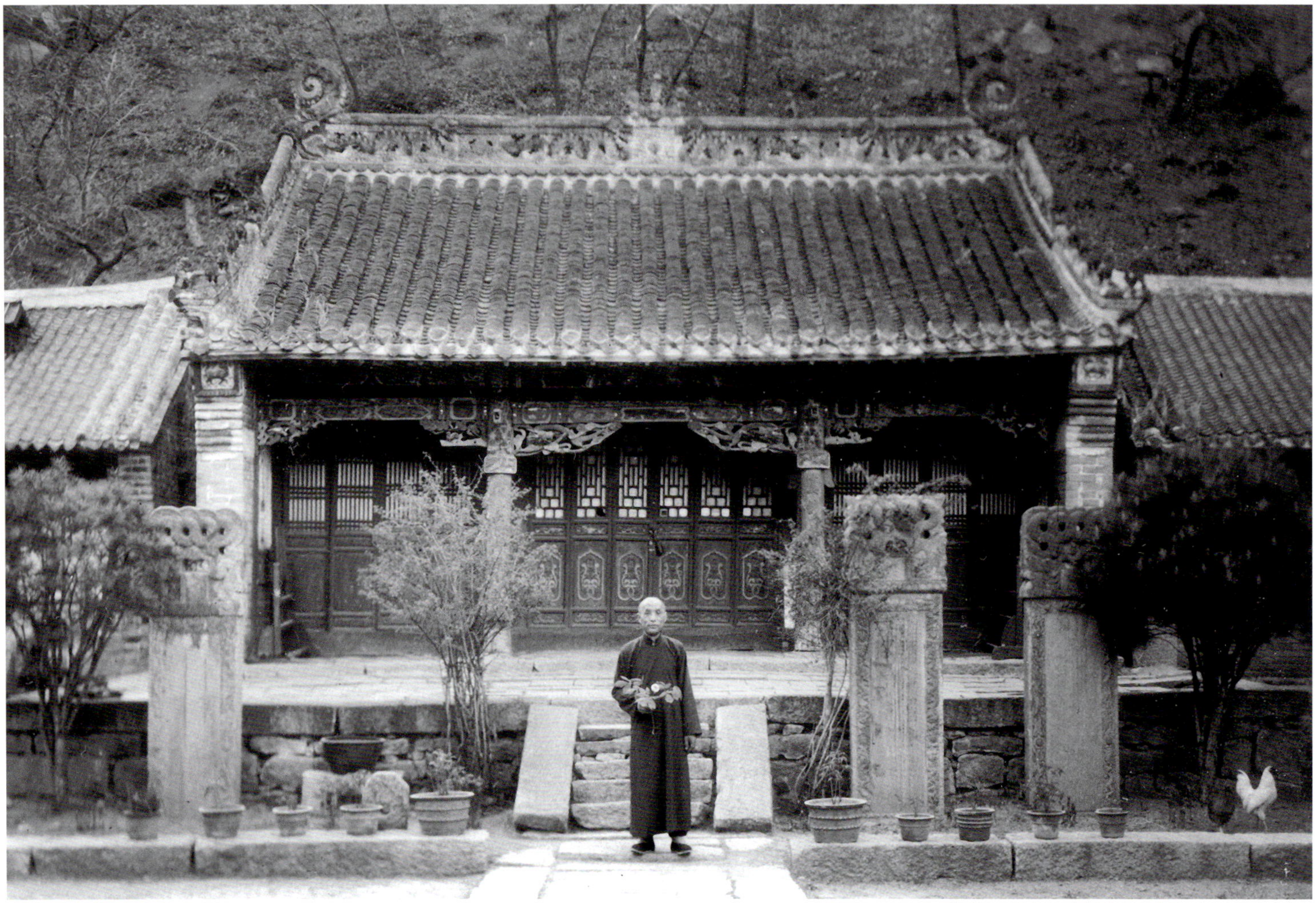

Fig. 6. Source photograph for Hung Liu's *The Botanist* (2013; cat. 44) by an unidentified photographer, 1920s. The photograph shows Liu Weihua, Hung Liu's grandfather, at Qianshan.

Fig. 7. Detail of *The Botanist*.

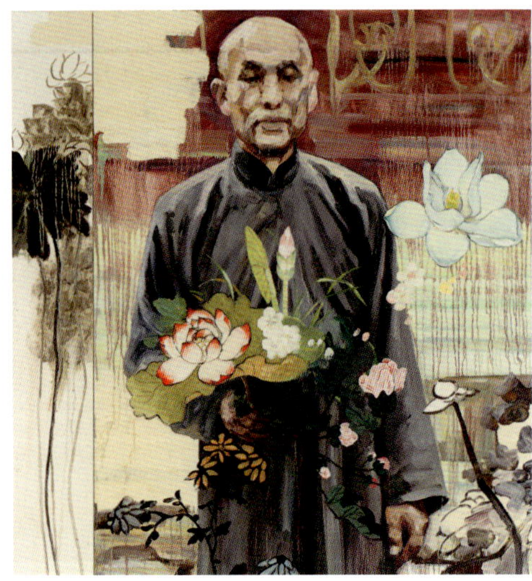

amounts of linseed oil. The drips she creates both purposefully and by chance are reminiscent of tears or the flowing water that exists constantly in her mind as a metaphor for her family's journey.[5] Liu considered the fluid temporal aspect of her work in a 1989 statement, when she described the interface between history and the contemporary moment as "the tension between the continuity of movement and the fixity of single moments . . . like the difference between cinema and photography, between the currents of history and the documents by which we fix and remember them."[6] Liu's use of family and historical photographs is an act of recovery as she sources the past and brings it into the present. Her conceptual framework of time is imbued with imagery of water. As a powerful element, water flows through her childhood memories and finds its way onto her canvases—both as subject matter and as media that invigorate the surfaces of her portraits. Liu's deliberate marks and improvised drips coexist to amplify the notion of time as simultaneously fleeting and continuous.

In 1972, Liu left the countryside during the Cultural Revolution to attend Beijing Teacher's College, where she studied until 1975 (fig. 8). She was not offered art history courses and had to learn about art on

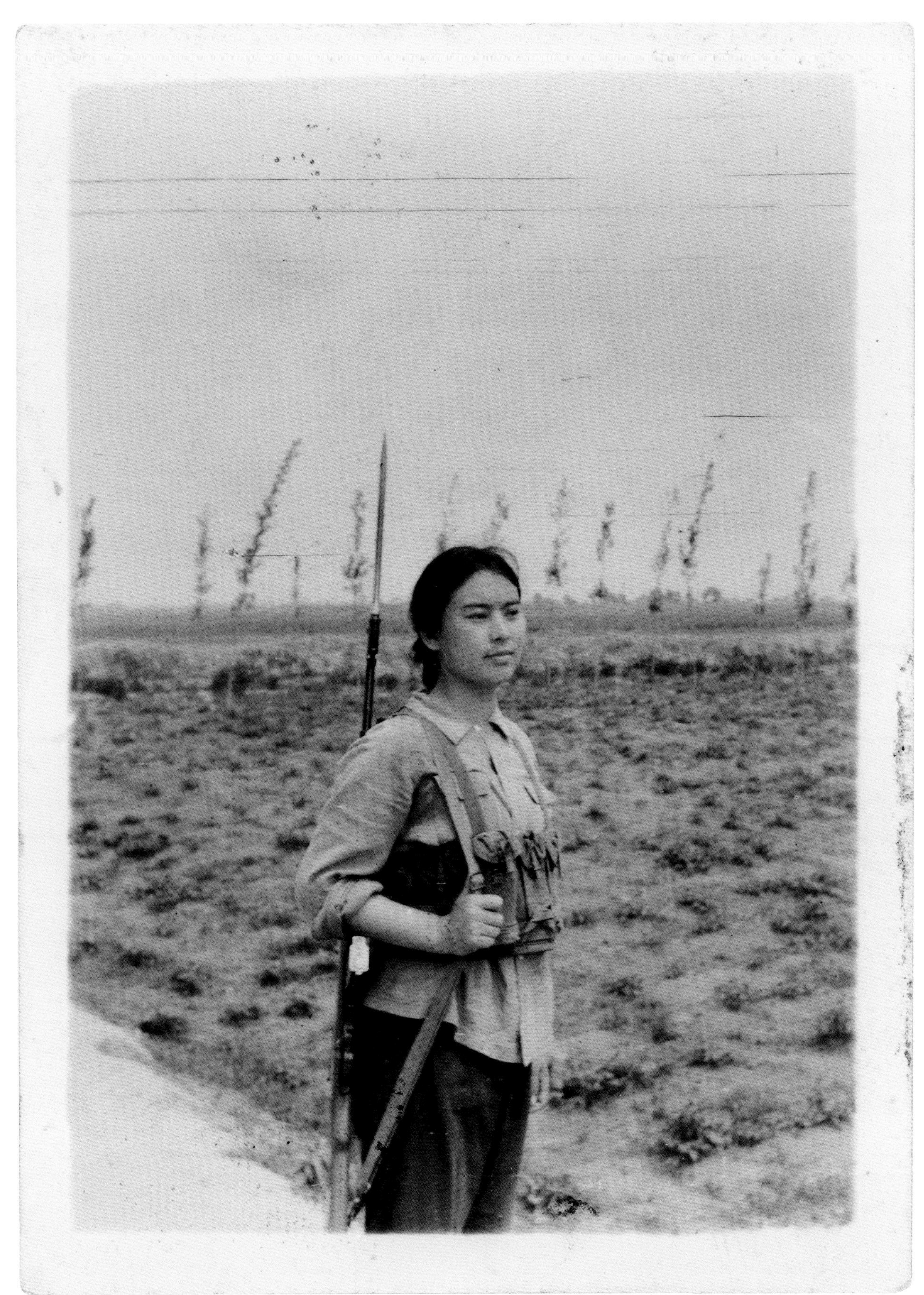

Fig. 8. Hung Liu during military training while a student at Beijing Teacher's College, 1973–74; source photograph for *Avant-Garde* (1993; cat. 20).

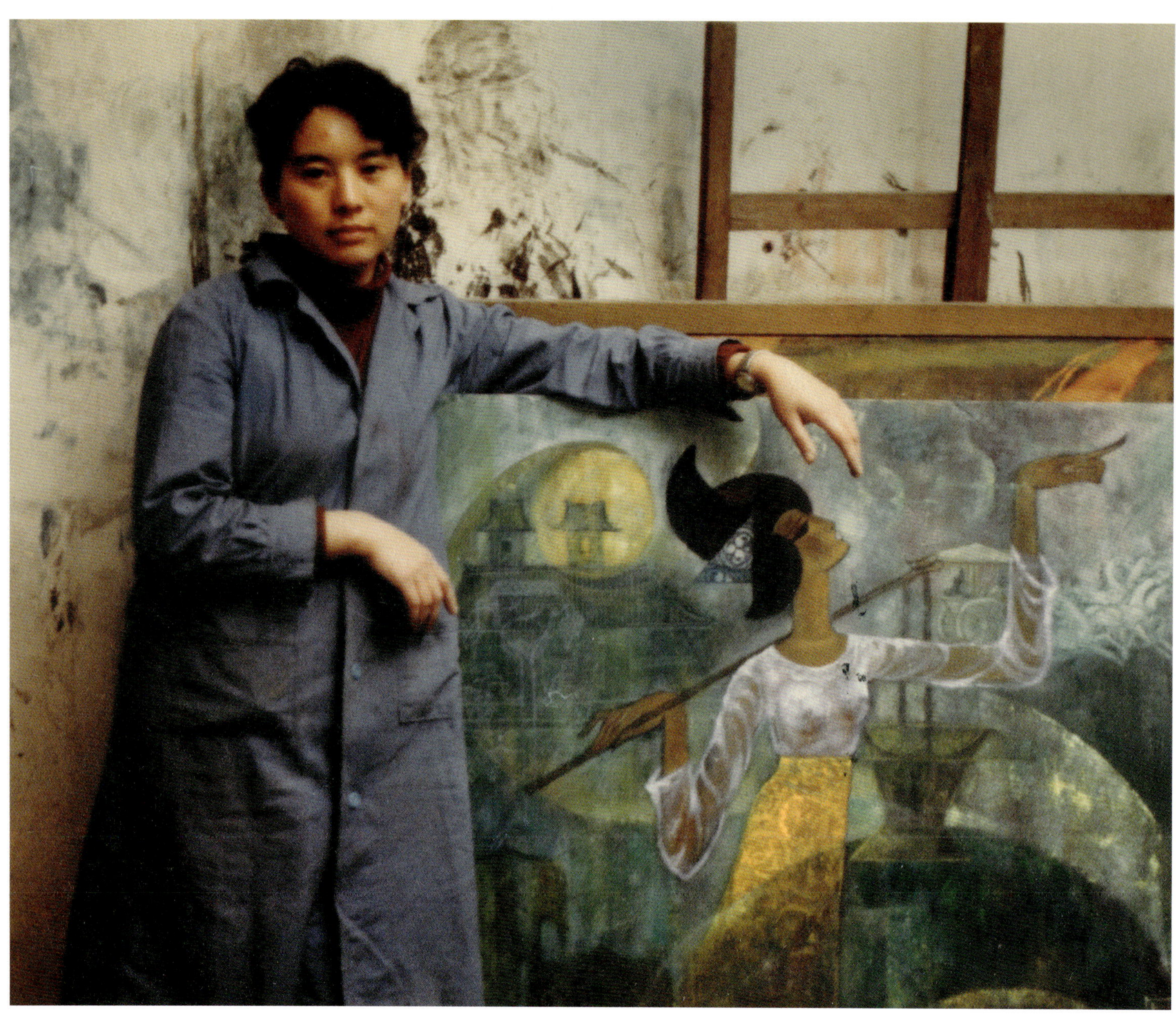

Fig. 9. Hung Liu as a graduate student, Central Academy of
Fine Arts, Beijing, 1980.

her own. Following graduation, she taught art to schoolchildren. From 1979 to 1981, she attended graduate school at the Central Academy of Fine Arts in Beijing, where she was forced to study portraiture in a traditional and academic way (fig. 9). Her focus on murals allowed her to have more freedom than other students, but the style of socialist realism, from the Soviet Union, was the guiding pedagogy at that time, and there was little room to deviate. Her approach would not shift until she left Beijing and immigrated to the United States.

In 1984, Liu left China to begin graduate studies at the department of visual arts at the University of California, San Diego. There, she worked closely with the foundational performance artist Allan Kaprow, known for the Happenings of the 1960s (fig. 10). This exposure to artists, critics, and theorists such as Moira Roth, Eleanor and David Antin, and Manny Farber, as well as fellow graduate students Lorna Simpson, Christine Tamblyn, Hal Fischer, Carrie Mae Weems, and Jeff Kelley (her future husband), invigorated and freed her conceptual thinking. Consequently, Liu's portraiture moved into a performative mode, one that amplifies the dynamic relationship between photography and painting, often through a sly humor that she uses as a form of critique. She began considering and experimenting with how this interplay between media could be activated in the transformation and renewal of historic imagery. The former instruction she had received in China, which discouraged copying photographs, was no longer a limiting factor, and she now felt liberated to interpret the figure more conceptually through source material.

Like Liu's mother—and later Liu herself, as a professor at Mills College—Liu's grandfather was a teacher who encouraged scholarship, innovative thinking, and creativity. Preserving the work he did, as a scholar of Qianshan's monasteries, has become important for Liu in her adult life, in large part because her grandfather was so active in her intellectual formation as a child. He instilled in her a sense of confidence and a spirit of determination. One time, when Liu was around five, she protested his critique of one of her drawings after he had assigned the drawing a score of 95. He listened to her explanation and then proudly marked out the 95, replacing it with a 100 (fig. 11). The picture offers a window into the tender relationship that the two of them shared, one of encouragement and creative engagement.

In describing her 2013 portrait *The Botanist,* Liu wrote:

I really knew my grandfather. I remember a lot of things: his face, his demeanor, his body language. He had hands that were very soft and big. So those kinds of things were very important for me as part of these paintings. When I was painting his shoes, I couldn't help but think, Grandma made these shoes! The memory, the way they looked, is very close to me, but they are all ghosts. They are with me all the time, but I cannot reach them.[7]

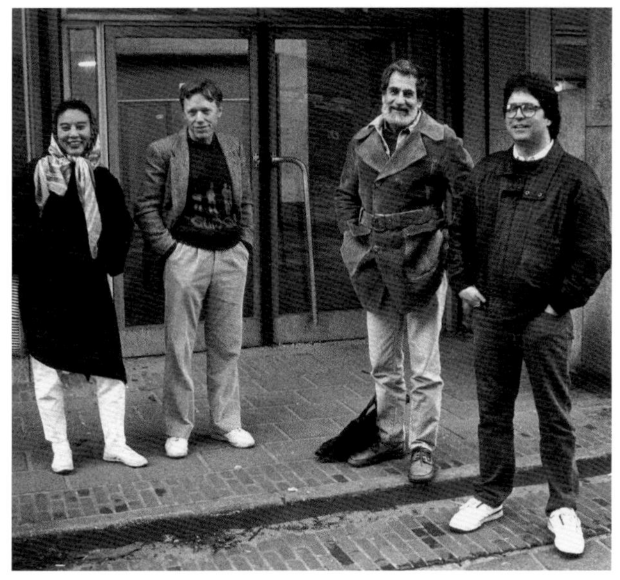

Fig. 10. From left: Hung Liu, Peter Kirby, Allan Kaprow, and Jeff Kelley, 1988.

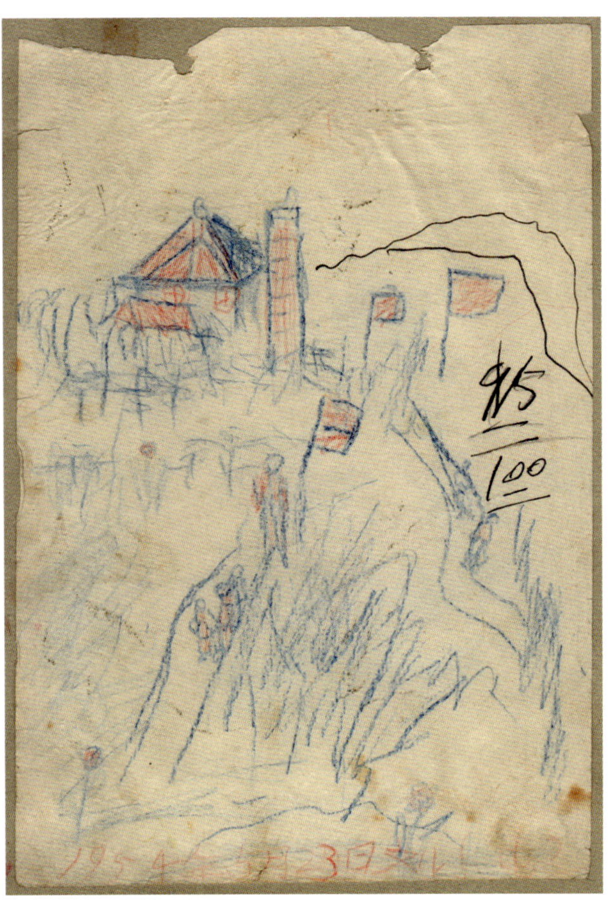

Fig. 11. Drawing by Hung Liu, graded by her grandfather Liu Weihua, 1954.

Similarly, her monumental portrait of her grandmother, who was four years older than her grandfather and married him when he was twelve or thirteen, in an arranged marriage, emphasizes her hands: "I painted her hands very strong because all her life she would make shoes, clothes and did laundry [by hand]. All her joints were arthritic and swollen."[8] Despite her grandmother's having never traveled to Qianshan, Liu painted a map of the mountain onto her grandmother's blouse to symbolically connect her to the place that occupied her husband's mind and soul and her support of his life's work (1993–2013; cat. 21).

Liu also vividly remembers her grandfather's visionary support of girls as equal to boys. She recalls her grandfather teaching her the "Ballad of Mulan" when she was just four or five, a narrative poem that she can still recite to this day. The poem is about the strength of a young girl, and in many ways, it epitomizes the feminism that Hung Liu subscribes to, "a feminism that comes from China. . . . It's the type of woman that I pay homage to, or you could say the type I've always hoped I could become, from Hua Mulan to Qiu Jin, these are truly outstanding women, and I admire them all. . . . The women I've known, beginning with my grandmother, were all incredibly strong; they could do anything, shoulder every burden."[9]

Whether she is portraying girls, prostitutes, workers, or migrant mothers, Liu transcribes the determined character that she recognized in her own mother, aunts, and grandmother to those otherwise anonymous women whose faces speak to her through historic Chinese photographs. For example, she has said of her painting *Goddess of Love, Goddess of Liberty* (1989; cat. 25), which depicts a woman with bound feet that point abjectly at the viewer, "I just want to startle the audience and convey the pain felt by our mothers."[10]

Liu's attraction to the historic Chinese images of prostitutes that she discovered in 1991, on her first trip back to China after seven years, might be seen in connection with her family's deep interest in photography as a tool for documenting and exposing secret lives and unknown stories, including her grandfather Liu Weihua's incorporation of the medium to aid in his research trips. In the 1920s and 1930s, Liu Weihua hired a photographer to follow his journeys to study Qianshan and its ecological systems, religious shrines, and the monks, priests, and nuns who dwelled there. The resulting five hundred photographs became source material for Liu's 2013 series of paintings about her grandfather's research trips. Her paintings based on these photographs offer insight into the depth of her family's interest in the ancient traditions of China and her wish to honor her grandfather's dream to be a *Jushi*. In 2002, forty years after his death, Liu Weihua's book was published, with the help of Hung Liu and her mother (figs. 12, 13).[11] In this regard, her practice of translating images from photographs is a personal journey as much as it is a means for restoring dignity and honor to those, like her grandfather, whose lives and work may be at risk of erasure.

Such an act of recovery closely aligns with the work of other conceptually minded artists, such as Glenn Ligon and Lava Thomas, who appropriate historical imagery to make visible a traumatic past and to move forward.[12] The viewer of Liu's paintings is constantly reminded of the close attention to detail that the artist has committed in reviving her subjects. Translating specific details into paintings activates a temporal layering effect, bringing those intimate recollections of the individuals back to her and ultimately conjuring for the viewers memories of their own families. As such, Lucy R. Lippard aptly refers to Liu's work as collage.[13] It becomes clear that the artist's deep reverence for her anonymous subjects is drawn from her respect for her family members—the sensory details of their lives are etched in her mind and are reawakened and reactivated when she paints. Liu wrote, "I communicate with the characters in my paintings with reverence, sympathy, and awe."[14]

Family photographs have traversed time and place with Liu, a reminder of the power that they hold in personal memory, allowing for threads of connection when physical contact has become impossible or has ended. "I think my mom was conscious to keep a record of how I grew up," Liu said, reflecting on why the ritual of studio photographs was such an important one in her upbringing.[15]

As Liu described her family photographs, she remembered details that are obscured in the black-and-white images—colors that jump out of the image and evoke historic symbolism, such as the red tie

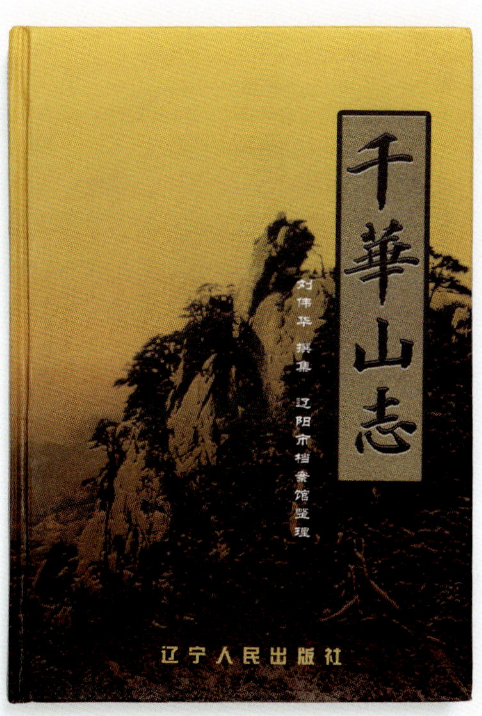

Figs. 12 and 13. Book by Liu Weihua, Hung Liu's grandfather, on the history and rituals of Qianshan, published posthumously by Liaoning People's Publishing House, Shenyang, 2002.

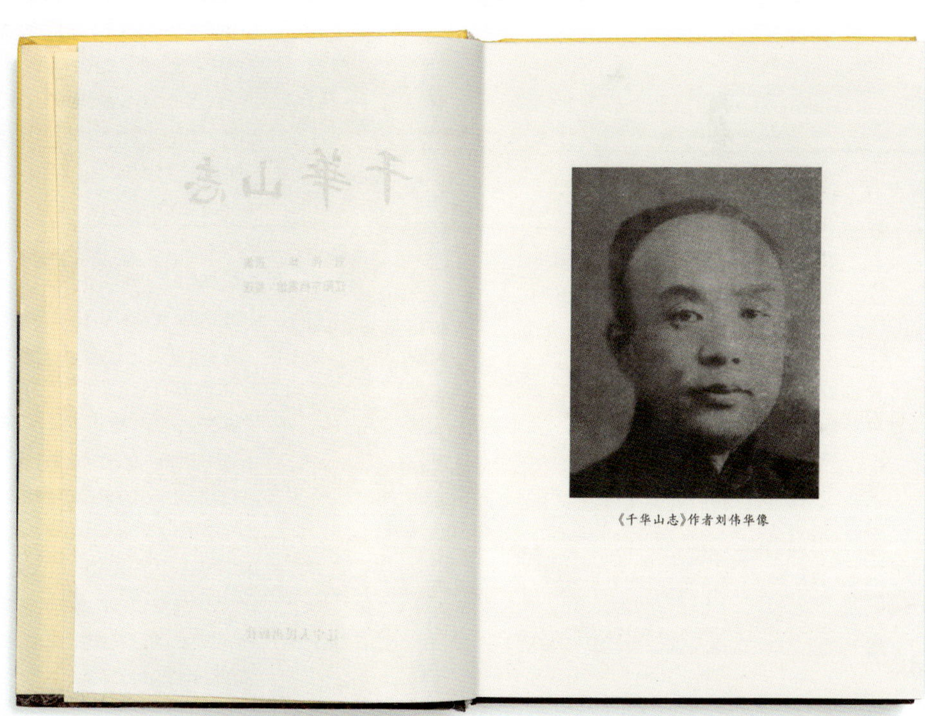

attached to her school uniform, directly borrowed from the uniforms of the Young Pioneers of the Soviet Union: "Colors are in our life, as well as in our memories and dreams. Sometimes they are so vivid, you can never forget the visual impacts."[16] She thought about the red scarf her mother knitted for her before she was sent to the countryside in 1968: "I remember she made it with the wool from unpicking an old pair of leggings. It's these things. I think there's something so human, so meaningful to them."[17]

Liu also recalled the clothes her mother sewed: "She loved to make clothes for me, especially when I was very young, and everyone used to say the clothes she made were very pretty. She was very much against making a dress very long so it could be worn for three years. The dresses she made were always very short and really vibrant. Sometimes the photographs of me were put on display by the studio as a way of attracting other customers."[18] The "Shirley Temple dress" that she made for Liu in the 1950s looked nothing like the dresses Chinese mothers routinely made for their daughters (fig. 14). It was short and playful and fulfilled her desire to dress Liu in an American style. Liu reminisced about the fun she had wearing it and described how she posed for a photographer in a storefront. These memories reveal the tender, loving side of their mother-daughter relationship, an aspect that is far less evident in the formal, much more formulaic studio portraits.

Portrait photographs and memories of their circumstances have the power of "summoning ghosts," a phrase Liu often uses to describe her work. They offer stories of a family's journey and help trace the impact of that journey on subsequent generations. Elaine Kim has described Liu's approach to historic photographs as akin to dealing with memory loss: the third-generation reproductions are often faded and grainy, but the image persists.[19] This play with memory and symbolism through photography brings to mind the work of theorist Roland Barthes, whose work in semiotics is important to Liu's practice. Liu explained, "In China, we always grew up with an innate awareness of semiotics. . . . When I was in China, philosophy as a subject in higher education was offered simply as Marxism and Mao Zedong's thought. In my work, both history and memory are not about the past, rather the present. In that sense, my work is more symbolic than only literal."[20] In Liu's own persistence to retrieve the subject, she reactivates memories. She brings the subject into view, larger than life, as monuments or archetypal versions of the ghosts held in the recesses of her mind. In her use of color, texture, form, and scale, the photographic portraits of her mother, her grandfather, her son, and herself expand on the possibilities of the studio and the documentary portrait to not only memorialize the people who formed her but also to hold on to them, carry them, and raise them up to impart a universal family story.

Through incorporating striking color, dripping paint, and large-scale dimensions, these portraits transport her family members

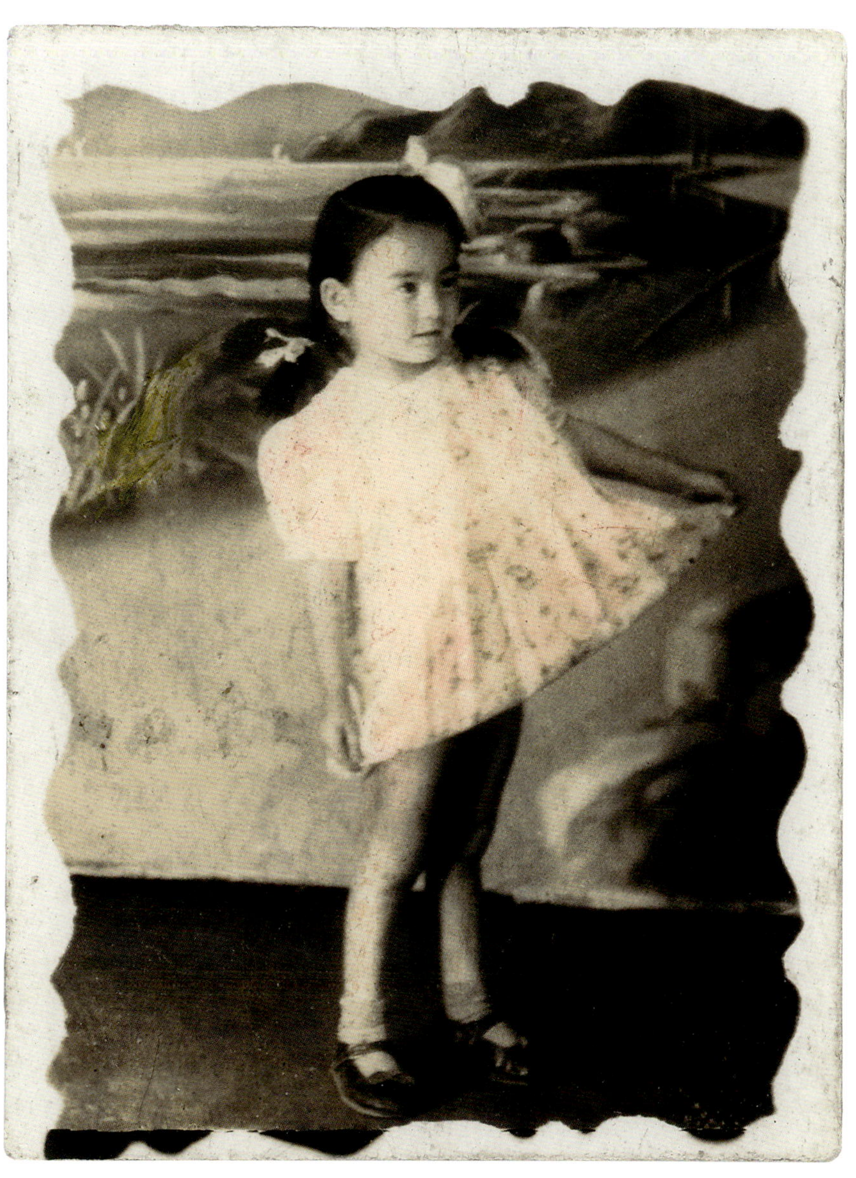

Fig. 14. Hung Liu in the "Shirley Temple dress" that her mother made for her, 1953.

into our contemporary moment while forcing viewers to look up, a performative act that references a child's looking up to his or her own elders. Like the parallel portraits that Liu subsequently made based on historic Chinese photographs, such as *Refugee: Opera* (2001; cat. 31), and those that are part of her current body of work, which are based on Dorothea Lange's archive, such as *Migrant Mother: Mealtime* (2016; cat. 47), Hung Liu crosses generational and cultural divides to transmit to the viewer a shared experience, evoking empathy and understanding. As she has explained: "When I tried to use colors to image and decode the old black-and-white photos, [it was] as if I could feel the subject's heartbeat and pulse, I felt the connection and understanding with her/him/them."[21] In Liu's work, color brings her emotional memory from the past into the present.

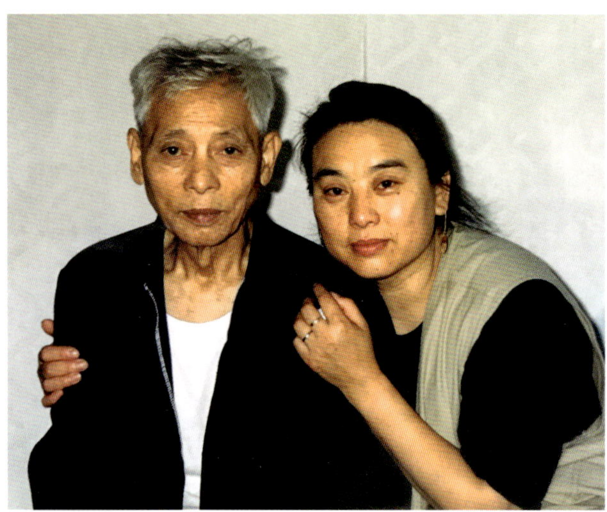

Fig. 15. Source photograph for Hung Liu's *Father's Day* (cat. 22), 1994.

Liu's family photographs and the portraits based on them are foundational to her concept of portraiture. The subjects are as much a part of her identity as all of her portraits are, whether or not she ever met the subjects or even lived during their lifetimes or shared in their cultures; they become part of her. She has explained, "After finishing a portrait of a person, I [feel] either I have adopted her/him as my family member, or they have adopted or accepted me as theirs. Our relationship has forever changed."[22] Similarly, for photographer Dawoud Bey, a successful portrait ceases to be an object and instead becomes a psychological experience.[23]

Liu's larger-than-life representations and shaped canvases are grounded in a combination of influences, from her training in mural painting and as a graduate student in Beijing to her conceptual explorations with Kaprow; they remove the subjects from a particular place so that they may be carried through time. Liu's portrait *Father's Day* (1994; cat. 22) provides an example of the way her family portraits move from the specific to the universal as they are activated by the viewer in the performative space of the museum. The story of Liu's relationship with her father, Xia Peng, is one of absence and searching, and ultimately of resilience. Having been raised by her mother, Liu grew up wondering about her father but only began searching for him in the early 1990s, after she had become a U.S. citizen. Upon receiving a phone call from a friend that her father had been located, she traveled from California to China to reunite with him when she was forty-six years old, in 1994—coincidentally on Father's Day. She found him on a rural work farm for elderly inmates near Nanjing, where he had been imprisoned on and off since 1948, the year of her birth, and subjected to years of hard labor. She feared she would not identify him as she scanned the elderly men around the camp, but she knew him immediately when she finally met him. It did not matter that he was worn and thin. She recounts that he stood with his head down and showed no emotion in front of the guards when she introduced herself to him. As she struggled to hold back the tears from streaming down her own face during their first encounter, she could not understand why he showed no feeling. Later, when they spent time at the camp alone together, talking through the night, he explained to her that he was no longer capable of showing emotion—that he had been trained in prison to bury his feelings.

Father's Day is based on a photograph (fig. 15). It is an oversize shaped canvas, one that allows her to "carry" the work, literally, and remove the subjects from any particular context. In considering the broader implications of Liu's tactics, Holland Cotter's discussion of Weems's use of historic photographs in her work is relevant: "The work is both an indictment of photography as enslavement, and a homage to long-dead sitters . . . who, under unknowable duress, gave their bodies and faces to the artist, to us, and to history."[24] Although the subjects of Liu's photographs of prostitutes, refugees, child migrants, and other marginalized figures are anonymous (cats. 24–40), they are nonetheless interwoven with the portrait of Liu's father, who was enslaved. They are also connected to the painter of the portrait, whose father was absent during her childhood, due to his removal from the family by the government. The face of Liu's father interfaces with the other enslaved subjects whom she paints. The specificity that Liu conjures in painting his condition and her "lifting" of him, both representationally in the portrait and metaphorically, in the form of the portrait, demonstrates how Liu transforms the specific to the universal.

While Liu created *Father's Day* from a recent photograph, made around the time of their reunion, she based the monumental portrait of her son on a much older snapshot (fig. 16). In *Little Artist* (1998; cat. 23), Liu presents Ling Chen as a toddler, just having drawn an image in chalk on the concrete floor. The activity was one he often enjoyed, despite Liu's mother's concerns about the dangers associated with inhaling chalk dust. In describing the portrait, Liu vividly recalled the red leather shoes her son wore and the texture of handsewn clothes made by her mother.[25] The source for the portrait is a black-and-white print, one of a group taken by a friend who visited Liu's family in Beijing around 1980. Liu recalls that when she saw the image printed, it was a revelation to view a family photograph that was spontaneous and not posed in the studio manner she had grown accustomed to in her youth.

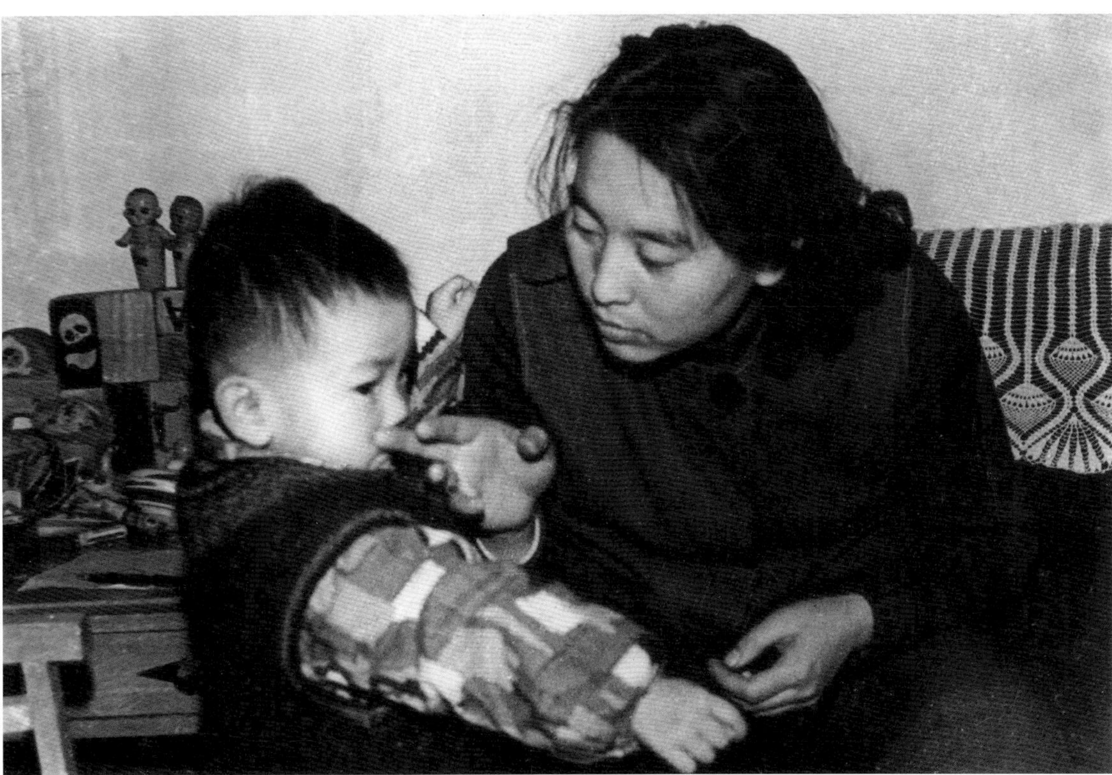

Fig. 16. Hung Liu with her son in Beijing, c. 1980. The friend who took this snapshot also took the one that Liu used as her source for *Little Artist* (1998; cat. 23).

Her delight in seeing this snapshot that focuses on a child—not the usual subject of grand portraiture—carries into Liu's portraits of orphans from the *Mission Girls* series (2002–3; cats. 32–40) and her paintings based on Dorothea Lange's photographs of migrant children during the Great Depression (cats. 45–52). In the interface between Ling Chen and those anonymous children, Liu captures the innocence of childhood across cultures and across time—an innocence that she constantly reminds us is at risk. With the pull Liu feels toward painting suffering children—Chinese refugees, the infants who are destitute and latch onto their mother to survive—she imagines the cries of her own son. These are echoes that she must have heard as a young mother when she, a newly divorced woman, left six-year-old Ling Chen in Beijing with her mother and grandmother so that she could bravely pursue graduate study in San Diego. She reproduces her son's visage and the other children she portrays to emphasize their value and importance as individuals and insist on their being seen, heard, and remembered. Her attraction to the mothers and children whom Lange photographed during the Great Depression are reminders that the vulnerability of children must be exposed in order to create societal change and create a better world for future generations.

Also embedded within Liu's paintings of children are memories that her mother shared with her of her own struggle as a refugee. When Liu addressed the San Francisco Women's March as one of the keynote speakers on January 21, 2017, she told the story of her family's escape from the battleground around Changchun, in 1948, when she was an infant:

> When I was six years old, my mother told me a story about that journey that I have never forgotten. She said that while fleeing the fighting around Changchun with countless other refugees—with no food and under fire—our family passed by a river. Sitting alone on that riverbank was a baby. The baby's mother had set it down and stepped into the river's rushing water. Nobody picked up the baby. Everyone just kept walking. I asked my mother if she would ever have drowned herself and abandoned me by the river. She looked at me and said, "I don't know."[26]

Later, in 1968, when Liu was sent to the countryside for proletarian reeducation during the Cultural Revolution, she worked among the youth as a peasant for 360 days a year for four years, growing wheat and corn. Her only escape in the evenings was to read forbidden novels that she and her friends hid under her pillow. They included *Jean-Christophe* by Romain Rolland, which recounts the story of St. Christopher, the patron saint of travelers. Liu was especially impacted by the description in the story of Christopher carrying a baby across a dangerous river. When the child became too heavy and the river grew more powerful, he asked the child to reveal his name. The child replied, "I am the day soon to be born."[27]

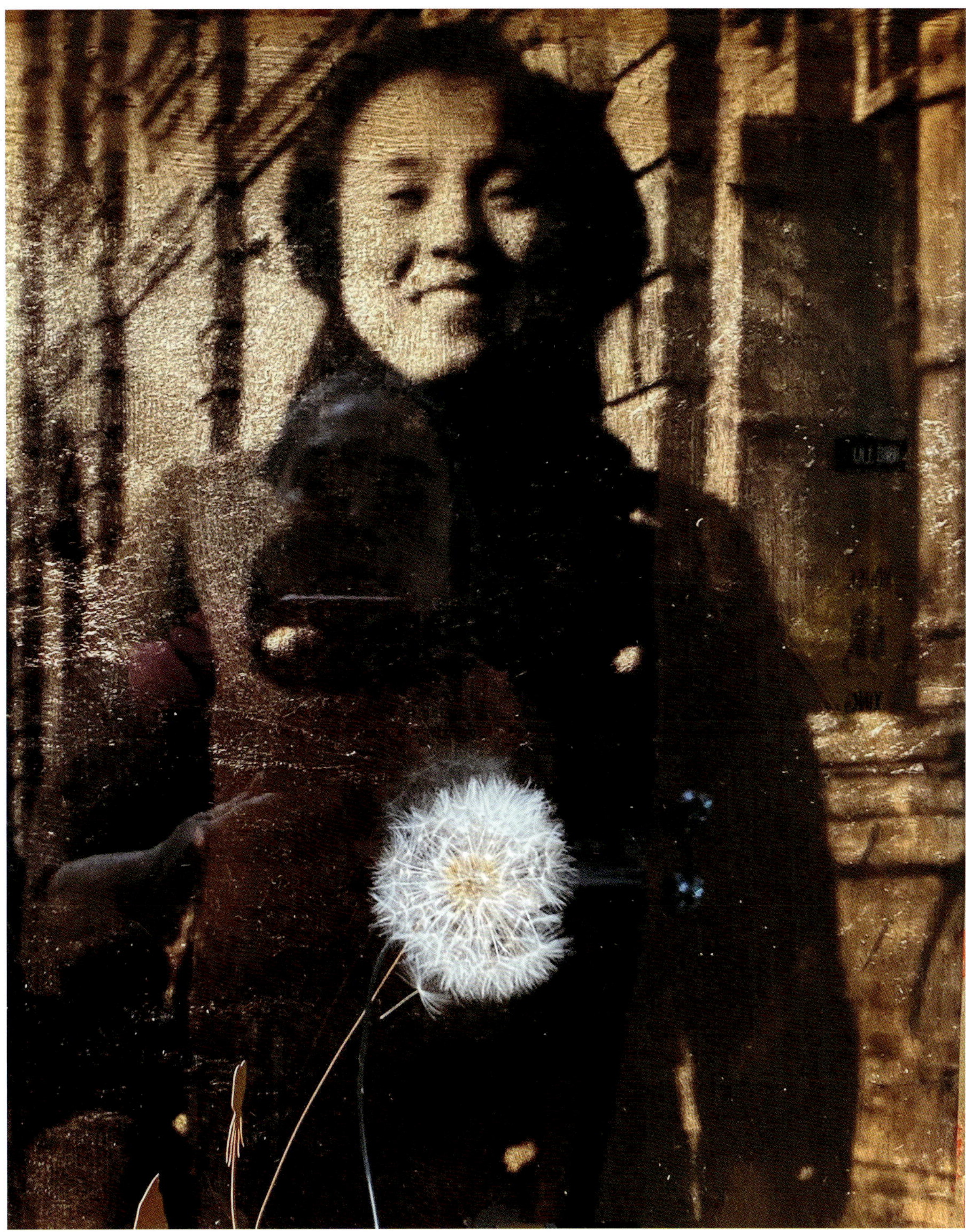

Fig. 17. Hung Liu created this photographic image on June 27, 2020, what would have been her mother's ninety-eighth birthday. She placed a dandelion in front of an original photograph of her mom as a way to reference their journey together. Liu is visible in the reflection.

In her temporal layering or interfacing of her specific family experience with anonymous historical subjects, Hung Liu makes a lasting impact on the history of portraiture and pushes the genre forward for future generations. The transformation of her marginalized, forgotten, historical subjects into monumental, heroic, contemporary figures happens through a process that she has described as "chemical to mineral."[28] From the chemical process of developing and printing photographs to the mineral of the oil paint that brings the subjects back to life, she carries her subjects and herself across the "dark and swollen" rivers of time, always with the memory of her mother carrying her and the hope of a new dawn (fig. 17).

Notes

Epigraphs: Hung Liu quoted in "Sixty Years on a Hard Journey for Art: A Conversation between Hung Liu and Wu Hung," in *Hung Liu: Great Granary*, ed. Wu Hung (Hong Kong: Timezone 8, 2010), 110, 100-101.

1. Hung Liu quoted in Rachelle Reichert, *Hung Liu: Qianshan, Grandfather's Mountain* (New York: Nancy Hoffman Gallery, 2013), 56.
2. The city of Changchun, now the capital of Jilin Province in eastern China, served as the capital of the Japanese puppet state from 1932 to 1945. It was defended by Chiang Kai-shek and his Kuomintang (Nationalist Army).
3. Hung Liu, phone conversation with author, April 13, 2020.
4. Hung Liu, phone conversation with author, April 13, 2020.
5. For a fascinating look at Liu's process, see a short video on KQED Spark, "Hung Liu," https://www.youtube.com/watch?v=LV8e43K2zCI, during which the artist quips, "Gravity is my secret collaborator."
6. Hung Liu, "Statement (1989)," quoted in *Contemporary Chinese Art: Primary Documents,* ed. Wu Hung, with Peggy Wang (New York: Museum of Modern Art, 2010), 269.
7. Hung Liu quoted in Reichert, *Qianshan, Grandfather's Mountain* 64.
8. Hung Liu quoted in Reichert, *Qianshan, Grandfather's Mountain,* 56.
9. Hung Liu quoted in Wu Hung, "Sixty Years," 109.
10. Hung Liu quoted in Elaine Kim, "'Bad Women': Asian American Visual Artists Hanh Thi Pham, Hung Liu, and Yong Soon Min," *Feminist Studies* 22, no. 3 (Autumn 1996): 589.
11. Reichert, *Qianshan, Grandfather's Mountain,* 8.
12. I am thinking specifically of Glenn Ligon's *Runaways* series, which incorporates imagery from nineteenth-century advertisements created by slaveholders, and Lava Thomas's *Mugshot Portraits: Women of the Montgomery Bus Boycott* series, where she uses as source material mugshots of African American women who were arrested for participating in the boycotts of 1955–56.

13. See Lucy R. Lippard, "Hung Liu: China Trade," in this book, esp. p. 80.

14. Hung Liu quoted in Kim, "Bad Women," 588.

15. Hung Liu, phone conversation with author, April 20, 2020.

16. Hung Liu, phone conversation with author, April 20, 2020.

17. Hung Liu quoted in Wu Hung, "Four Moments in Hung Liu's Art," in *Summoning Ghosts: The Art of Hung Liu,* by René de Guzman et al. (Oakland, Calif.: Oakland Museum of California; Berkeley: University of California Press, 2013), 24.

18. Hung Liu quoted in Wu Hung, "Four Moments in Hung Liu's Art," 23–24.

19. See Kim, "Bad Women," 585. Kim also points to repetition and the act of copying as a form of meditation and prayer.

20. Hung Liu, email message to author, July 14, 2020. See Roland Barthes, *Camera Lucida: Reflections on Photography* (New York: Hill and Wang, 1980).

21. Hung Liu, phone conversation with author, April 20, 2020.

22. Hung Liu, phone conversation with author, April 20, 2020.

23. Dorothy Moss, *The Outwin 2016: American Portraiture Today* (Washington, D.C.: National Portrait Gallery, 2016), 19.

24. Holland Cotter, "Testimony of a Clear-Eyed Witness," *New York Times,* January 23, 2014.

25. Hung Liu, phone conversation with author, May 15, 2020.

26. Hung Liu, transcript of speech delivered at the San Francisco Women's March, January 21, 2017.

27. Hung Liu, San Francisco Women's March speech.

28. Hung Liu, phone conversation with author, May 15, 2020.

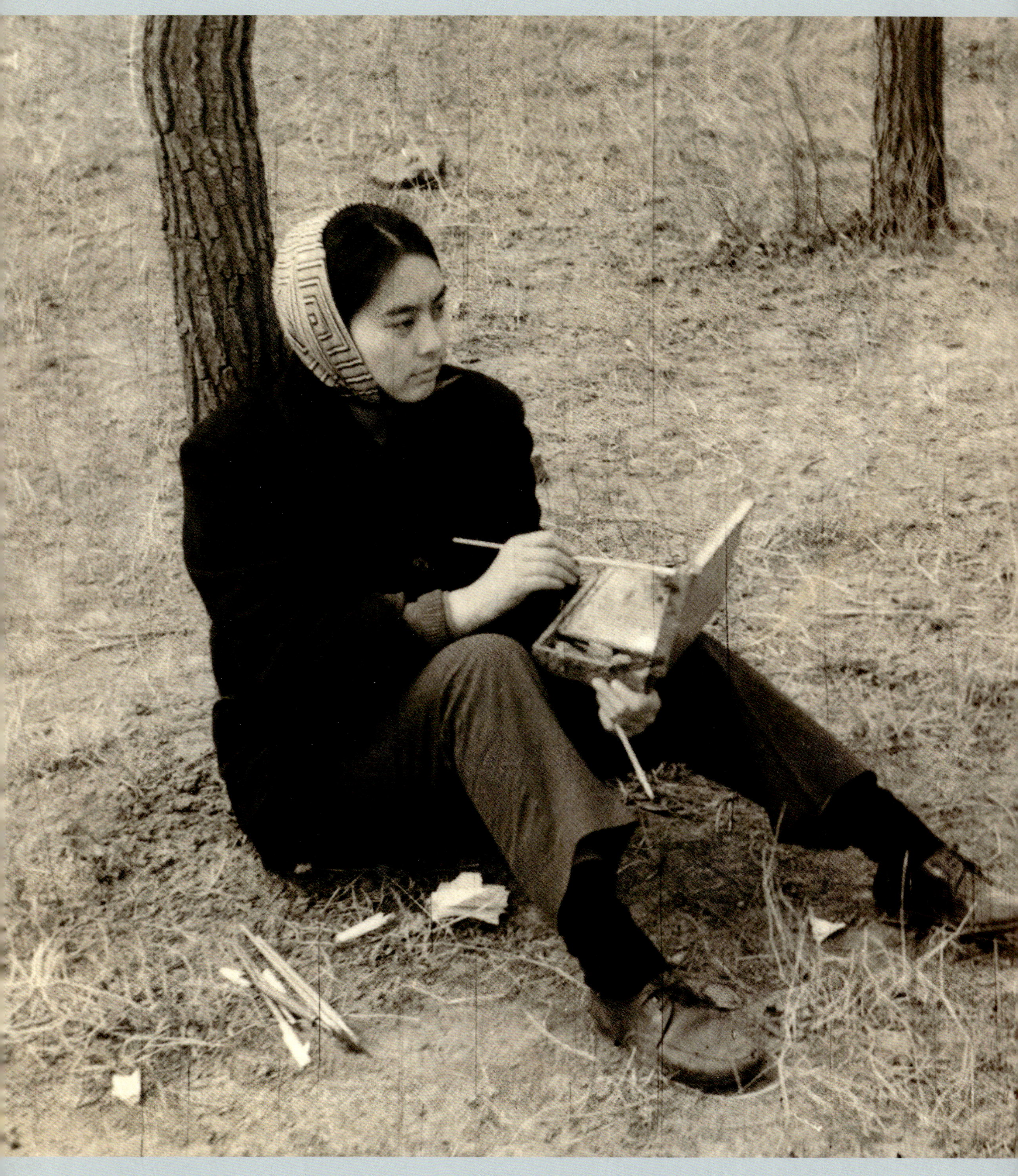

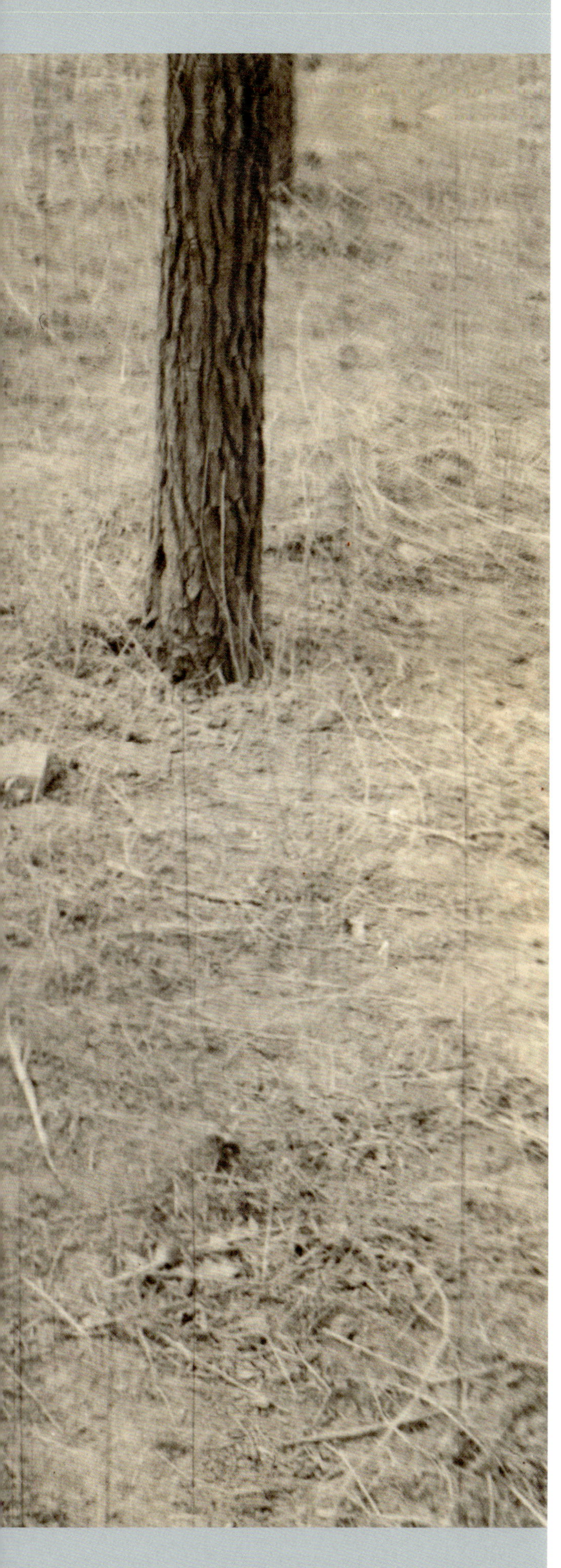

NANCY LIM

PICTURING THE CULTURAL REVOLUTION

Hung Liu's Early Work

In 1968, under Mao Zedong's sweeping "Down to the Countryside Movement," twenty-year-old Hung Liu was resettled in rural China for proletariat reeducation. In the wide farmlands of Dadu Lianghe, fifty miles north of Beijing, she labored for four years, joining seventeen million other "sent-down youth" who had been exiled from the country's urban centers and charged with the creation of a Communist utopia. Liu threshed rice and bound corn, dug trenches of frozen mud during winter, fertilized fields and collected wood; and in the scarce moments between, she survived on meager rations of grain, cooking oil, and soap. As the days grew into seasons that passed into years, she felt the heavy endlessness of her exile, uncertain when it would end. When the occasional plane flew overhead, she wondered, "Is it coming to take us away from here?"[1]

Surprisingly, Liu's most reliable, if sporadic, moments of rest were delivered through the village's political meetings, convened to broadcast the Communist Party's newest instructions. Because attendance counted toward time in the fields, people diligently made themselves present—and then napped, breastfed their children, or finished their needlework and other household chores. "Nobody listened," Liu recalled, and indeed, so long as their bodies were visible, active participation was irrelevant.[2] Their labor and devotions could be applied elsewhere—to sewing, to chatting—such that this space of civic gathering and propaganda transmission became redefined, by the villagers themselves, as a sphere of rest, autonomy, and even self-determination. Liu, who soon came to feel the same motivating freedom, picked up her pencil and started sketching.

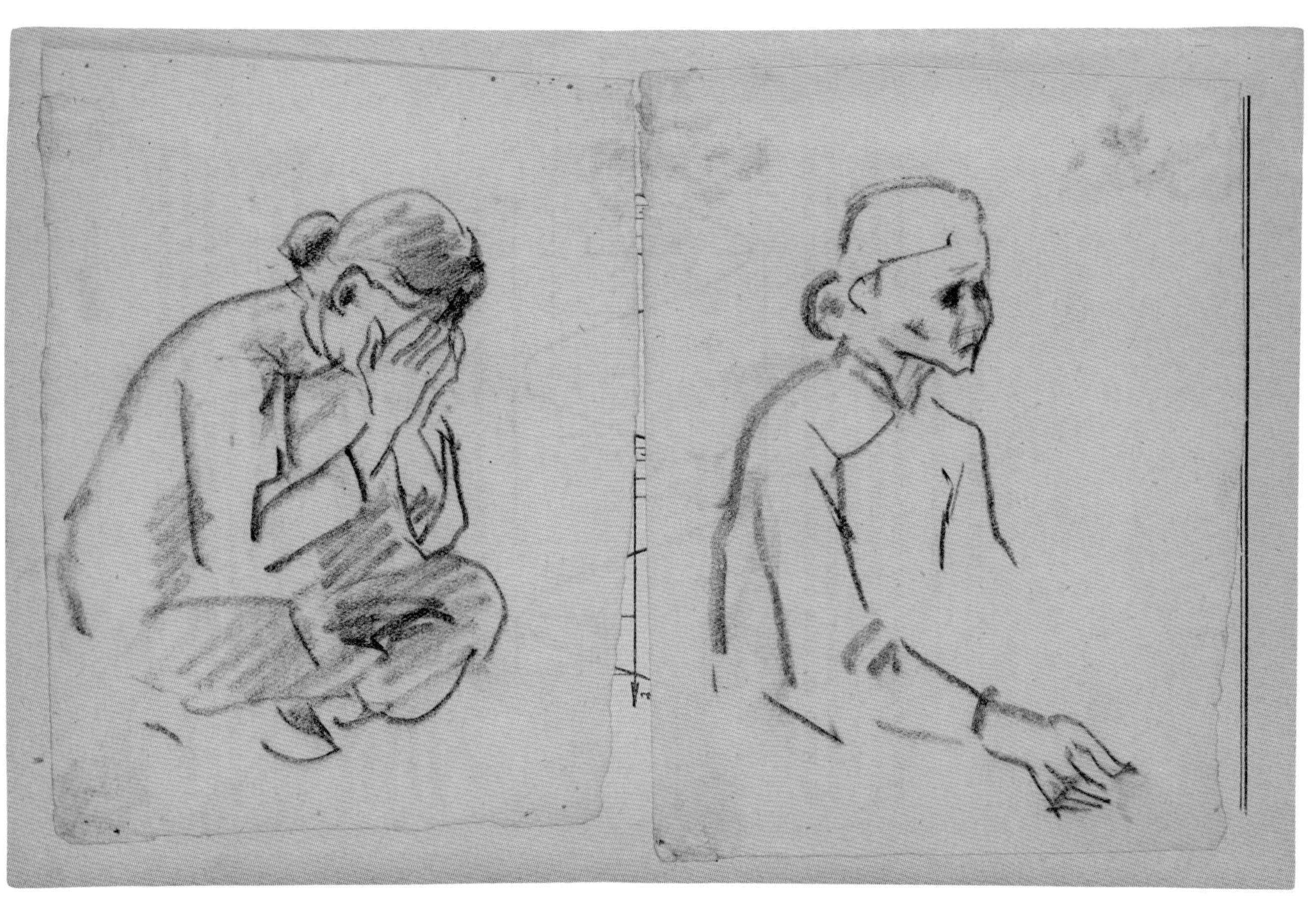
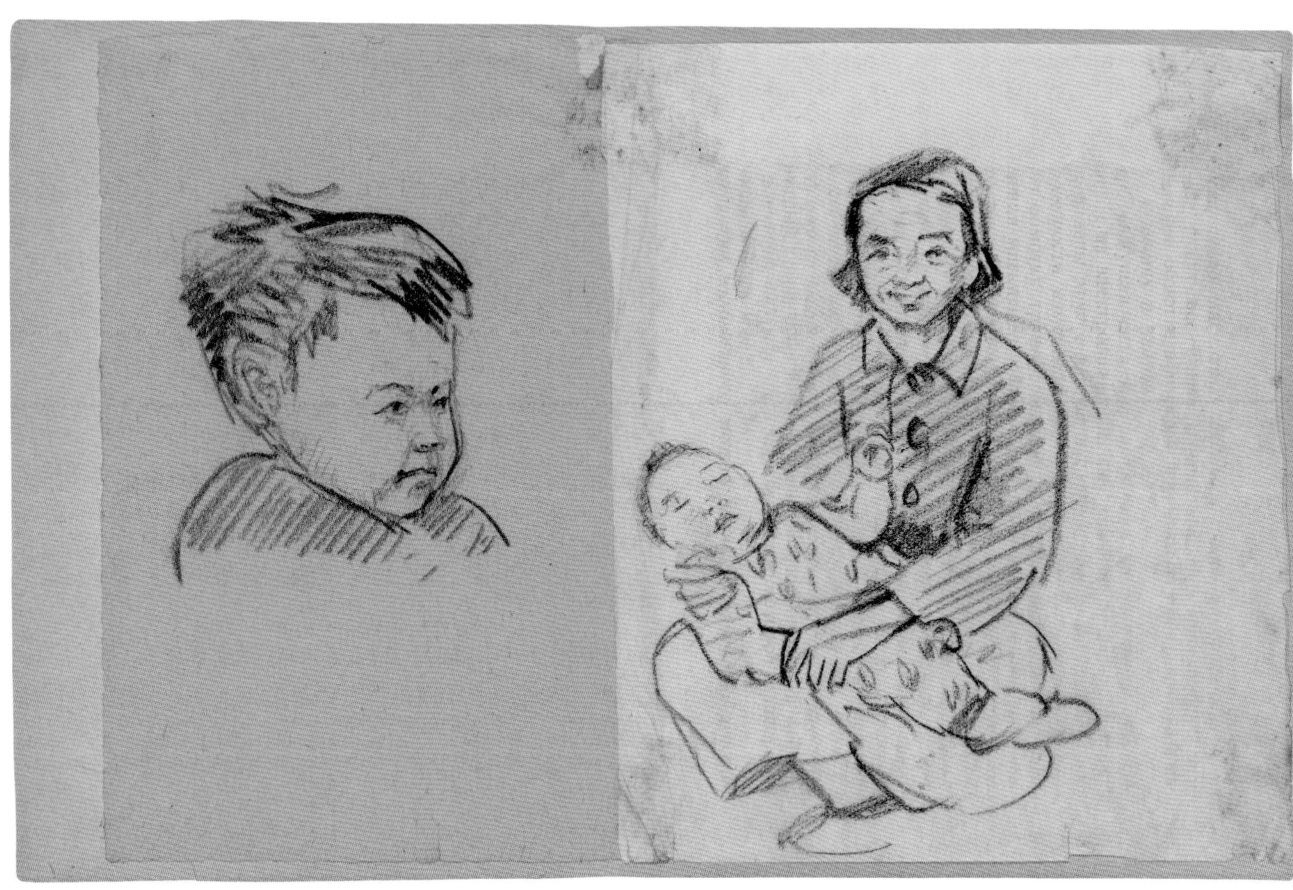

She drew the villagers around her, reinscribing their inattentive, dreaming bodies onto her paper pad. With soft graphite lines, she rendered pant legs and slumped shoulders; other times, she explored more narrative details: a toddler dozing in his mother's lap or an elderly woman mending her shoes (figs. 1, 2). Sketched within a minute or two, the drawings are casual and schematic, reflecting Liu's decision to bypass technical veracity in favor of speed. Despite their concision, however, the sketches indulged the artist's curiosity for the expressive humanity around her. From childhood, she had shown an acute sensitivity to personalities who crossed her path; she drew careful portraits of each visitor to her mother's home, and during her middle and high school years, while receiving formal instruction at art clubs and the Beijing Children's Palace of Culture, she painted landscapes *en plein air* and sketched live models and plaster busts. These foundational experiences seeped into Liu's drawing practice in the village meetings, connecting her earlier days of art-making to her new reality of enforced labor and limited creative supplies.

Thus, while the sketches appear as simple impressions of the scenes around her, the fragile continuity she was able to recover, between her previous and current lives, suffuses the images with a self-preservationist impulse.[3] This same drive inspired her to subscribe to *Peking Weekly*, a Communist magazine published in English. Her proficiency in "the language of imperialism,"[4] which she had learned at her mother's insistence, proved an invaluable resource; reading its pages, she recalled, "gave me the feeling that I hadn't been 'reformed' into something like the clods of earth in the fields around me, stupefied and numb to it all."[5] Drawing, too, became a hopeful, even redemptive, act, as it threaded, however tenuously, her reality with both her past and glimpses of an alternate present.

As villagers became acquainted with Liu's sketches, they eventually began asking for posed portraits, curious to engage in more deliberate self-presentations. Liu happily obliged, and together she and the villagers embarked on more self-conscious interpersonal terms that gave formal shape to their respective roles as sitter and artist (cats. 5–7). She turned her gaze to her own visage as well, drawing each element with time and detail, from the braid slung over her shoulder to her headscarf's shaded drapery (fig. 3).

Ultimately, it was not the act of drawing that alone held redemptive capacity; it was also her relationships with the neighbors. Their increasingly nuanced dynamic produced drawings wholly distinct from their high-profile counterpart: the "portraits" on view in the propaganda circulating furiously in urban centers (fig. 4). Ideological missives in the country's rural areas were often not visual in scope; they tended to be broadcast aurally, through loudspeakers and at village meetings, to accommodate low literacy rates and a disinterest in spending meager disposable income on the Communist daily paper. But in Beijing, throughout Liu's childhood and on her irregular

Opposite top: Fig. 1. Hung Liu
Sketches of a woman in Dadu Lianghe, 1968–71
Graphite on paper, each 5 × 4 in. (12.7 × 10.2 cm)

Opposite bottom: Fig. 2. Hung Liu
Sketches of villagers in Dadu Lianghe, 1968–71
Graphite on paper, left: 5½ × 3½ in. (14 × 8.9 cm); right: 5½ × 4½ in. (14 × 11.4 cm)

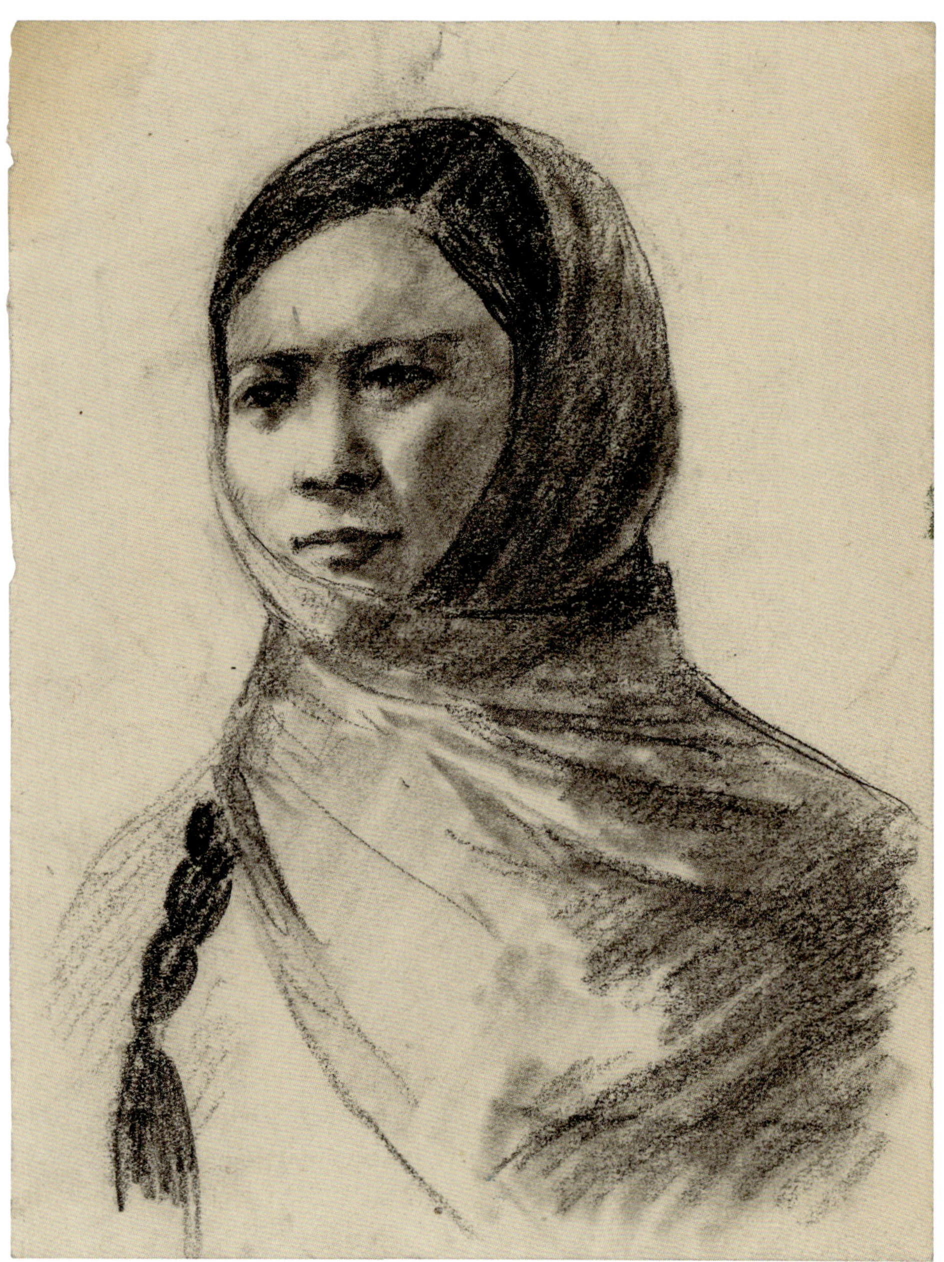

Fig. 3. Hung Liu
Self-Portrait, 1968–72
Graphite on paper, 7 × 5¼ in. (17.8 × 13.3 cm)

trips home to visit family during exile, the Party's posters, statues, flyers, and billboards saturated the visual landscape. Readers of Mao's Little Red Book were typical protagonists, as were laborers in sociable conversation, their figures framed by a colorful backdrop of factories or fields. Meant to reify an optimism for the country's health and productivity, and disavow the realities of the catastrophic Great Leap Forward, these featured bodies were invariably reduced to key symbolic components so as to ensure a narrative legibility: resolute eyes and a directional gaze, crisp hand gestures such as bold, raised fists, and ruddy cheeks whose hue of Communist red was Party-dictated in meticulous efforts to bolster a sentimental patriotism.

Despite Liu's childhood immersion in these spectacles, she understood clearly that the relationship between these depictions

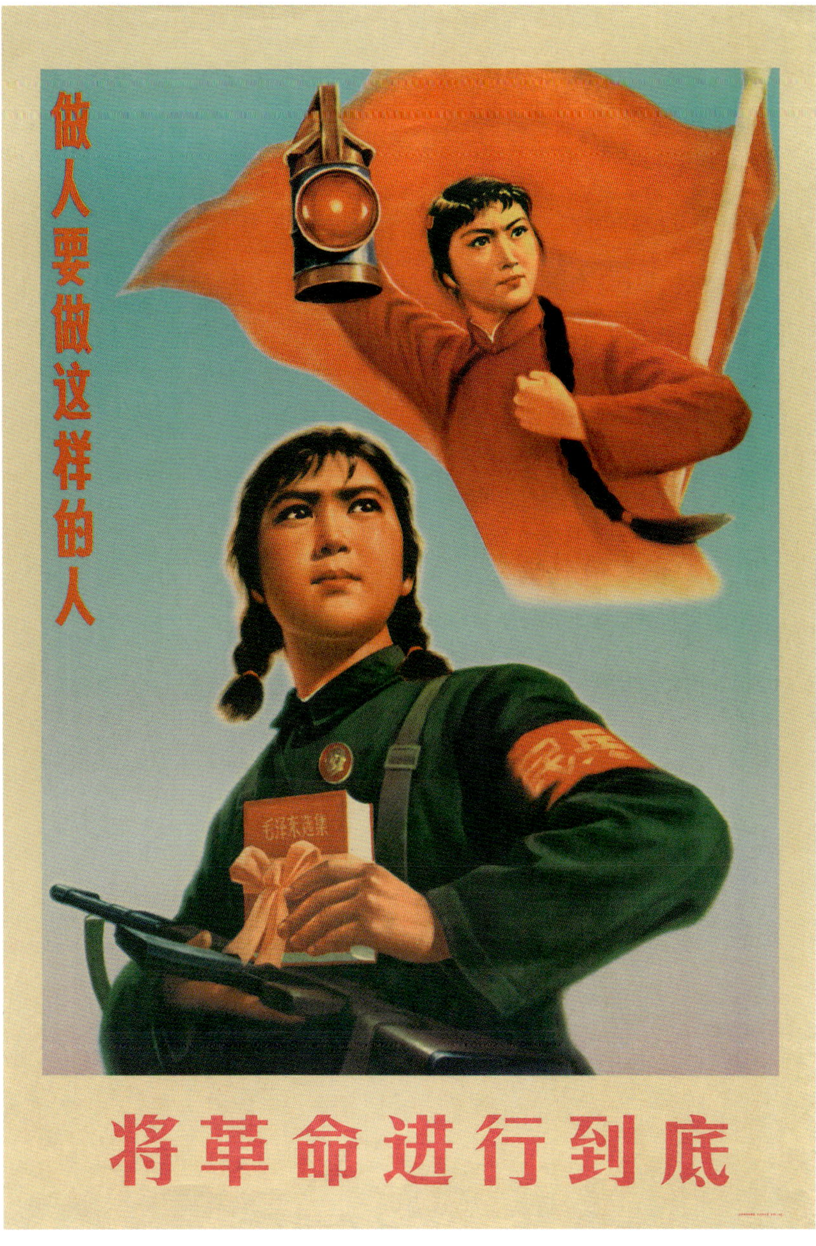

Fig. 4. Shan Lianxiao
I Want to Live Like Her (Carry on the Revolution to the End), 1968
Poster
Collection of Shaomin Li

and reality was tenuous. "When I was in the countryside on a rainy day when our pants were dirty," she recalled, "no one had a smile on their face like on the posters. In the war, no one posed heroically."[6] This romantic "pseudo-realism," as one author has called it, inspired Liu's own coinage: "socialist surrealism," intended as a play on the phrase "socialist realism," the aesthetic China had adopted from the Soviet Union in the mid-1950s and disseminated throughout the country's public spaces and educational settings. (Even when the universities reopened in 1972, the prescribed academic training rested fully on this model, despite its basis in the Western canon and bourgeois Platonic ideals.) In the context of a state that mandated even the precise hue of red for Mao's cheeks, the freedom Liu experienced while sketching quickly and unconstrained—first in the meetings and

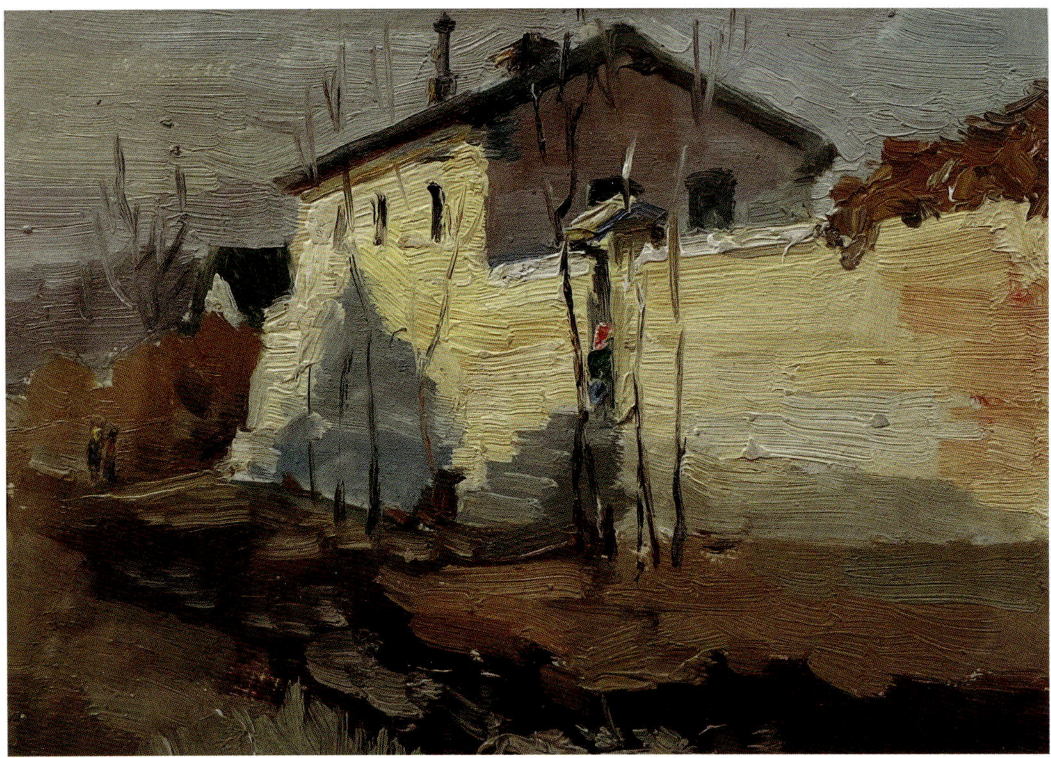

Fig. 5. Hung Liu
My Secret Freedom 19, 1972–75
Oil on paper, 5 × 7 in. (12.7 × 17.8 cm)
San Francisco Museum of Modern Art. Purchase, by
exchange, through a gift of Peggy Guggenheim

eventually in the village—became its own joyful defiance. "That was my chance," she said. "I loved it—nobody cared, you know. In the city, everybody knows what you are doing. But in the village, they cut me some slack."[7]

Liu's unrelenting search for hopeful paths became fundamentally characteristic. When she finally left Dadu Lianghe in 1972 to begin university in Beijing, she sought relief from the strictures of the state's art curricula by escaping each morning to the outskirts of the city, alone, to paint subjects in formats and mediums guided purely by personal will rather than the will of the state. This led to speedy, postcard-sized landscapes of fields, outhouses, dirt paths, and shacks, and she delighted in these humble exercises of color and form (fig. 5). But in their refusal to depict a rosy-cheeked Mao or other Party-approved motifs, the landscapes incited questions from Liu's watchful roommate (who had earned the nickname "Government") about her commitment to a proletariat future. Liu ignored the surveillance and continued painting, hiding some under her bed to dry and throwing most others away. By the time of her graduation in 1975, she had produced more than five hundred of these paintings, keeping faith, day after day, in art's deliverance of a singular kind of freedom.

Presaging such future acts were her sketches in the village. Casual but insistent, discreet but public nonetheless, they were ultimately an assertion over the dominion of representation. And it is this that makes them elementally important in Liu's oeuvre. They rejected the Party's sanctioned vision of the ideal citizenry, as well as the tonal monotony of its visual tropes to which she had become so attuned from years of immersion. Instead, her explorations of Dadu Lianghe's body politic dignified its individuals as such, rather than as mass signifiers. Even while sketching quickly and broadly, she attended to the specificity of every person, drawing them unencumbered by ideological missives and asserting instead their freedom to inhabit a physicality—as exhausted laborers, as breastfeeding mothers, as daydreaming children.

Liu sometimes drew isolated body parts in her sketchbook as well (fig. 6). A floating limb, for instance, torques, droops, and materializes in space. But rather than intending her study of the hand as practice toward a Communist lexicon of didactic gestures, such as the pointed index finger or the open, outstretched palm, she pursued the particularities of its form entirely outside the symbolic realm. Indeed, all throughout her years at the village, Liu's sketches remained unmediated by the government's propaganda tactics and its dependence on the optics of revolution and spectacle. This was notable during a period of enormous pressure to engage with politicized representation, whether as viewer or artist, reader or author. Her sketches abided instead by a humanity—in the interpersonality that generated them, in her embrace of the body's expressions, in her honesty in transcribing what she saw, and in Liu's vision itself.

Fig. 6. Hung Liu
Sketch of villagers in Dadu Lianghe,
1968–71
Graphite on paper, 5¼ × 7½ in.
(13.3 × 19.1 cm)

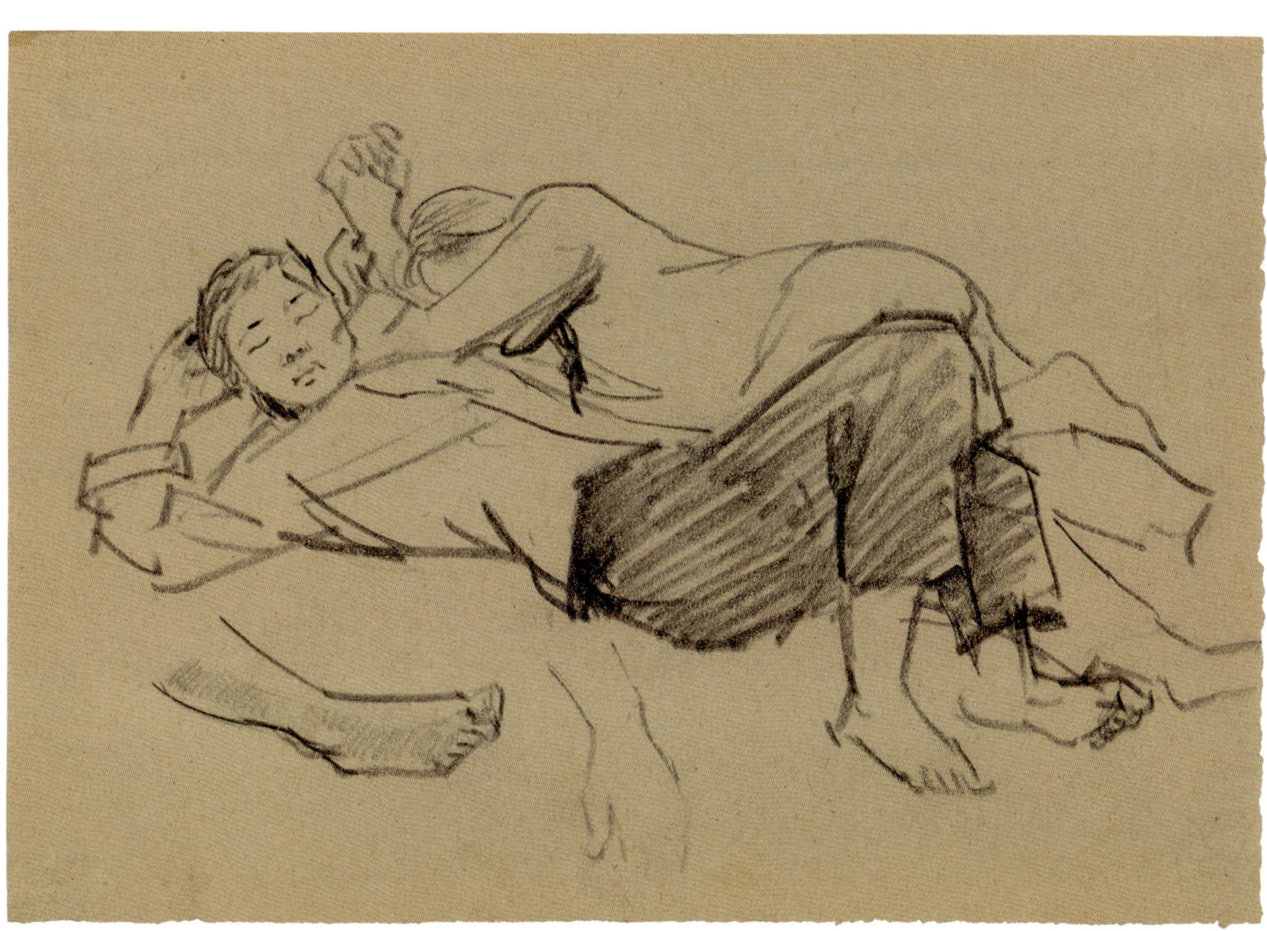

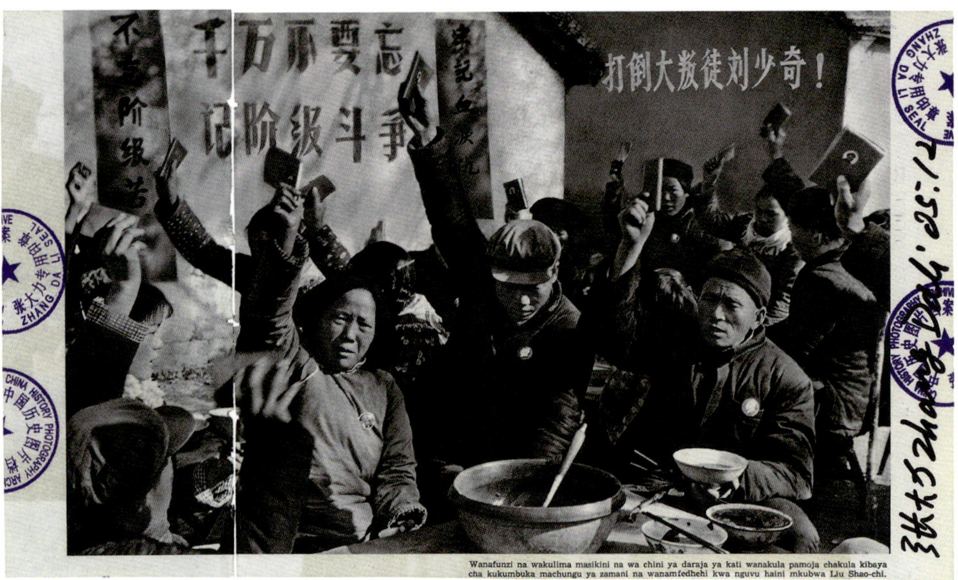

《人民画报》1969年2月（斯瓦希里文版）P25"程庄农业劳动学校"，编辑和出版者：人民画报社，社址：北京阜成门
外北礼士路车公庄大街，电话：89.2127电报挂号：3973 印刷者：北京新华印刷厂，厂址：北京阜成门外北礼士路车公庄
大街，电话：89.5073 电报挂号：0456，总发行处：邮电部北京邮局，订购处：全国各地邮电局所，代订代售处：全国各
地新华书店，国内售价每册1元，本报图片文字如需复制请注明转载本报，代号：2-7，总248期，本报用汉、朝鲜、俄、
英、德、法、日、越南、印度尼西亚、印地、西班牙、阿拉伯、瑞典、斯瓦希里、意大利、乌尔都十六种文字刊印，
《People's Pictorial》February 1969 (Swahili language edition), p. 25 "Chengzhuang Agriculture Labour School". Edited by
People's Pictorial Press: Address Beilishi Road, Chegongzhuang Avenue, Fuchengmenwai, Beijing, tel. 89.2127, trunk line 3973.
Printed by Beijing Xinhua Printing Factory: Address Fuchengmenwai, Beilishi Road, Chegongzhuang Avenue Beijing, tel. 89.5073,
trunk line: 0456. Distributor: Ministry of Post and Telecommunications Beijing Post Office; Subscription Office: any local post
office in the nation; sale and subscription office: any local post office in the nation and the Xinhua Bookstore; domestic sale price: 1
CNY. Any reproduction of images and texts must be registered with the Pictorial. Book no. 2-7, issue 248. The present issue has
been printed in Chinese, Korean, Russian, English, German, French, Japanese, Vietnamese, Indonesian, Hindi, Spanish, Arabic,
Swedish, Swahili, Italian, and Urdu.

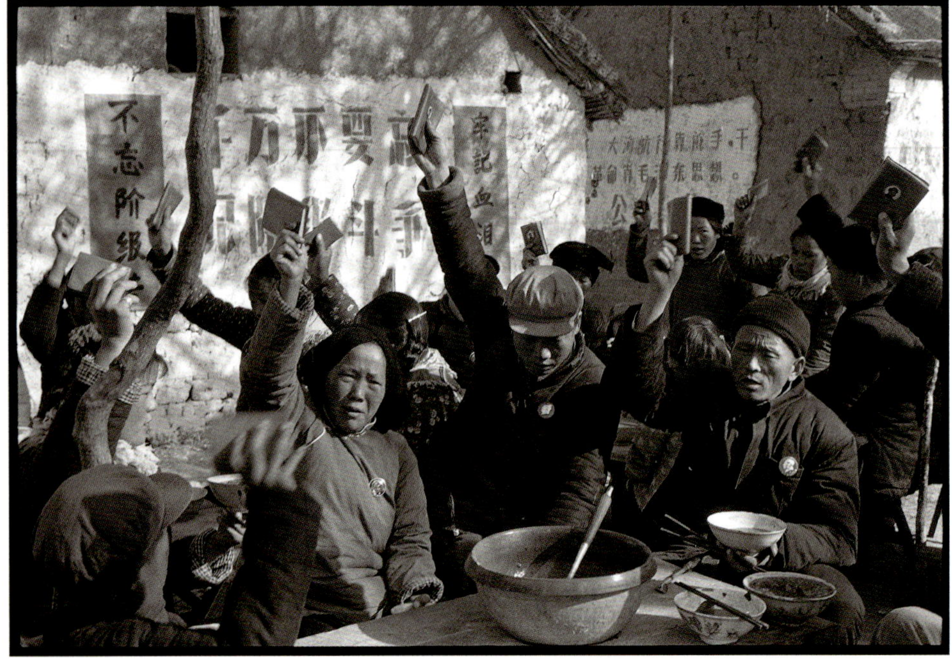

Fig. 7. Zhang Dali
*Second History 85: Chengzhuang
Agriculture Labour School,* 2003–10
Chromogenic print
44⅛ × 23⅝ in. (112 × 60 cm)
Courtesy of the artist and
Eli Klein Gallery

原版黑白底片档案144465
Original black and white negative, Archive no. 144465

This approach profoundly shaped her photographs as well. That photography even emerged as a possibility for Liu is striking. Cameras had become rare in China's cities (most were smashed or confiscated), and vernacular photography had all but disappeared. Any extant knowledge of the medium was marshaled by the state to train a new school of photographers, and this rising generation produced extensive "documentations" of the nation's revolutionary progress. Their photos were then enhanced in the darkroom: retouchers whitened Mao's teeth, purged compositional distractions (or foes), and even tinted bowls of soup to impart an appearance of bounty (fig. 7). The final images "originated in life but [were] higher than life," as one retoucher famously said, and state channels zealously disseminated these parallel, fictive visualizations of the country—a new world construction.[8]

Prior to 1970, Liu had never used a camera. Additionally, her exposure to the medium was limited to studio portraits with family, occasional snapshots with classmates, and the ubiquitous propaganda throughout the city. But as she and a friend were preparing for their departures in 1968, he left his camera with Liu for safekeeping, anticipating that otherwise it would be destroyed at the military camp to which he had been assigned. Nearly two years into Liu's reeducation, she abruptly remembered its existence after overhearing villagers discussing their photo IDs. Thus, by chance and sudden recall, she found herself with a camera during one of the most consequential times of Chinese life and at a critical moment in twentieth-century world history.

Liu waited patiently for one of her permitted trips to Beijing to acquire rolls of film. This was no easy task; as a sent-down youth rather than a state photojournalist, she was an emphatically atypical customer at the photo supply store she visited. But with money borrowed from her mother, she managed to purchase several rolls, even learning from the salesman how to load them, and upon her return to the farm, she began taking pictures of friends. Liu experimented with shutter speed, lighting, and focus, grasping for a technical foundation however she could, all while taking care with her ever-diminishing number of exposures. When she eventually turned to the villagers with requests to take their portraits, some responded warily: "The only time in my life I had my picture taken was when the Japanese occupied [northeast China and] I had to put it on my ID card," Liu recalled hearing.[9] Others feared the gauzier but widespread superstition that the camera would steal their souls.

With time, however, she gained their trust, their comfort with each other tracking their mutual comfort with the medium—especially after she gifted them the photos, painstakingly developed in a corner of her mother's home (cats. 1–4). In the absence of a darkroom, she would wait for nightfall to begin, and then, using secondhand chemicals and a lightbulb she painted red, work through the night to develop the portraits, eventually scavenging an enlarger to scale her photos from thumbnail size to larger sheets. "And then I carried my

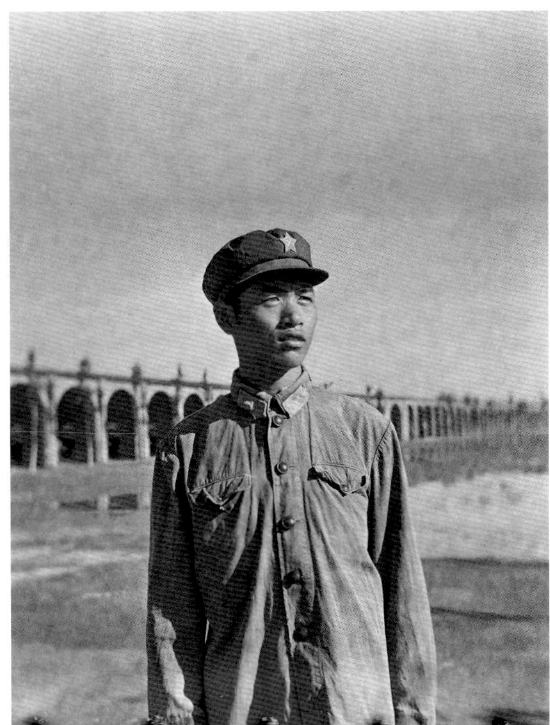

Fig. 8. Hung Liu
Soldier, 1970–72
Photograph

pictures like my harvest back to the village," she said. "The [people there] were all amazed."[10]

At first glance, Liu's images seem to align neatly with conventions of propaganda and studio portraiture. She depicts her subjects from chest up, occasionally stretching the frame to show their bodies in full, and they often stand outdoors, posing in a field at high noon. In a few cases, Liu applies these conventions in a duplicative attempt—one photo features a uniformed youth standing before an elaborate bridge, a trope of Communist progress (fig. 8). But on the whole, she uses architecture as a compositional aid: doorjambs outline the body, while large walls anchor it in space. In her general refusal to produce crisp, politicized images populated by symbols and tropes, the buildings that are present tend to dissolve, becoming specters in the periphery, while other times they appear arbitrary or accidental. Even Mao's portrait, if visible, hangs companionably beside other memorabilia, all the wall's elements on candid display rather than dutifully minimized or erased (fig. 9). "I had this great satisfaction and pleasure that I could do something so casual so they didn't have to go to town and to the effort of putting on new clothes," she said of her honest and low-key approach to these shots. "They could just stand in front of the fence or whatever."[11] Her ambivalence about the background differed sharply from the constancy of her interest in the human subject, who holds almost total visual primacy in this series. Unlike propaganda's

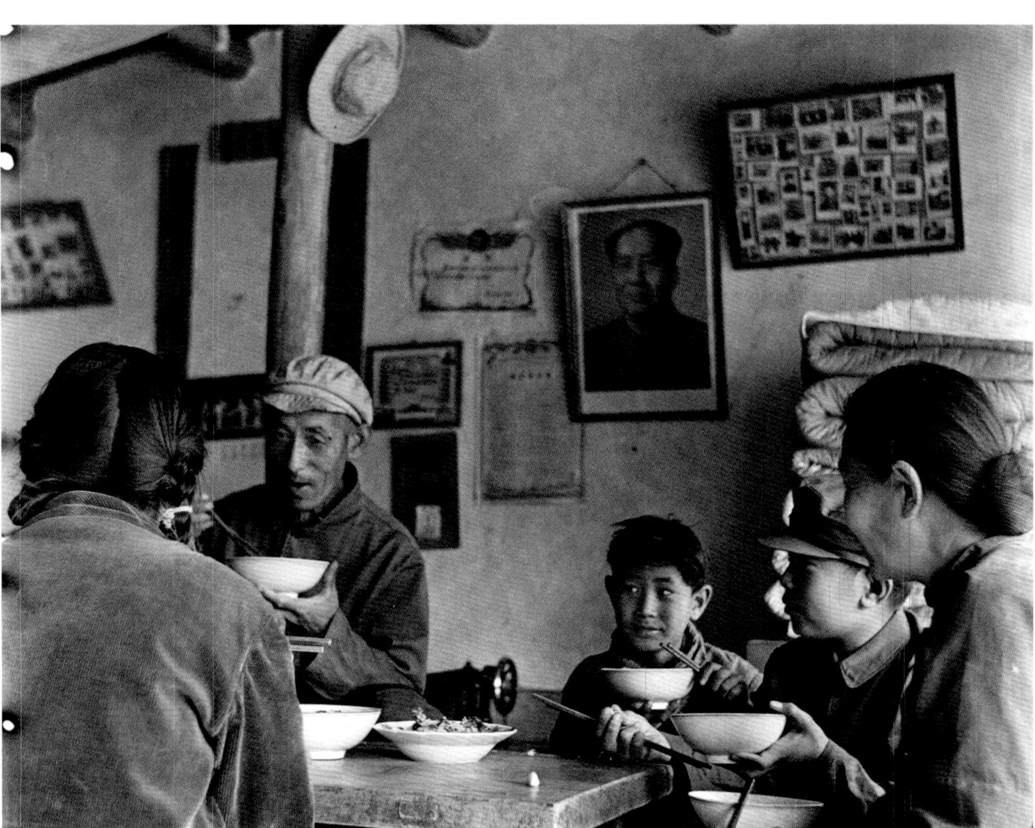

Fig. 9. Hung Liu
Village Photograph (Peasant Family
Dinner), 1970–72
Photograph

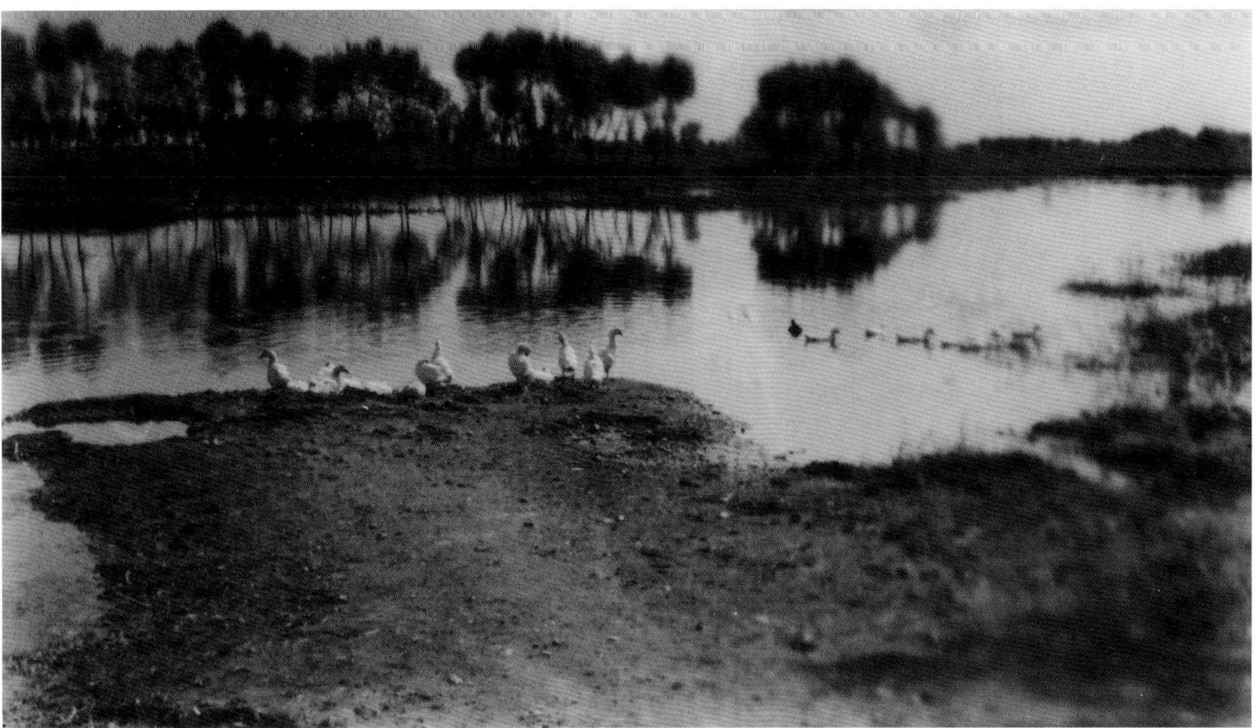

Fig. 10. Hung Liu
The River's Awakening, c. 1970
Photograph

narrow focus on political subjectivity, Liu's tender documents of humanity radiate with her subjects' richness and complexities. These portraits are heightened by her "mistakes," such as eyes that closed at the click of the shutter or mouths that froze mid-sentence—all those bodily disobediences that only photography could surface (cat. 4).

For a time, Liu took her camera to a river near town that reminded her of Russian paintings she had studied as a child. The resulting photos were themselves painterly, the shadowy trees and the water's dappled surface so lyrical they drew dangerously close to the individualistic, "bourgeois" pictorialism considered punishable in China's cities (fig. 10). Their lush, excessive poetry connects them to her village portraits, and this shared quality reveals Liu's overall focus on photos beholden to the pleasures of sight—both naked sight itself and sight as revealed through the camera lens and on the printed sheet. Already in this incipient period of her career, she believed intensely in the vitality of image-making beyond prescribed state functions. This understanding led her to regard her photographs as acts of sensuousness that explore embodied life and embrace the joys of vision.

She then tied this—in her photos, her sketches, and all of her practice to come—to the pleasures of interpersonal communion, which she deepened through gifts of her work to the villagers. These offerings contain hidden worlds of time and care, from her nocturnal experiments in the darkroom to her long and unreliable truck rides back to the village from Beijing. She called them her "harvest," and

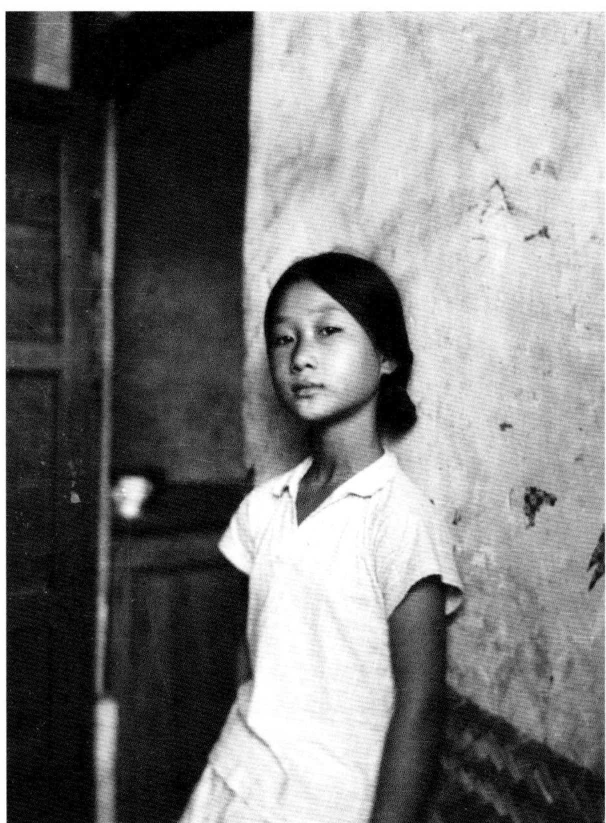

Fig. 11. Hung Liu
My Little Swan, 1970–72
Photograph

indeed she tended to them, developed them, and then gave them away. While certainly "a gesture of solidarity between the city girl and her rough-hewn subjects," as one author has described, they were above all a bestowal, to herself and those around her, of memory.[12] Her photos and drawings, and their subsequent circulation, were joyful provocations to the systematic erasure of history ignited by Mao's condemnation of the past. Whether eagerly or against their will, people throughout urban centers burned family portraits and destroyed other cherished mementos. In this context, Liu's images are willful, as modest as they initially seem, enacting in these early, formative years what would come to be a lifelong devotion to remembrance and the unassailable worthiness of memory (fig. 11).

Notes

1. Hung Liu quoted in "Sixty Years on a Hard Journey for Art: A Conversation between Hung Liu and Wu Hung," in *Hung Liu: Great Granary,* ed. Wu Hung (Hong Kong: Timezone 8, 2010), 80.
2. Hung Liu, oral history interview by Joann Moser, April 25–29, 2010, Archives of American Art, Smithsonian Institution, Washington, D.C.: 81–82.
3. See Alan Atkinson, *Hung Liu: Now and Then* (Norman: University of Oklahoma, Fred Jones Jr. Museum of Art, 2008), 11.
4. Hung Liu quoted in Wu Hung, "Sixty Years," 68.
5. Hung Liu quoted in Wu Hung, "Sixty Years," 77–78.
6. Hung Liu quoted in Karen Smith, "Hung Liu: Thunder in My Heart," in *Summoning Ghosts: The Art of Hung Liu,* by René Guzman et al. (Oakland, Calif.: Oakland Museum of California; Berkeley: University of California Press, 2013), 96.
7. Hung Liu, oral history interview, 82.
8. The retoucher, Chen Shilin, is quoted in Marine Cabos, "The Cultural Revolution through the Prism of Vernacular Photography," *Art and Vernacular Photographies in Asia* 8, no. 1 (Fall 2017): n.p. Also see Wu Hung, ed., *Zooming In: Histories of Photography in China* (London: Reaktion, 2016), 205.
9. Hung Liu, oral history interview, 83.
10. Hung Liu, oral history interview, 83.
11. Hung Liu quoted in Kathleen McManus Zurko, ed., *Hung Liu: A Ten-Year Survey, 1988–1998* (Wooster, Ohio: College of Wooster Art Museum, 1998), 32.
12. Atkinson, *Now and Then,* 11.

PLATES
Part I

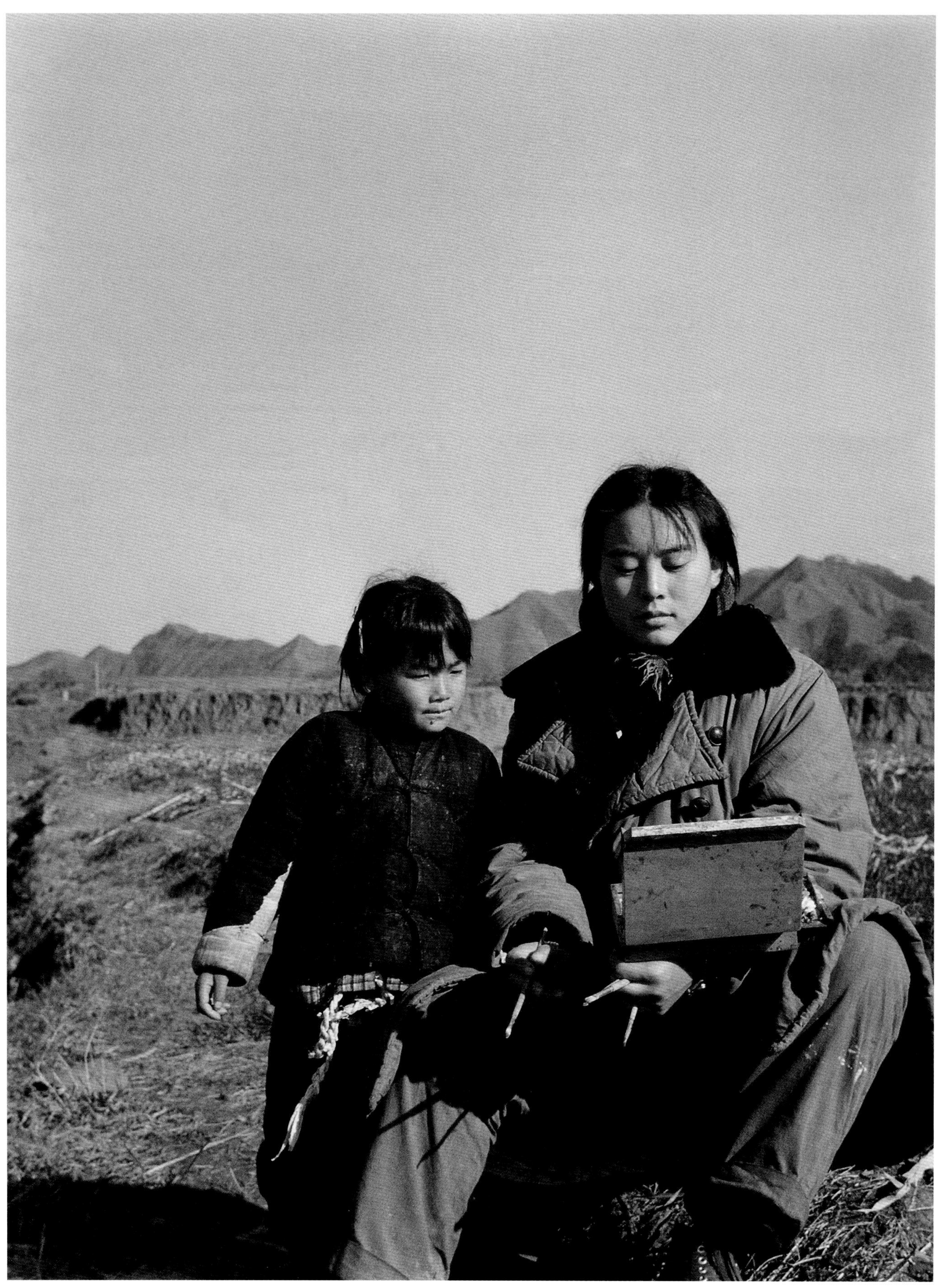

1. *Village Photograph 4* (Paint Box), 1970–72 (printed later)
Photograph
24 × 18 in. (61 × 45.7 cm)

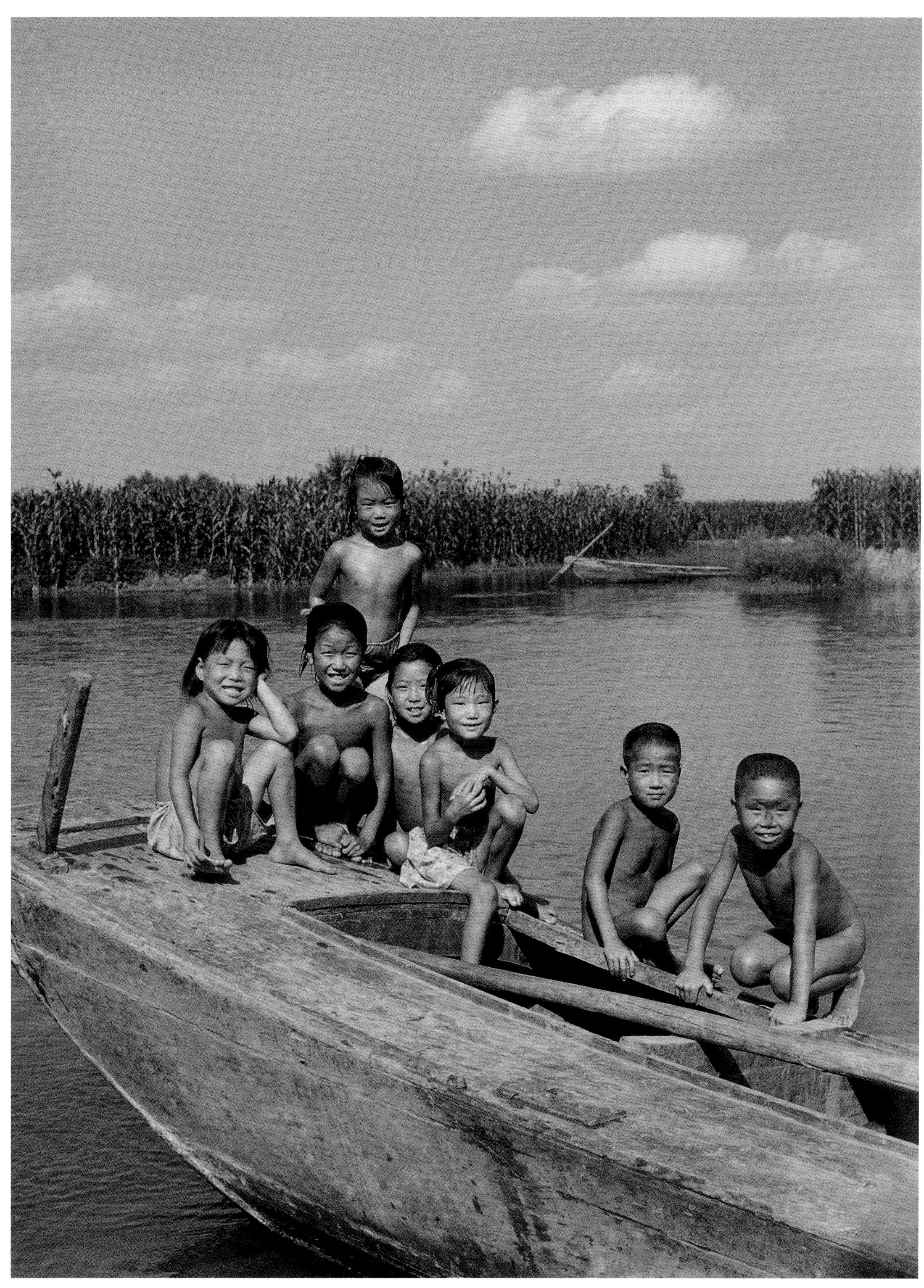

2. *Village Photograph 10* (Water Children), 1970–72 (printed later)
Photograph
24 × 18 in. (61 × 45.7 cm)

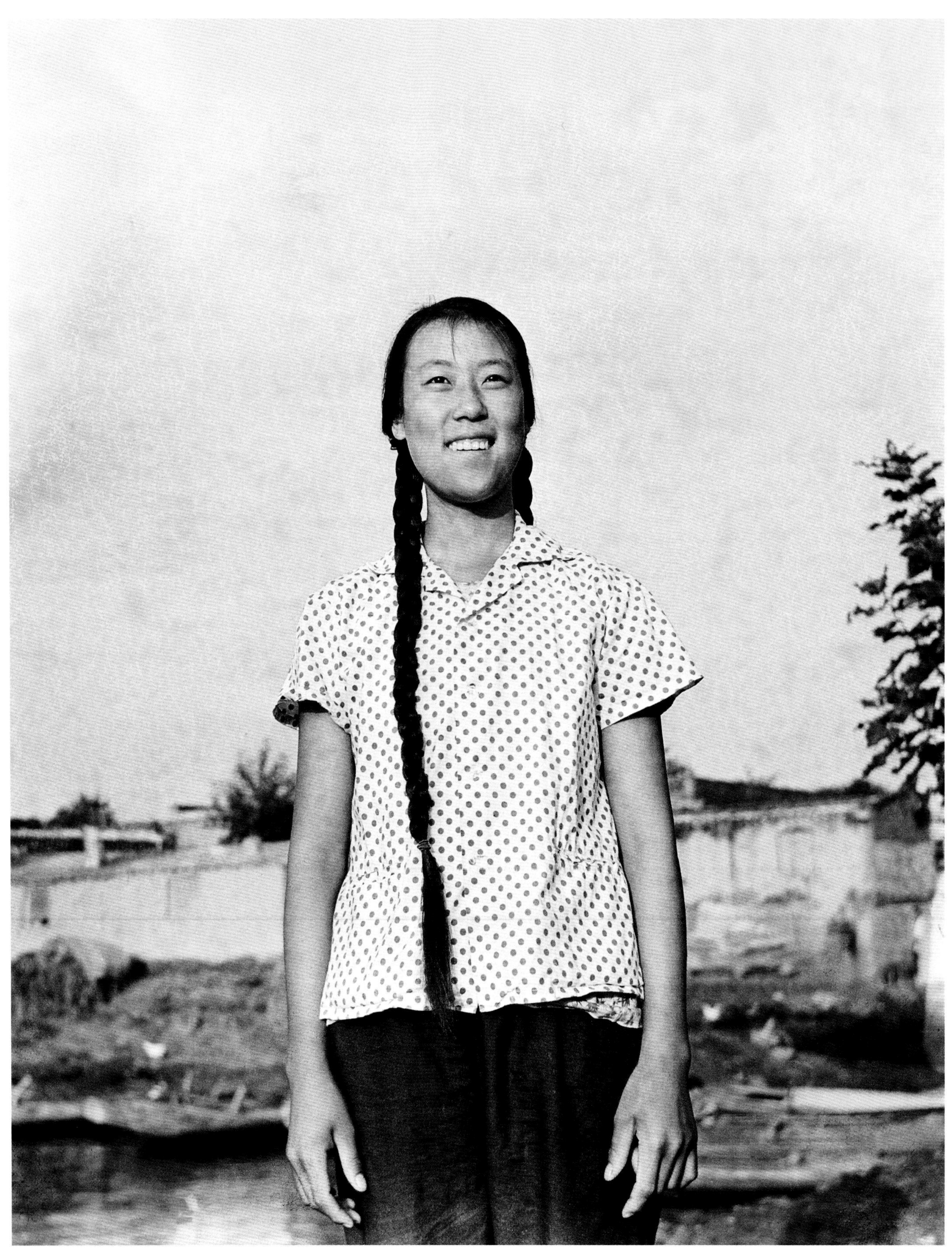

3. *Village Photograph 8* (Her Village), 1970–72 (printed later)
Photograph
24 × 18 in. (61 × 45.7 cm)

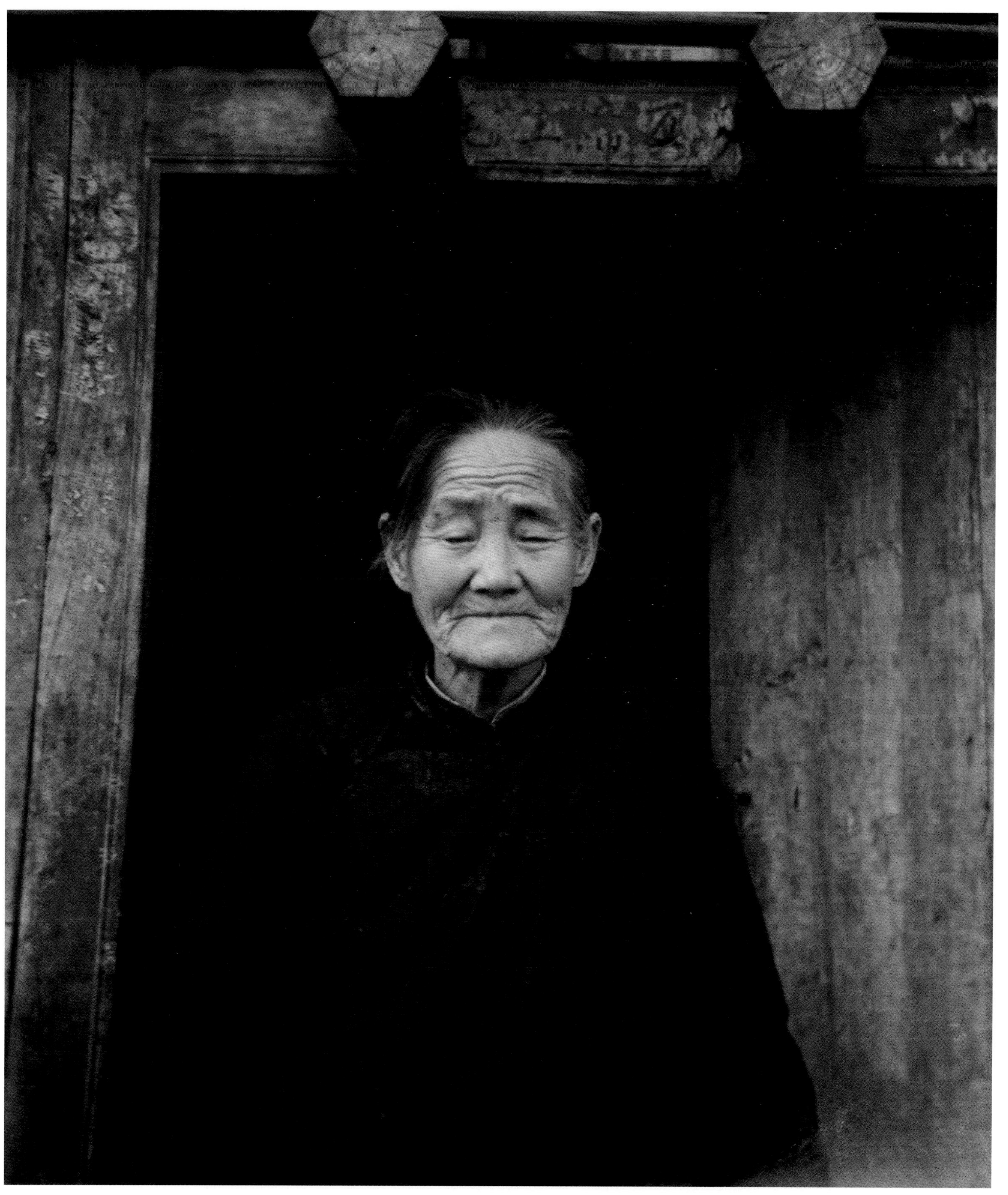

4. *Village Photograph 5* (Peasant Grandma), 1970–72 (printed later)
Photograph
24 × 18 in. (61 × 45.7 cm)

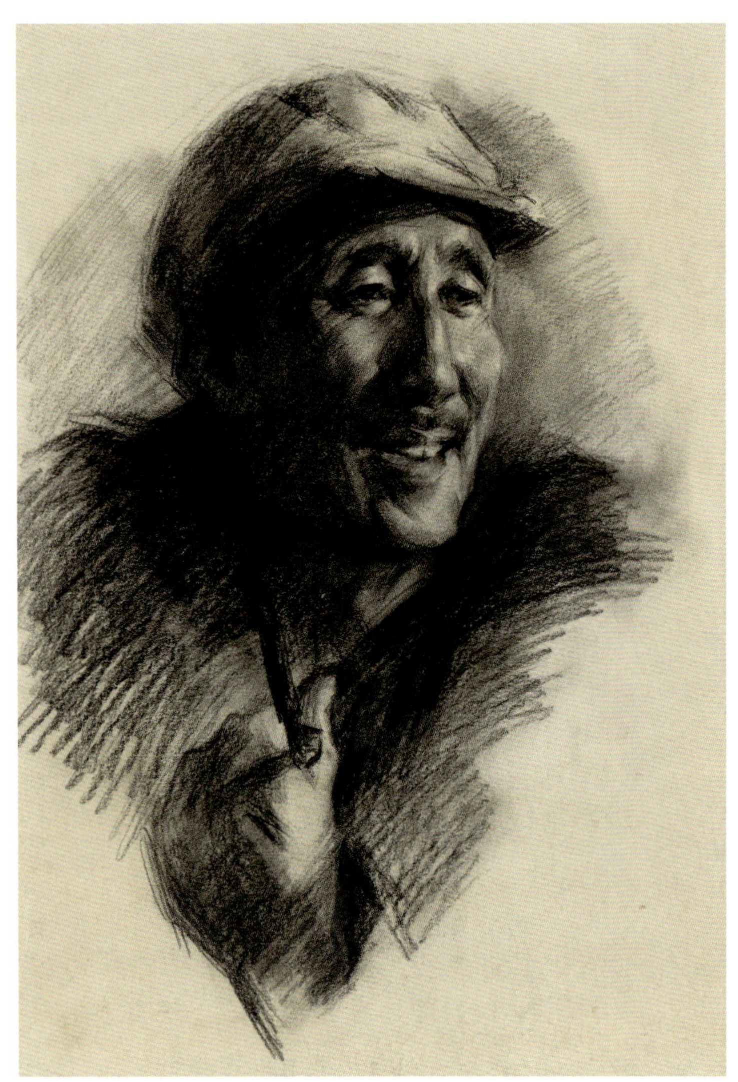

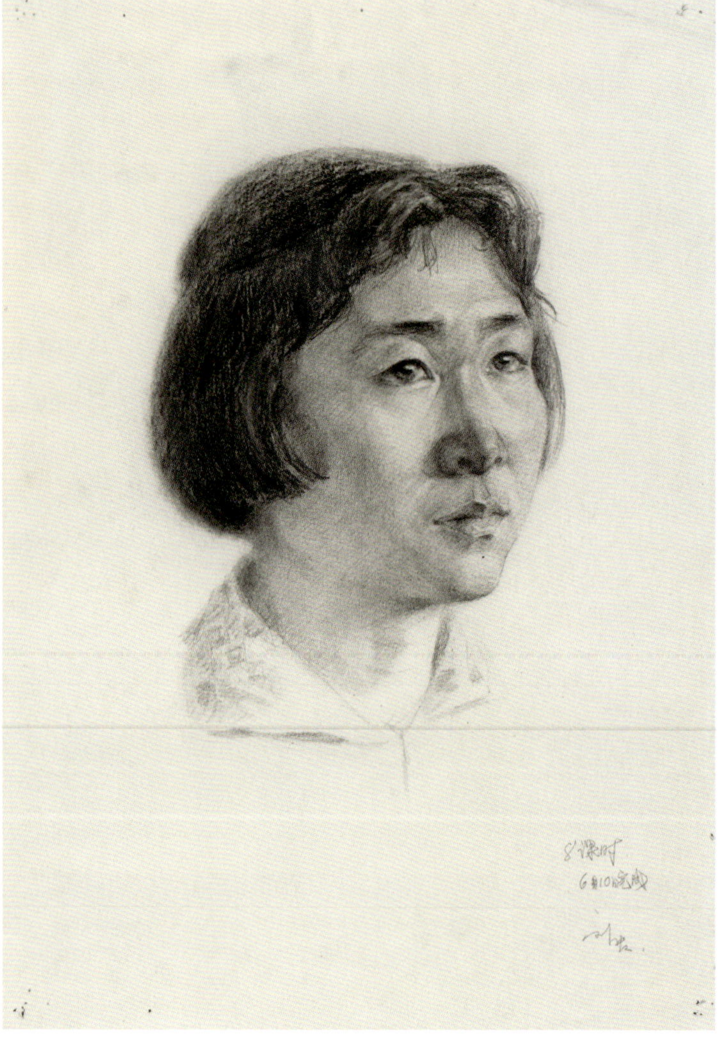

5. *Man with Coat and Hat,* 1972–75
Charcoal on paper
15½ × 10½ in. (39.4 × 26.7 cm)

6. *Young Woman,* 1972–75
Charcoal on paper
12 × 8 in. (30.5 × 20.3 cm)

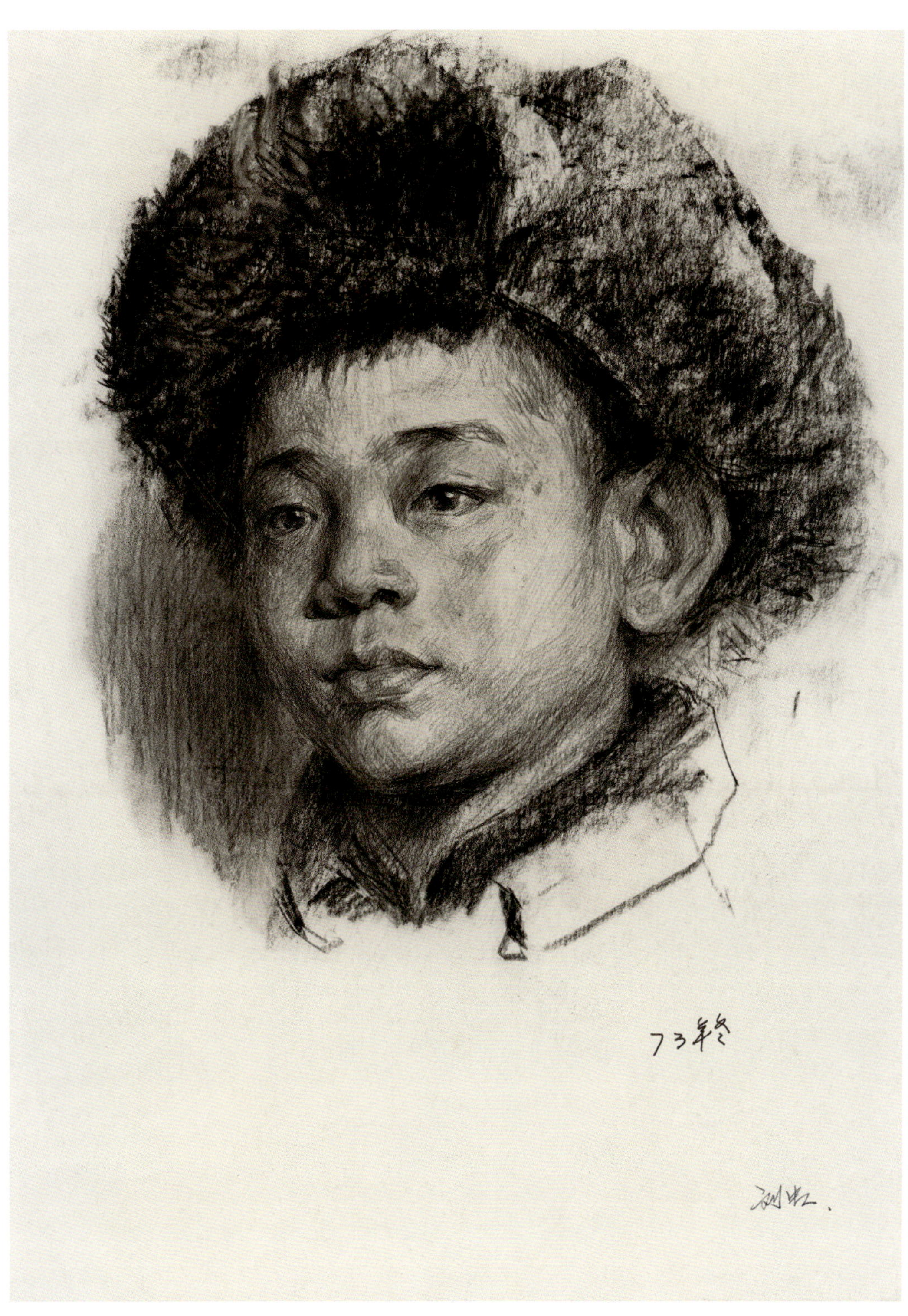

7. *Boy with Hat in Winter,* 1973
Charcoal on paper
12 × 8 in. (30.5 × 20.3 cm)

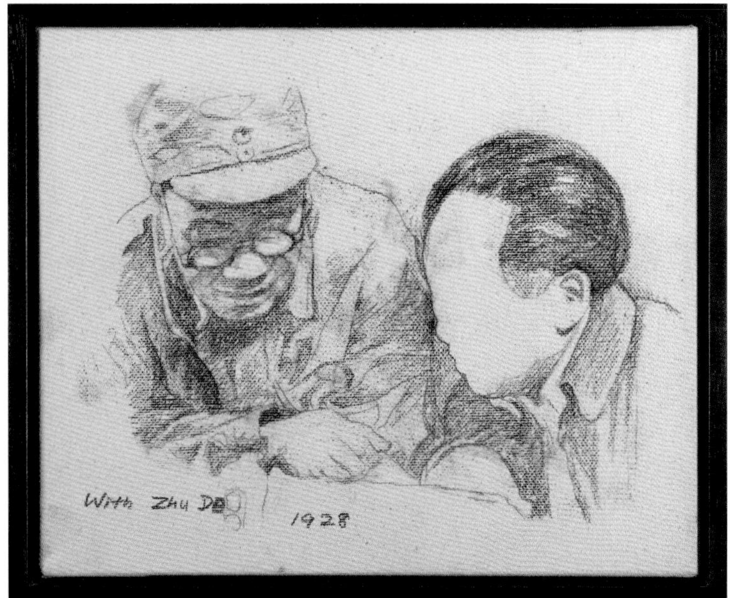

8

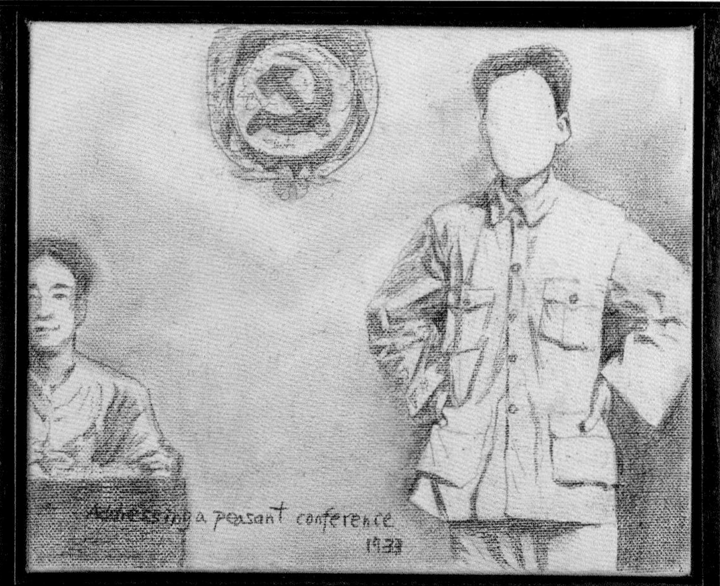

9

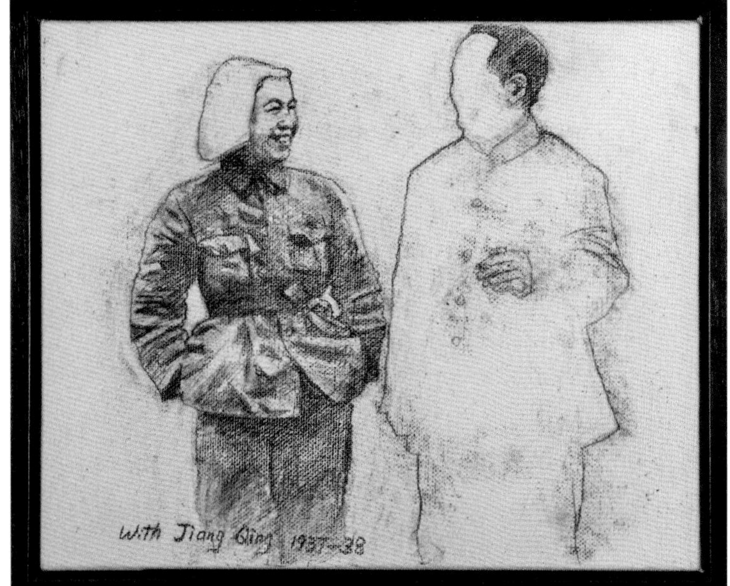

10

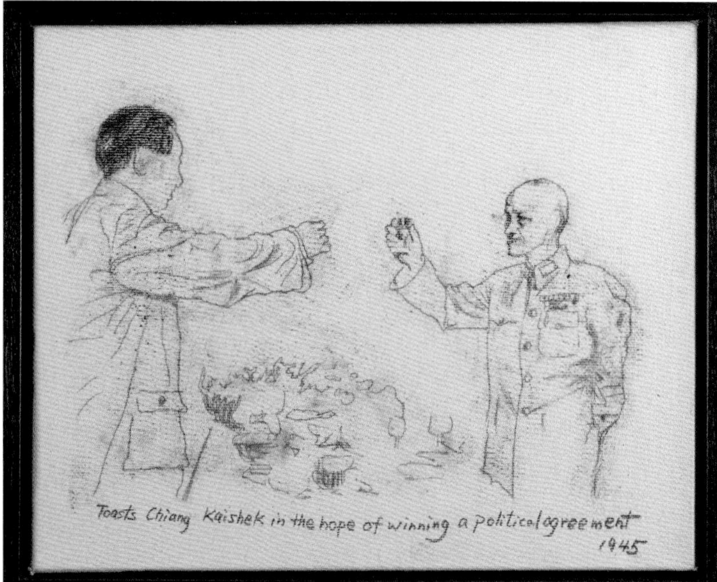

11

8 through 17. *Where Is Mao?*, 1988
Graphite on canvas
Each 8 × 10 in. (20.3 × 25.4 cm)
Gift from Vicki and Kent Logan to the Collection of the Denver Art Museum

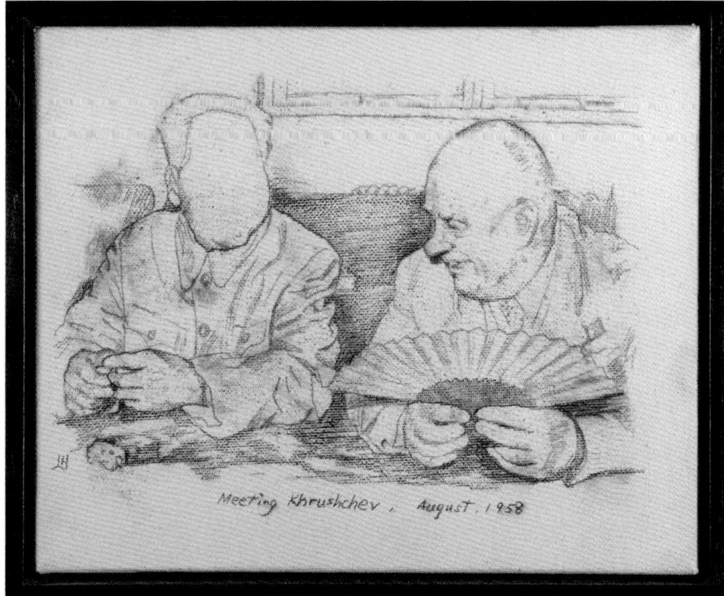

12

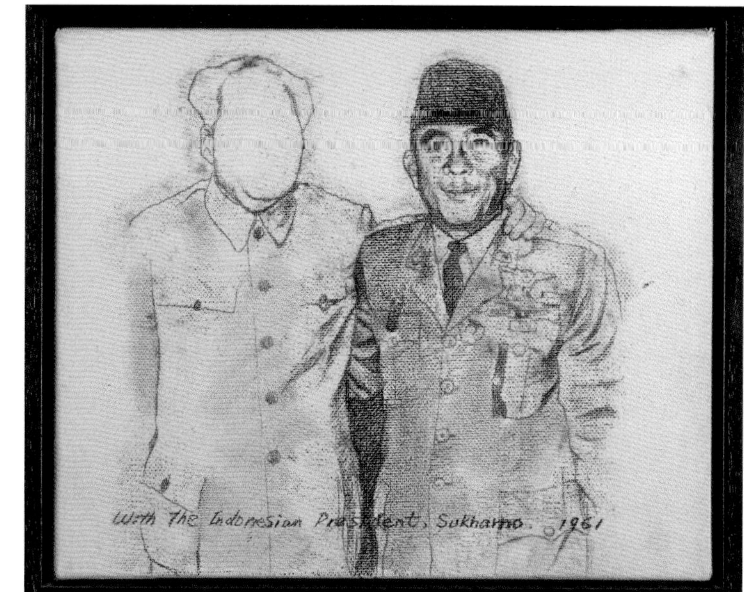

13

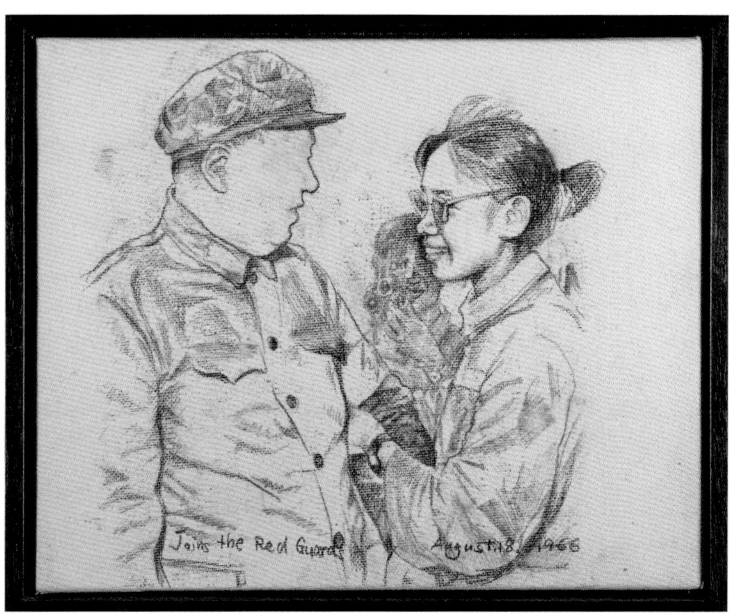

14

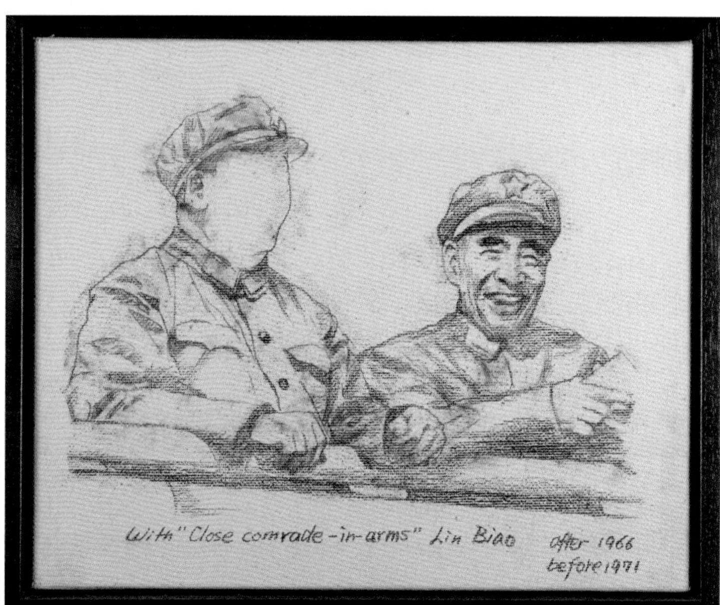

15

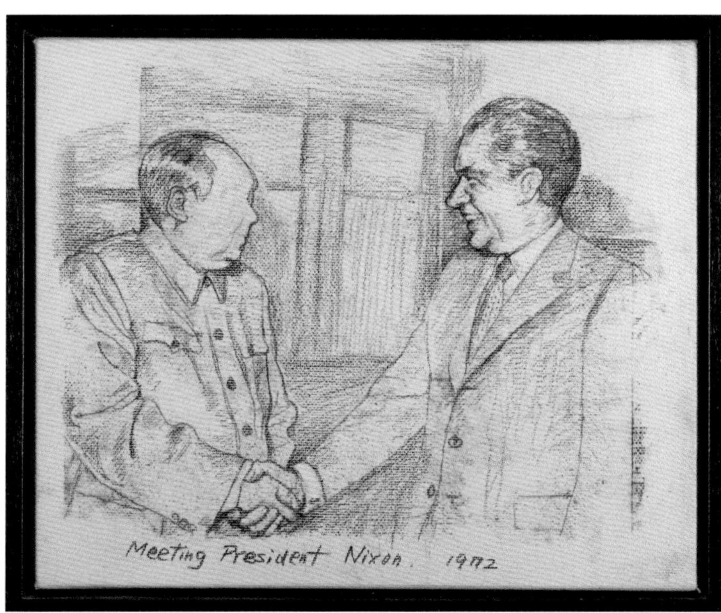

16

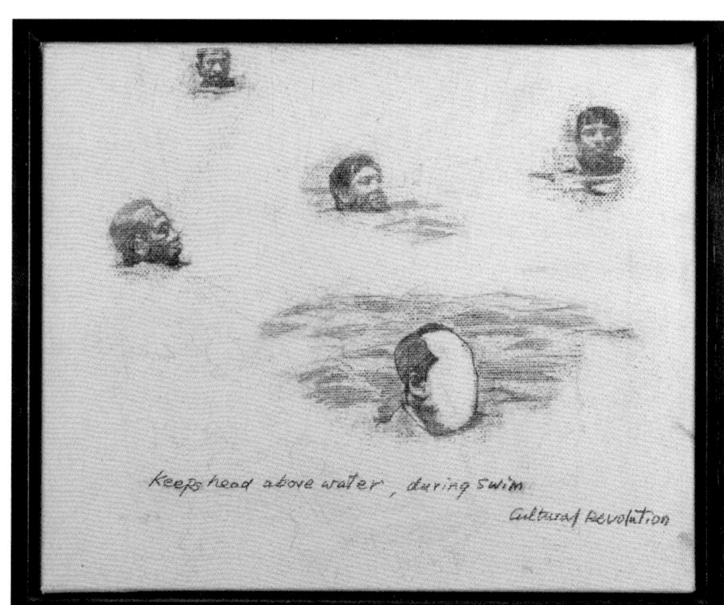

17

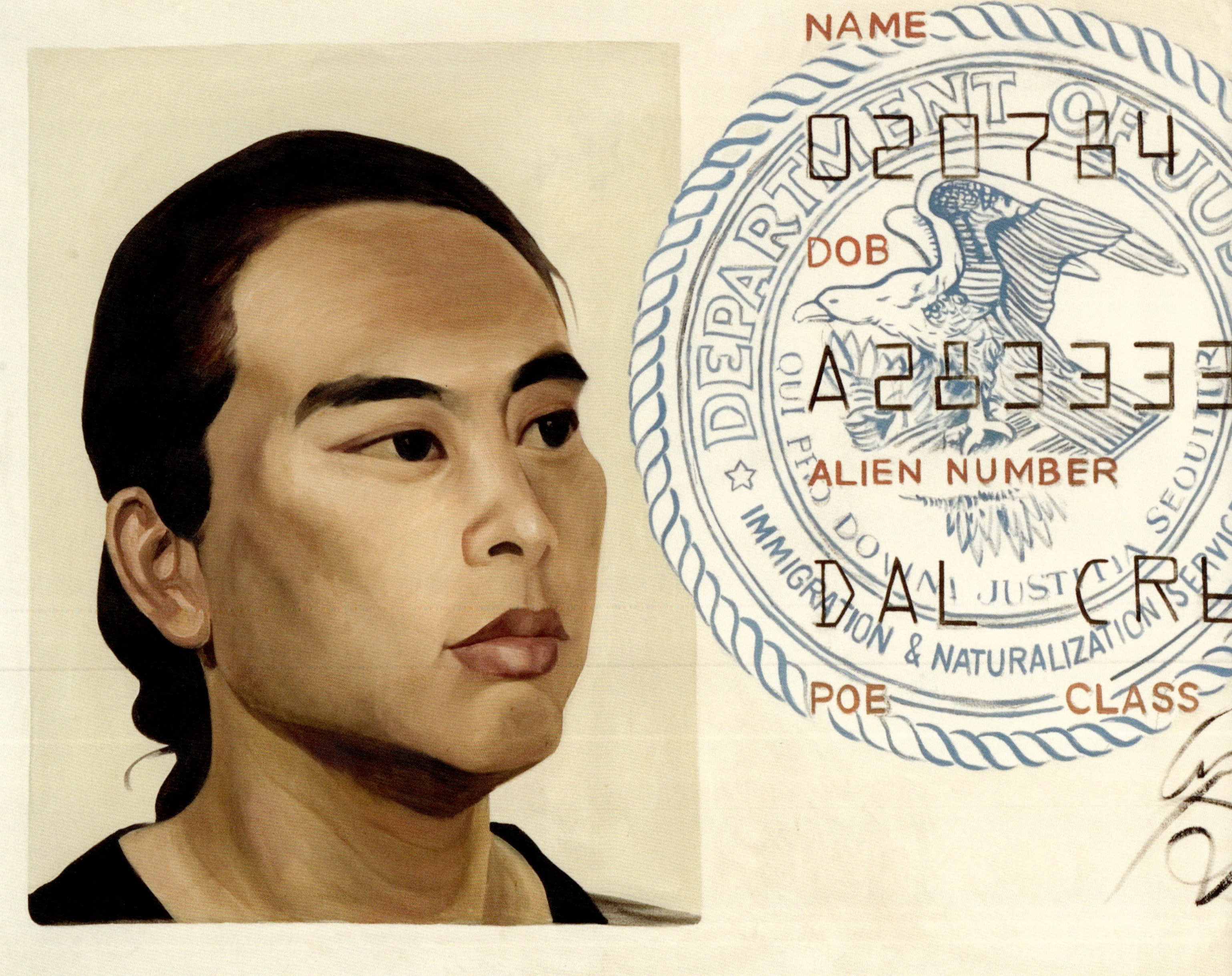

18. *Resident Alien,* 1988
Oil on canvas
60 × 90 in. (152.4 × 228.6 cm)
Collection of the San José Museum of Art. Gift of the Lipman Family Foundation

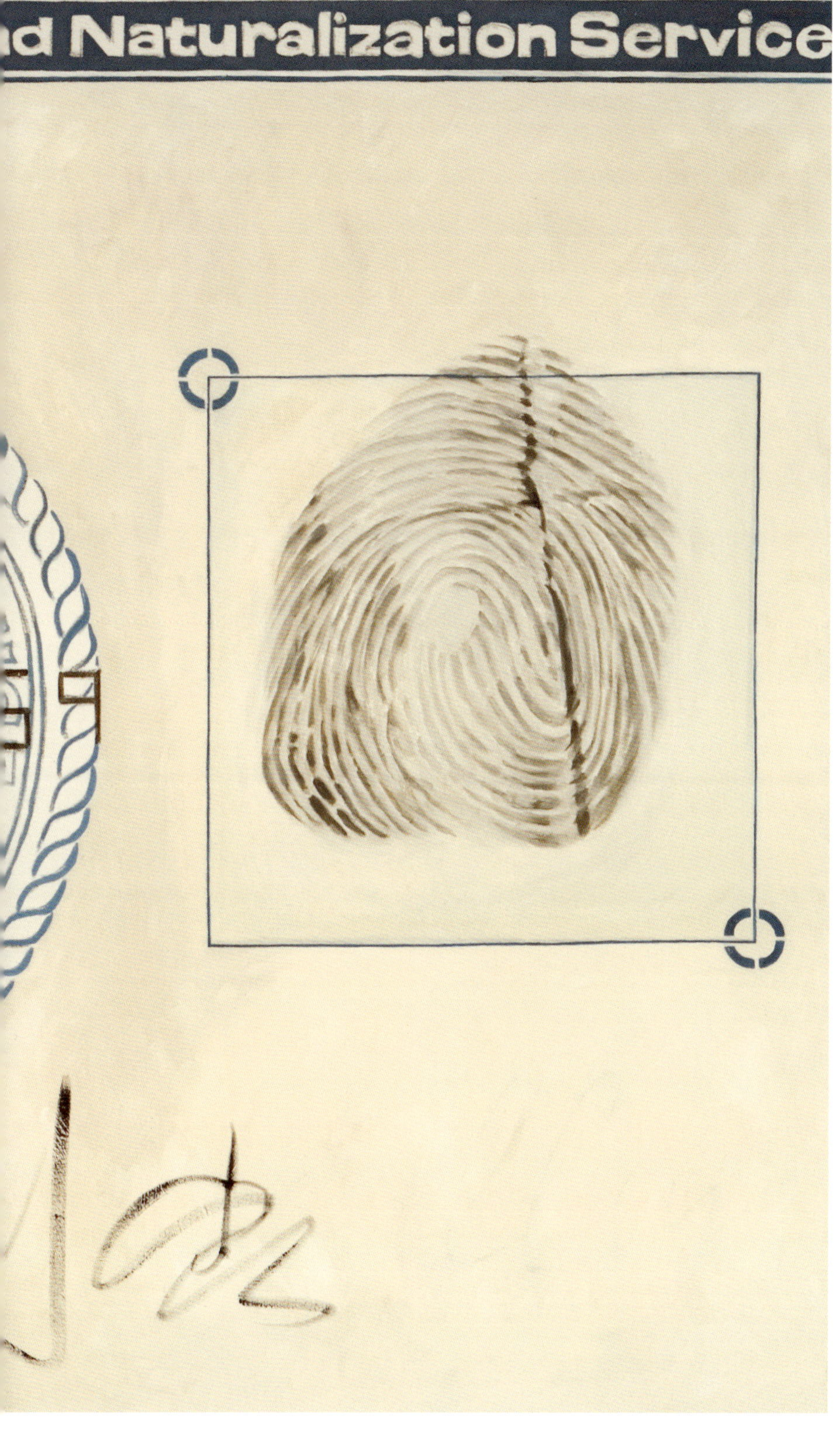
ALIEN
nd Naturalization Service

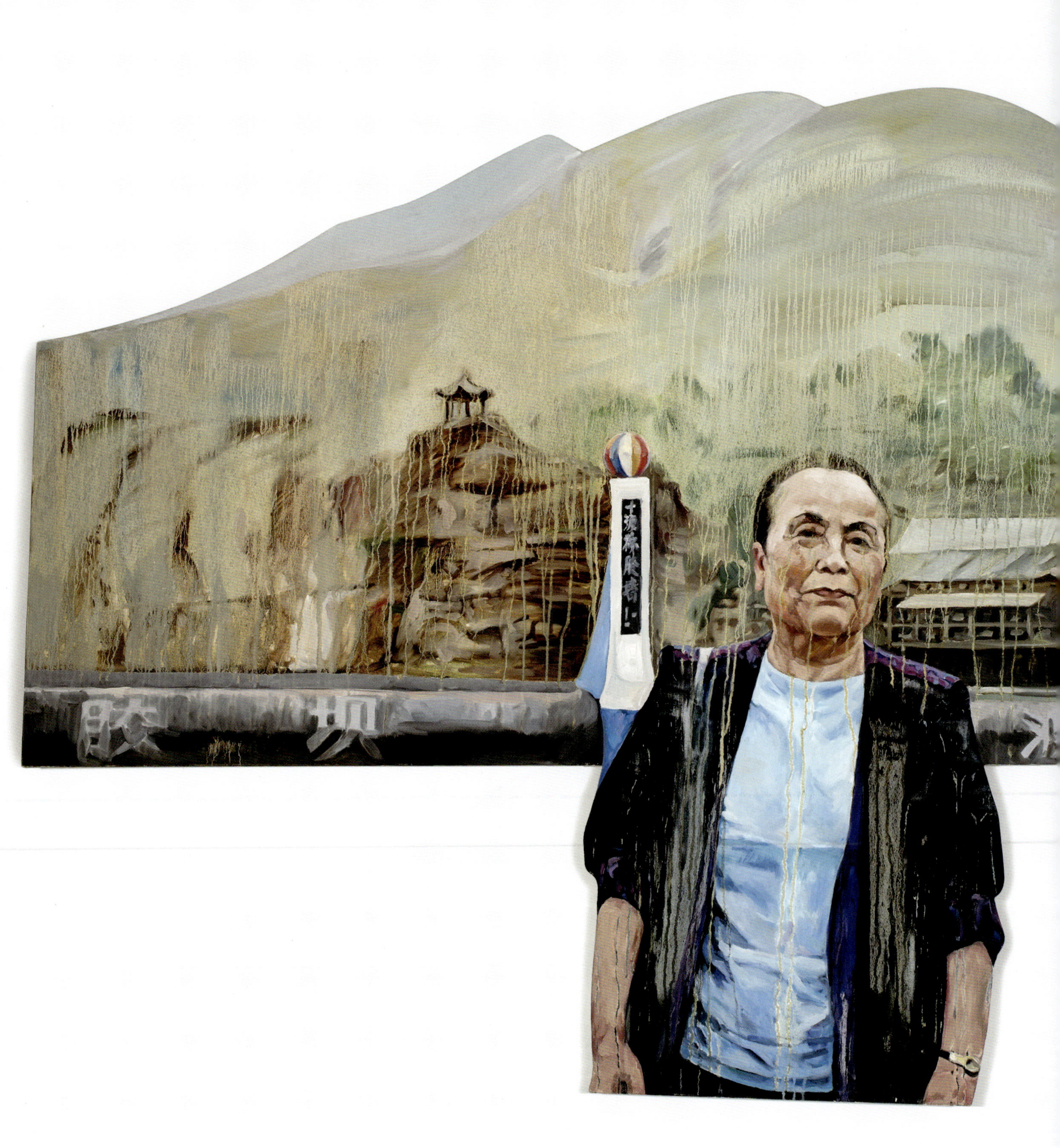

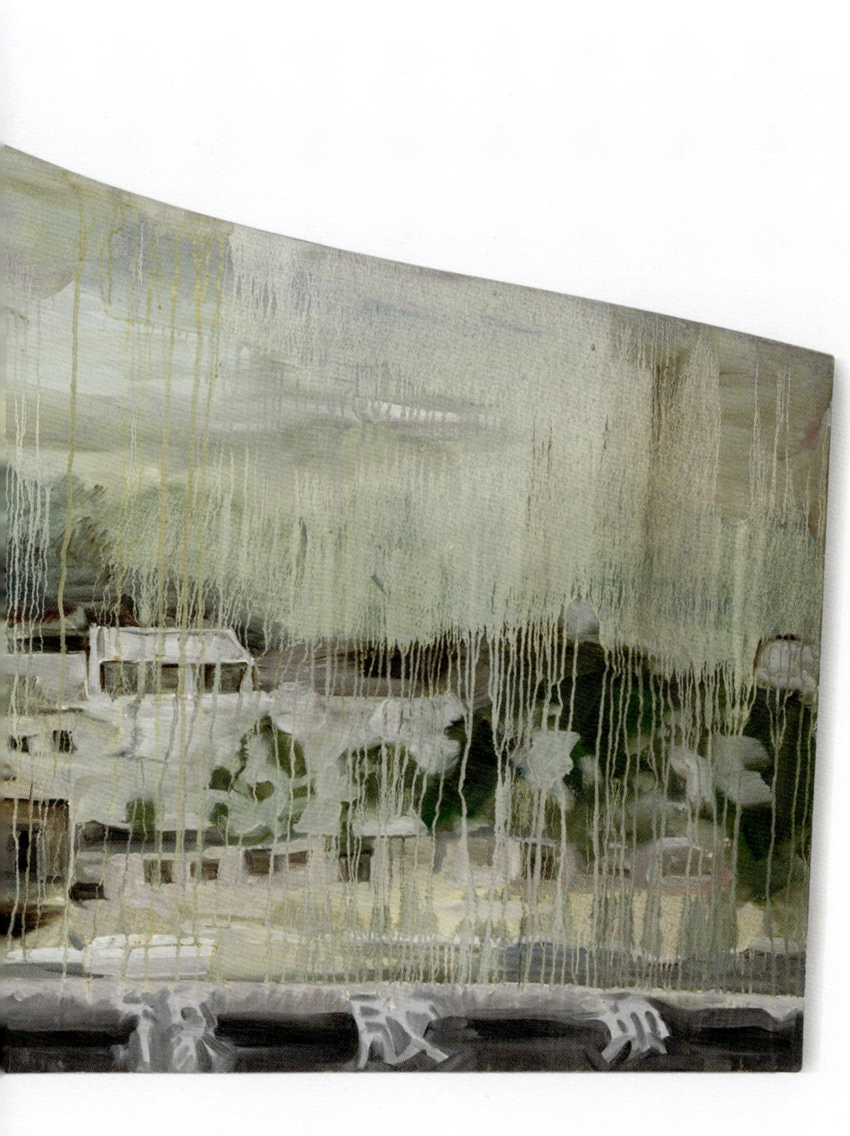

19. *Ma,* 1993
Oil on shaped canvas
59 × 96 in. (149.9 × 243.8 cm)
Allen Memorial Art Museum, Oberlin College, Oberlin, Ohio.
Oberlin Friends of Art and R. T. Miller Jr. funds

20. *Avant-Garde,* 1993
Oil on shaped canvas and wood
116 × 43 in. (294.6 × 109.2 cm)
San Francisco Museum of Modern Art. Gift of Hung Liu and Jeff Kelley

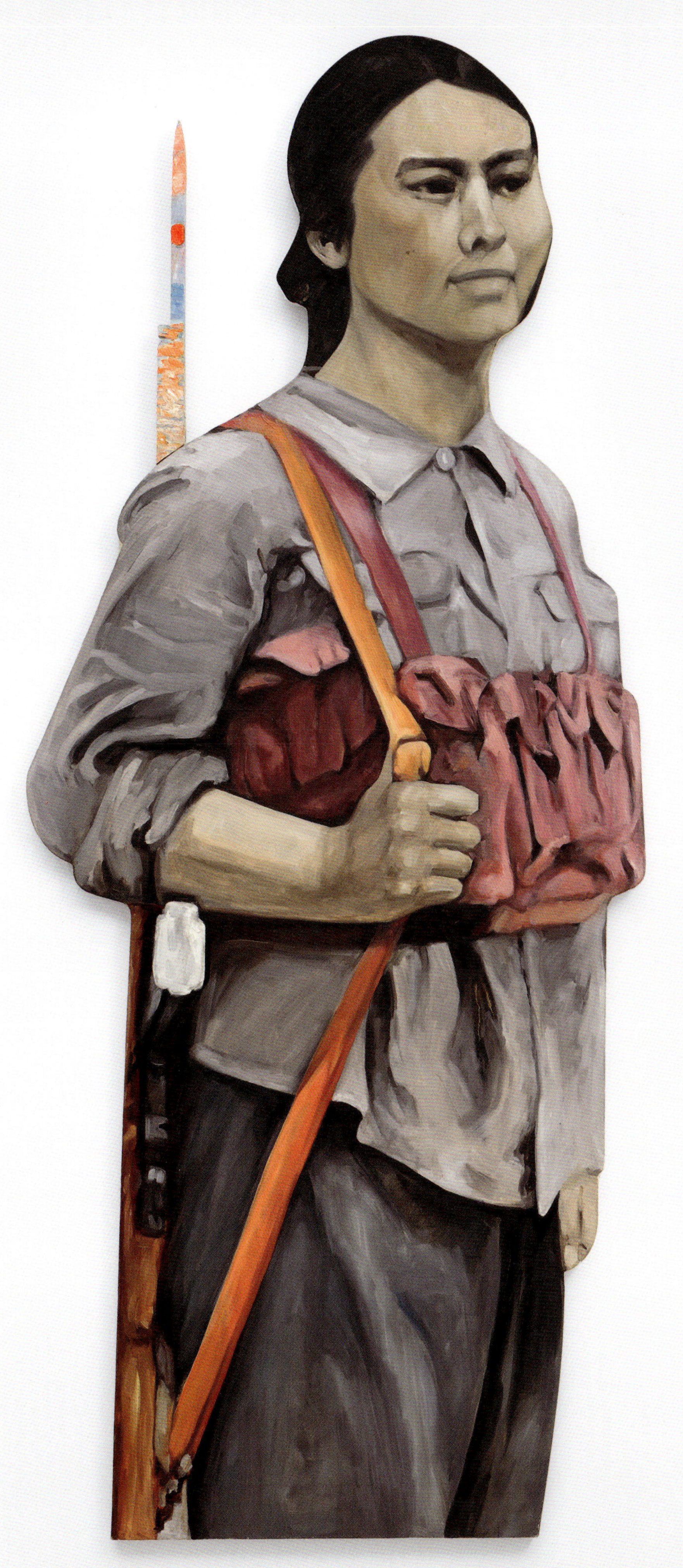

21. *Grandma,* 1993 and 2013
Oil on shaped canvas and antique architectural panels
99 × 55 in. (251.5 × 139.7 cm)

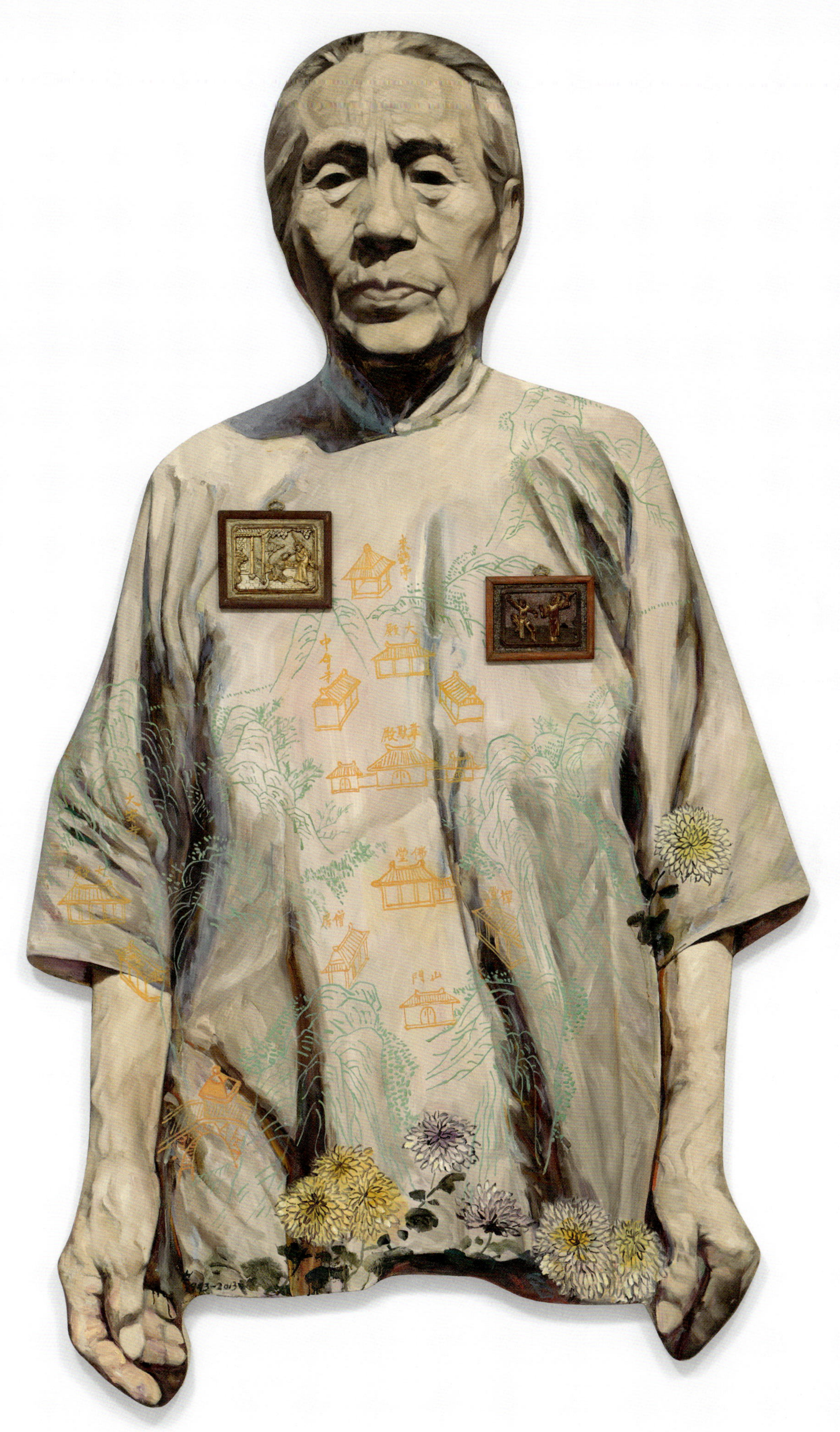

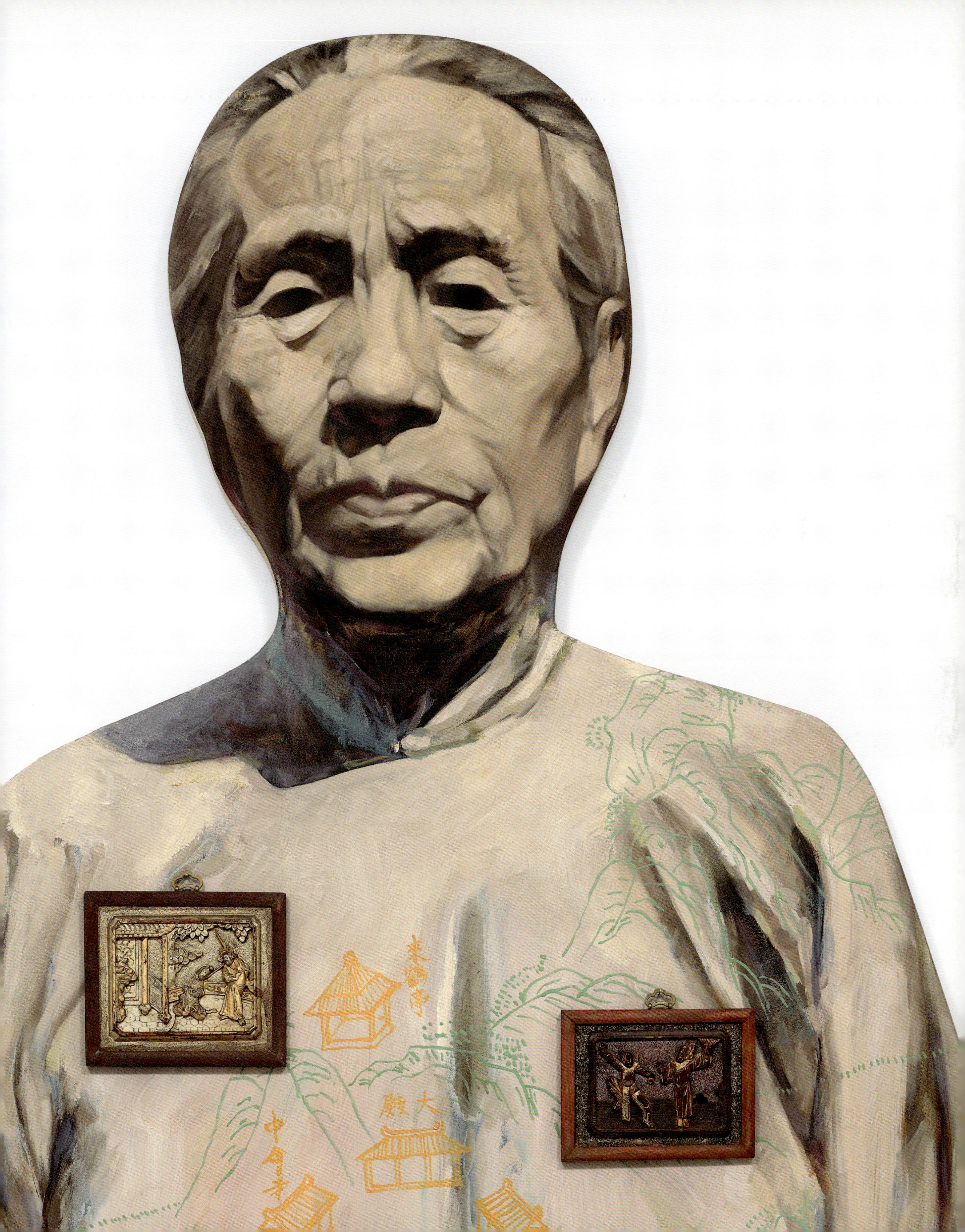
未鶴亭
大殿
中身者

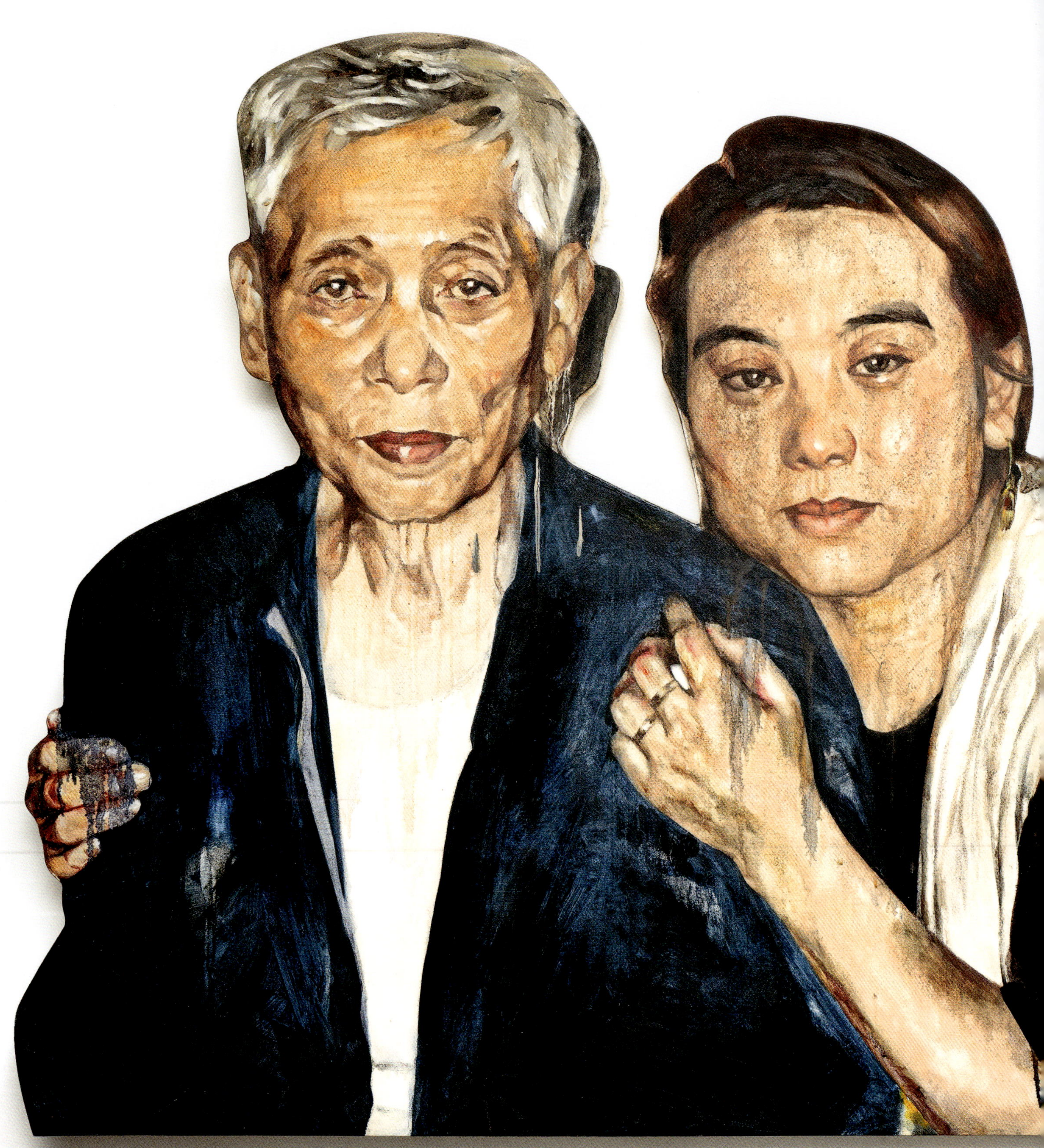

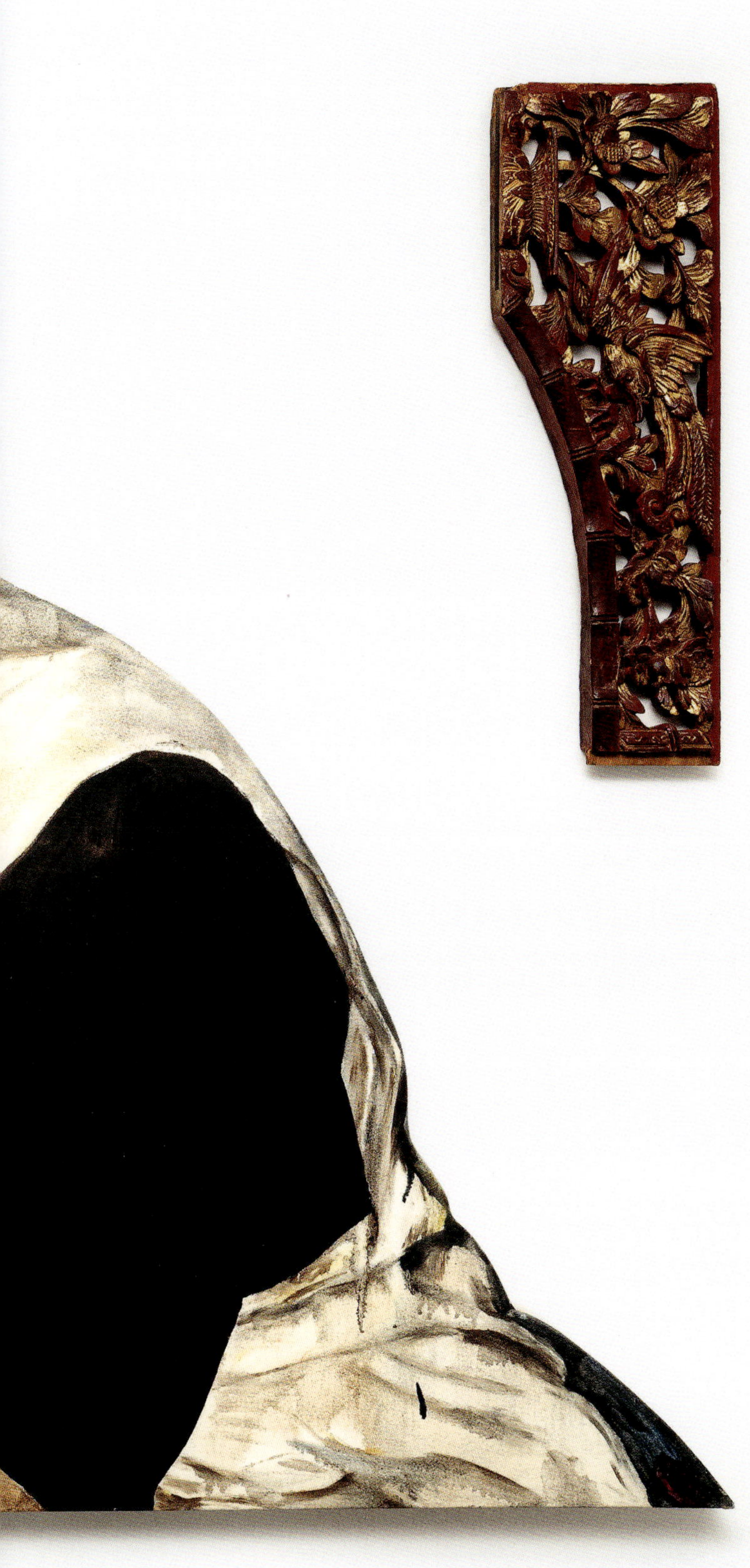

22. *Father's Day,* 1994
Oil on shaped canvas and architectural panel
54 × 72 in. (137.2 × 182.9 cm)
Entrust for Ariel Steinbaum

23. *Little Artist,* 1998
Oil on canvas
80 × 80 in. (203.2 × 203.2 cm)
Bill and Christy Gautreaux Collection, Kansas City, Mo.

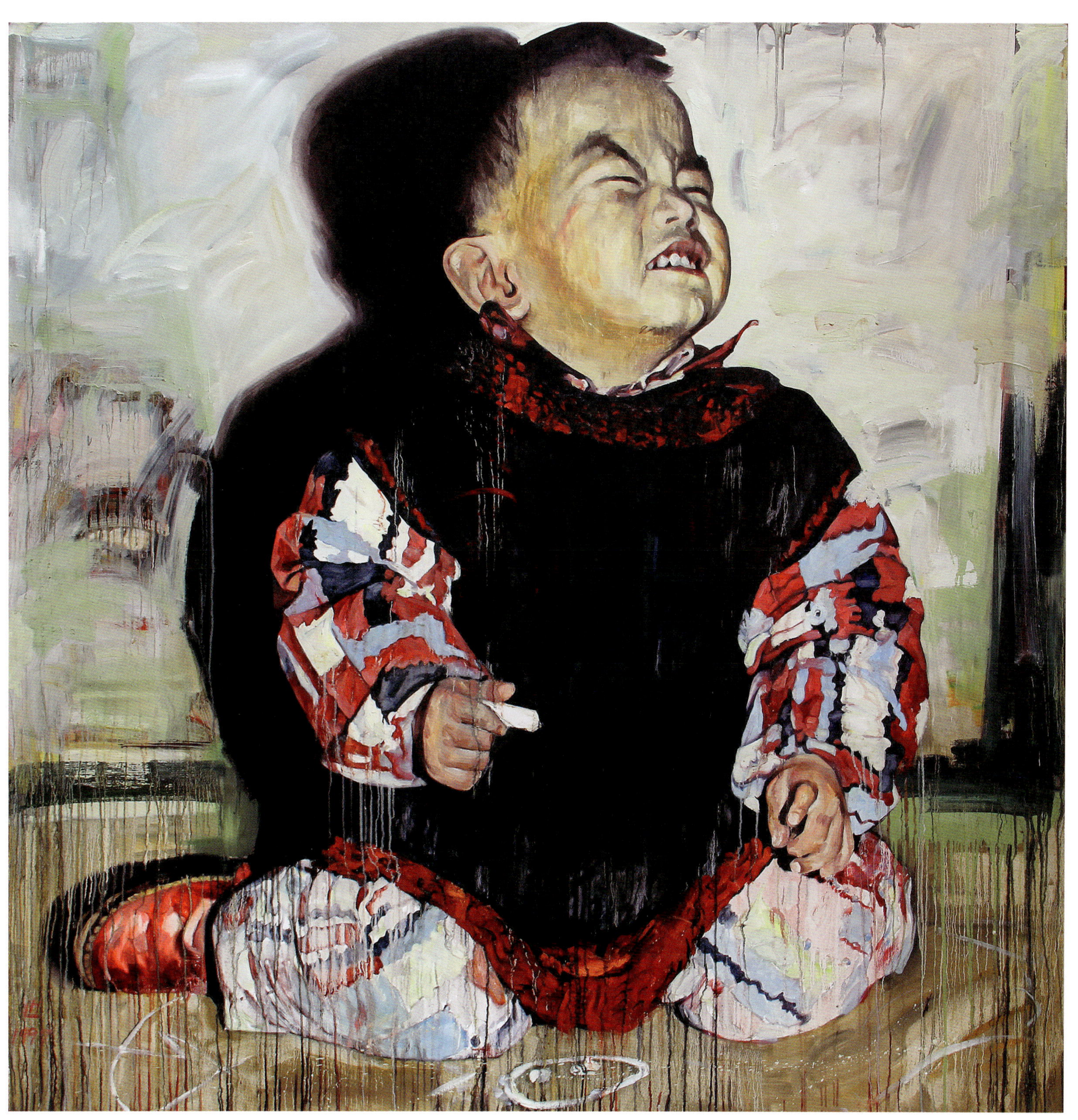

24. *Miss Y,* 1993
Oil on shaped canvas and architectural panel
80 × 40 in. (203.2 × 101.6 cm)
Collection of Nancy and Peter Gennet

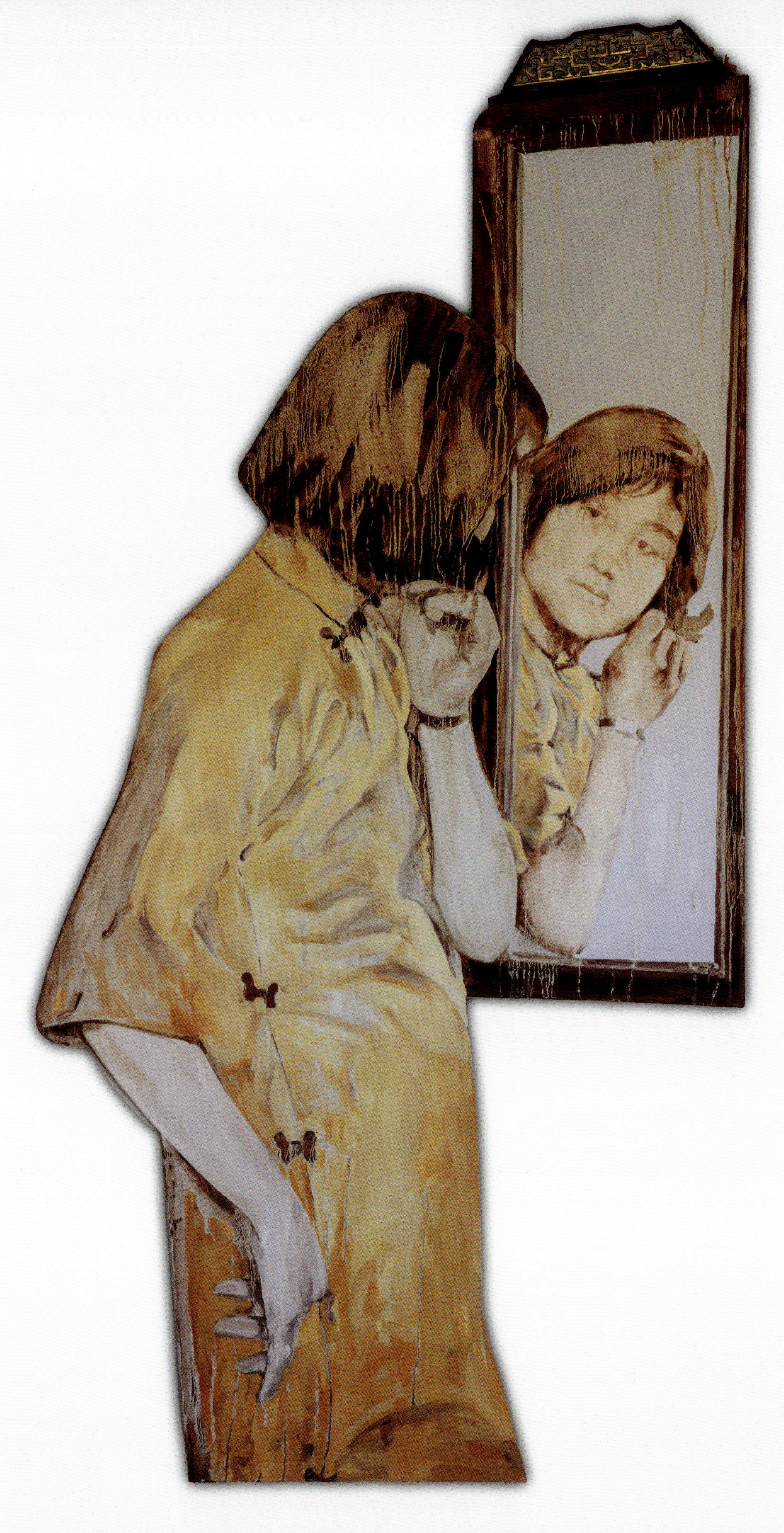

25. *Goddess of Love, Goddess of Liberty,* 1989
Oil on canvas with wooden bowls, slate, and broom
72 × 96 in. (182.9 × 243.8 cm)
Dallas Museum of Art. Museum League Purchase Fund

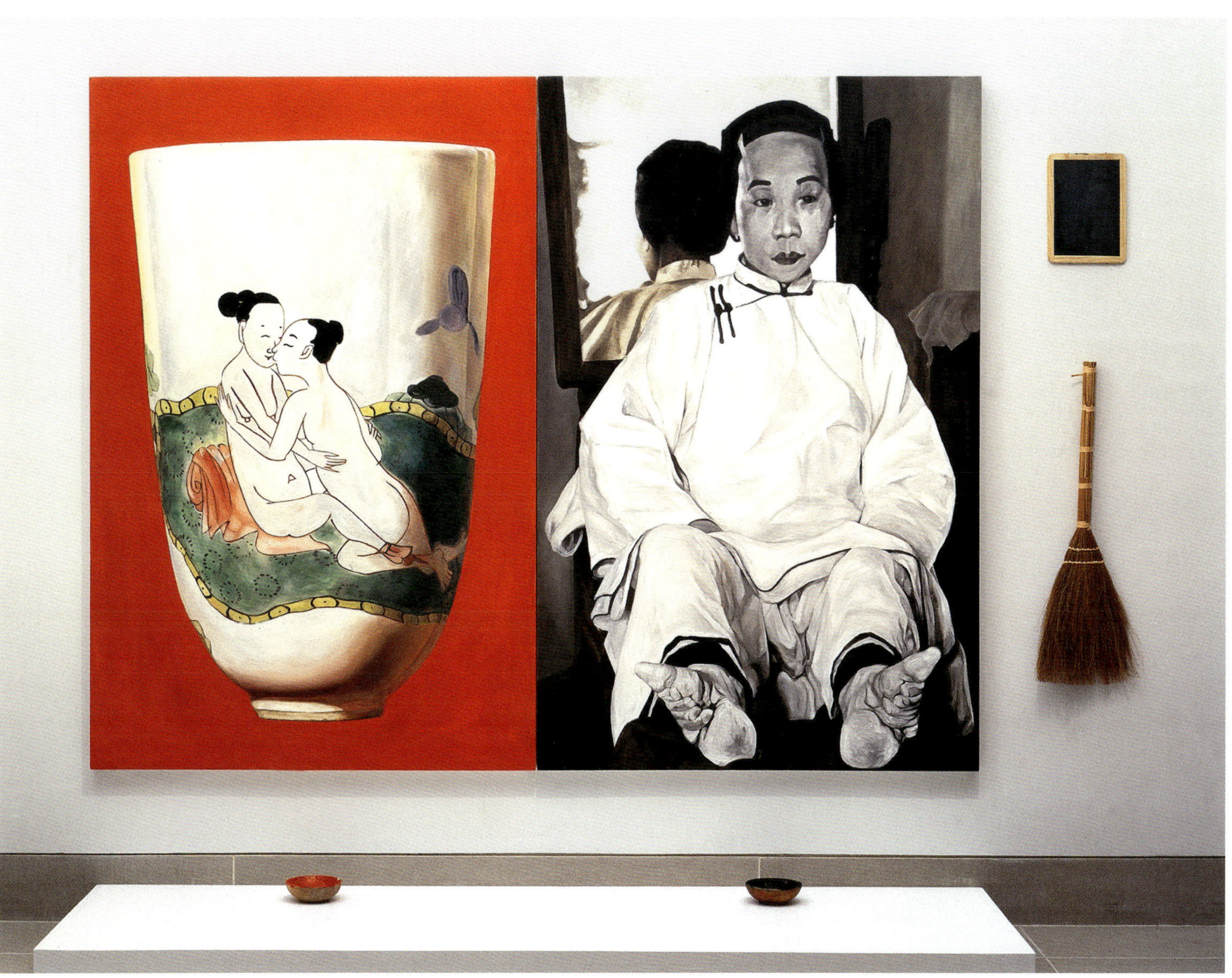

26. *Madonna,* 1992
Oil on canvas, gold leaf, wood, and antique architectural panel
79 × 40 in. (200.7 × 101.6 cm)
Estate of Esther S. Weissman

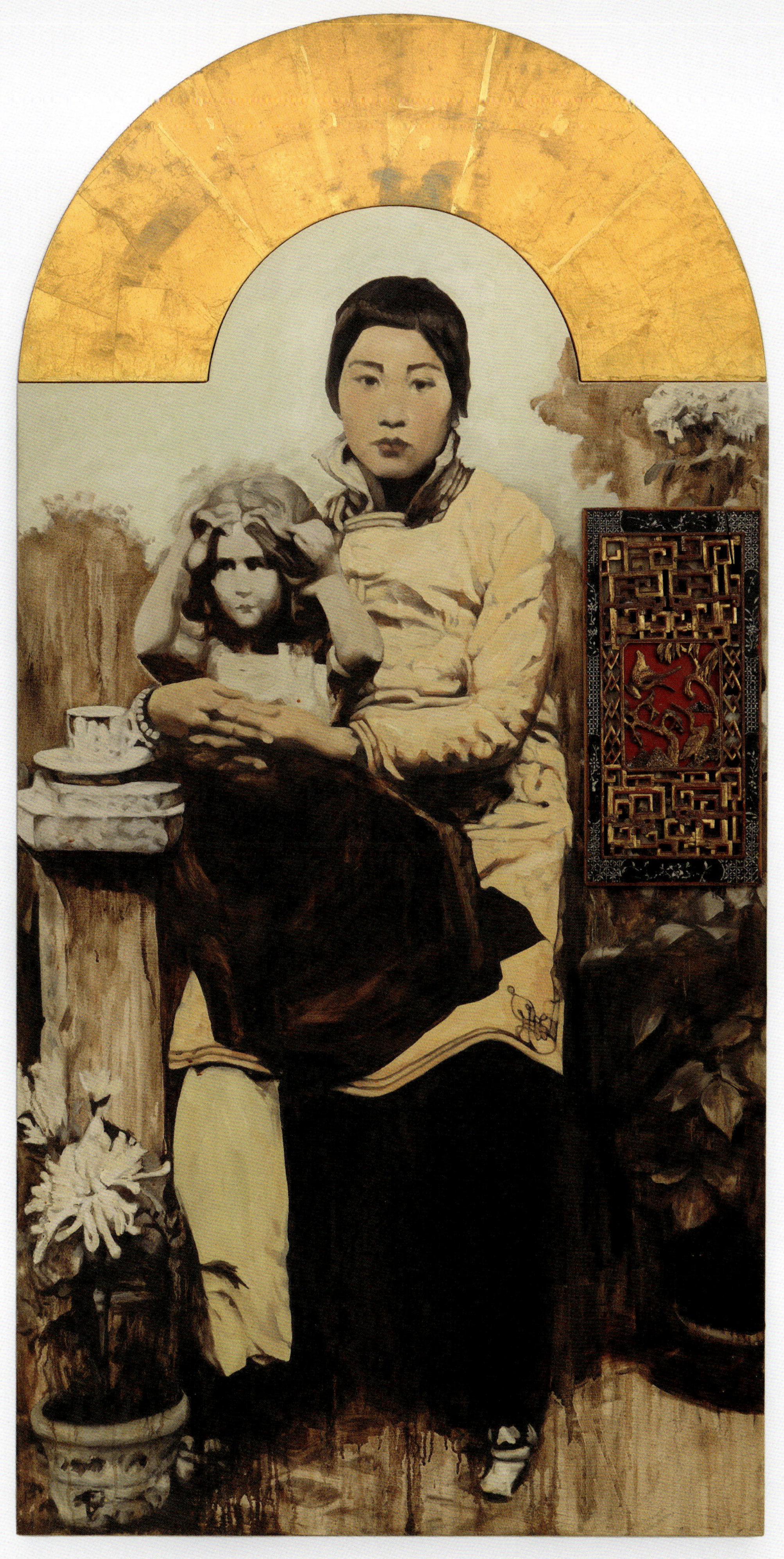

27. *Imperial Consort,* 1996
Oil on canvas with painted wood
48 × 38 in. (121.9 × 96.5 cm)
Collection of Janet L. Holmgren

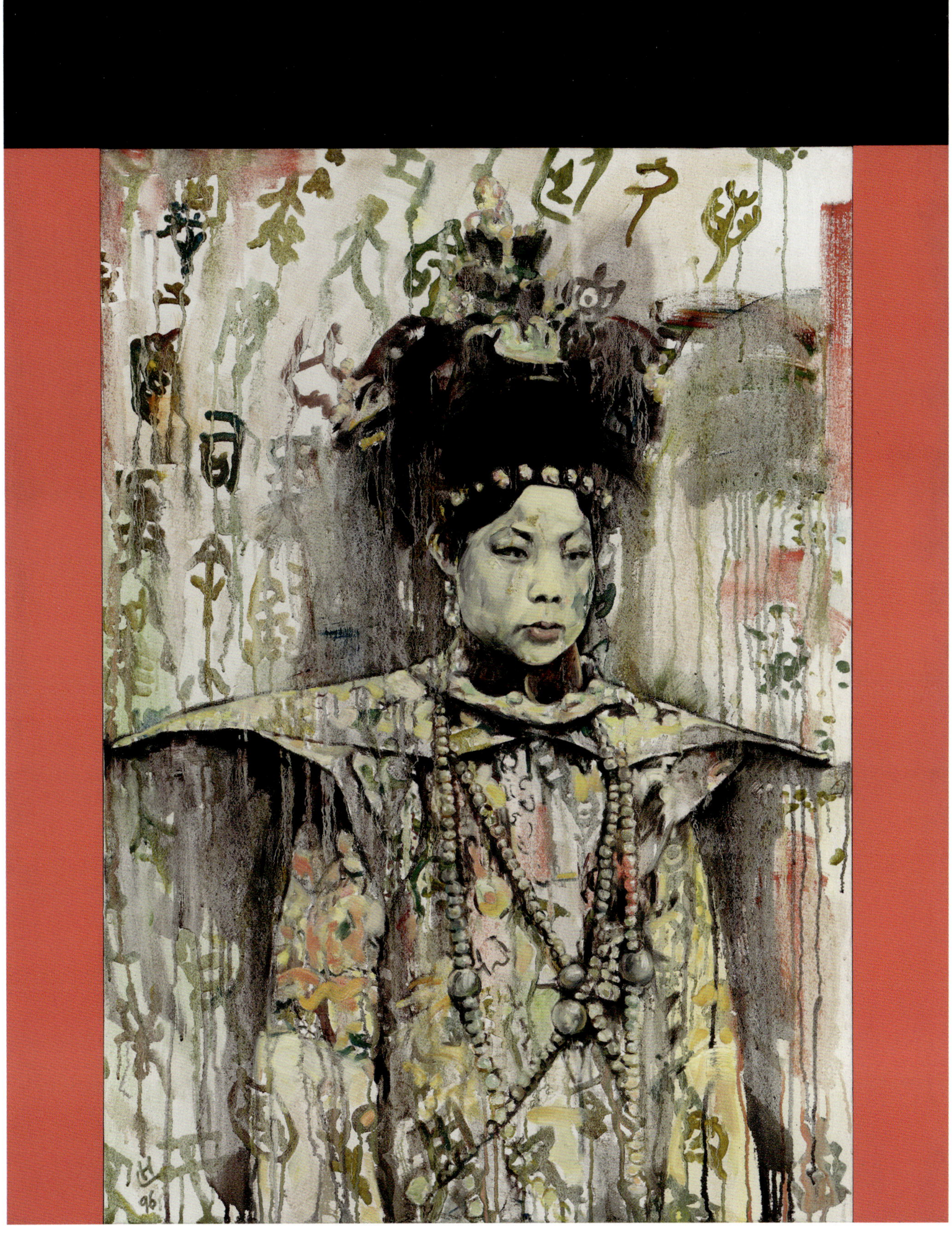

28. *Chinese Profile II,* 1998
Oil on canvas
80 × 80 in. (203.2 × 203.2 cm)
San José Museum of Art. Museum purchase with
funds contributed by the Council of 100

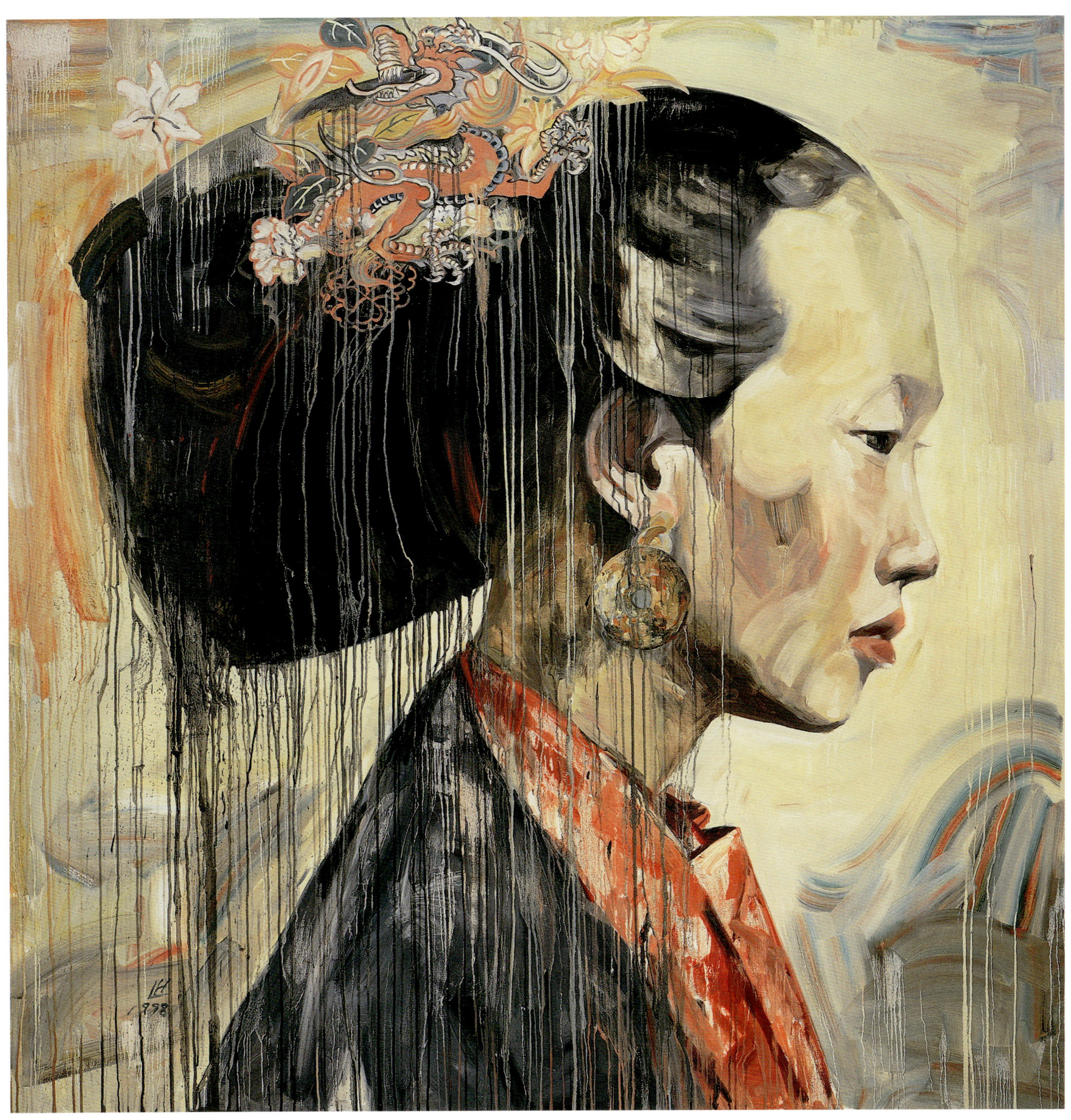

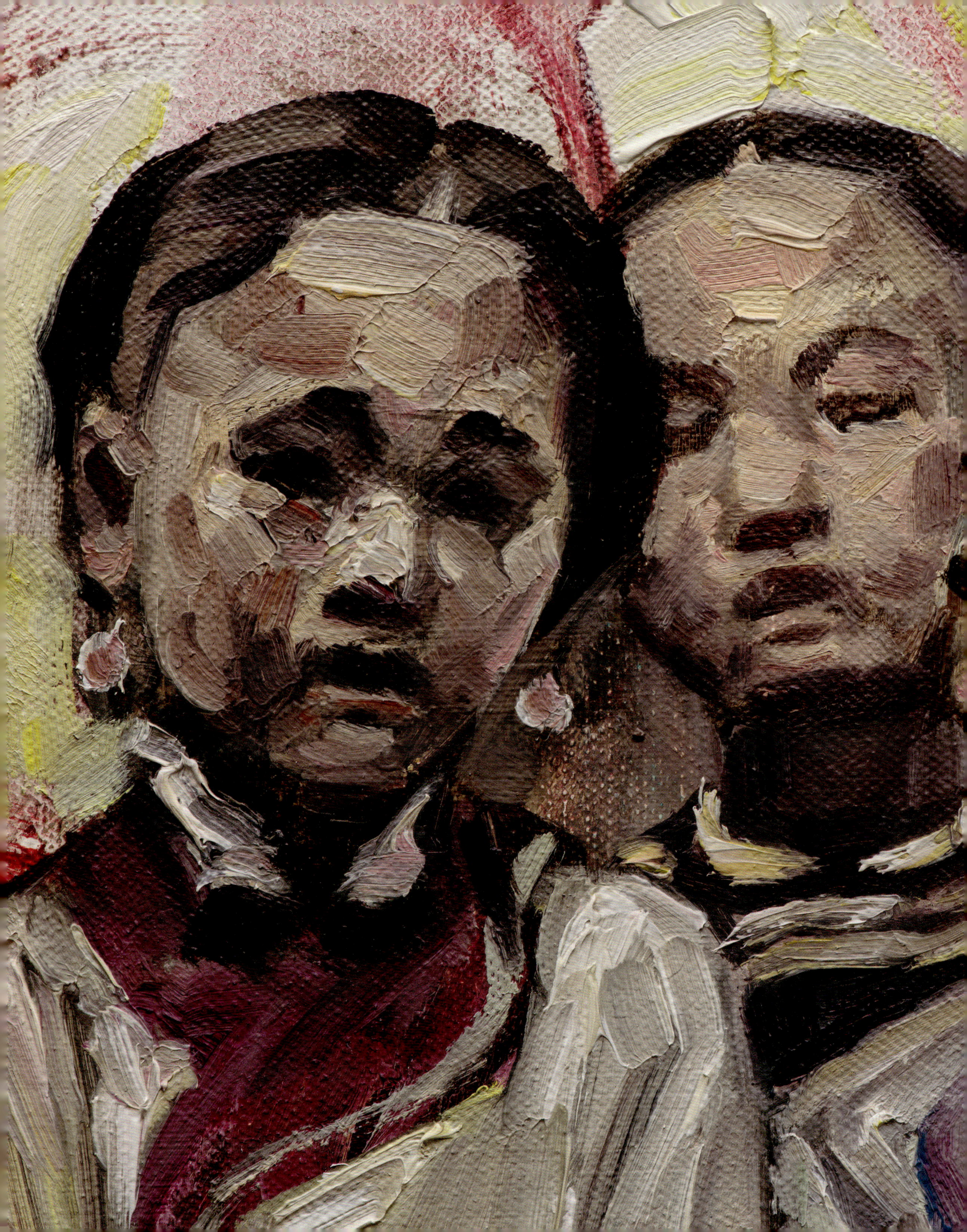

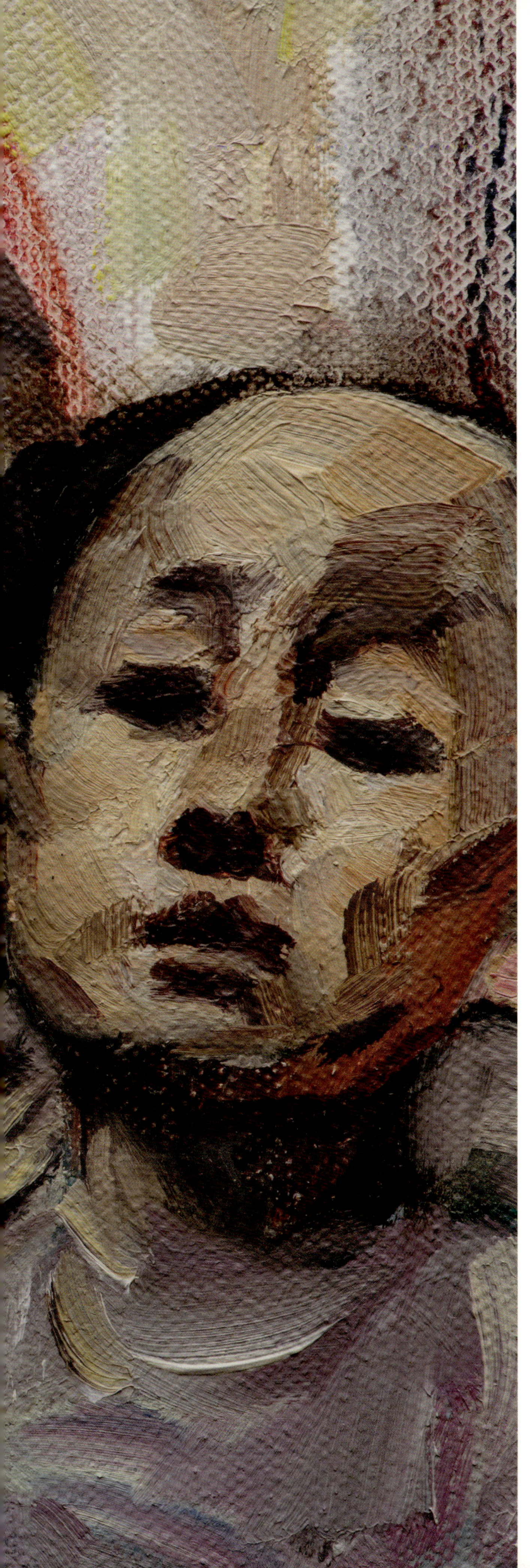

LUCY R. LIPPARD

HUNG LIU
China Trade

Portraits—human faces and eloquent bodies—have always been at
the core of Hung Liu's art. There are some unpeopled works, but they
are rare. And when there are people, there are "portraits" of people,
often in action, fully integrated with their body language, which con-
stitutes as important an element as their facial features. It is a hard-
ened viewer who cannot be moved by this combination, which makes
the work's messages inescapable. This is not the conventional defini-
tion of portraits. Until fairly recently, the portrait genre was limited to
the upper classes who could afford to hire skillful and accommodating
interpreters. These days, we use the word "portrait" loosely, as in
"portrait of an era." The term is no longer restricted to an image of
someone sitting up straight and uncomfortably still, with a few signi-
fying accoutrements.

Before the twentieth century, some artists did record the existence of the anonymous exotic, the foreign, the enslaved, and the
imprisoned, but they made no indication of the misery behind such
figures. When enslaved children were shown lurking in the backgrounds of nineteenth-century portraits of their master or mistress,
they were made to appear content, or at least ordinary. Liu, on the
other hand, puts marginalized people back into the frame, on center
stage, painting them with the energy and compassion of a participant.
Her portraits (in the broadest sense, as I use it here) do not depict
"sitters," but rather, real people *standing;* perhaps they stand for hope.

Liu's images, most of which derive from old photographs, are
engagingly intimate. One of Liu's gifts, after all, is her empathic mode
of communication. Since 1984, when she left her professorial position
in Beijing to study art in the United States, she has negotiated

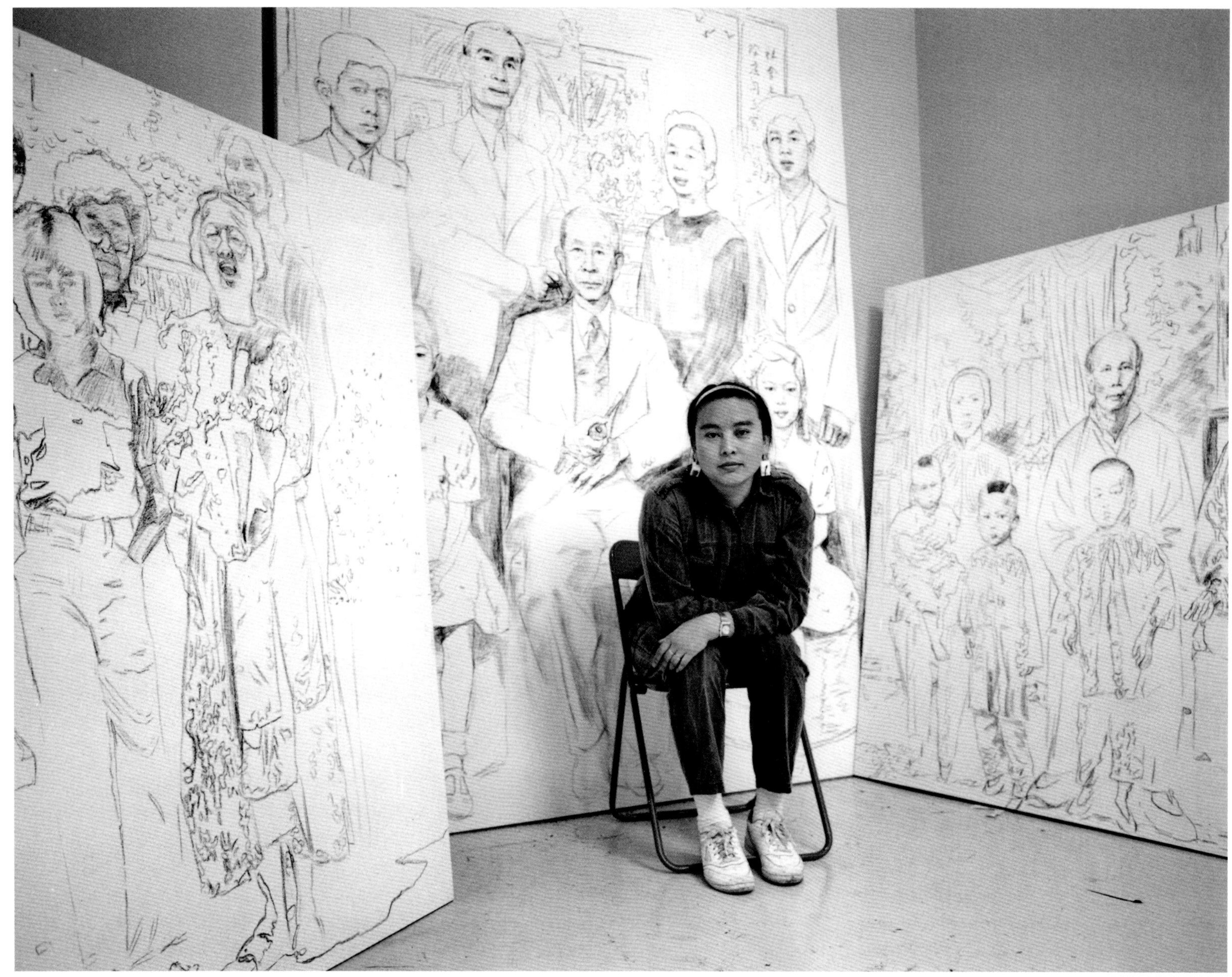

identities from Chinese to Chinese American to pretty much American. But assimilation has never been her goal. Like all immigrants, she has struggled with the prevailing "American Dream" and "melting pot" mythologies. For all the "Americanization" she has experienced over the last thirty-six years (including an enduring marriage to Jeff Kelley, a respected American art writer), she continues to address the whole person in her portraits, which means incorporating the role of China in both individual and social histories. In 1988, during a residency at San Francisco's Capp Street Project, Liu noted that she was trying "to invent a way of allowing myself to practice as a Chinese artist outside of Chinese culture. Perhaps the displaced meanings of that practice—reframed within this culture—are meaningful *because* they are displaced" (fig. 1).[1]

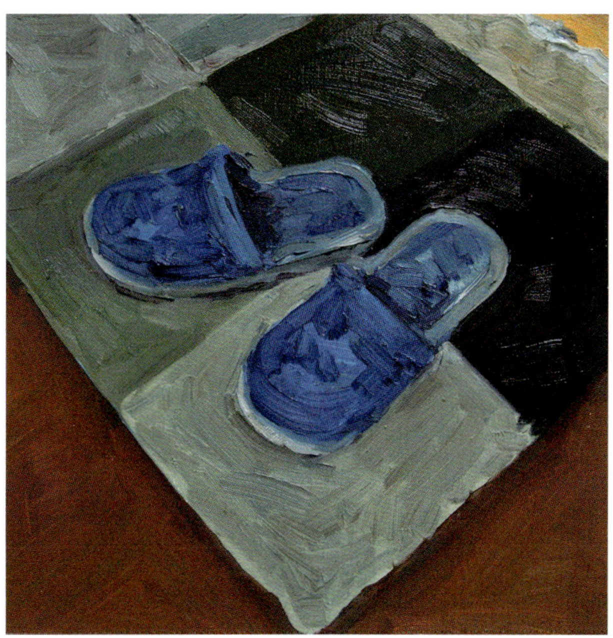

Fig. 2. Hung Liu
To Live 23: Slippers, January 17, 2012, 2012
Oil on canvas, 12 × 12 in. (30.5 × 30.5 cm)

In most cultures, women are the self-defined caretakers and tellers of family histories. (I serve that role in my own family, though I have only boys to inherit it.) A year after her mother died in 2011, Liu painted a series of "portraits" of the suddenly empty apartment in Beijing, including the phone on which they had spoken daily, keeping the channels open (figs. 2–4). All families offer insights into a broader political landscape, but those of immigrants are particularly riveting, given the challenges of cross-cultural negotiations. And how do cultural and "racial" differences—in looks, in meaning, in education—affect an all too often xenophobic American audience? In 1984, thirty-six-year-old Liu arrived in the United States with twenty dollars in her pocket; she would have failed the "merit" (income) test recommended for immigrants by the Trump administration. (She and her son, Ling Chen, became U.S. citizens in 1991.) Artists, after all, are assumed to be progressive, although the same cannot be said of art institutions, which are just now scurrying to catch up with the undeniable multiculturalism of the United States. Given the blatant national anti-immigrant climate today, it is all the more important that work like Liu's be acknowledged and made publicly visible.

For good reason, Hung Liu's unique biography is emphasized by writers on her art, myself obviously included, because until recently her subjects have been the Chinese people she left behind, the China she left behind, and the drastically changed China she revisits. She returned for the first time in 1991 and again in 1994, when she found the long-imprisoned father she had never known; she was six months

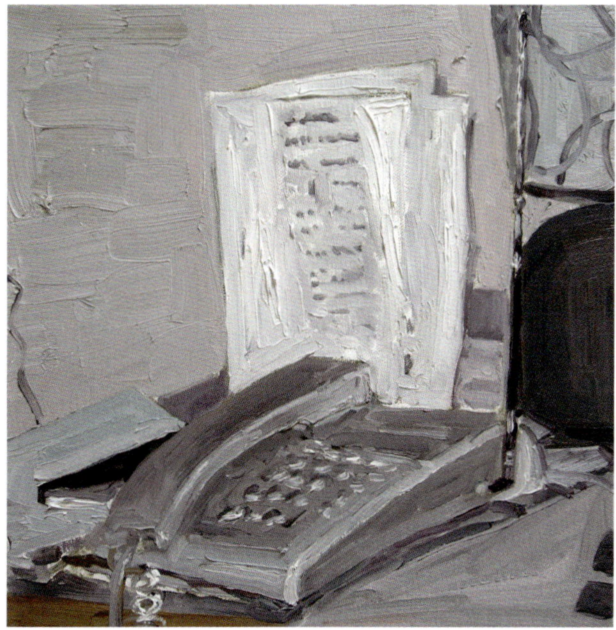

Fig. 3. Hung Liu
To Live 26: Telephone, January 20, 2012, 2012
Oil on canvas, 12 × 12 in. (30.5 × 30.5 cm)

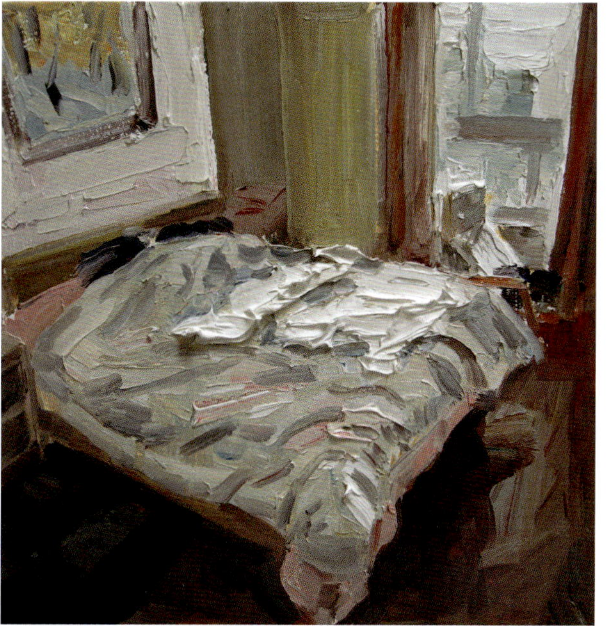

Fig. 4. Hung Liu
To Live 33: Bed, January 27, 2012, 2012
Oil on canvas, 12 × 12 in. (30.5 × 30.5 cm)

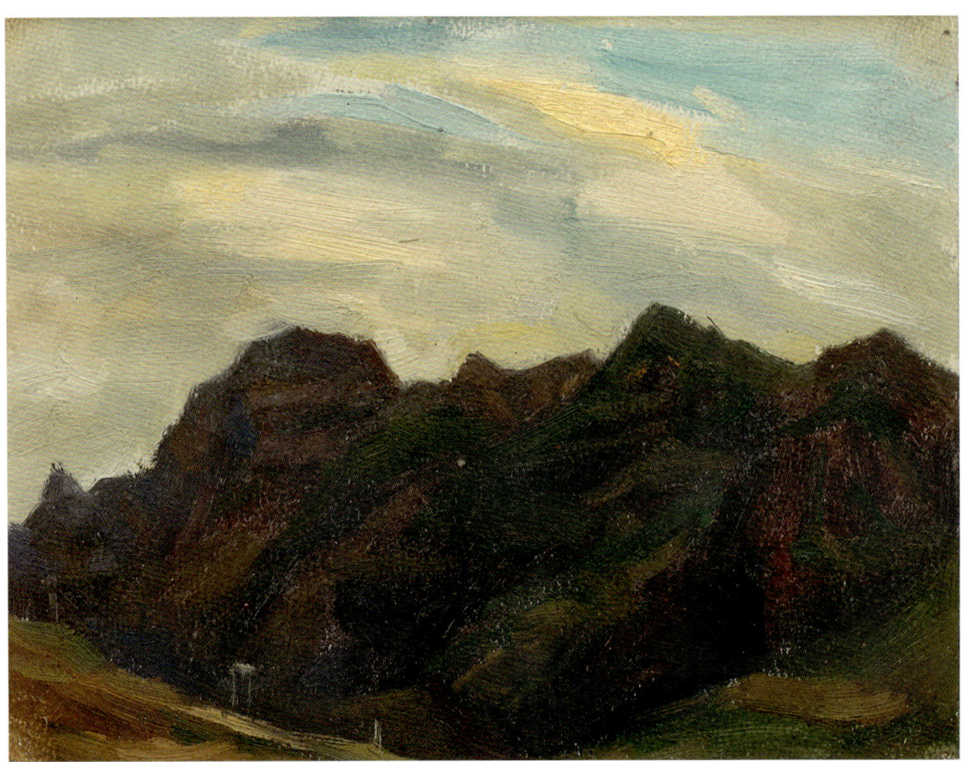

old when, as a nationalist soldier, he was captured by the Communist army. The reunion was commemorated by a poignant double portrait of her and her father, *Father's Day* (cat. 22). (Liu maintained her connections to China. Her beloved mother often made lengthy visits to her in the United States, and her son is now married to a Chinese woman; they live in New Jersey.)

Liu specializes in portraits of the exploited, abandoned, and hardworking people she had known during China's Cultural Revolution (1966–76). For four years, she was exiled from her family and education to be "reeducated" as a farmworker. She managed to reeducate herself—just as the government claimed, though hardly the way they had planned—surreptitiously drawing, photographing the villagers among whom she worked, and reading banned books. Difficult as the experience was, it also gave her unique insights into indoctrination, hardship, and discipline. She emerged from this mind-threatening situation stronger and more determined, with a firsthand sympathy for those who worked physically, for those who could not escape as she finally did.

When Liu arrived in the United States to study at the University of California, San Diego (UCSD), she was imbued with the Chinese aesthetic prejudice against painting portraits from photographs,

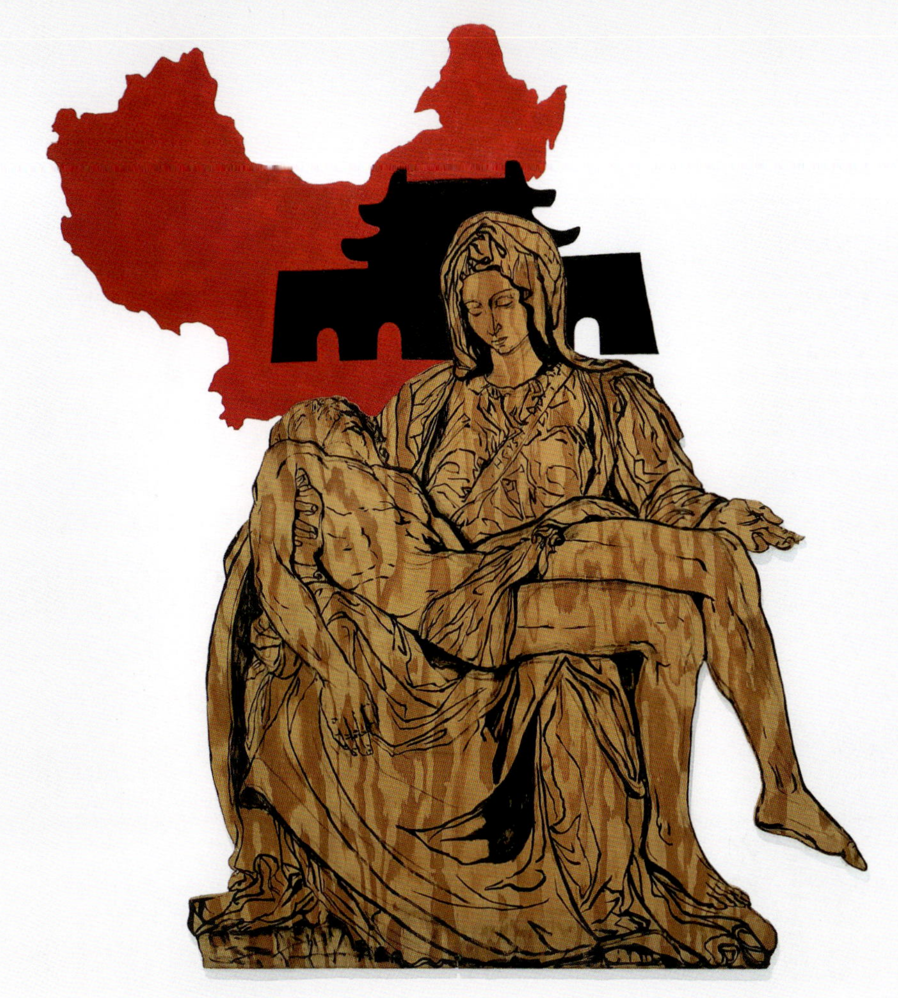

which was considered a lesser task than working from life. She has described herself and her fellow art students in Beijing as "brothers and sisters," all devoted to perpetrating the same style, the same message. Her drawings from 1972 to 1975, created when she was in her twenties, are exquisite, and "old-fashioned" in American art world terms (cats. 5–7). The covertly painted plein-air landscapes from that period now titled *My Secret Freedom* reveal her focus on ancient Chinese paintings (fig. 5). Before emigrating, she had worked with the cave drawings at Dunhuang and painted a monumental mural at her alma mater, the Central Academy of Fine Arts in Beijing.

Even after UCSD, she found herself reluctant to deploy political overtones, recalling the serious risks of such forays in China. Liu was already interested in the layers of Chinese public speech, traditional Chinese spectacles, and political propaganda. Then, on June 4, 1989, the tragedy of Tiananmen Square jolted her into artistic action. For an installation that year at the Woman's Building in Los Angeles, she made plywood cutouts.[2] In one cutout, a woman displays her grotesquely bound feet; below her, we see the body of a slain student, and nearby, the Goddess of Democracy, the icon of the Chinese Student Movement. Another was titled *Chinese Pieta* (fig. 6). Other paintings on the subject followed soon after.[3]

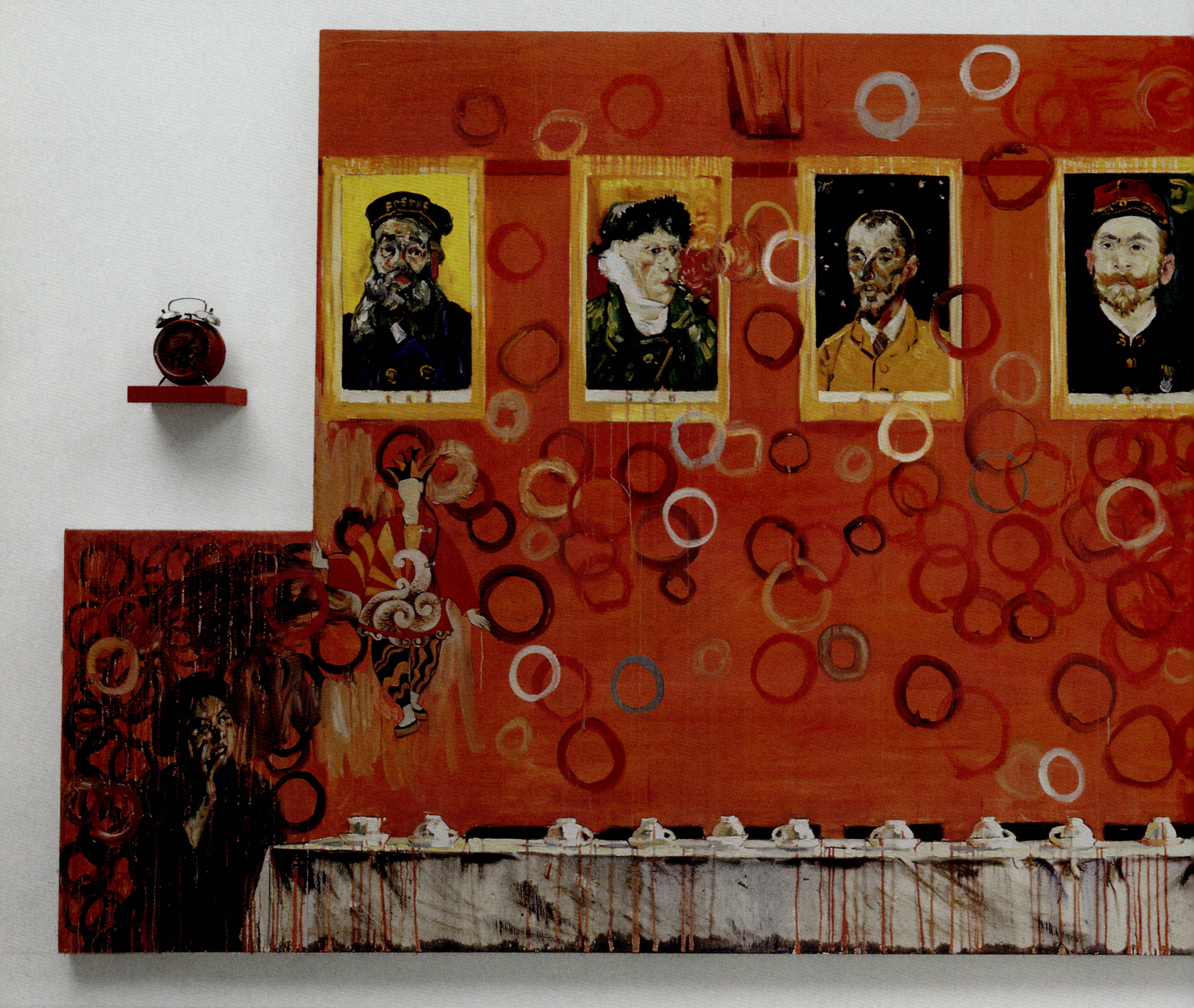

Fig. 7. Hung Liu
Modern Time, 2005
Oil on canvas with lacquered wood and Cultural Revolution
clocks, overall: 66 × 168 in. (167.6 × 426.7 cm), diptych

As she learned unfamiliar conceptual art practices from Allan
Kaprow and others at UCSD, Liu began to work with old photographs.
"As a painter," she has said, "I am interested in subjecting the documentary authority of historical photographs to the more reflective
process of painting. I want to both preserve and destroy the image."[4]
She revitalized anonymous subjects—women with bound feet, women
sold into prostitution, children in state care, forgotten laborers—developing her own "Western" style by transforming her sources, her photographic "bank of images" from the bad old imperial years, but never
deviating from the core of China. Dignity is always a subtext.

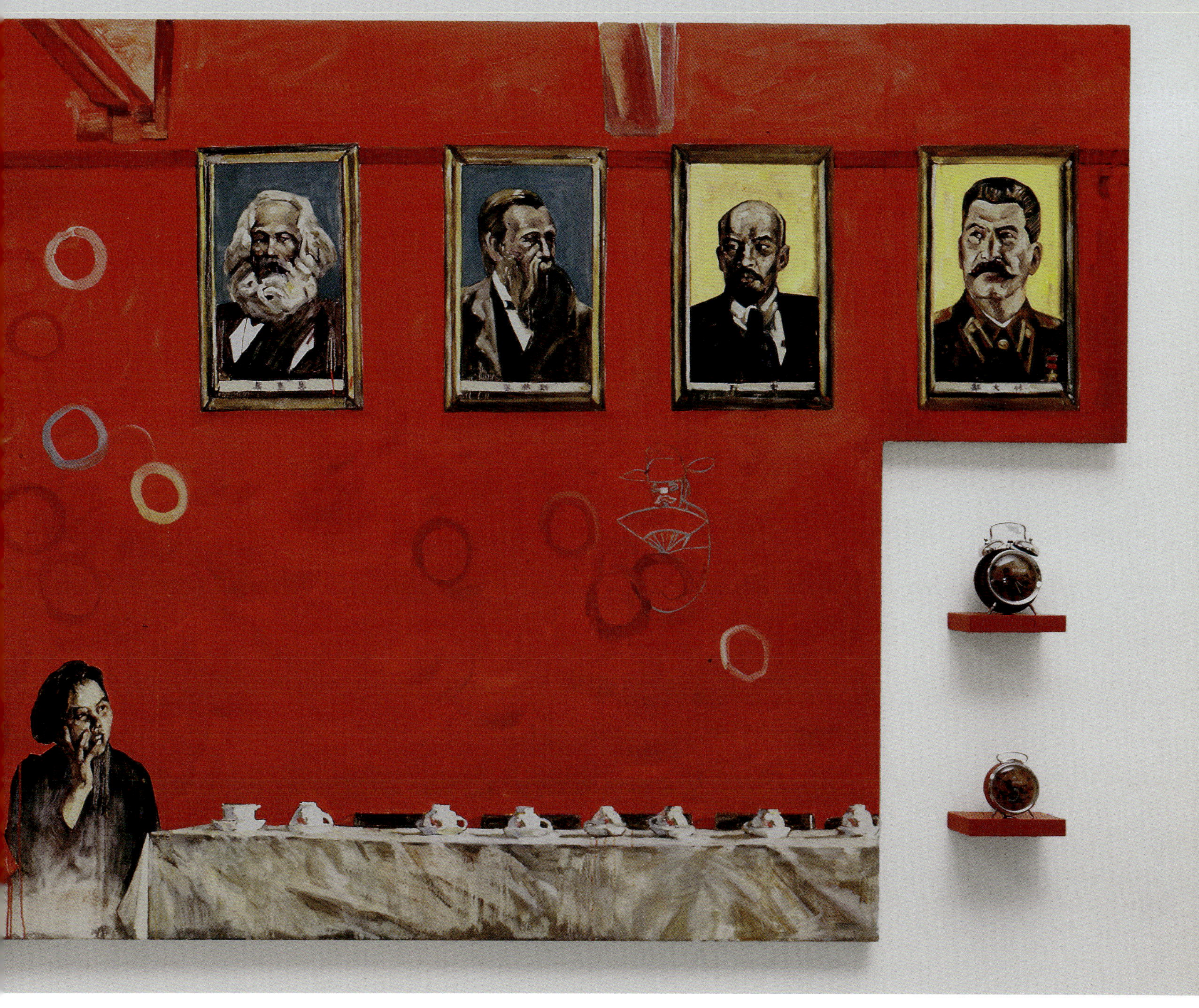

While painting from photographs, Liu's focus "has shifted steadily from their content to their temporality."[5] Her shaped canvas *Modern Time* (2005) incorporates actual alarm clocks on shelves. On one side are portraits by Van Gogh; on the other, portraits of Marx, Engels, Lenin, and Stalin (fig. 7).[6] Many of the images she used came from photographs taken by the American photographer John Thomson from 1868 to 1872, at a time when Western colonialism was filtering into China. Moira Roth has noted how European art history served to mediate between the originals and the meanings of Liu's paintings.[7] A later example, *Miss Y* (1993), based on a photograph from the 1920s

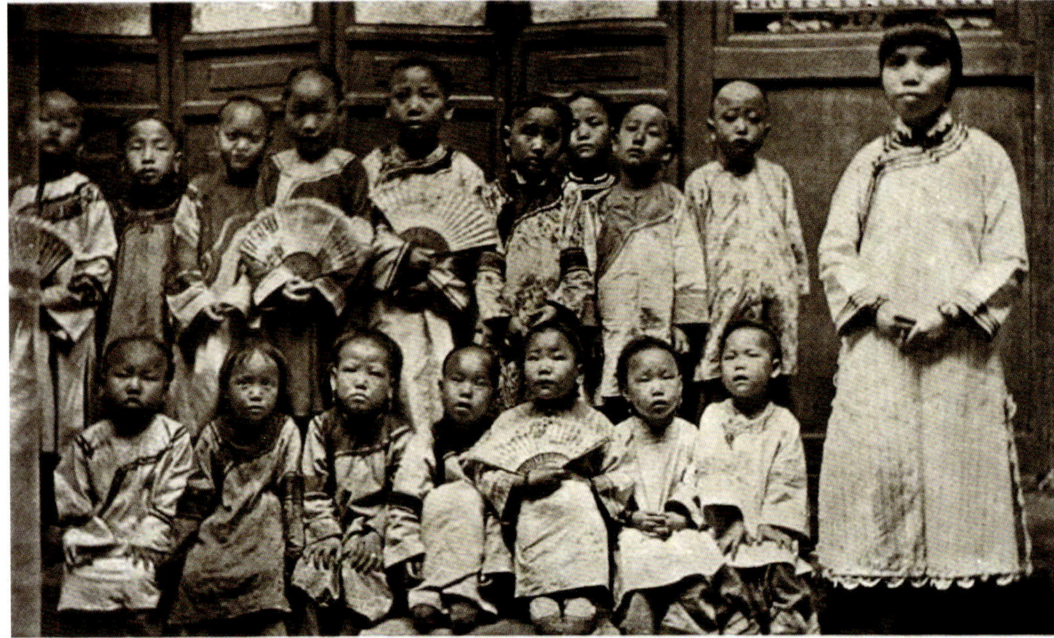

Fig. 8. Source photograph for *Mission Girls.*

or 1930s, shows a young woman looking at herself in a mirror, her hair and dress modern and Westernized (cat. 24).

When Liu was shown an album of nineteenth-century photographs of prostitutes (some of whom look to outsiders like miserable royalty), the contrasts and similarities between poverty and exploitation were a continuing grist to her mill. For instance, she based her portrait series of small, sad, orphaned "mission girls" (2002–3; cats. 32–40) on a late nineteenth-century group photograph that she broke down into small, loosely rendered canvases (fig. 8). Not in this series, but certainly related, *Sister Hoods* (also known as *Sisters in Arms,* 2003) is a touching image of solidarity: three tiny girls arm in arm, bundled in quilted jackets (fig. 9). These are heartrending images by any standard, but in the Southwest, where I live, they evoke the tales of so many Native American children who were forced from their families and into boarding schools where they were shorn of their customs, their languages, and their cultures. In both cases, colonialism took its toll.

The "gaze" is one of the instruments that brings us back to Liu's subtle exposure of the past. A prostitute with bound feet, uncomfortably posed like a Western odalisque, nevertheless has a level gaze that communicates to the viewer the strength demanded to play this role, to live this life. Griselda Pollock has commented on this "returned gaze" as an antidote to Orientalism,[8] and Margo Machida has discussed the "reverse mirroring" practiced by Asian American artists raised in the West.[9] Their expressive faces defy the Western bias that all Asians "look alike."

It was only recently that Liu completed her first project without relying on any Chinese references. Working from Dorothea Lange's

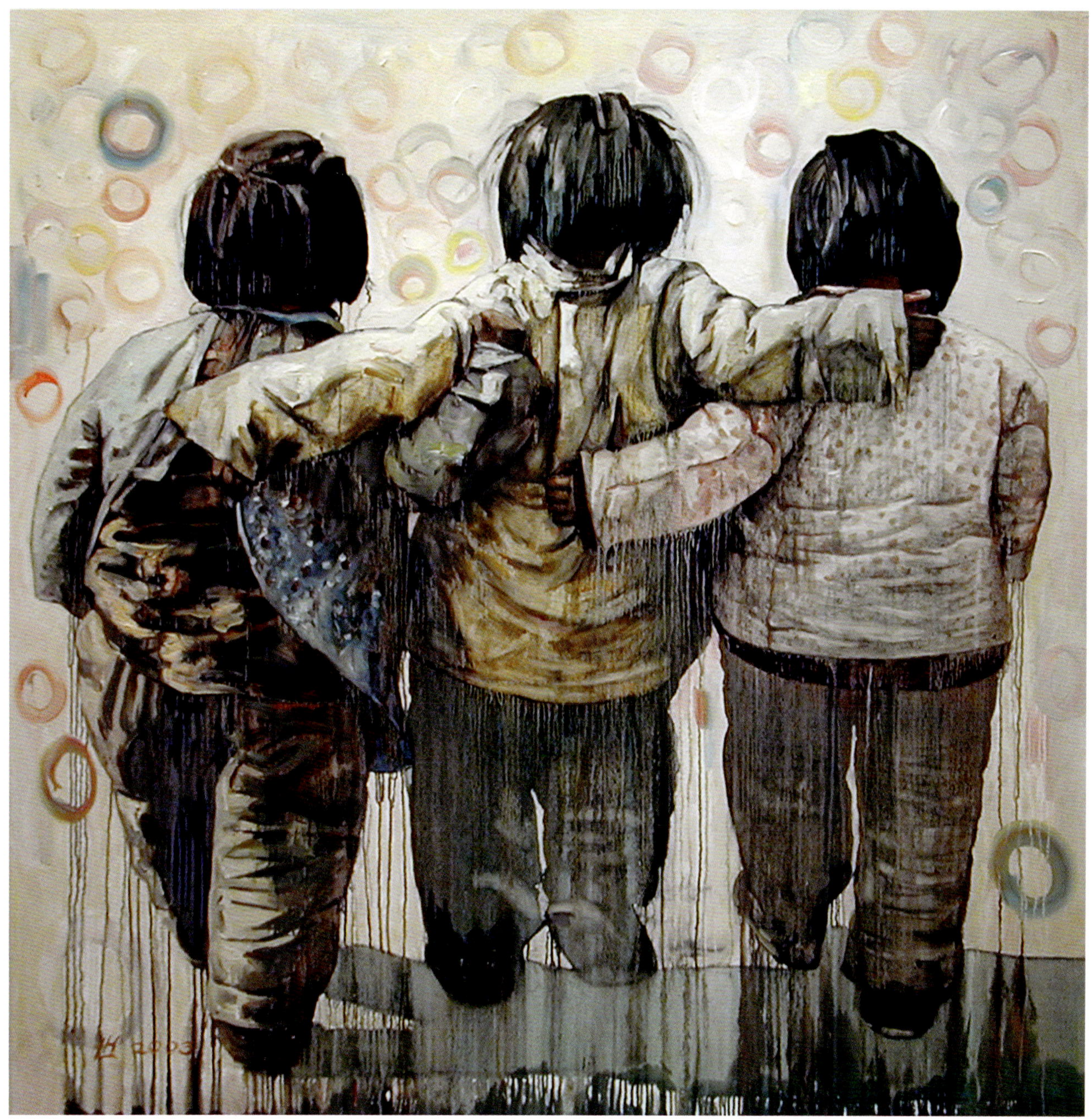

Fig. 9. Hung Liu
Sister Hoods (Sisters in Arms), 2003
Oil on canvas, 72 × 72 in. (182.9 × 182.9 cm)
Collection of Robert A. and Julie T. Berlacher

Dust Bowl photographs, most notably the photographer's famous *Migrant Mother,* Liu sought to broadly critique the suffering brought on by ecological crises (see cats. 45–52). However, given the Trump administration's recent policies on the U.S.–Mexico border, she does not deny the local parallels: "Sometimes art isn't 'about' something so much as near it," she observed.[10] Finally, these are portraits in the sense that we usually understand the word. Even in Liu's "action paintings," such as *Corn Carrier* (1999), the facial expressions are compelling (fig. 10). Liu endows her subjects with her own strengths,

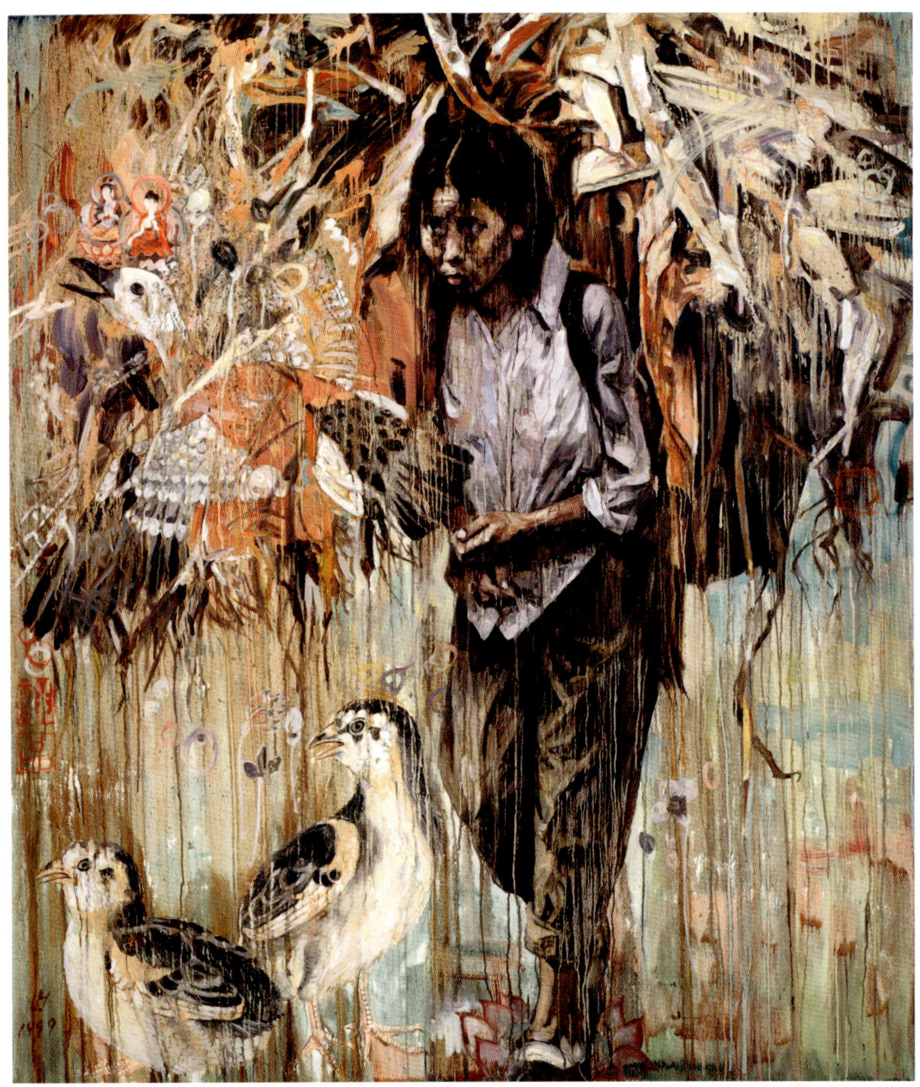

Fig. 10. Hung Liu
Corn Carrier, 1999
Oil on canvas, 80 × 70 in. (203.2 × 177.8 cm)
Private collection

inherited from generations of women crippled with bound feet, their intelligence communicated by their level gazes. As Donald Kuspit has observed, this is in effect "Liu's own rebellious gaze—the rebellious gaze of her art."[11]

Most of Liu's paintings are layered, a form of collage. The dripping paint that is her trademark (it has been interpreted as tears) acts as a veil between past and present, persuading the viewer to look through it to an unfamiliar reality. She has described this technique as "preserve and dissolve."[12] It also serves to mask or "modernize" Liu's extraordinary skill at realist painting, based in socialist realism despite her experience-based rejection of the happy, heroic peasant cliché of the Mao years. Her use of juxtaposition in the many diptychs reflects her own dual roots and commitments.

The transition of Chinese to American is the theme of her *Chinese in Idaho* series (2004–6; cats. 41–43), which features Polly Bemis (1853–1933), a Chinese woman who was sold into the slave trade and ended up in Idaho during the Gold Rush (fig. 11; cat. 43). Her marriage to an American saved her from the anti-Chinese immigration furor, and after his death, she became a local businesswoman on a small ranch near the Salmon River. Liu's portraits of Bemis, taken from battered photographs that span more than two decades, show her in her garden, with pets, with her husband, in an apron, and once in an elegant dress. The suggested parallels with the artist's own trajectory are obvious.

The collage effect is primary in the appeal of Liu's paintings. The palimpsest of "nature" and humanity—flowers, birds, and butterflies layered over faces and bodies—is aesthetically decorative, yet meaningful. Whores are given flower names, and bound feet are called "lotus hooks." (Liu has compared this unnatural practice to Bonsai.) The recurring cranes are auspicious omens for travel, certainly a major part of the artist's life. The ubiquitous rings, superimposed on many paintings, have roots in ancient calligraphy, and can signify

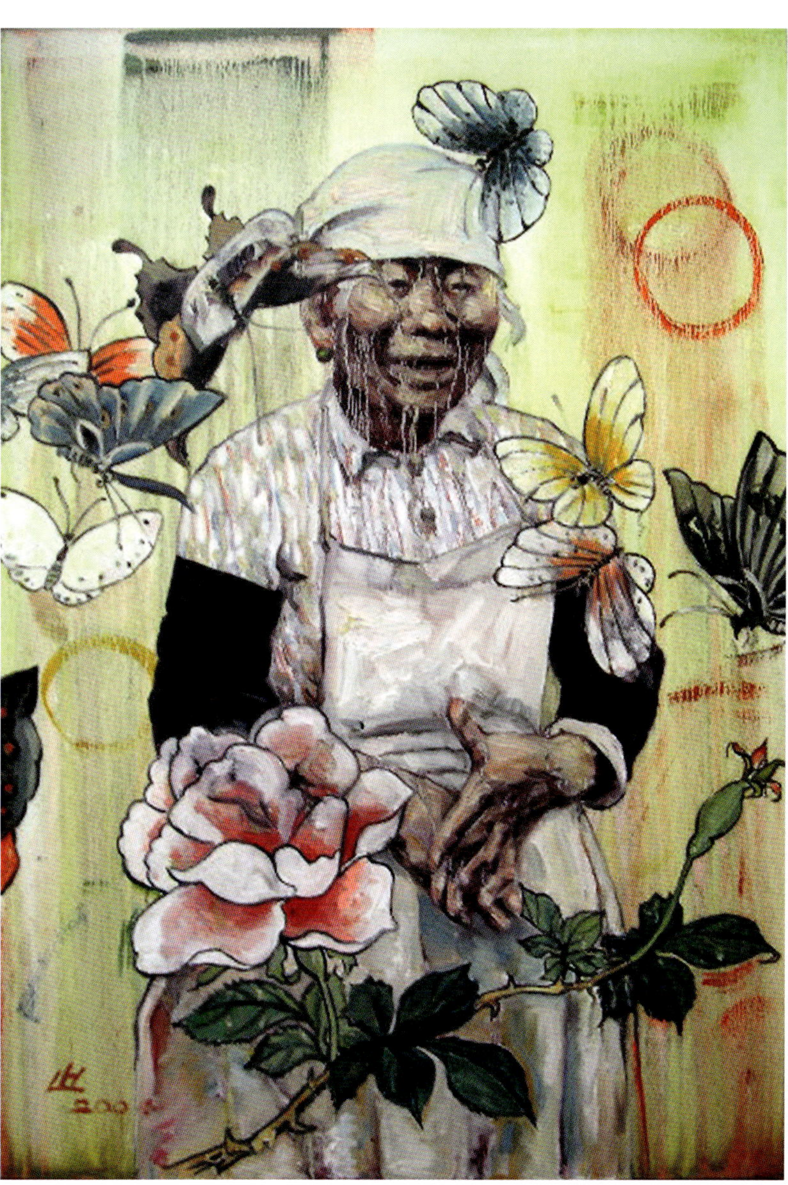

Fig. 11. Hung Liu
Chinese in Idaho Portrait I, 2004
Oil on canvas, 36 × 24 in. (91.4 × 61 cm)
Private collection

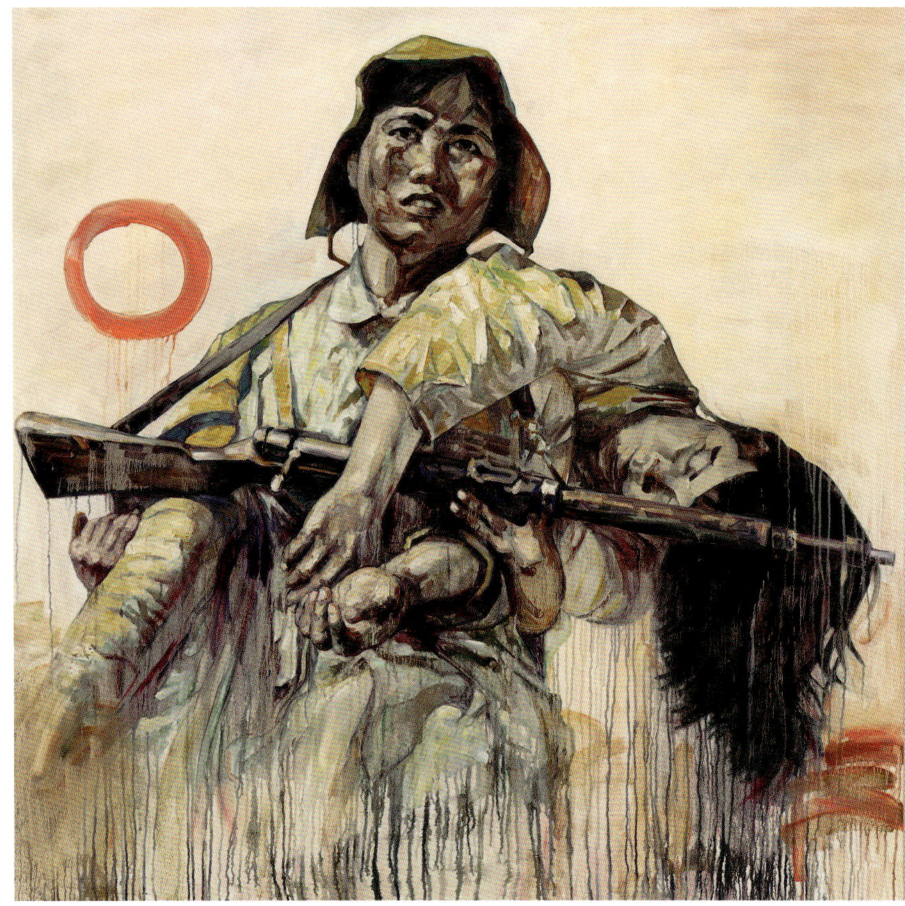

Fig. 12. Hung Liu
Tis the Final Conflict, 2007
Oil on canvas, 66 × 66 in. (167.6 × 167.6 cm)
Collection of Roselyne Chroman Swig

wholeness, but Liu cites their transience: "they're also light and airy—like when you blow bubbles—and full of hope."[13] They can also be read as ghostly metaphors for the ways in which history returns to haunt us, separating the subject from the present, presenting simultaneous existences in the then and the now. "I shifted my artwork from socialist realism, the style in which I'd been trained," she said, "to social realism; and it transformed my personal identity crisis to a crisis of cultural collision."[14]

Liu's *Red Flag Flowing* (2012) and *Hi Ho* (2011) are executed in the style of patriotic propaganda booklets from the era, and Kelley has described the paintings as "tender lessons in socialization, at once charming and eerie."[15] But with these works, Liu also commemorates the artists who succumbed to imposed standards and lost their art during the Cultural Revolution.

Liu's early self-portrait *Resident Alien* (1988; cat. 18), for which she took on the parodic name "Cookie, Fortune," is free of dripping pigment and decorative overlays, as is her series *Portraits of a Chinese Self* (2013). And her *Rat Year* diptychs (2008; 2020) are double portraits of herself and what might be called her "spirit animals." Together, Liu's self-portraits offer an unadorned visual autobiography. This is the self that has survived, and thrived, but remains faithful to its origins, or perhaps to the self that is unable to escape them. Since the early 1990s, of course, China has become a major player in global

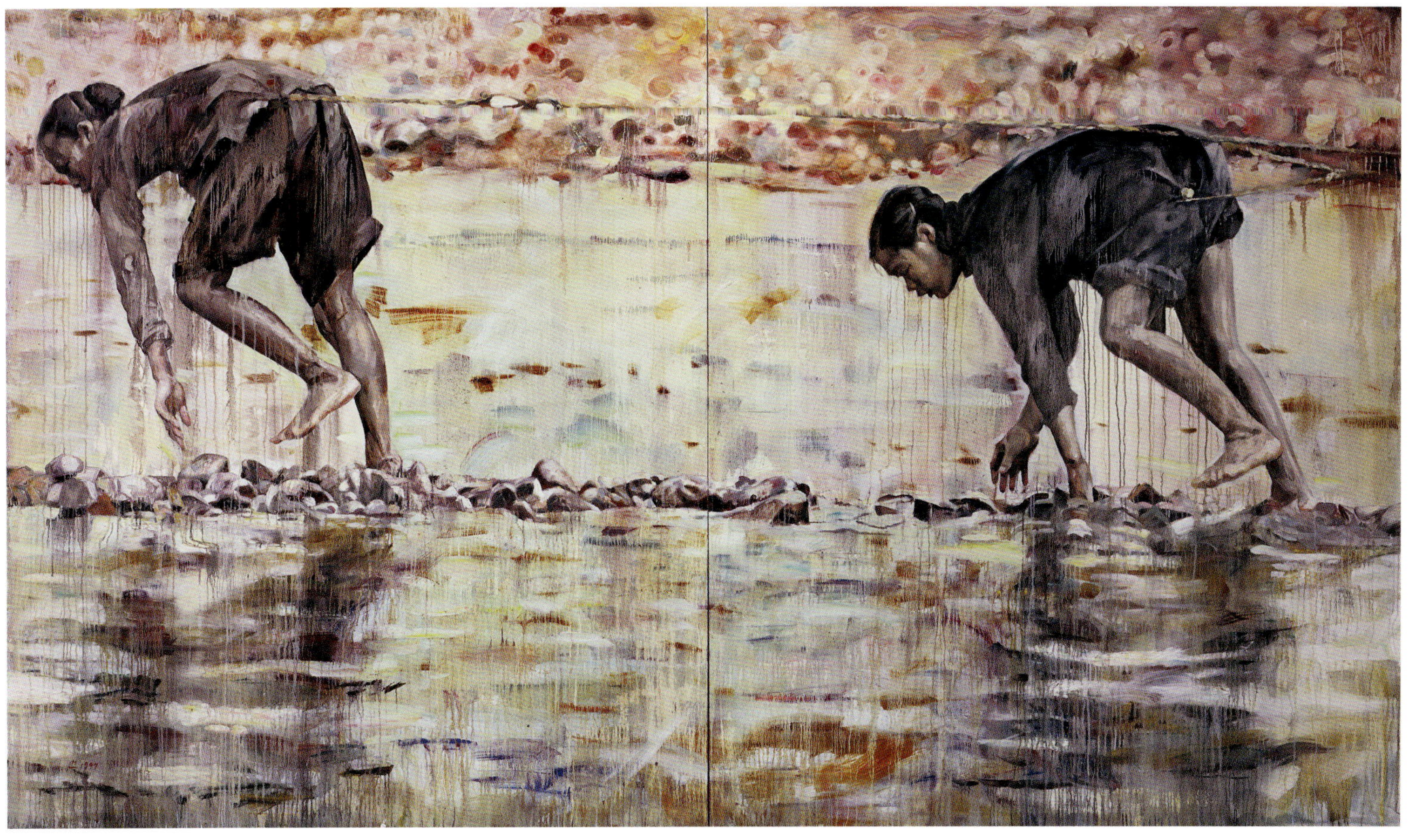

Fig. 13. Hung Liu
Mu Nu (Mother and Daughter), 1997
Oil on canvas, overall: 80 × 140 in.
(203.2 × 355.6 cm), diptych
Kemper Museum of Contemporary Art,
Kansas City, Mo. Museum purchase

contemporary art worlds. In 2008, Liu had her first solo show in her home country, at the Beijing Art Gallery, within the old Imperial Granary complex, a rare survivor of architectural modernization in Beijing.

It is clear that, despite the unique trajectory of her life story, Liu has played the roles so many of us play—mother, daughter, partner. She identifies as a feminist artist, with caveats about her feminism's origins in her Chinese life and her admiration for heroic women, not so much the American movement, though it has welcomed and included her.[16] Much of her work focuses on the redemption of marginalized women through what might be called the body politic. The drastic changes in gender roles brought on by the Maoist republic are evident in the full body of her work, from the beautiful and beautifully dressed concubines with bound feet to the heroic warrior women who "hold up half the sky" (so long as they get with the program). The heroic depictions of women in the Mao days, like the Red Lantern Girls during the Boxer Rebellion, deeply impressed Liu's generation. One of her early influences was *Daughters of China,* a 1949 film by Zifeng Ling about resistance to the Japanese occupation. It was the source of Liu's powerful painting series of 2007, which includes *Tis the Final Conflict,* a portrait of a mourning female soldier carrying the body of a comrade (fig. 12). In *Mu Nu* (1997), a mother and daughter, almost indistinguishable from men, are roped together as they haul a boat along a canal—men's work, the downside of equality (fig. 13).

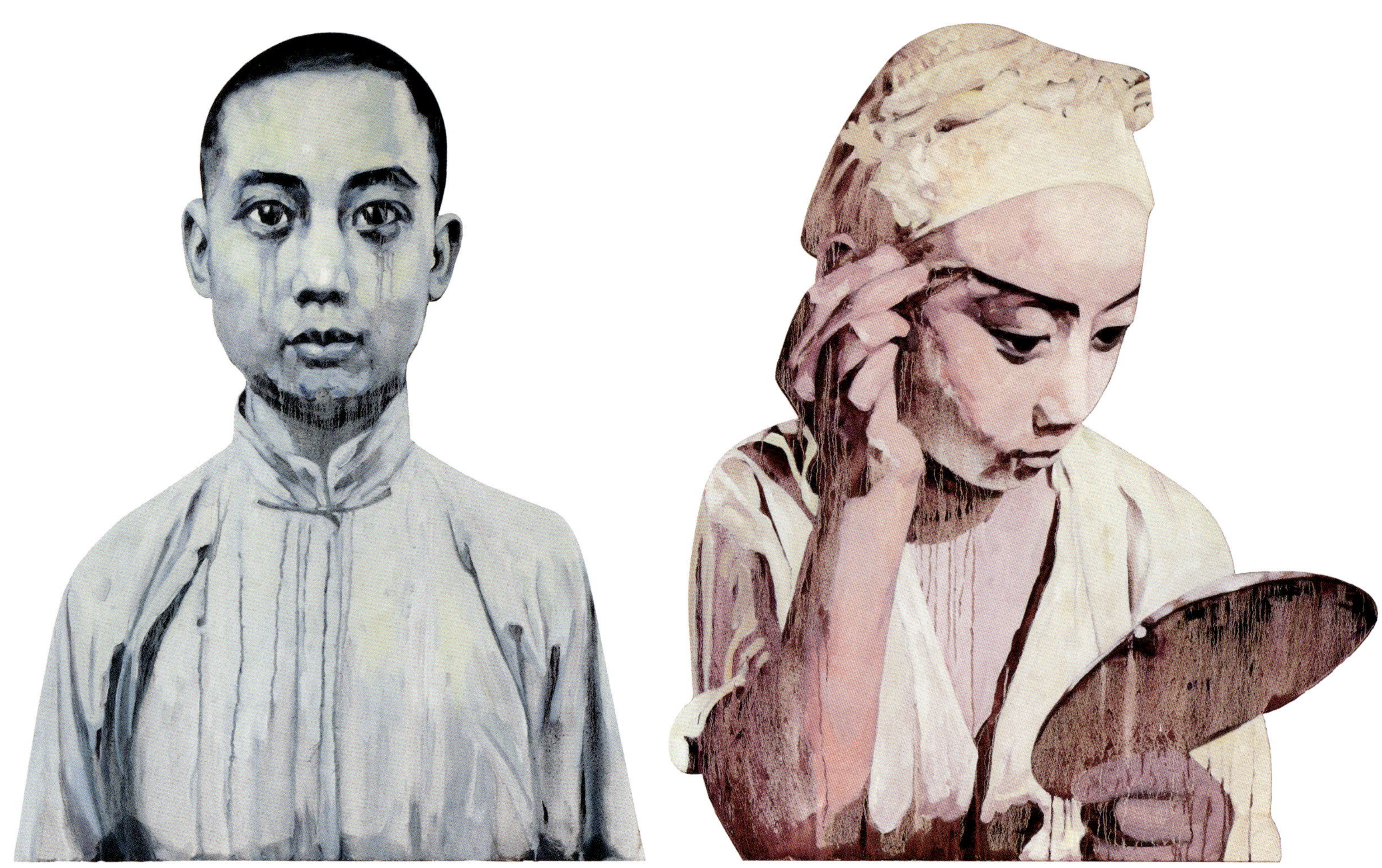

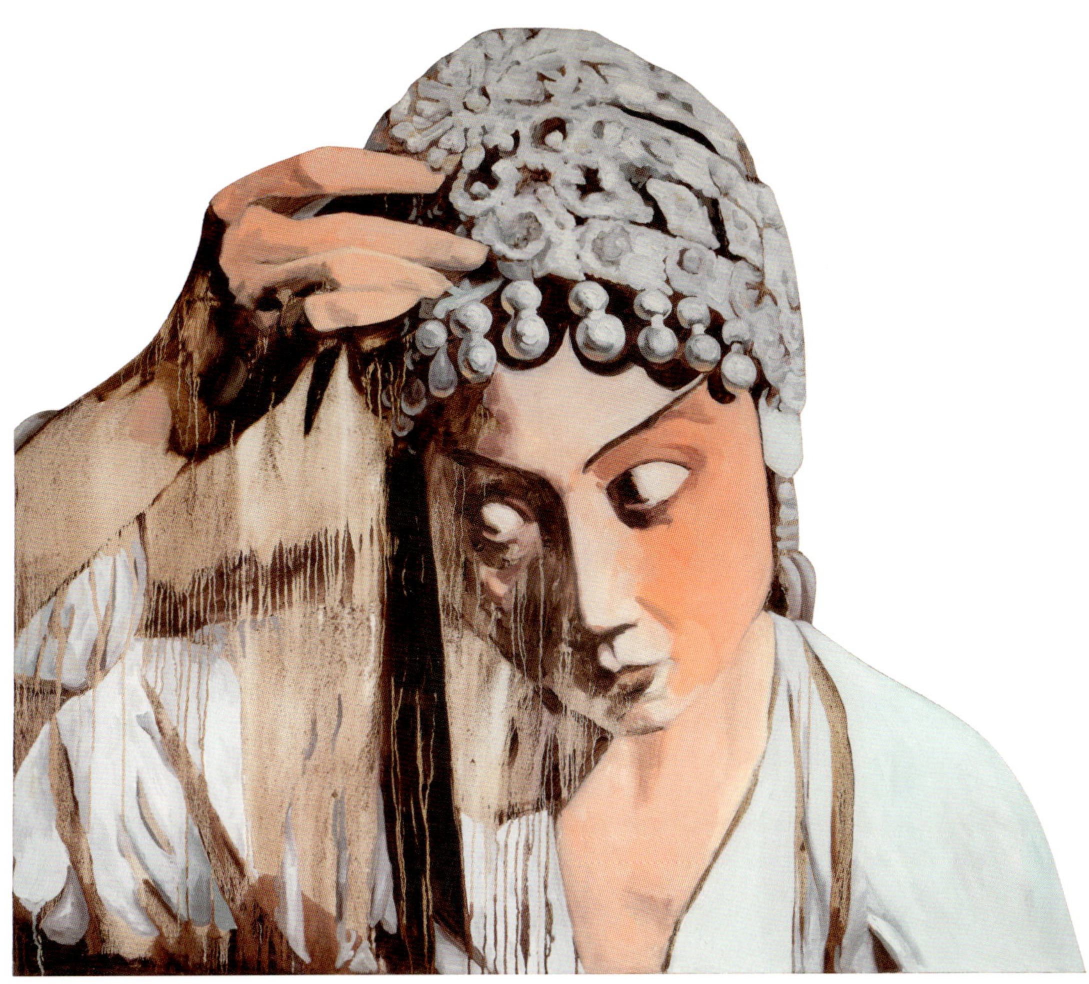

Fig. 14. Hung Liu
Blue Boy, 1993
Oil on shaped canvases, overall: 48 × 130 in.
(121.9 × 330.2 cm), triptych
Private collection

Gender and gender roles have long preoccupied Liu. In *Blue Boy* (1993), an androgynous young man (actor Mei Lanfang) is making himself up as a woman, as all roles in the Peking Opera were played by men (fig. 14). Liu quotes Lu Xun, who remarked that the men in the audiences thought about the women portrayed by male actors, while the women thought about the men playing them.[17] In Liu's *Madonna* (1992), based on an old photograph, a young Chinese prostitute (ironically standing in for the "virgin" Mary, complete with implied halo) holds a Western plaster bust of Cupid, who looks like a girl child (cat. 26). In another ambiguous example, *Goddess of Love, Goddess of Liberty* (1989), two women are apparently making love, though they have been described as a woman and a "soft" man (cat. 25).

Liu's art disproves the adage about East and West: "never the twain shall meet." Recontextualizing both Orientalism and Occidentalism, she has become an effective post-Orientalist. In recent works like *South* (2017) and *Sanctuary* (2019), she has addressed subjects such as immigration and prejudice in the United States (cats. 49, 50). Liu continues to carry the burden of memory as it slips back and forth between fact and fiction, her own and that submerged in the lives of others: "I want my work to be a comfort to people I've never known."[18]

Notes

1. Hung Liu, "Artist's Statement, 1988," typescript, from *Resident Alien,* Liu's Capp Street Project installation. The exhibition was presented in San Francisco's Monadnock Building, 685 Market Street, from August to October 1988. The Capp Street Project Archive is held at the California College of the Arts, Oakland Campus. See California College of the Arts, "Vault," https://vault.cca.edu.
2. Leah Ollman, "Paintings, Text Speak of the 'Trauma' in China's Body Politic," *Los Angeles Times,* September 15, 1989.
3. See, for example, *Peeking Opera* (1989), 120, and *Trauma* (1989).
4. Hung Liu, "Seven Poses," *Women in the Arts* (Fall 2008): 22.
5. Wu Hung, "Four Moments in Hung Liu's Art," in *Summoning Ghosts: The Art of Hung Liu,* by René de Guzman et al. (Oakland, Calif.: Oakland Museum of California; Berkeley: University of California Press, 2013), 37.
6. A number of works in Liu's earlier series *Where Is Mao?* (1988; cats. 8–17) feature global leaders meeting with Mao, whose features are erased.
7. Moira Roth, "Interactions and Collisions: Reflections on the Art of Hung Liu," in *Hung Liu: Sittings* (New York: Bernice Steinbaum Gallery, 1992), n.p.
8. Griselda Pollock, "Hung Liu: Odalisque," in *Fresh Talk/Daring Gazes: Conversations on Asian American Art,* ed. Elaine H. Kim, Margo Machida, and Sharon Mizota (Berkeley: University of California Press, 2003), 119–22.

9. Margo Machida, "Seeing 'Yellow': Asians and the American Mirror," in *The Decade Show: Frameworks of Identity in the 1980s* (New York: Museum of Contemporary Hispanic Art; New Museum of Contemporary Art; Studio Museum in Harlem, 1990), 109–27.

10. Hung Liu quoted in Jonah Winn-Lenetsky, "Hung Liu: Catchers," *THE Magazine* (September 2019): 57. The emotional *Refugee: Mother and Son* (1999) offers another parallel to current events.

11. Donald Kuspit, quoted by Alison Ferris, in *Hung Liu: Tales of Chinese Women* (Sheboygan, Wisc.: John Michael Kohler Arts Center, 1994), n.p. See also Donald B. Kuspit, *Hung Liu* (San Francisco: Rena Bransten Gallery, 1993), 4.

12. Hung Liu quoted in Bill Berkson, "Hung Liu, Action Painter," in René de Guzman et al., *Summoning Ghosts,* 128.

13. Hung Liu quoted in an interview with Cynthia Barber: Cynthia Barber, "Comfort and Joy: Interview with Hung Liu," *Printmaking Today* 14, no. 1 (Spring 2005): 34.

14. Hung Liu quoted in Roth, "Interactions and Collisions," n.p.

15. Jeff Kelley, "Hung Liu: Chronology," in de Guzman, *Summoning Ghosts,* 199.

16. See Wu Hung, "Sixty Years on a Hard Journey for Art: A Conversation between Hung Liu and Wu Hung," in *Hung Liu: Great Granary,* ed. Wu Hung (Hong Kong: Timezone 8, 2010), 109. This lengthy interview offers a particularly insightful overview of Liu's life and career.

17. Lu Xun quoted in Wu Hung, "Four Moments in Hung Liu's Art," 23.

18. Hung Liu quoted in Barber, "Comfort and Joy," n.p.

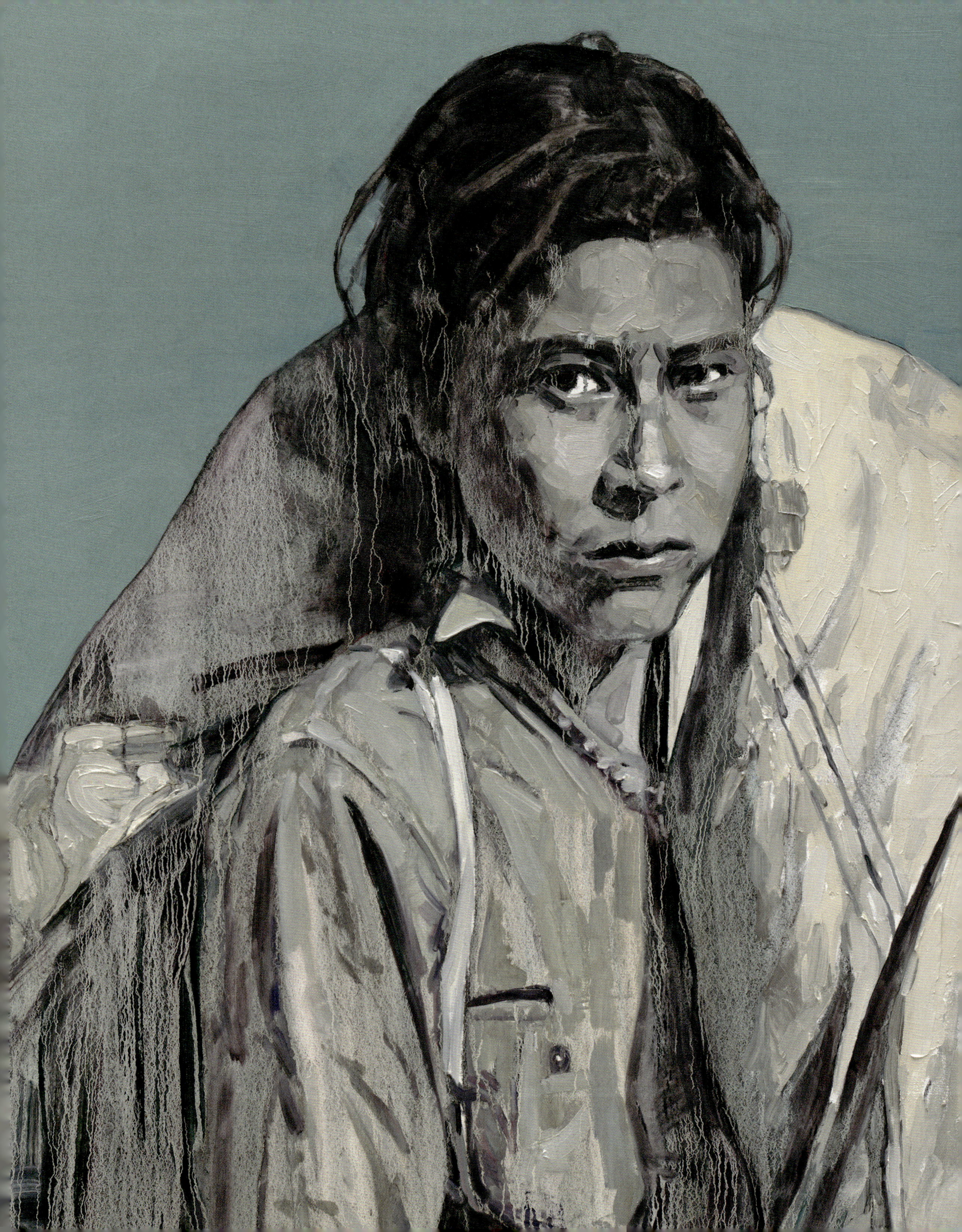

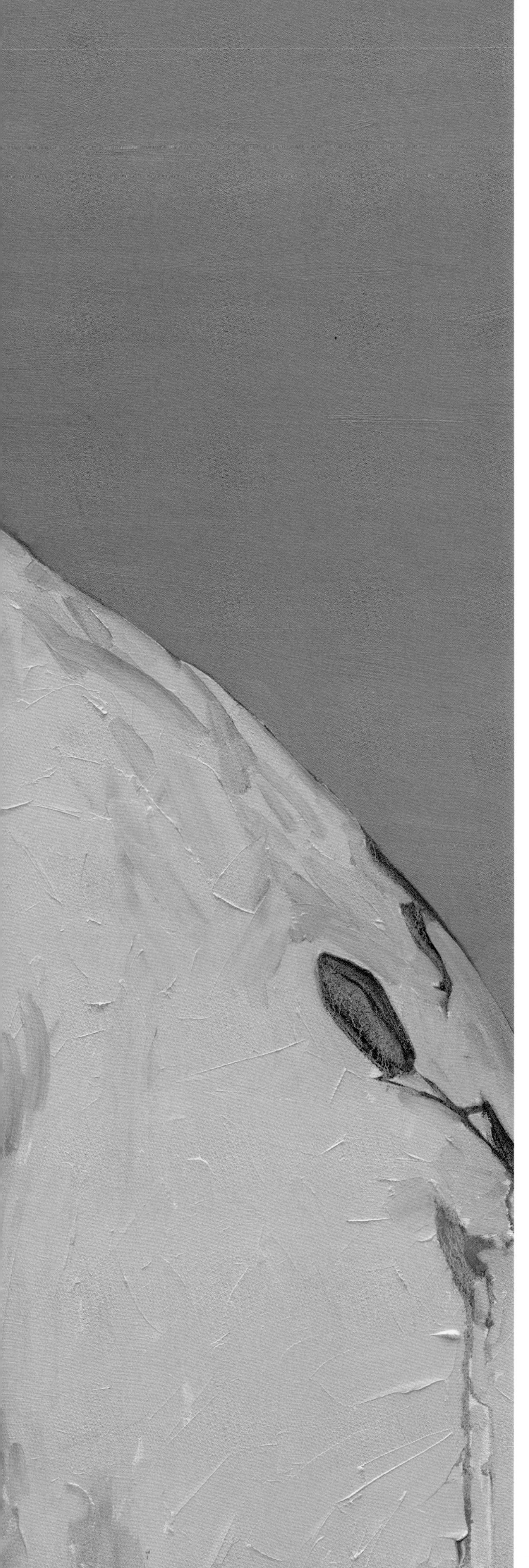

ELIZABETH PARTRIDGE

DEEPLY FAMILIAR

Hung Liu and Dorothea Lange

The good photograph is not the object. The *consequences* of the photograph are the object, so that no one would say, "How did you do it? Where did you find it?" But they would say, "That such things could be." —Dorothea Lange

I paint from historical photographs of people; the majority of them had no name, no bio, no story left. Nothing. I feel they are kind of lost souls, spirit-ghosts. My painting is a memorial site for them. —Hung Liu

In 2015, Hung Liu drove to the Oakland Museum of California, only a few miles away from her studio. There, in the quiet of the library, she pored over the archives of the great American photographer Dorothea Lange (1895–1965).[1] Flipping through big, black binders, she encountered thousands of images—archival prints, proof sheets, negatives, and other memorabilia (fig. 1). Liu became absorbed by Lange's photographs. She stared intently at each portrait, taking in the smudgy dirt, the wrinkles, the worries, the hope and joy. "I love human faces," she has remarked. "The face tells you so much. And the photograph is like a frozen moment, like frozen time. That moment. That face, forever."[2]

At first glance, Lange may not seem to have much in common with Liu. Born in a different century, on a different continent, she is best known for her black-and-white representations of Americans during the Great Depression, whereas Liu often paints from photos of Chinese society's "outcasts." As Liu discovered, however, their trajectories reveal remarkable parallels, particularly with regard to portraiture.

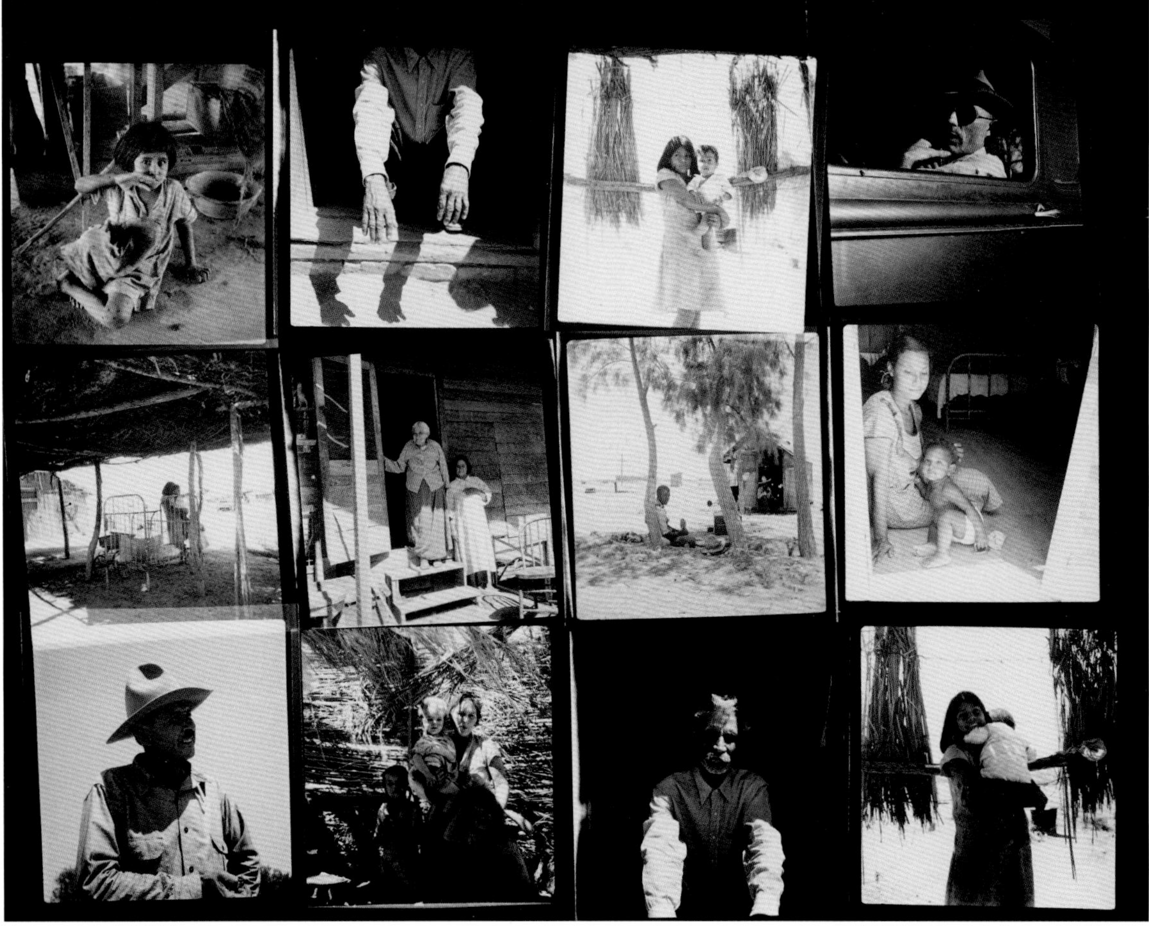

By merely scratching the surface, we begin to see that both artists witnessed political upheaval and endured personal trauma. Each
demonstrated strength and bravery in the face of adversity. In their
own ways, Lange and Liu grew from difficult circumstances to become
resolute artists, whose work honors ordinary people caught in extraordinary, disruptive times. The more closely we look, the more these
connections come into focus.

Liu was only an infant when her parents carried her in their desperate flight from Changchun, China. It was 1948, and Communist
forces ringed the city, locking in the Kuomintang (Nationalist) soldiers,
who were trying to hold the area that was embroiled in the civil war.
The residents trapped inside were first hungry, then starving. Liu's
parents, along with several members of her mother's desperate family,
left on foot, determined to escape.

Liu, of course, has no memory of this flight, but it shaped her
life profoundly. When her family reached the Communist forces,
her father, an honest man, told them the truth: he was a captain in the
Kuomintang army. The Communists consequently took most of their
meager possessions and sent Liu's father to a "liberation camp" while
Liu and her other relatives were permitted to travel.

As the family walked on and on, they came to a river. A baby sat
quietly beside the water. The mother had jumped in and drowned,

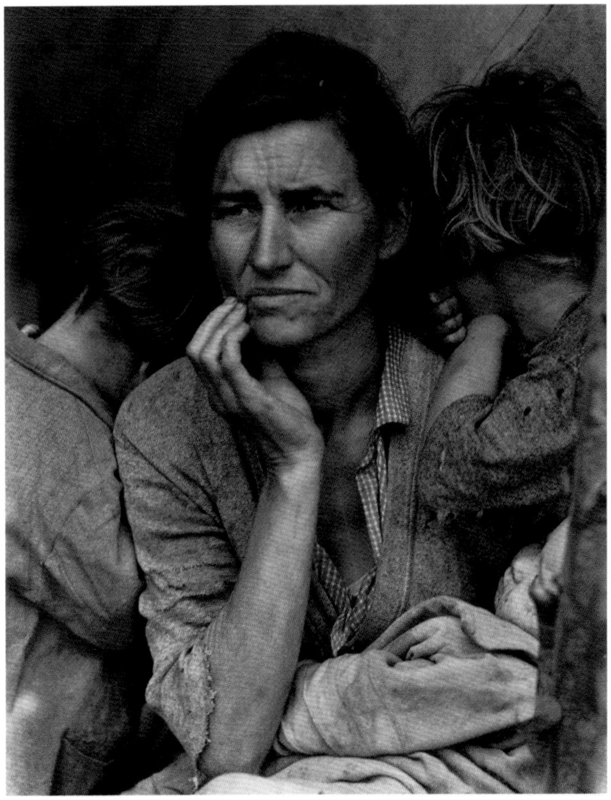

Fig. 2. Dorothea Lange
Migrant Mother, Nipomo, California ("Destitute pea pickers in California. Mother of seven children. Age 32"), 1936
Prints and Photographs Division, Library of Congress, Washington, D.C.

leaving her child. No one stopped, no one picked up the baby. No one could. Fleeing by the thousands, the refugees were barely able to help themselves.

"When refugees are escaping a disaster, it involves thousands of people running away with their families," Liu recalled years later. "No one is able to look out for anyone else."[3] Though Liu understood why no one could help the baby, the story, told to her by her mother, has long haunted her. What drove that woman to abandon her baby? How could she have gone into the river so undaunted, the water closing over her, leaving no ripple in the flow of history?

Heavy rains fell one evening as Liu's family continued their journey. They huddled together under a sheet. Liu's mother sat cross-legged all night with Liu in her lap, trying to shelter her baby from the worst of the weather. A month later, Changchun fell to the Communists. Liu's family realized their chances of survival would be best if they returned to the city. They had no idea of her father's whereabouts or if he was even alive.

Decades later, as she searched for resonant images to paint, Liu was often drawn to photographs of mothers and their young, vulnerable children. In 2001, she painted *Refugee: Opera,* which presents an exhausted, fleeing mother holding her baby, who nurses from her nearly empty breast (cat. 31). It is a heartbreaking image to look at, but at least the child has a mother and, perhaps, some nourishment.

Later, when Liu was painting from the photographs that Lange took on assignment for the Farm Security Administration (FSA), she passed over *Migrant Mother* (1936), Lange's most memorial image, taken near Nipomo, California (fig. 2). Instead she focused on six other photos of the family from the series (fig. 3). In Liu's painting, *Migrant Mother: Mealtime* (2016; cat. 47), Florence Owens Thompson cradles her sleeping baby, who appears close in age to the baby in *Refugee: Opera.* Another young child leans her head on Thompson's shoulder. And in front of all three is an ominously empty tin plate. A different country, but the same theme: unfed children, desperate refugee mothers. Tragically, it was a reoccurring theme in twentieth-century China.

By 1960, a massive famine had gripped the country, a result of Mao Zedong's "Great Leap Forward," begun three years earlier, and Liu, her mother, and her mother's family moved on to Beijing. Then in 1961, after doing extremely well on the qualifying exams, thirteen-year-old Liu entered an elite girls' boarding school, the Girls' Middle School attached to Beijing Normal University. School was a natural fit for Liu. She studied hard and excelled. Interested in drawing and painting from an early age, she was able to take art classes as well. Though her family still had no news of her father, his Kuomintang service cast a shadow on them. In school, students were required to take either Russian or English. Most wanted to take Russian, but realizing that Liu would never be allowed to travel to Russia, her mother enrolled her in English. It opened up a world of new literature for the budding artist.

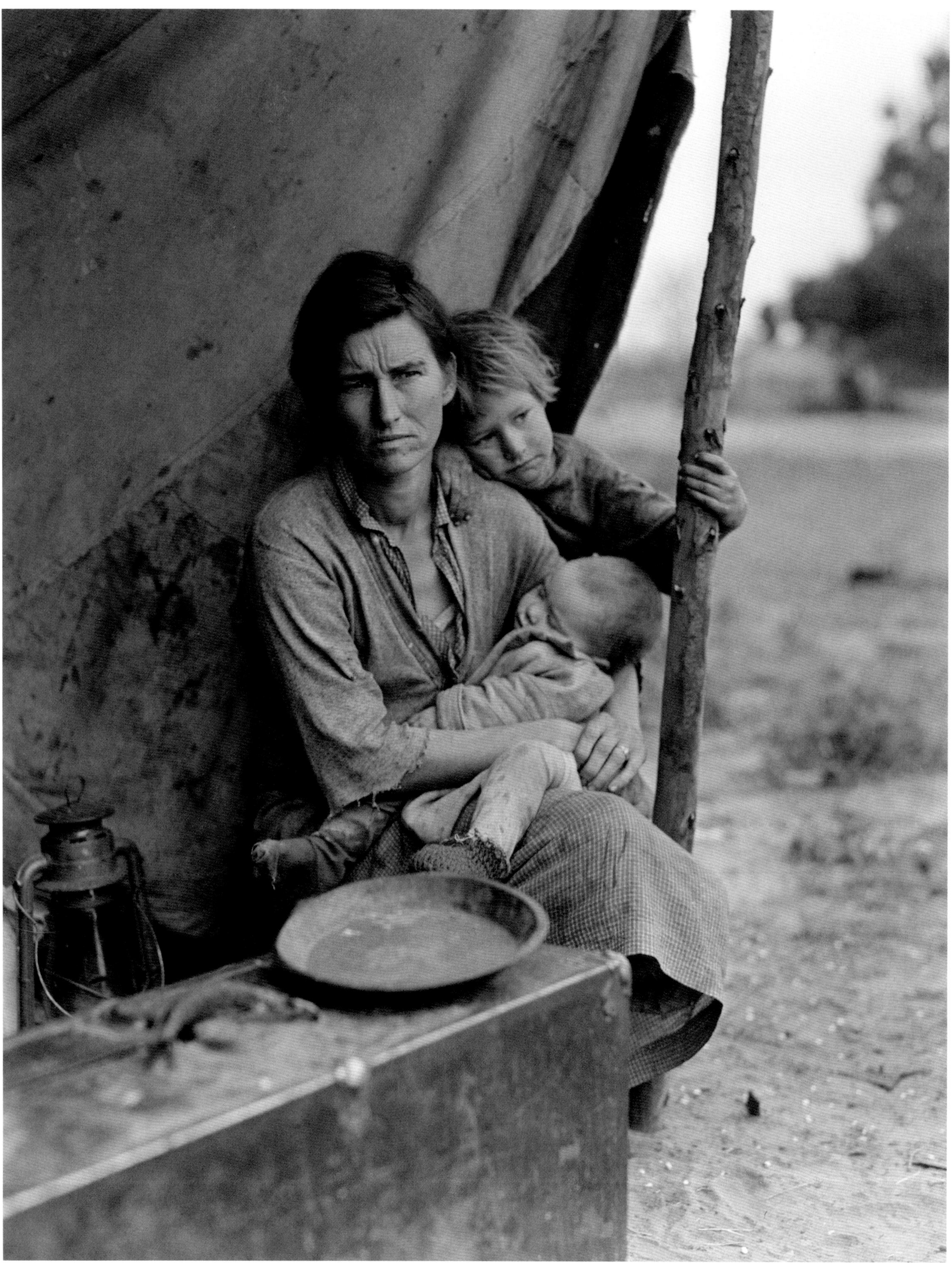

In the spring of 1966, during Liu's last year of high school, the Cultural Revolution began. To purge China of "counterrevolutionary" influences, Mao encouraged Communist youth, known as Red Guards, in violent rebellion. Educators, said to be poisoning students with Western ideology, were a prime target. Liu was not allowed to join the Red Guards. Her all-consuming interest in studying led other students to call her "*baizhuan,*" or "apolitical." Being baizhuan was perilous: it was only one small step away from being considered a counterrevolutionary. Liu had not seen her father since she was six months old, but his affiliation with the Kuomintang continued to pose problems. After all, the reasoning went, she had been raised by the woman who had married him.

Shortly before Liu's class was supposed to graduate in July, Beijing Normal University was in total chaos. Regular academic classes came to a standstill as Mao's exhortations against educators galvanized some of the students. Still living in the dorms, the Red Guards at Liu's school spun increasingly out of control, and on August 5, a group forced the deputy principal to run up and down the stairs of the six-story dormitory building until she was exhausted. When she could barely crawl, they beat her. The horrified janitor loaded her onto a cart used for moving garbage and took her to the hospital, but it was too late to save her.

Liu was not at school that day. Other students whispered to her what had happened. The next morning, an announcement came over the loudspeaker that the deputy principal had died, but no details were given. It was a searing moment for Liu. She saw, firsthand, how easily the truth could be erased and how impossible it was for others to speak up. "Suddenly, overnight, the revolution had started," Liu said later. "I saw these Red Guards, who had been very modest, even shy girls, friendly and sensitive, who studied hard, and who respected their teachers, transformed into demons. They used a belt to beat people and even set up a detention center at school."[4]

Over the next few months, several thousand people—many of them educators—were publicly humiliated, tortured, and killed in Beijing by the Red Guards. But as the violence escalated, Mao came up with a new plan. He decided high school and college students should be reeducated and demanded that they all be sent to work with peasants in the countryside. In 1968, Liu was first ordered to leave Beijing for Inner Mongolia, but because she was an only child, she was soon reassigned to a village about fifty miles outside of Beijing, closer to her mother, aunt, and grandmother. This way, she would be nearby if she was needed to take care of her elders.

For Liu, used to books and studying, work in the countryside was physically demanding and unending. The villagers grew wheat and corn, a little paddy rice, and a few vegetables (fig. 4). Though the labor was always arduous, harvest time was by far the hardest. They pulled up each wheat plant by the roots so the stalks could be used for cooking fires. Nothing was to be wasted. Each morning, loud speakers in

Fig. 3. Dorothea Lange
"Migrant agricultural worker's family. Seven children without food. Mother aged thirty-two. Father is a native Californian. Nipomo, California," 1936
Prints and Photographs Division, Library of Congress, Washington, D.C.

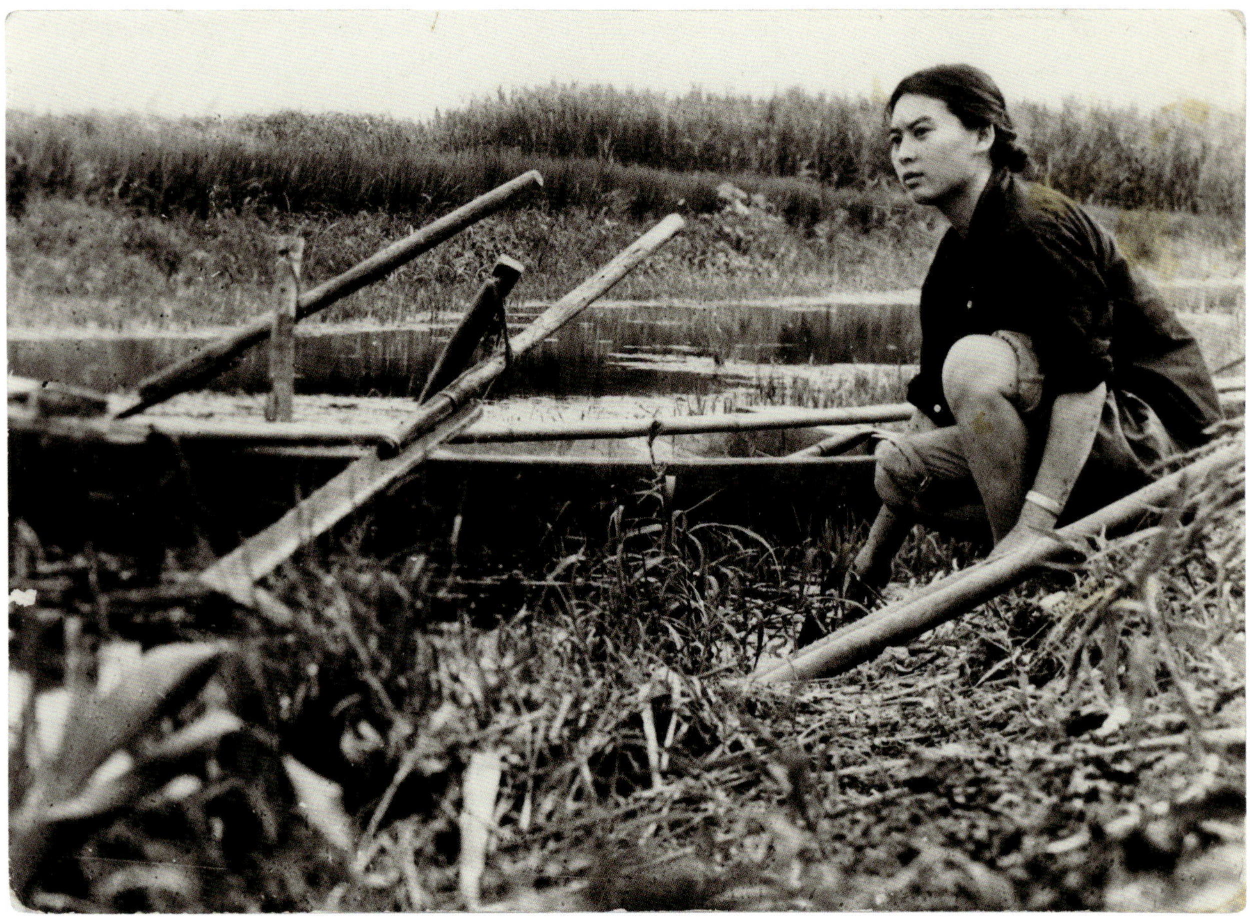

Fig. 4. Hung Liu working in the fields in Dadu Lianghe, China, c. 1968–72.

the village blared out at wake-up times, and everyone had to be up well before dawn. By the time the sun emerged, the workers' faces and clothes were splattered with wet, heavy mud. It was like nothing Liu had ever experienced. "We went through to the bottom," she said of being sent to the countryside. "The bottom of the bottom."[5]

One night, when the corn was nearly ripe, it was Liu's turn to watch over the fields to protect the crop from thieves and animals. She was paired with a peasant she called "Big Brother." Hearing a rustling noise, the two of them quietly sneaked closer to the sound. When they snapped on a flashlight, they saw a man stealing corn. To their shock, it was a man the villagers all affectionately called "Uncle," one of the poorest people in the community. His wife was sick and could not work, and they had five ragged, underfed children.

Big Brother paused for a few seconds, then moved forward. He began pulling corn off the stalks and stuffing it into Uncle's bag. Liu was frozen in place until Big Brother whispered to her to come help. Uncle was so stunned at what he was witnessing that he stopped picking corn. Liu and Big Brother filled his sack and heaved it up onto his shoulder.

The next day, Liu saw Uncle but did not give the slightest indication she had helped him the night before. The consequences for him and his family would have been unimaginable. Blame would also have fallen heavily on her and Big Brother. Liu recently reflected on the memory: "I learned, big-time, the rule of regulation. Compassion and humanity overrule all of that."[6]

At the end of the first year, like the other workers in the village of Dadu Lianghe, Liu was given an accounting of the money she had earned, based on how much work she had done. Many of the peasants were in constant debt, never able to get ahead. Liu found she had not made enough to get out of debt herself, but the hard work quickly made her strong. At the end of the following year, she was paid around two dollars.

Prior to leaving home in 1968, one of Liu's friends had asked her to take his Shanghai Seagull 120 twin-lens reflex camera. He was being sent to a military labor camp, where he would be under more intense scrutiny than Liu, and his belongings would be searched. Just owning a camera marked him as a member of the bourgeoisie.

Liu had never used a camera, but she was intrigued: "One day, I said [to myself], I have a camera, I can use it," she recalled. "I bought a roll of 120 film. . . . It was scary, exciting."[7] Liu set up a rudimentary darkroom by painting a light bulb red and borrowed money from her mother to buy photo paper, chemicals, and a cheap enlarger. Once back in the countryside, she occasionally was able to take pictures of the villagers who trusted her (cats. 1–4). Many in the commune had only seen photographs of themselves on their ID cards when the country was under Japanese occupation during World War II.

Liu had to be extremely careful not to get caught with the camera, and she had no idea how long she would have to remain in the countryside. "Because you are already kicked out from the city," she said. "You become illegal in the city."[8] Books—hard to come by after many were burned—were surreptitiously passed from hand to hand between the students. For Liu, it was not only a shortage of food to eat but also "no spiritual food either."[9]

In Lange's photographs of the Great Depression, Liu found familiar themes of deprivation, dislocation, and rural poverty (fig. 5). "The kids, for many days, they didn't wash their face. I saw the country kids just like this, their faces all covered by dirt, or snot," she said. "I know exactly no bathing, no water, no food." For Liu, Lange's photos are "almost a first-hand experience with American farmers and the migrant families."[10]

Two years in the countryside became three years, and then four. There was no choice for Liu or for any of the other students living and working in the villages. "Your life," she explained, "your future, is all in the hands of the Great Leader."[11] In Lange's many images, Liu may have seen a painful remembrance of what it was like to see her world flipped upside-down, to have no control over her own destiny. Like Liu, the people Lange photographed had been forced from one place

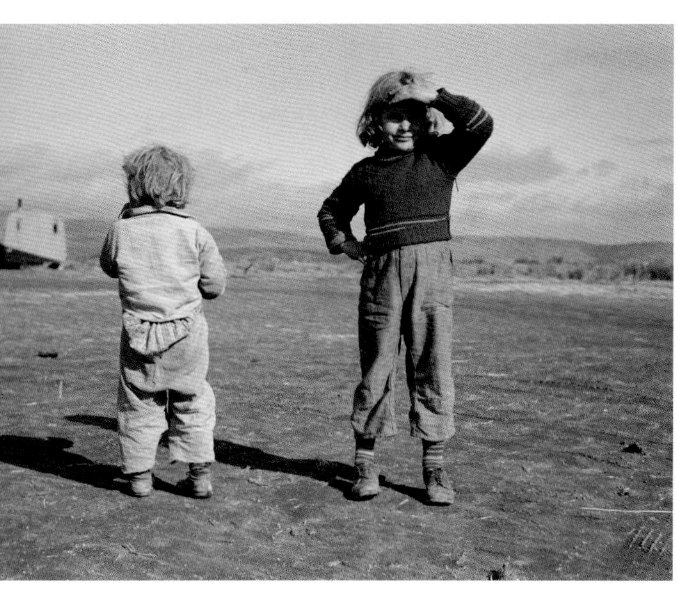

Fig. 5. Dorothea Lange
"Migrant children. Merrill, Klamath County, Oregon. In unit of FSA (Farm Security Administration) mobile camp," 1939
Prints and Photographs Division, Library of Congress, Washington, D.C.

in their country to another, unsure of their future, wondering if life would get better or if that was only a hopeless, fleeting, dream.

On rare occasions, while working out in the fields, Liu would see a plane fly overhead, and for a moment, she would remember there was a bigger world out there, a world beyond her daily work, beyond her freedom-denying ration card, a world where cameras would not have to be concealed. There was a place, she reminded herself, where she would be free to be an artist.

Growing up in Hoboken, New Jersey, Dorothea Lange never spent considerable time in the countryside, but like Hung Liu, her early life was marked by sudden and abrupt changes. In 1902, when she was seven, she contracted polio, which left her with a dropped right foot and a rolling gait. A few years later, Lange's father abandoned the family, and Dorothea, her mother, and little brother moved in with her mother's parents. It was a precipitous fall from a grand, spacious house to a crowded flat.

It also meant Lange took the ferry into New York City every day and walked from her mother's job as a librarian in Manhattan to PS 62. Other children called her "Limpy." Out walking on the street, her mother would admonish her to "walk as well as you can."[12] Having polio, Lange said later, "was the most important thing that happened to me, and formed me, guided me, instructed me, helped me, and humiliated me."[13]

Returning home each day after school, she had to make her way through the Bowery, stepping around drunks and bums. But she was learning an important skill that would be critical to her photography. Later she called this her "cloak of invisibility." It allowed her to observe while having no attention paid to her presence. "I knew how to keep an expression of face that would draw no attention, so no one would look at me. I can turn it on and off. If I don't want anybody to see me, I can make the kind of a face so eyes go off me," she said.[14]

After high school, she apprenticed with several photographers, then in 1918, when she was twenty-three, she headed west on an around-the-world trip that ended when all her money was stolen in San Francisco. She opened a portrait photography studio there, and before long, amassed the "cream of the trade."[15] After her marriage in 1920 to the painter Maynard Dixon, known for his vast Western landscapes, Lange was soon managing a thriving business while coping with the demands of raising two sons and a stepdaughter.

Looking down from the second-story window of her studio in 1933, she watched the homeless, unemployed men as they gathered at the corner, unsure of which way to go next. She picked up her bulky Graflex and headed out onto the street, determined to photograph what she was seeing, develop the negatives, make a print, and get it up on the wall of her studio, all in twenty-four hours. She wanted to "just grab a hunk of lightning."[16] Lange saw something compelling in a sober line of men waiting at a soup kitchen, run by a woman known

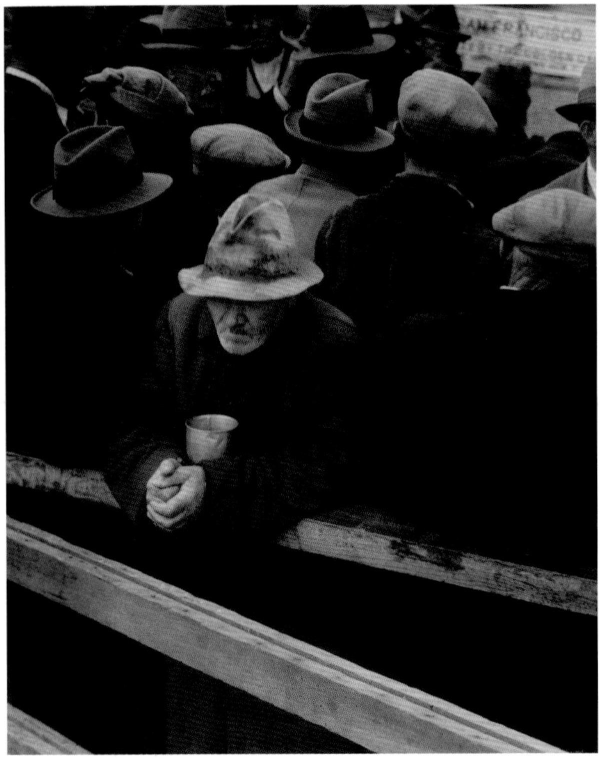

Fig. 6. Dorothea Lange
White Angel Bread Line, San Francisco, 1933
Gelatin silver print, 10¾ × 8⅞ in. (27.3 × 22.6 cm)
The Museum of Modern Art, New York. Gift of Albert M. Bender

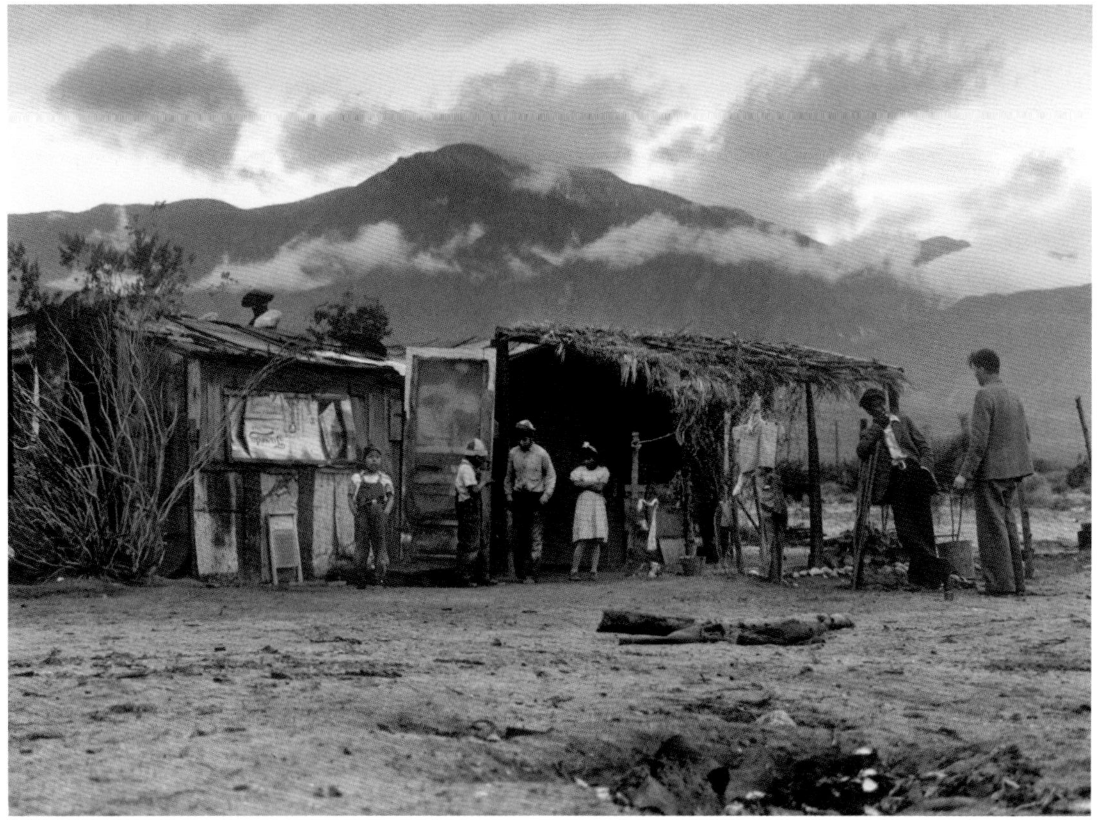

Fig. 7. Dorothea Lange
Coachella Housing, Coachella Valley, California, 1935
Gelatin silver print,
6⅞ × 9½ in. (17.5 × 24.1 cm)
The Dorothea Lange Collection, the Oakland Museum of California. Gift of Paul S. Taylor

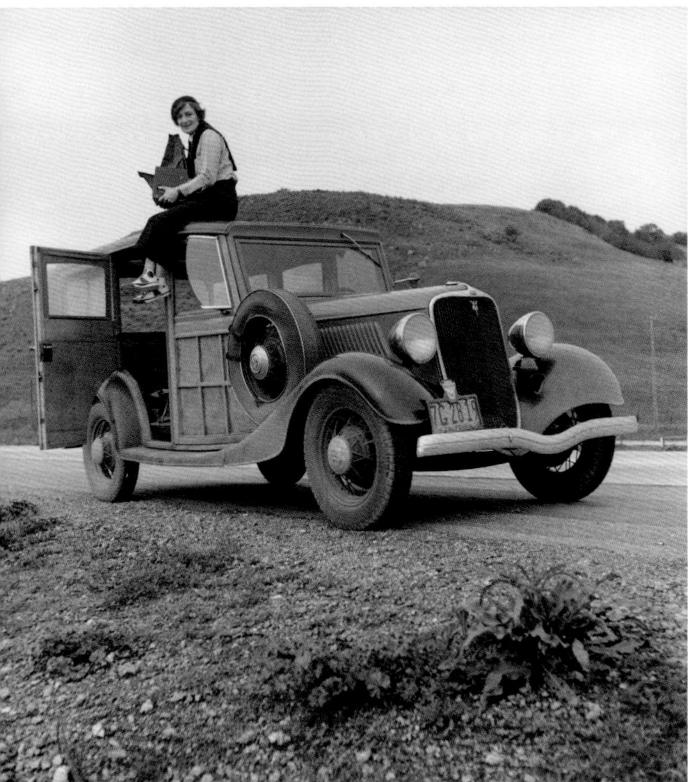

Fig. 8. Dorothea Lange while working in California as a Resettlement Administration photographer, 1936. Prints and Photographs Division, Library of Congress, Washington, D.C.

as the "White Angel." That very first day she took her haunting photograph *White Angel Bread Line* (fig. 6).

Lange's early photographs of her forays onto the streets of San Francisco caught the attention of Paul Schuster Taylor, an economics professor at the nearby University of California, Berkeley. Determined to record the plight of Mexican immigrants and Dust Bowl refugees in the California fields, Taylor hired Lange to collaborate on his field research. In March and April 1935, she accompanied him with her camera, documenting conditions in the Imperial Valley (fig. 7).

It was not long before Lange closed her studio, divorced Dixon, and married Taylor. While out on the road working together, Taylor taught her to listen to what people could tell her: "The words that come direct from the people are the greatest."[17] She would listen intently, then sit down on the grass or in her car to write down their exact words, using the information she'd gleaned to write extensive captions for her images (fig. 8). Sometimes she synthesized what she had learned to make an acute observation that might not be readily apparent, as she did in identifying "Future voter & his Mexican father" (fig. 9).

In 1936, Lange began working for the Resettlement Administration (later the Farm Security Administration), a New Deal agency created by Franklin Delano Roosevelt that sought to document the effects of the Great Depression. Though each photographer worked independently, others included Gordon Parks, Marion Post Wolcott, and

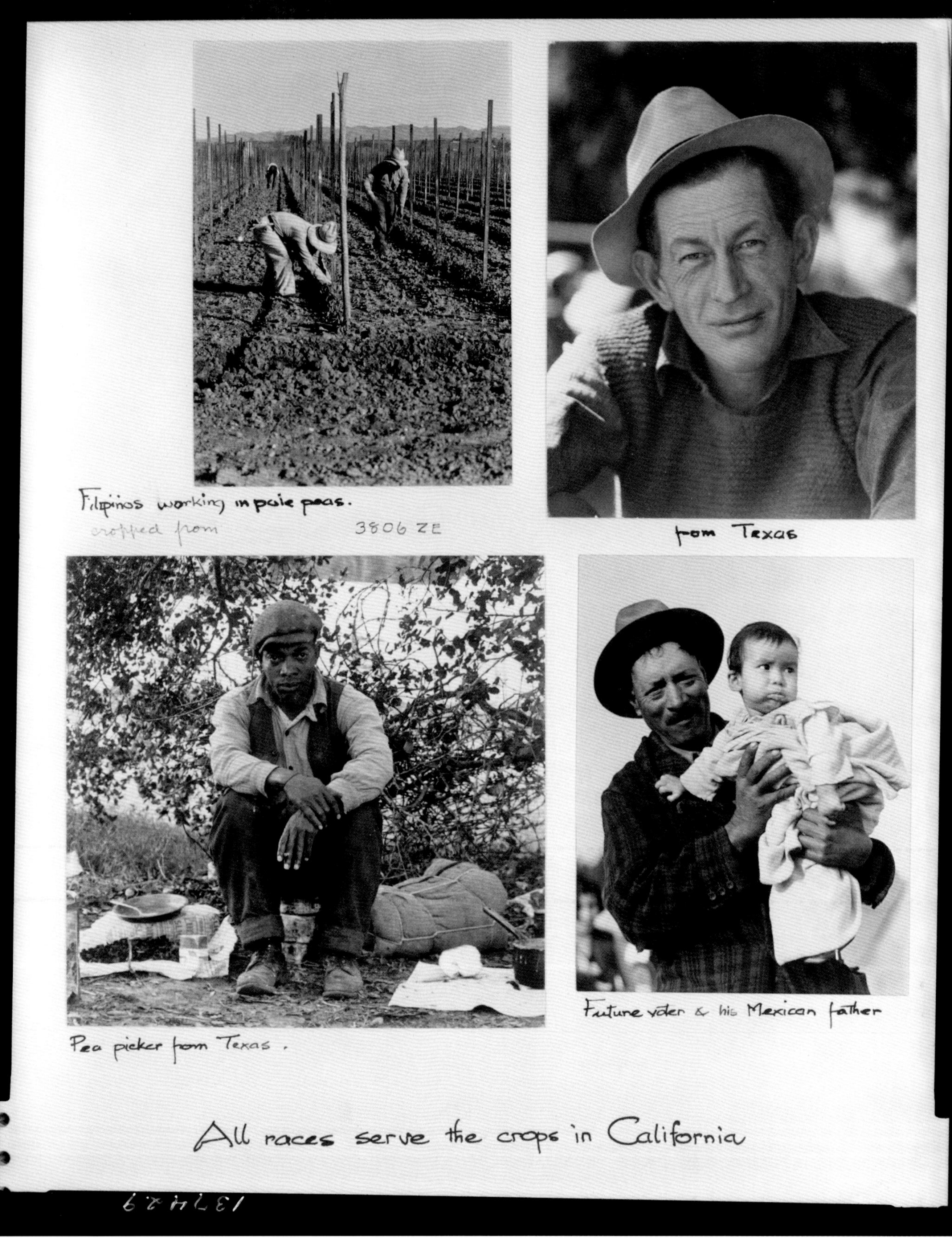

Fig. 9. Dorothea Lange
"All races serve the crops in California," 1935
Prints and Photographs Division, Library of Congress,
Washington, D.C.

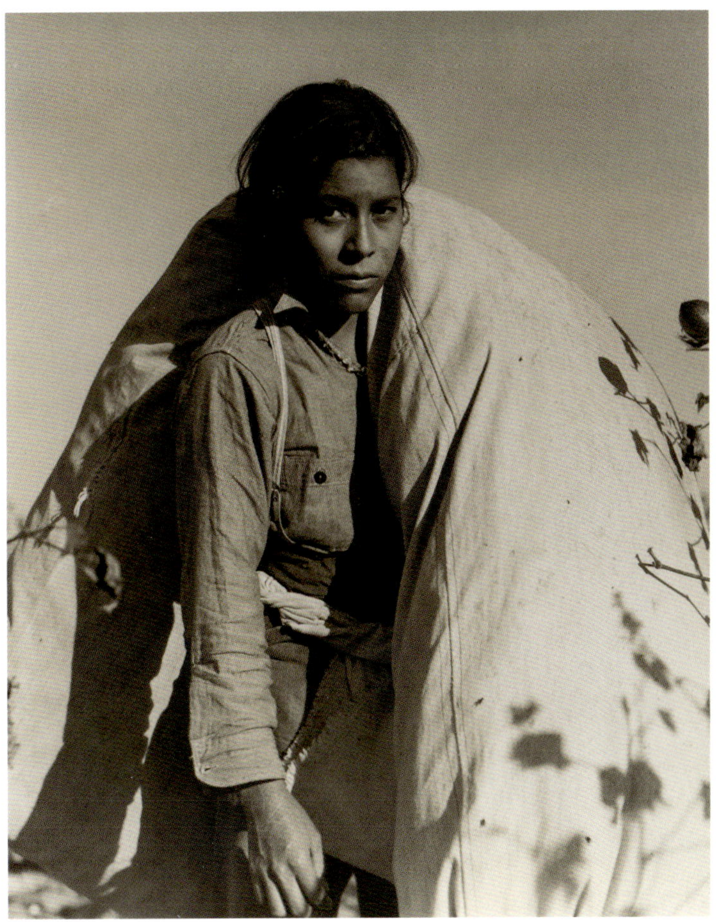

Fig. 10. Dorothea Lange
Young Cotton Picker, San Joaquin Valley, 1936
Gelatin silver print, 9½ × 7³⁄₁₆ in. (24.1 × 18.3 cm)
The Dorothea Lange Collection, the Oakland Museum
of California. Gift of Paul S. Taylor

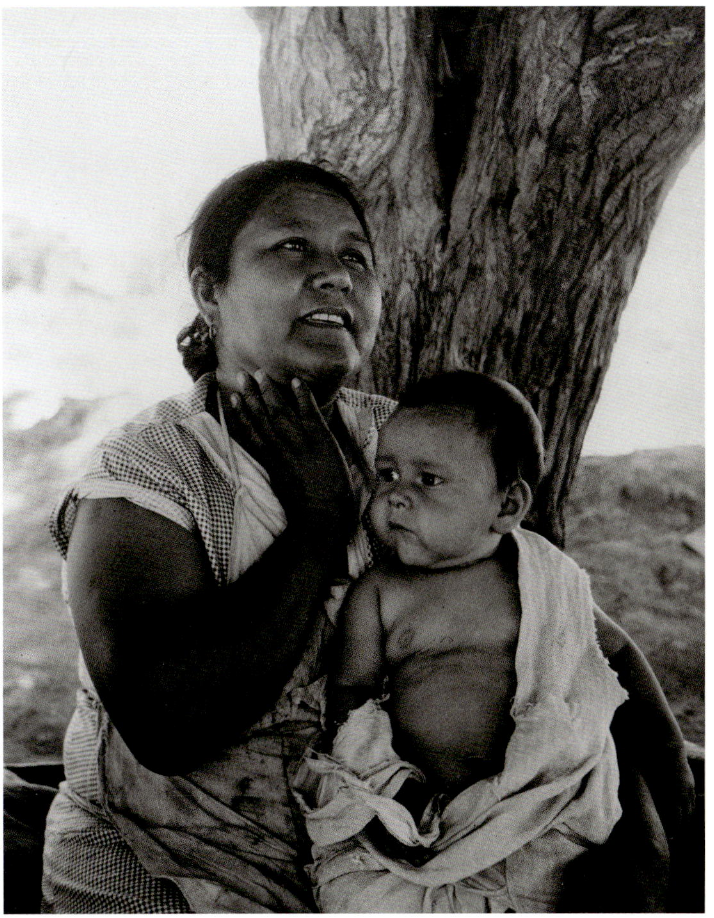

Fig. 11. Dorothea Lange
"Mexican mother in California: 'Sometimes I tell my
children that I would like to go to Mexico, but they
tell me, *We don't want to go, we belong here,*'" 1935
Prints and Photographs Division, Library of Congress,
Washington, D.C.

Walker Evans. Living on the West Coast, Lange received many assignments to cover conditions of migratory farmworkers in the fields of
California (figs. 10, 11).

For the next few years, she made frequent trips, photographing
migrants' broken cars and makeshift shelters, their dirty, threadbare
clothes, and their attempts to keep their tents and clothes clean
and their children fed. She showed them beset by adversity but sur-
viving. Leaving the fields of California, she took several long trips
across the United States, driving through the Southwest, the Dust
Bowl, Texas, and the South (fig. 12). "I had to get my camera to regis-
ter the things about those people that were more important than how
poor they were—their pride, their strength, their spirit," Lange said.[18]

Over and over again, she worked herself to the point of exhaustion.
But she had an urgent need to show the conditions of the migrants,
and she threw herself wholeheartedly into her assignments. Some

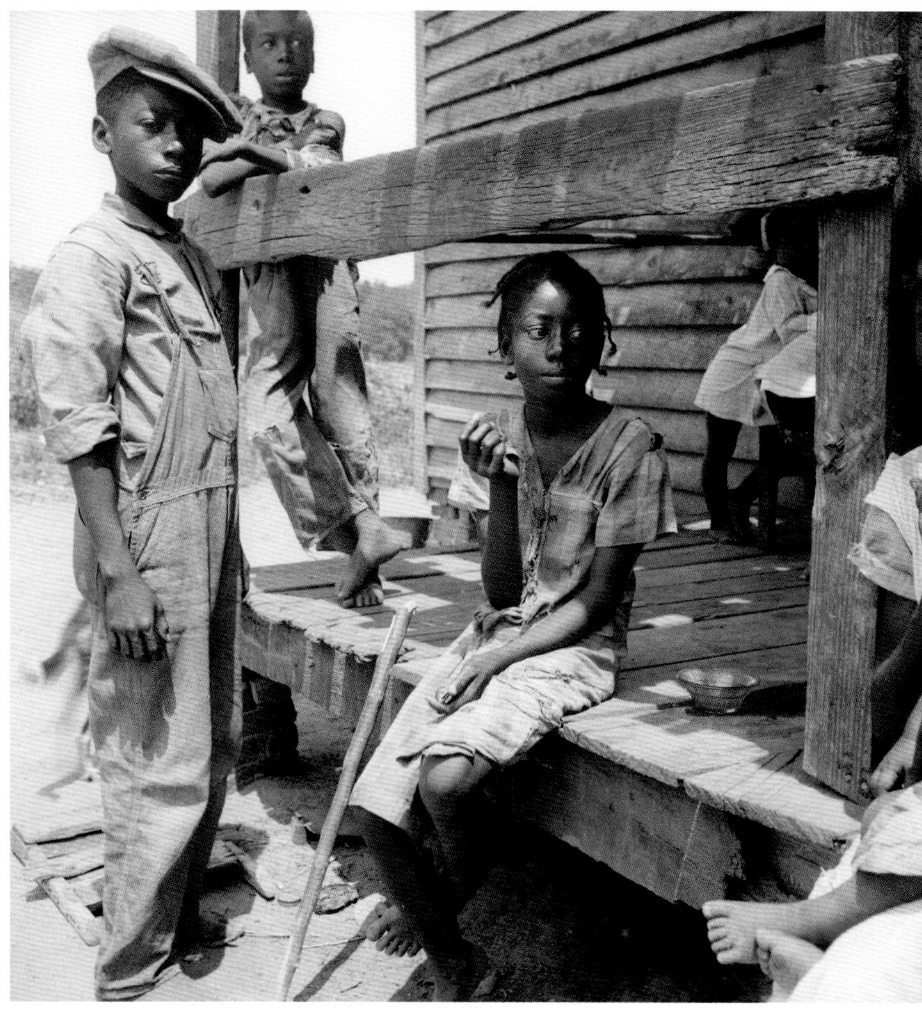

criticized her photographs and those of the other FSA photographers as having crossed the line from documentation to propaganda, specifically for Roosevelt's New Deal agricultural programs. Lange, however, refused to be led into a semantic argument: "Everything is propaganda for what you believe in, actually, isn't it?" she asked. "The harder and the more deeply you believe in anything, the more in a sense you're a propagandist. Conviction, propaganda, faith. I don't know, I never have been able to come to the conclusion that that's a bad word."[19]

In 1972, after four years in the countryside, Liu was accustomed to life under the rigid rules of Communism, but her path forward nonetheless led her to become a painter, creating propaganda murals for the government. Colleges had begun opening again in 1970, and she managed to get a coveted spot at the Beijing Teacher's College in the department of revolutionary art and literature. The previous year's pupils had been genuine "worker-peasant students," recruited from the countryside. The year Liu enrolled, students were mostly "rusticated youth" like she was.

After graduation in 1975, Liu began teaching art at the Jingshan School, an elite elementary and high school in Beijing. She married a man who worked in an observatory, and they soon had a son, Ling Chen. But shortly after the birth of their son, Liu and her husband divorced.

Determined to keep honing her artistic skills, she applied to graduate school in 1979 and was accepted at the Central Academy of Fine Arts in Beijing, where she majored in mural painting. Here, Mao's ideological goals dictated a stylized form of painting based on Soviet socialist realism. People working in factories and fields across China were portrayed as well-fed, cheerful, and proud. This schism between what Liu had experienced and the propaganda she painted was huge. As a muralist, she often worked on exhibitions that showed the misery people experienced in the old society, before Communism, and how "happily they lived now under the socialist system," Liu said. Arts and literature were "just part of the revolutionary machine."[20]

When she could, Liu slipped away with a wooden box hidden under her clothes. Inside were a set of oil paints, a little brush, and a thin compartment where she could hide a finished painting. Back at school, she would sneak the wet painting under her bed for a few days until it dried, then tuck it out of sight. It was a way for her to put aside the blatantly untrue propaganda art she was instructed to paint and follow her own creative urge. It wasn't about the final result, but "it was the process that was so lifesaving," she said.[21]

In 1980, Liu had a friend carry a few slides of her work to the University of California, San Diego (UCSD), to see if they would admit her to study art. Afterward the friend warned Liu not to get too excited, as the administrator had seemed uninterested. But the visual arts department had never had an applicant from China, and the faculty members were fascinated by Liu's work. In 1981, she was accepted into the master's program. Almost ready to graduate from the Central Academy, she figured she would soon be free to go to the United States to study. "But what it actually meant was the beginning of my own Long March," she recalled, "a Long March full of great hardships."[22]

One Chinese bureaucrat after another stood in Liu's way, refusing to let her leave the country. Desperate to attend UCSD, she fled to Hong Kong. She had heard that from Hong Kong she could go to Uruguay and then on to the United States. But she didn't have the five thousand dollars it would cost to even try. Deeply discouraged and afraid she might even be thrown in prison for trying to leave China, she returned home.

UCSD assured her they would keep her application open, and Liu continued to fight for her chance to go to the United States. At the same time, she was determined not to waste time and explored new fields in art, studying ceramics and the ancient arts of calligraphy and seal carving. Finally, in 1984, she was given permission to leave China. After nearly four years of waiting to get a passport from the Chinese government, it took only minutes to get a visa at the U.S. embassy. Leaving her son with her mother, Liu packed two big suitcases and boarded a plane for the first time in her life.

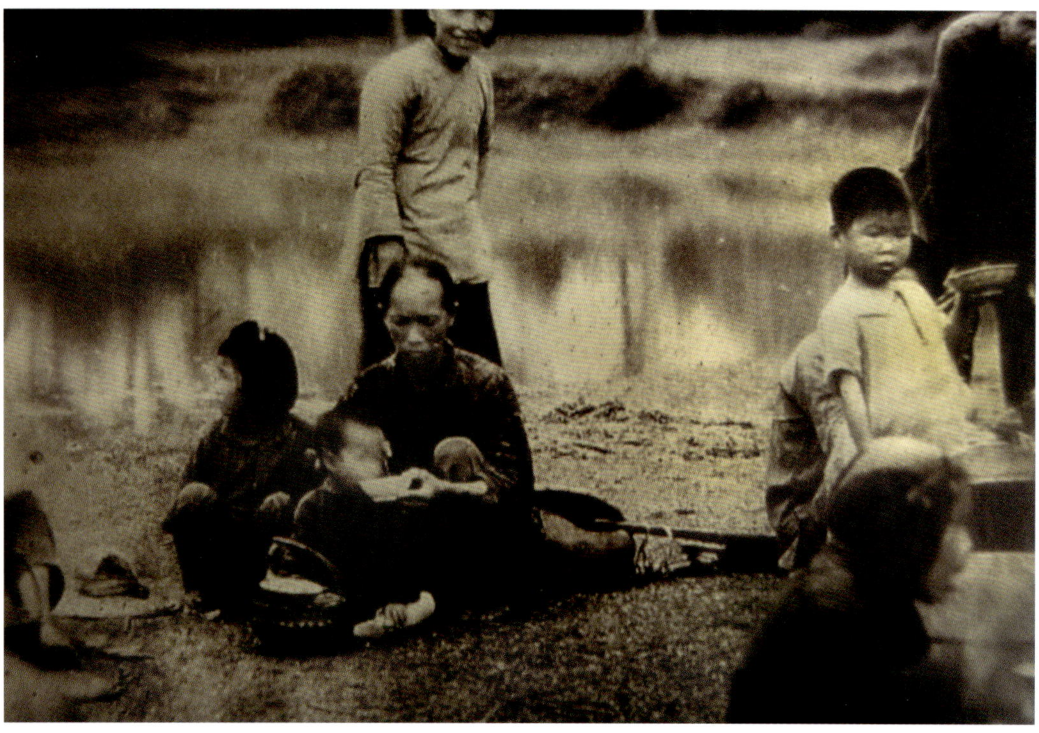

Studying art at UCSD was astonishing to Liu. Allan Kaprow, who helped develop the Happenings of the 1960s, set the freewheeling, exploratory tone of the department. In one of Liu's classes, he took everyone to a garbage dump and unloaded a couch, chairs, and buckets of house paint from the back of his truck. Then he told his students to do whatever they wanted. "I was shocked," said Liu. "You know, in China, you have a concept, you do a drawing, you do all the preparation before the painting, all this academic stuff." Liu watched a student open a paint can and pour it on the sofa. She looked at Kaprow, waiting to be told what to do. But he didn't say anything. Finally, she picked up a paintbrush and thought, "What am I going to do?"[23] The class turned out to be very liberating. "Probably when I think back," Liu said, "the way I improvise while I paint today goes back to that moment in the dump with Allan Kaprow at UCSD."[24]

Liu soon married her classmate Jeff Kelley, and her son joined them in California, where Liu took a teaching job at Mills College in Oakland. For the next several decades, her work often centered around Chinese subjects. These sharply contrasted with the energetic, pink-cheeked workers, peasants, and soldiers she had portrayed for propaganda murals. Working from archival photographs, she painted Chinese society's outcasts: prostitutes and thieves, rebels and soldiers. She also began to incorporate historic photos of the early Chinese in

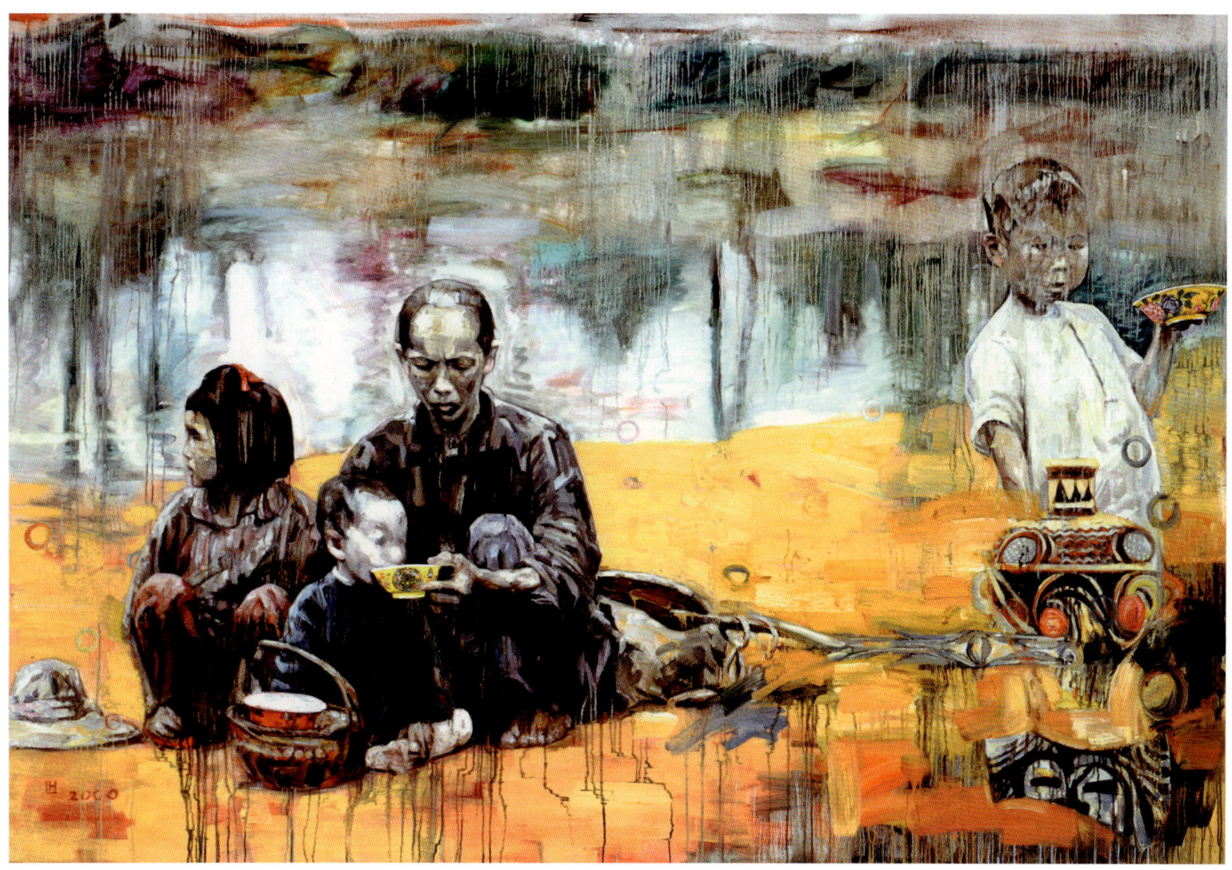

Fig. 14. Hung Liu
By the Rivers of Babylon, 2000
Oil on canvas, 78 × 114 in. (198.1 × 289.6 cm)
Private collection

the United States, those who had immigrated to "Gold Mountain" after the discovery of gold in the Sierra foothills in 1848. These immigrants had learned to make their way as Chinese in the United States, as Liu was doing now.

On a trip back to China, Liu discovered an old photo of a refugee sitting by a river with her children. "The woman is feeding a little kid some food," said Liu, describing the photo (fig. 13). "They have their basket. They're tired from their travel, and on their right side, there's a boy holding a bowl, trying to help himself."[25]

In 2000, Liu set to work making a painting from the photo with some important changes. "They have very shabby bowls, some broken even," Liu explained. "But I switched it to the most expensive antique bowls from the imperial palace, like it's invaluable antique bowls and Neolithic-period pottery pieces . . . even though they're poor, they're homeless, but they still have a very rich heritage. Maybe they don't even know about it, but I want to offer them this, from me." The resulting painting is *By the Rivers of Babylon* (fig. 14).[26]

Like so many of the people Liu painted, those caught by Lange's camera are often nameless, their lives unheralded. Liu felt compelled to honor them, not because of an intellectual impulse but rather as a result of a deeply visceral response. "I am not naïve," she has affirmed.

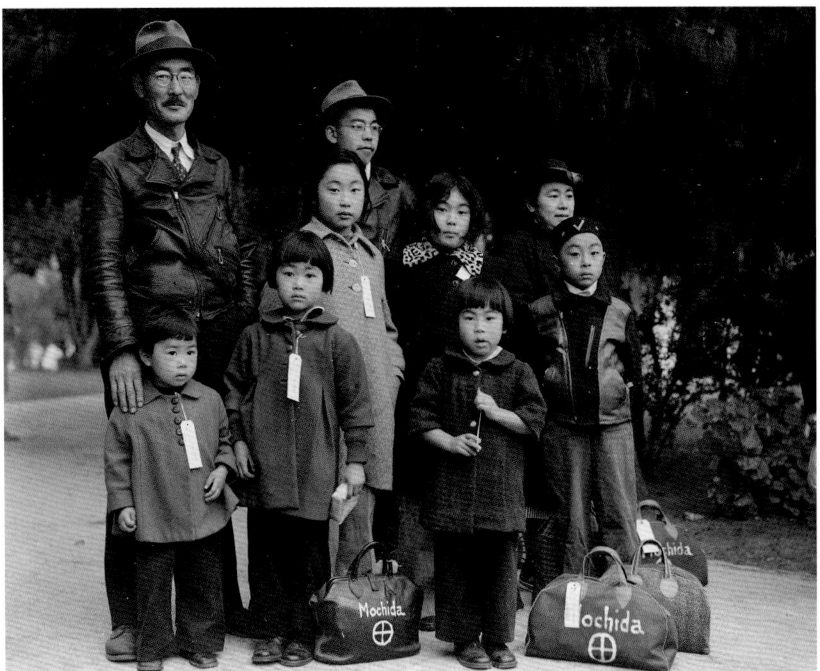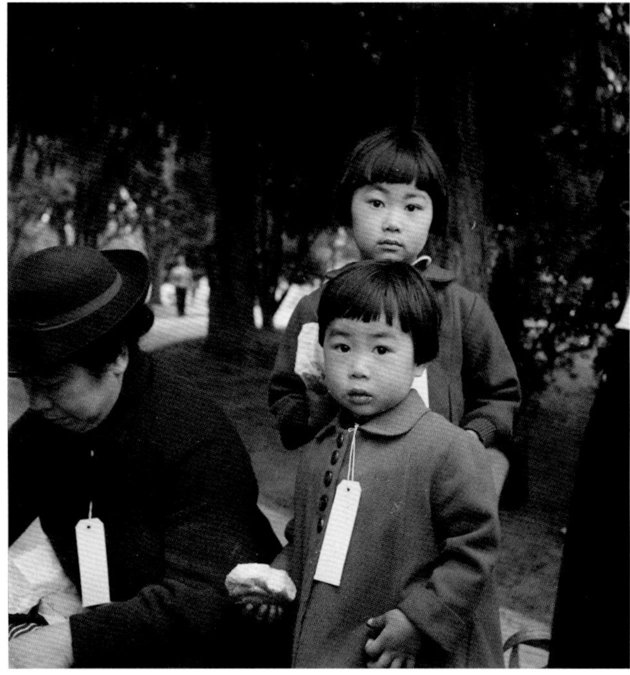

Figs. 15 and 16. Dorothea Lange

Members of the Mochida family await evacuation bus in Hayward, California, following Executive Order 9066, 1942.

National Archives and Records Administration, Records of the War Relocation Authority, Washington, D.C.

"A photograph doesn't tell the truth and nothing but the truth." But in Lange's work, she observed something deeper. "Lange tried to photograph as a form of protest: the truth, the real picture. That's what I like about her; she shows us the real picture."[27]

Lange's archive includes images from her government assignment photographing the incarceration of Japanese and Japanese Americans during World War II for the War Relocation Authority, though the complete set of images is held at the National Archives. The military wanted a photographic record to show the process was "orderly and humane." Strict constraints were imposed on Lange by the military (no photographing the guard towers or barbed wire, always be closely accompanied by a guard). For Lange, the suspension of civil liberties for the Japanese Americans was devastating. On this assignment, her personal "conviction, propaganda, faith" was in direct conflict with the aims of the government, but she was determined to make her own historical record. "This is what we did," she said later. "How did it happen? How could we?"[28]

Liu found several of Lange's photographs of the incarceration especially compelling. In one series of images taken on May 8, 1942, Lange focused on the Mochida family as they waited for the evacuation bus (fig. 15). Everyone wore thick paper tags with family identification, as seen in a close-up of two girls (fig. 16). Liu added two folded-paper cranes to her own composition (fig. 17). As a child, Liu had been taught to make paper cranes by her mother and other adults, who guided her small hands to make all of the requisite creases. It was not until she was an adult, however, while visiting Hiroshima and Nagasaki in the 1990s, that she saw "the countless colorful paper

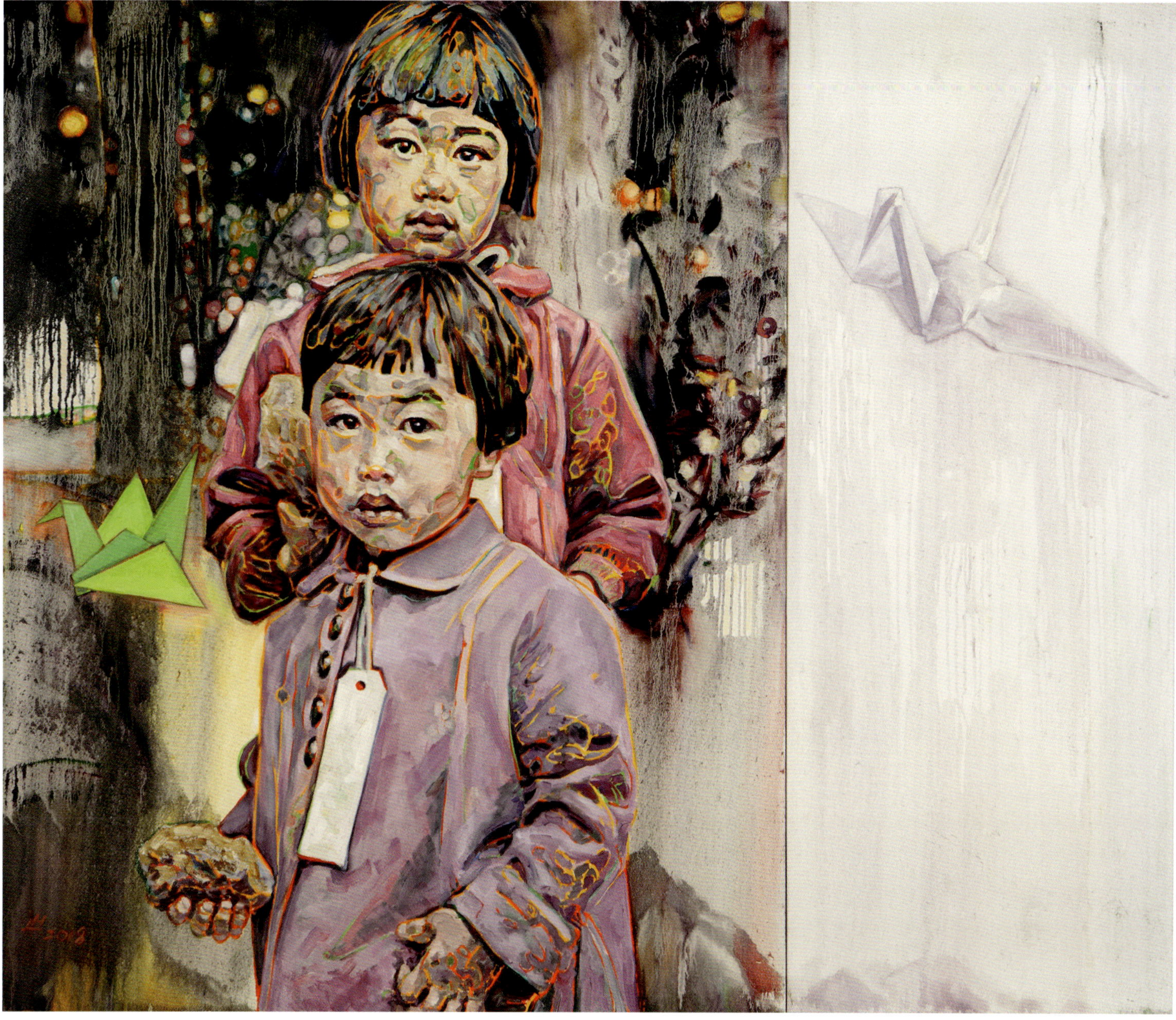

Fig. 17. Hung Liu
Internees, 2018
Oil on canvas, 60 × 72 in. (152.4 × 182.9 cm)
Private collection

cranes" and became aware of "the elevated symbolism and layered meaning." Having observed the cranes in Japan, folded by people of varying ages and backgrounds, she remarked: "They are really a collective of mourning, praying, and worshipping for mankind. Therefore, I offered *my* cranes to the little sisters who were about to be sent away."[29]

Time after time, Liu has returned to the quiet library at the Oakland Museum to view Lange's archive. Without the years of back-breaking toil in the fields, Liu certainly would not have resonated so profoundly with Lange's photographs. The faces and roughened hands of those who worked the land were deeply familiar. All knew lean times and hunger, regardless if they were called farmers, peasants, or laborers. Through close looking and extended periods of concentration, Liu has come to feel as though she knows the people Lange portrayed. "They are all my relatives," Liu remarked. "We don't need a language, but we can communicate across time and space. There is something beyond that links us."[30]

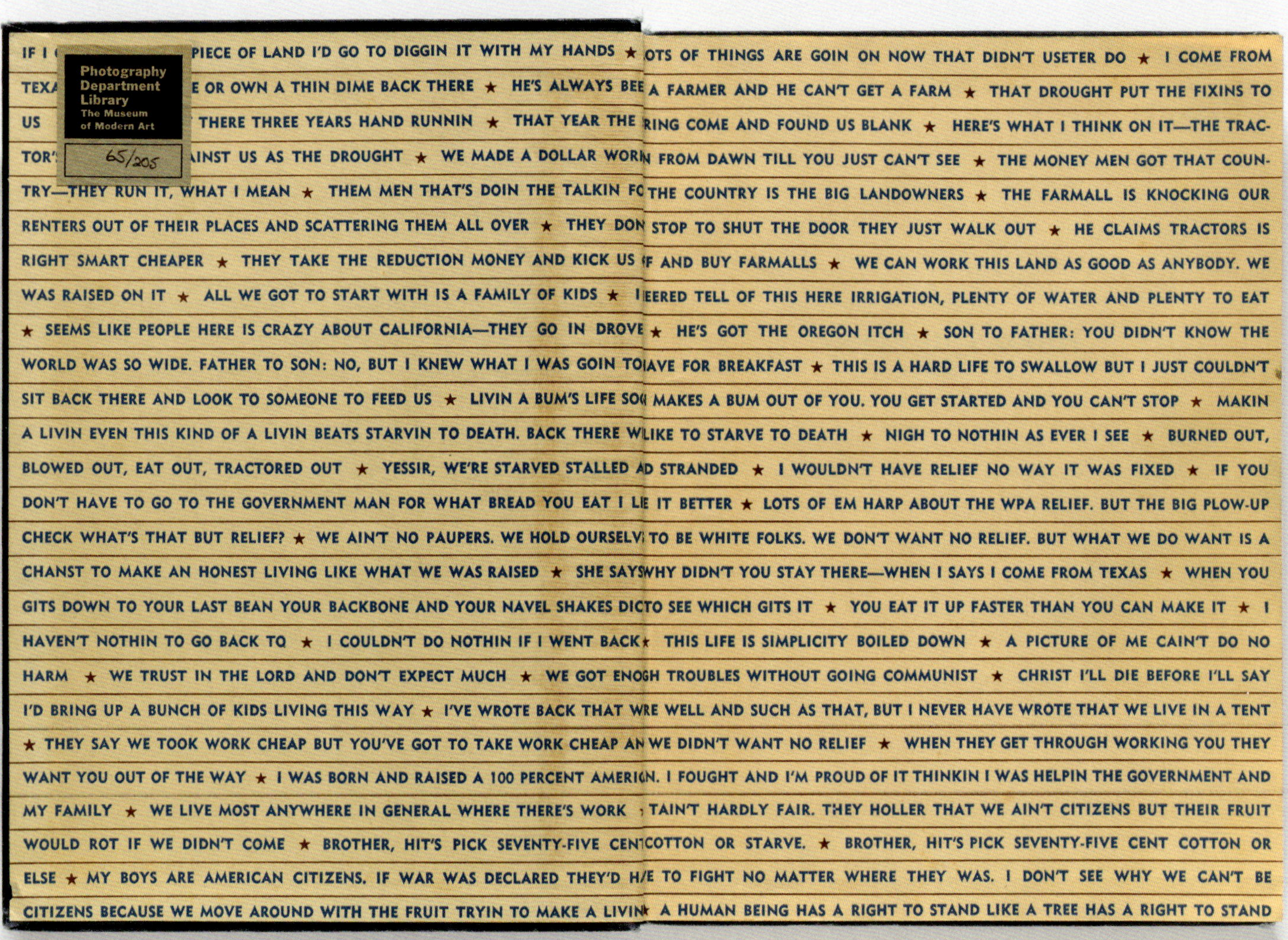

Fig. 18. Dorothea Lange and Paul Schuster Taylor, *An American Exodus: A Record of Human Erosion* (New York: Reynal and Hitchcock, 1939), endpapers. The Museum of Modern Art, New York

Notes

Epigraphs: Dorothea Lange, KQED San Francisco Audio Recording, 1964, Dorothea Lange Archives, Oakland Museum of California.

Hung Liu, interview with author, January 20, 2020.

1. While Lange's body of work for the Farm Security Administration (FSA; originally the Resettlement Administration) is held at the Library of Congress, a number of her FSA images are included in the Dorothea Lange Collection at the Oakland Museum of California, either as duplicate prints or on proof sheets. In total, the Oakland Museum holds more than 25,000 of Lange's negatives and proof sheets and around 6,000 archival prints, along with her field notes and other memorabilia.
2. Hung Liu, interview with author.
3. Hung Liu quoted in "Sixty Years on a Hard Journey for Art: A Conversation between Hung Liu and Wu Hung," in *Hung Liu: Great Granary* , ed. Wu Hung (Hong Kong: Timezone 8, 2010), 63.
4. Joann Moser, "A Conversation with Hung Liu," *American Art* 25, no. 2 (Summer 2011): 80.
5. Hung Liu, interview with author.
6. Hung Liu, interview with author.
7. Moser, "Conversation with Hung Liu," 83.
8. Hung Liu, interview with author.
9. Hung Liu, interview with author.
10. Hung Liu, interview with author.
11. Hung Liu, interview with author.
12. "Dorothea Lange: The Making of a Documentary Photographer," interviews conducted with Suzanne Riess, 1960–61 (Berkeley: University of California, Bancroft Library; Berkeley: Regional Oral History Office, 1968): 6, https://digitalassets.lib.berkeley.edu/roho/ucb/text/lange_dorothea__w.pdf.
13. "Making of a Documentary Photographer," 17.
14. "Making of a Documentary Photographer," 16. See also the author's interview with Meghna Chakrabarti, "Dorothea Lange from Her Goddaughter's Perspective," WNYC, January 20, 2014, https://www.wnyc.org/story /dorothea-lange-from-her-goddaughters-perspective/.
15. "Making of a Documentary Photographer," 18.
16. Dorothea Lange, interview with Richard Doud, May 22, 1964, Archives of American Art, Washington, D.C., https://www.aaa.si.edu/collections /interviews/oral-history-interview-dorothea-lange-11757.
17. Lange, KQED Audio Recording.
18. Lange, KQED Audio Recording.
19. "Making of a Documentary Photographer," 181.
20. Moser, "Conversation with Hung Liu," 84.
21. Moser, "Conversation with Hung Liu," 99.
22. Hung Liu quoted in Wu Hung, "Sixty Years," 88.
23. Moser, "Conversation with Hung Liu," 87.
24. Moser, "Conversation with Hung Liu," 87.
25. Moser, "Conversation with Hung Liu," 96.
26. Hung Liu, oral history interview by Joann Moser, April 25–29, 2010, Archives of American Art, Smithsonian Institution, Washington, D.C.,61.
27. Hung Liu, interview with author.
28. Lange, KQED Audio Recording.
29. Hung Liu, email message to author, July 2, 2020.
30. Hung Liu, interview with author.

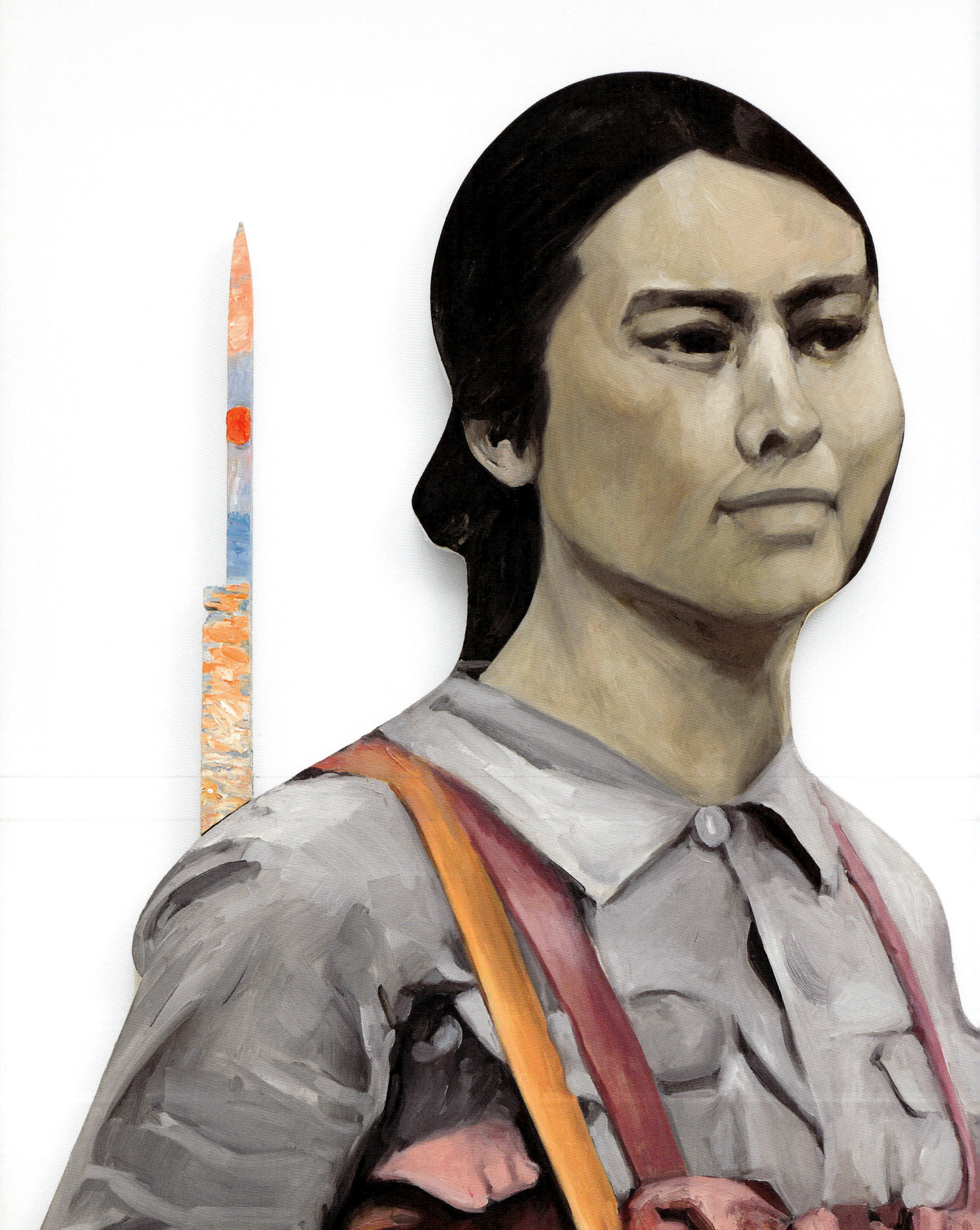

PHILIP TINARI

HUNG LIU

Passer-by

In the far northern corner of Caochangdi, a village halfway between Beijing and its airport, the muted joy of late spring bursts out on a leafy afternoon in May. It is Hung Liu's year, the Year of the Rat. It is also China's Olympic year, 2008. The capital's ubiquitous countdown clocks, digitally ticking since shortly after the city won its bid to host the Games back in 2001, have fewer than one hundred days to go. The air is thick with anticipation, and short on particulate matter, as the factories have already been shut and car traffic has been halved. The season finally in full bloom, and the first of two consecutive days of exhibition openings under way, Liu is showing her paintings, important paintings, to a giddy mix of well-wishers: the professionally engaged, the casually curious, the potentially acquisitive. A hundred or so visitors have gathered inside the renovated warehouse, filling it with the vivacious din of small talk in English, French, and Mandarin, spilling out into the courtyard. A gallery honed from industrial space, itself set on former farmland, home to a Brussels-born dealer and his Beijing-born wife: all in keeping with the way things seem to be going. Art districts are everywhere, radiating outward from the largest of them all, the nearby Factory 798.

After some time, a group of fervent supporters unlike any already present appears at the reception area: the artist's mother, now in her eighties, proudly holds up a copy of the new book she has written on her daughter's life and work while a band of Liu's high school classmates arrives in tow to celebrate. They hug and laugh and hover in proximity to the artist and to one another, survivors all. The exhibition is titled *Prodigal Daughter,* and there are plenty of fatted calves to be killed (figs. 1, 2).[1]

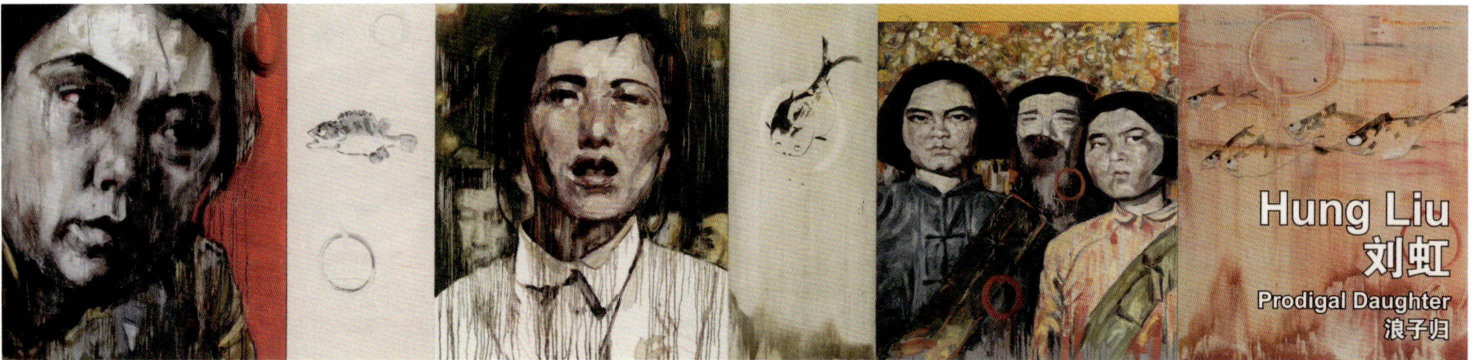

Fig. 1. Flyer for Hung Liu's exhibition *Prodigal Daughter*, 2008, F2 Gallery, Beijing.

The story of Hung Liu—her becoming, her departure, her sojourn, her return—has been told again and again, so much that the biographical and macrohistorical narrative of her life readily colors the critical reception of her art. Her path follows familiar scripts: the wandering hero Odysseus, the monk seeking enlightenment on a Journey to the West. Her biography unfolds against circumstances of consequence: the Cultural Revolution, Reform and Opening, a New Era. She came from China to the United States in 1984, at a moment of both awkwardness and optimism, when "engagement" was the doctrine, even if neither side could predict what that would entail. As she familiarized herself with California, she encountered people who did not yet know what to make of a "Chinese contemporary artist," a discursive, aesthetic, and political construction that would only settle into the wider consciousness a few years later, after the student movement met its bloody end at Tiananmen and her younger colleagues began to seek new possibilities abroad.

Fast forward to November 2019. After a full turn of the Chinese zodiac, on the cusp of another Rat Year, we are waiting, optimism fading, for the necessary approvals to open *Hung Liu: Passer-by* at UCCA Center for Contemporary Art, the museum that I direct in Beijing. Sitting just a few kilometers away from where the 2008 exhibition was presented, UCCA's registrars learn that the shipping of Liu's artworks from public and private collections throughout the United States cannot begin until the relevant municipal cultural authorities issue the necessary paperwork: a stilted notice of approval on red-letterhead paper with a circular seal stamped in vermilion at lower right, a document prosaic and decisive. I am in Shanghai for an art fair, and the team back in Beijing is understandably nervous. After

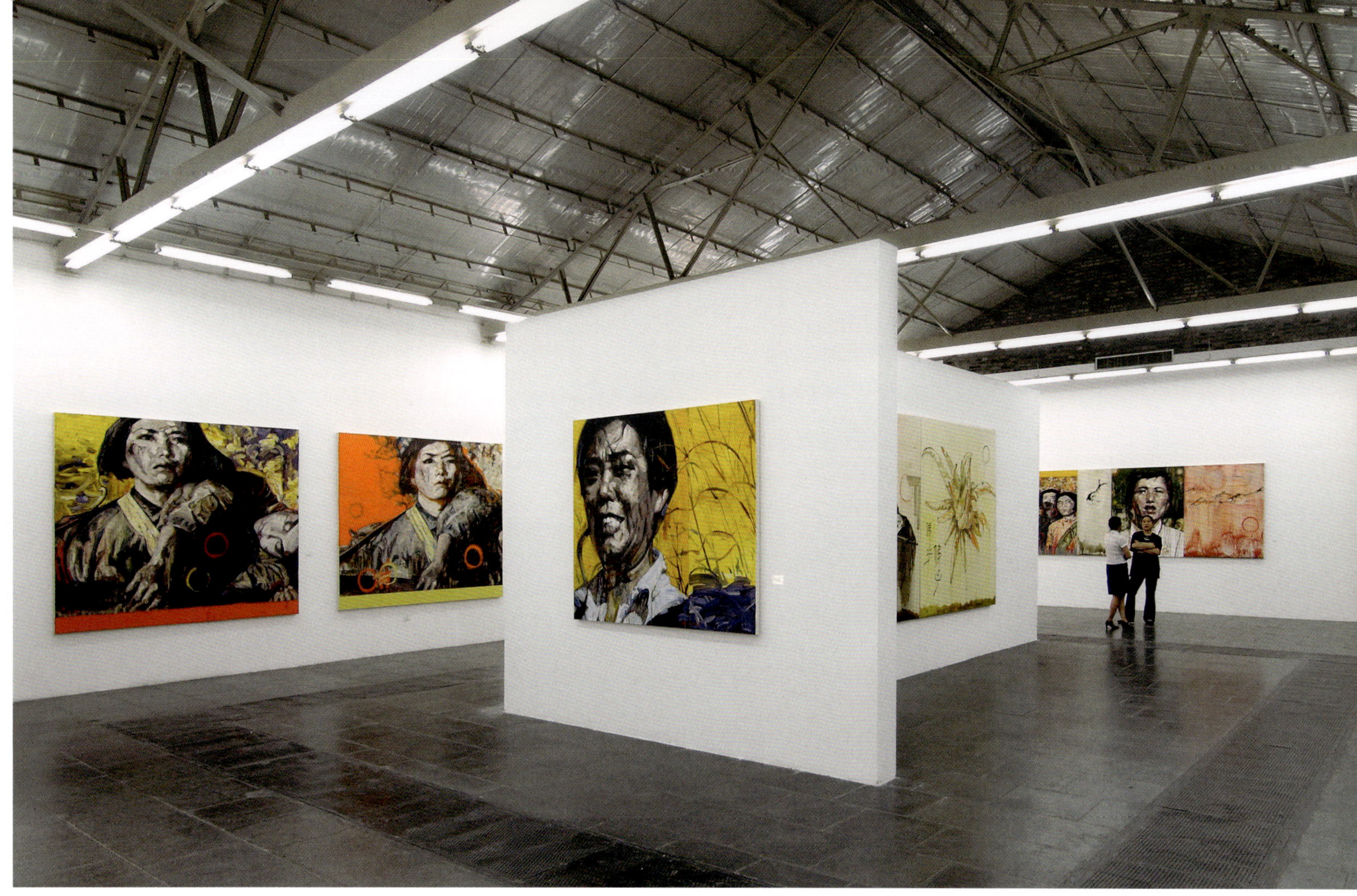

Fig. 2. Installation view of *Prodigal Daughter,* 2008, F2 Gallery, Beijing.

receiving a dribble of new information, I call Liu from the west bank of the Huangpu River, where Emmanuel Macron has just opened a new outpost of the Centre Pompidou. The good news, I tell Liu, is that a synod of experts will be convened to review our request. The bad news, I think to myself, is that the experts, once convened, tend to never say yes.

A lot has happened since 2008. I've remained in Beijing, progressing from a freelance critic to the leader of an organization, and Liu has completed hundreds of paintings, mounted a dozen exhibitions, and finished her teaching career at Mills College. China is now the world's second-largest economy. The United States has begun, even accelerated, its slide into autocracy. I am on the phone now, in Shanghai, speaking with Liu, in Oakland, an American in China explaining to a Chinese in America why her works might not be able to trace the trajectory that has become so fundamental to both our lives.

I cross the street in front of the Pompidou West Bund against the light. An hour later, a friend texts me a snap of a monitor attached to the traffic signal, displaying photos of my brazen act of jaywalking from several angles, my name as pulled from a facial-recognition database, and the message, "You have broken the law." Another week

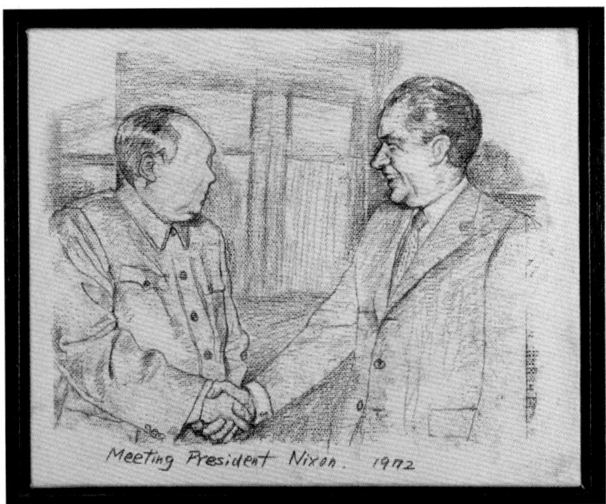

Fig. 3. Hung Liu
Meeting President Nixon, 1972 from the series
Where Is Mao? (1988; cats. 8–17)
Graphite on canvas, 12 × 14 in. (30.5 × 35.6 cm)
Gift from Vicki and Kent Logan to the Collection of
the Denver Art Museum

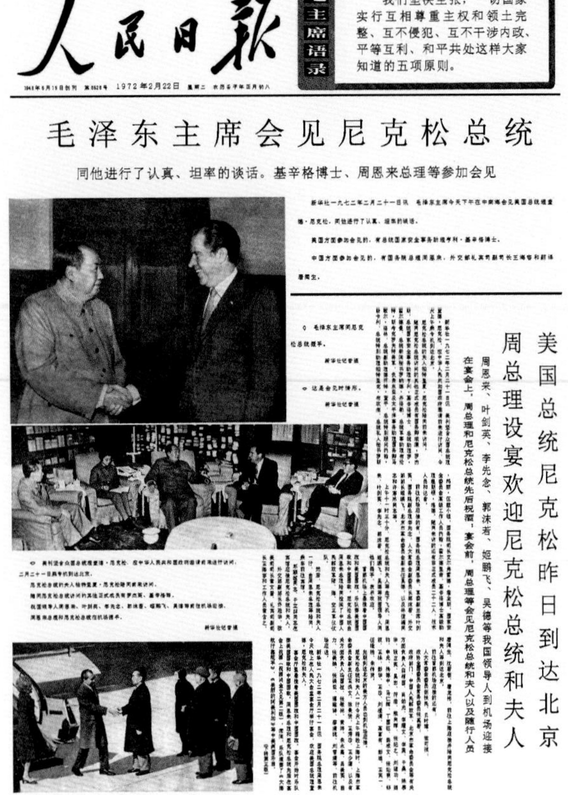

人民日报

毛主席语录

我们坚决主张，一切国家实行互相尊重主权和领土完整、互不侵犯、互不干涉内政、平等互利、和平共处这样大家知道的五项原则。

1972 年 2 月 22 日

毛泽东主席会见尼克松总统

同他进行了认真、坦率的谈话。基辛格博士、周恩来总理等参加会见

美国总统尼克松昨日到达北京

周总理设宴欢迎尼克松总统和夫人

Fig. 4. Front page of *People's Daily,* February 22, 1972.

of waiting goes by, increasingly futile. The next Tuesday, in Hong Kong, having rebooked into a Kowloon-side hotel to avoid the tear gas in Central, I draft a letter to the exhibition's would-be lenders, get Liu's approval, and "leak" it to the *New York Times*.[2] "As you have likely read, there has been a tightening of the civil sphere in China in recent years. There has also been an increase in tension between Liu's native and adopted countries of China and the United States," the letter goes. "Topics that were once relatively open for discussion are now increasingly scrutinized. An exhibition that might have been green-lighted a few years ago must now be canceled."

A few weeks later, Liu and I are together on the night when the show should have opened, not in Beijing among her paintings, but at a stately home in the Berkeley Hills, among her friends. Speeches are given from the landing as the assembled try to make sense of the situation. She speaks beautifully to her story, the twists and turns of a life that have taken her from wartime Manchuria to an elite girls' high school in the capital, out to the countryside, back to the Central Academy, onward from there to San Diego and San Antonio, to Oakland and Santa Fe and Sun Valley, and elsewhere in between. The momentary brightness of that afternoon in May 2008 has faded. The promise of a frictionless world in which her existential dialectic might resolve into a synthesis of so much that is good about China and the United States will go unfulfilled. It has come to seem less a promised land than a fleeting interregnum. She stands that night above the crowd, in a house above the fog, bearing witness. It is what she does best.

As Liu has spent her life toggling among grand narratives, she has directed her artistic practice toward examining and deconstructing them. The present exhibition begins in earnest with a series of works in graphite she made in 1988, after early People's Republic news photographs, under the rubric *Where Is Mao?* (figs. 3, 4; cats. 8–17). It ends with a series of paintings from three decades later, channeling the Depression-era photographs of Dorothea Lange, an entirely different kind of propaganda (cats. 45–52). These two bodies point to the scope of her vision and her project. The decision to at once render and omit Mao fits into a longer arc of examination and critique by Reform-era conceptual artists of the visual culture of high socialism. In each of Liu's drawings, the leader's face appears as the missing element; its oblong contours and poking hair-wings are outlined but incomplete. Their creation coincides with experiments by the painter Wang Guangyi, then in China, placing the "standard image" (as the approved portrait of Mao was known) behind an orthogonal grid of the sort used to facilitate collective attempts to paint that image at scale (fig. 5). In Wang's works, an invisible armature becomes an inescapable confine. Liu does something else, eliding the chairman in a series of scenes otherwise indelibly imprinted on the memory of a generation: swimming the Yangtze, glad-handing Nixon, receiving a Red Guard. The humility implied by her consummately skilled, compositionally tentative monochromes carries the

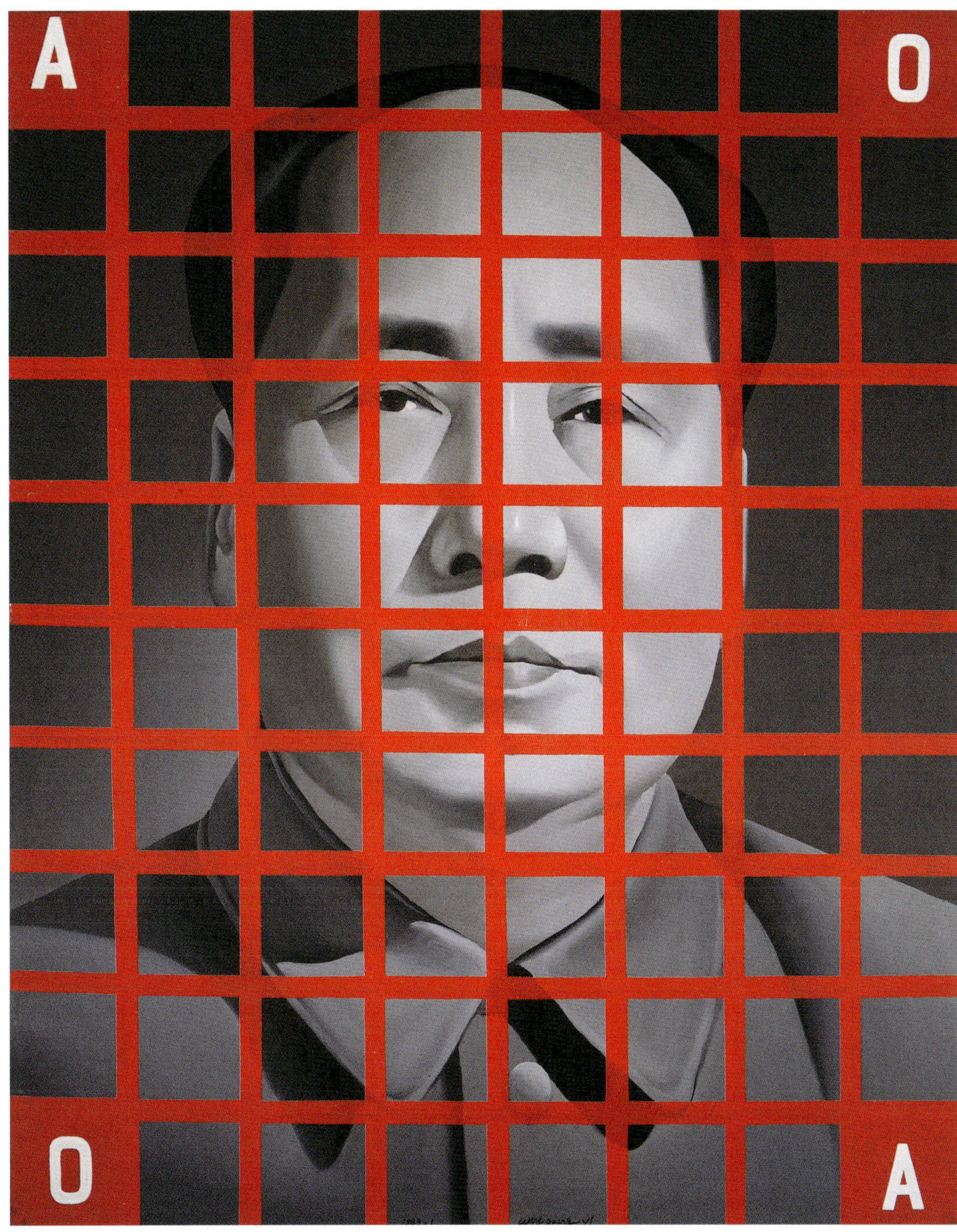

Fig. 5. Wang Guangyi (b. 1957)
Mao Zedong: Red Grid No. 2, 1988
Oil on canvas, 57⅞ × 46¹/₁₆ in. (147 × 117 cm)
M+ Sigg Collection, Hong Kong

force of her critique. They appear at once as studies for something greater yet to come and as assertions of fragility and contingency. They render the Great Helmsman diffident, literally effaced. Perhaps, they imply, this could all be erased.

The idea of Liu eking out these interrogations of the People's Republic's founding father in the same year she asserted her own complex relationship to the United States in *Resident Alien,* that career-defining painting of her green card, perplexes and delights,

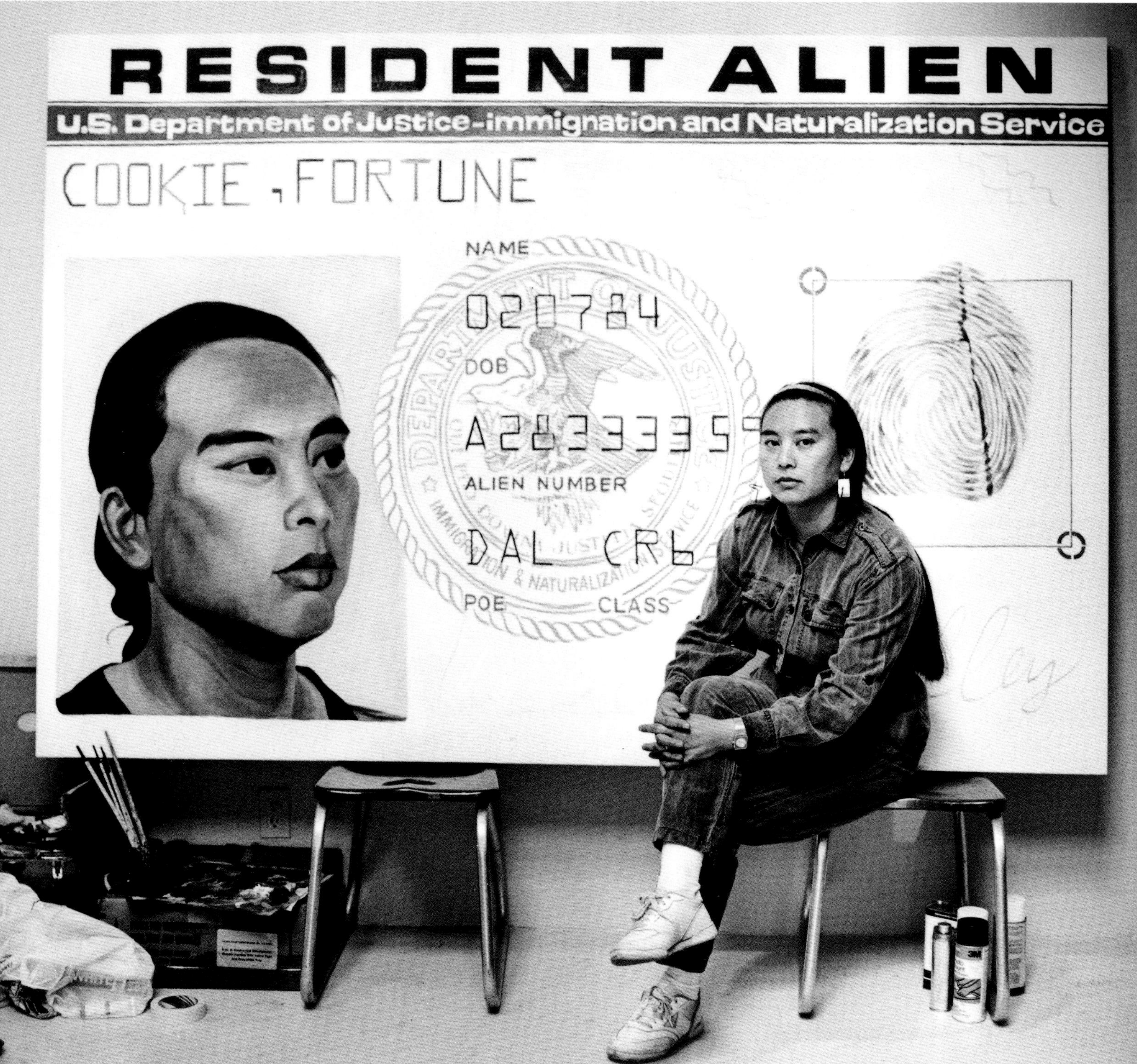

Fig. 6. Hung Liu with her painting *Resident Alien* (cat. 18) during her artist residency at Capp Street Project, San Francisco, 1988. Capp Street Project Archive at California College of the Arts Libraries, San Francisco, Calif.

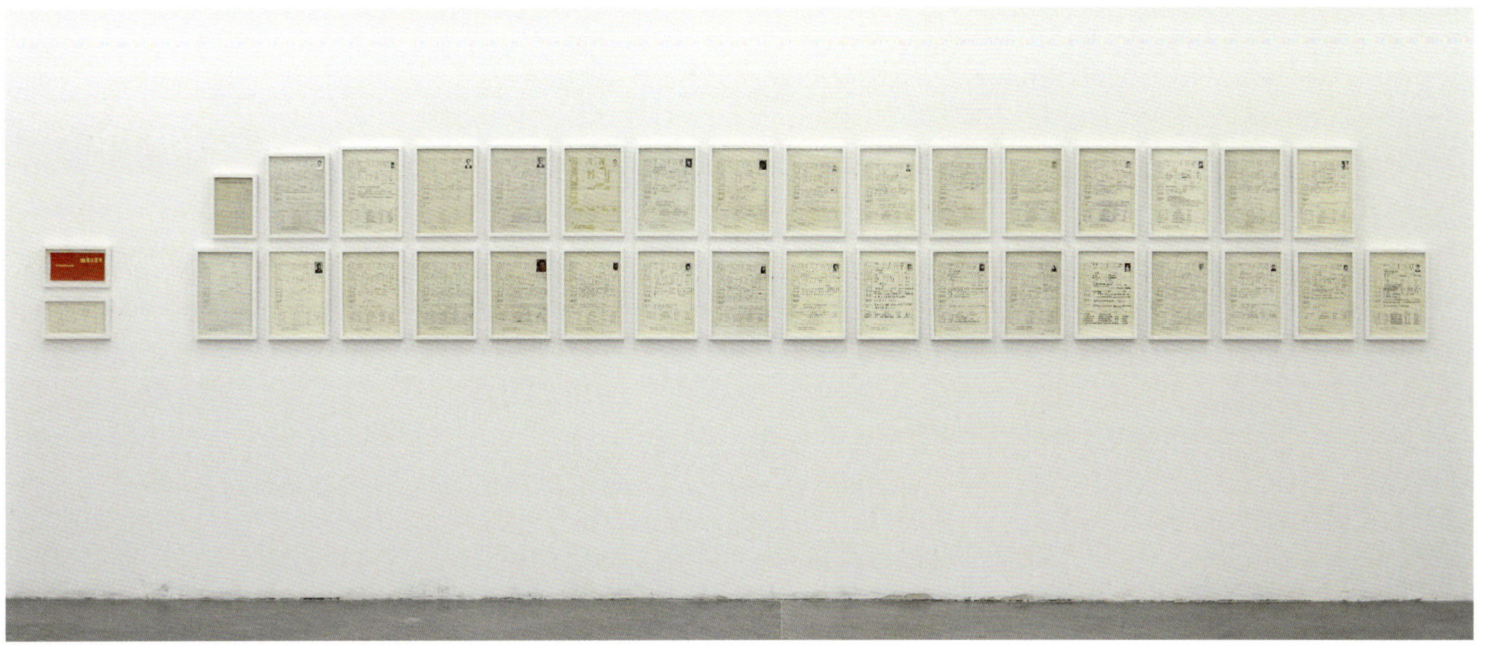

and then makes sense (fig. 6; also see cat. 18). One thinks of Liu, conflicted, processing her earlier history even as she begins to critically embrace her new identity. It is tempting at this moment of canonized struggles and long-postponed reckonings to place her self-portrait as "Cookie, Fortune" into a story we now think we know, a story of diversity and multiculturalism, tolerance and enlightenment. But is she straightforwardly calling out prejudice, or is there another kind of critique at work?

Looking at some of the elements that make up this painting—a governmental seal, a thumbprint, an ID photo, a signature—one might be reminded of a project by the late pioneering conceptualist Geng Jianyi from the same year, 1988, in which he circulated a questionnaire to all the artists and critics slated to attend a major conference in Huangshan to debate the proper forward path of the avant-garde (figs. 7, 8). Geng's forms looked at first like bureaucratic necessities until you read along and realized that the questions were devolving into absurdity: "What is your favorite animal? Your favorite plant? Have you ever, at any time, for any reason, been punished or rewarded for anything at all?"

Was Liu's call-out in *Resident Alien* directed only at the inaccuracies and injustices of the Immigration and Naturalization Services and the inventions and ellipses of immigrant identity? Or might it also have been a sigh of wary bemusement at the realization that life in the United States, as in China, is regimented by basic technologies of governance, full of statements to be sworn to the best of one's knowledge, documents to be filed away for safekeeping, offices in which to wait?

Much of the writing on Liu's work has rested on the rhetorical premise that she was liberated by, and eternally grateful for, her

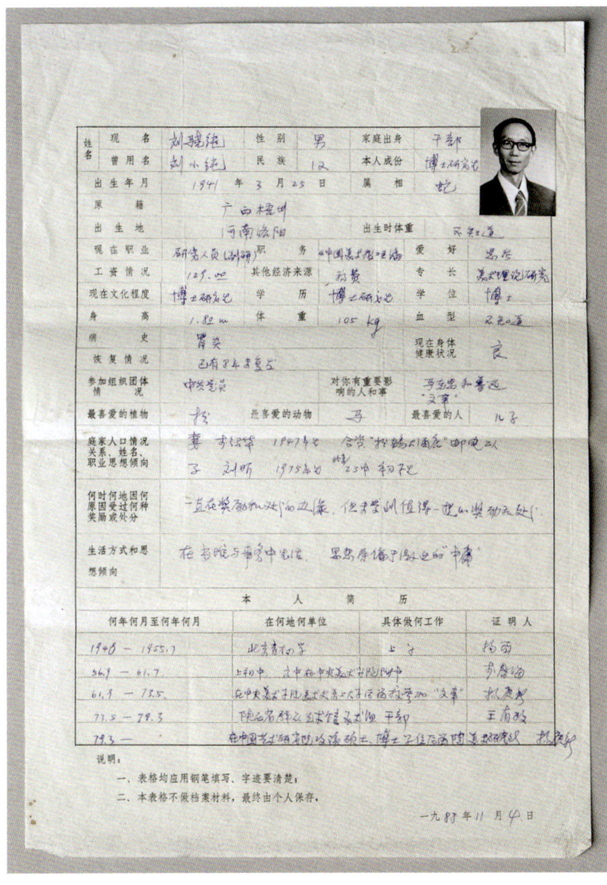

Figs. 7 and 8. Geng Jianyi (b. 1962)
Form and Certificate (*Can Be Confessed*), 1988
Photographs of forms filled out by hand
ShanghART Singapore

midlife transition of citizenship and subjectivity. And indeed Liu herself has spoken about this basic tension between her innate Chineseness and the never-ending process of becoming American. William L. Fox points to the reversing of her birth date on *Resident Alien,* from 1948 to 1984, as "a declaration of Liu's freedom from the strictures of social realism."[3] In this telling, realism, which has remained the driving force of Liu's artistic practice from her student days onward, is conscripted into service as an oppressive force to be overcome. Liu's emergence from the conventions of Sino-Soviet revolutionary representation becomes an allegory of some larger, more meaningful liberation of the soul. Thus construed, modifications to the basic realist template call out for additional scrutiny. As John Yau asked, in relation to the dripping motif that emerges in her paintings in the 1990s and becomes prevalent after 2000: "What about the drips? What might they stand for? Are they meant to be tears, both the women's and ours? Or is the painting dissolving in front of us?"[4]

But what if realism is not something Liu ever felt the need to escape? What if instead we defer judgment, treat it as a conscious, formal choice, arrived at or retained after an inventory of possible options and programs at the artist's disposal to which we, the viewers, are simply not privy? The artist William Kentridge has attributed his own grounding in another breed of figuration to the cultural privations of late-Apartheid South Africa (fig. 9). The country's deserved pariah status precluded meaningful artistic exchange, protecting him throughout his artistic education from the ossifying abstract formalism or high-gloss conceptualism to which he might have gravitated if let loose in London or New York during the 1970s and 1980s. Writing on the quiver of realistic techniques and motifs at work in John Currin's 2003 Whitney retrospective, the critic Peter Schjeldahl asked, "If, after all, we are not striding a hallelujah trail to Utopia—if the past, far from being left behind, inundates the present, and high and low culture defy being separated—why not directly avail ourselves of whatever, having once pleased, may please anew?"[5] Liu's figurative realism has a related air of confident defiance. It was never not valid, and yet, the reassessments of the past few years have made it somehow even more potent. Its relationship to photography—that stigmatized shortcut of her academic training, arrived at in the 1990s as a way to both preserve and destroy images of the ordinary—adds new layers, transgressive and memorializing.

How then to think of Liu as a "Chinese artist," or in relation to the field of "Chinese contemporary art," or to do neither of those things? Her arrival in the United States in 1984 came just as an experimental art scene gained traction in studios, classrooms, and editorial offices throughout China. Reading Hal Foster's *Art in America* travelogue from that year or looking at film footage of Andy Warhol's visit to Beijing in 1982, one finds little evidence of advanced practice.[6] Indeed, the first self-consciously theorized national avant-garde movement is known as the '85 New Wave, after the year it is understood as having

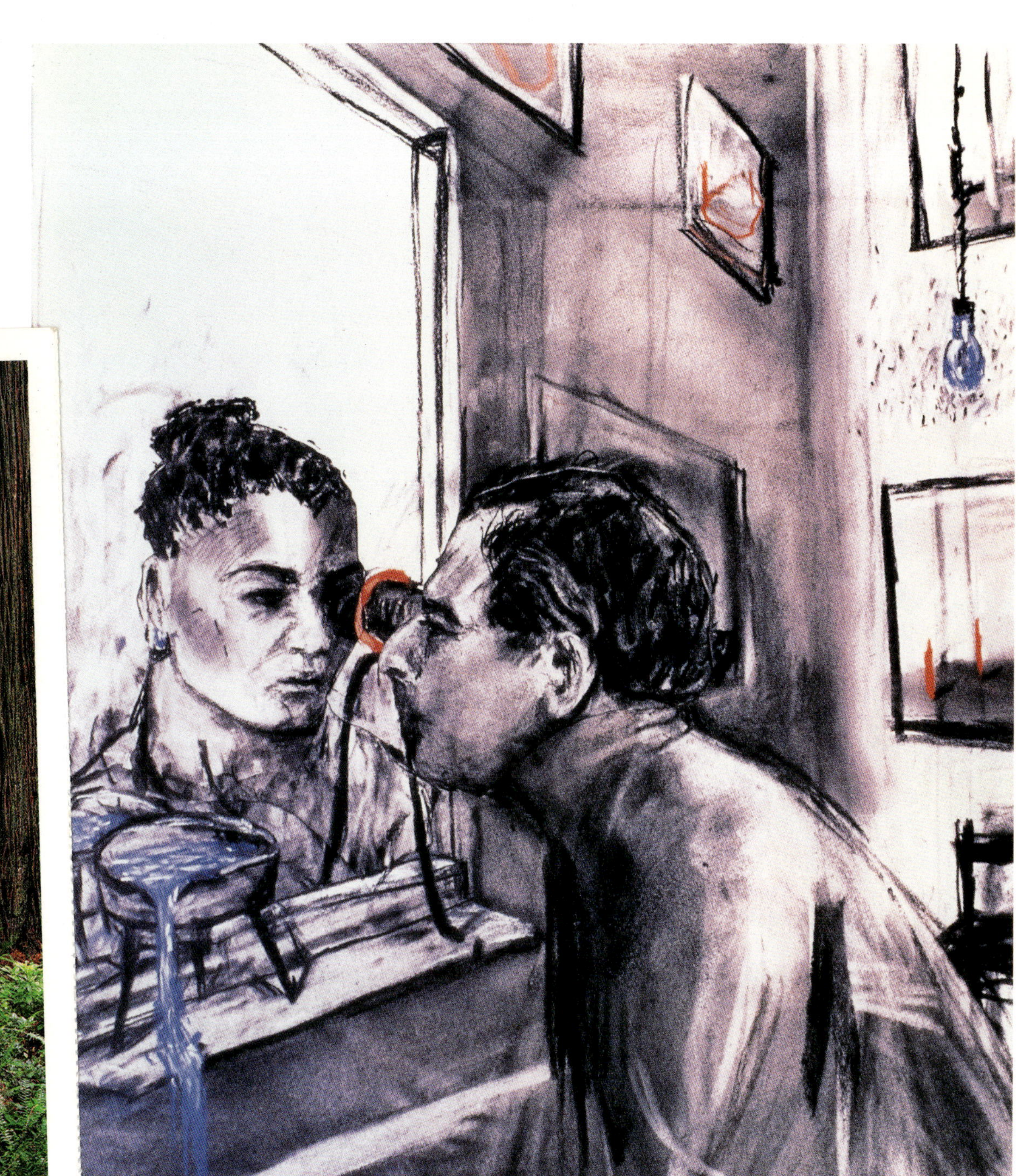

Fig. 9. William Kentridge (b. 1955)
Felix in Exile, 1993–94
Still from color video, trans. from 35 mm film
Solomon R. Guggenheim Museum, New York. Purchased with funds contributed by the Peter Norton Family Foundation and by the International Director's Council and Executive Committee Members: Ann Ames, Edythe Broad, Henry Buhl, Elaine Terner Cooper, Dimitris Daskalopoulos, Harry David, Gail May Engelberg, Linda Fischbach, Ronnie Heyman, Dakis Joannou, Cindy Johnson, Barbara Lane, Linda Macklowe, Peter Norton, Willem Peppler, Denise Rich, Simonetta Seragnoli, David Teiger, Ginny Williams, and Elliot K. Wolk, 2000

emerged. As that movement crested in the late 1980s, Liu was immersed in the realities of a new context, with its new obligations and inheritances, semiotics and hermeneutics, tensions and distortions. Meanwhile, within a few weeks of each other in the spring of 1989, artists in China mounted an exhibition summarizing the trends of the previous few years best known by its "No U-Turn" poster (fig. 10), and curators in Paris organized an exhibition at the Pompidou they billed as "the first global contemporary art exhibition." The existence of a Chinese avant-garde would not become common knowledge to a fraction of the American art world until the mid-1990s, and even then,

117   Hung Liu

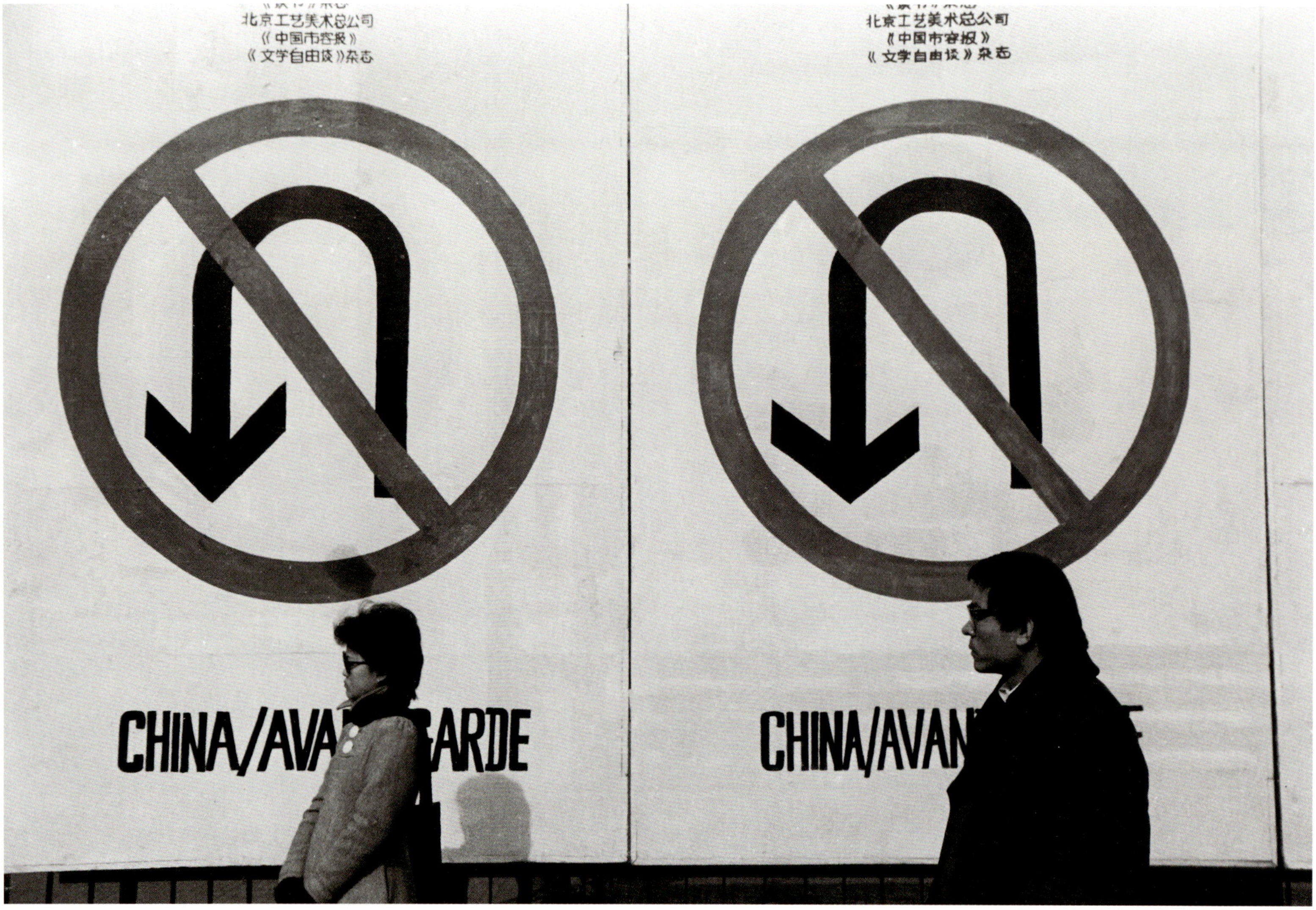

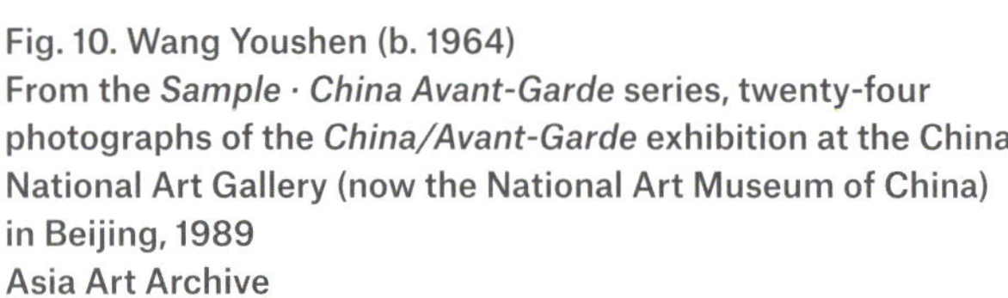

Fig. 10. Wang Youshen (b. 1964)
From the *Sample · China Avant-Garde* series, twenty-four photographs of the *China/Avant-Garde* exhibition at the China National Art Gallery (now the National Art Museum of China) in Beijing, 1989
Asia Art Archive

it remained of limited concern for years to follow. Throughout the 1990s, artists arrived from China, looking to make careers and follow Liu's path. But by the 2000s, faced with a rising tide of interest and resources at home, and having grown tired of being asked to speak only "in terms of" or "on behalf of" their homeland, few Chinese artists traveled to the United States for more than an opening or a residency.

Around this time, as China neared its own moment of global emergence, bicontinental mobility allowed Liu to establish a presence in the Beijing art world. If her status in the scene was rooted in high-profile projects such as the Central Academy of Fine Arts canteen mural that she completed in 1984 (see p. 175), or her television painting show a decade earlier, it was deepened and renewed through a series of personal and artistic encounters with junior colleagues who made temporary or extended homes in the United States in the years after she immigrated.

A productive artistic friendship with Ai Weiwei, begun while the
two were students doing fieldwork in the caves of Dunhuang in the
late 1970s and renewed during Ai's 1980s New York period, led to
conversations throughout the 1990s and 2000s. Liu Xiaodong and
Yu Hong, products of the same Central Academy oil-painting department, became friends and interlocutors after introducing themselves
at one of Liu's openings during their extended New York honeymoon
in 1993. Numerous others, admirers from the early years, emerged as
fellow travelers during the final chapter of her mother's life, as her
visits became more frequent and the capital's artistic atmosphere
quickened in pace and deepened in seriousness. Key to Liu's standing,
alongside her myriad attainments, was the simple fact of her birth a
few years earlier than most who had come to populate this sphere:
the irreplaceable status that comes from being the "big sister," the
"auntie," the karmic obligations owed to one's seniors, however slight
the age gap may be. Liu reveled in this reverie, though I have to think
that her profound familiarity with other, darker moments in China's
modern story made her understand how precious and precarious the
era of Olympic openness actually was.

The whiplash of the constant Sino-American toggle aside,
throughout this period, Liu continued to do what she always had. She
settled in as a working artist, employed as a professor at a women's
college founded by East Bay settlers, beloved by students, making
paintings from a studio in downtown Oakland that she bought at the
turn of the millennium, showing each summer at her galleries in
Santa Fe and Sun Valley, and every few years at museums around the
country. She was free from the daily vicissitudes of artistic experimen-
tation and official repression of Beijing in the 1990s, and then free
later from the all-consuming grandiosity of a society on the verge of
something new in the 2000s. Hers is not the sad story common to
ecologies in transition of the artist who left too early. Relieved of the
daily decisions of where and when and on what to compromise, she
went about her work. In some ways, the life she built even resembled
the life she might have eventually found had she never left the Central
Academy of Fine Arts, had the Central Academy of Fine Arts been
situated somewhere else: a life of practice and dedication, planning
and execution, elaboration and refinement. Subjects and devices have
come into her work, been handled, set aside. The record of daily learning grows ever longer, ideas and images layering recursively (fig. 11).

This is perhaps the ultimate paradox of a life and a career spent
between what have emerged as opposite poles in a new geopolitical
configuration, with malice toward neither. For all the time and distance between Liu today and her birth in Changchun a few months
before Mao declared the Chinese people to have stood up, she is
always bound to be perceived to speak, on some level, for the nation.
Rather than seeing this as a slight, we might better understand it as a
duty lovingly and carefully executed, a durational performance even,
like the daily calls she made to her mother in Beijing for years upon

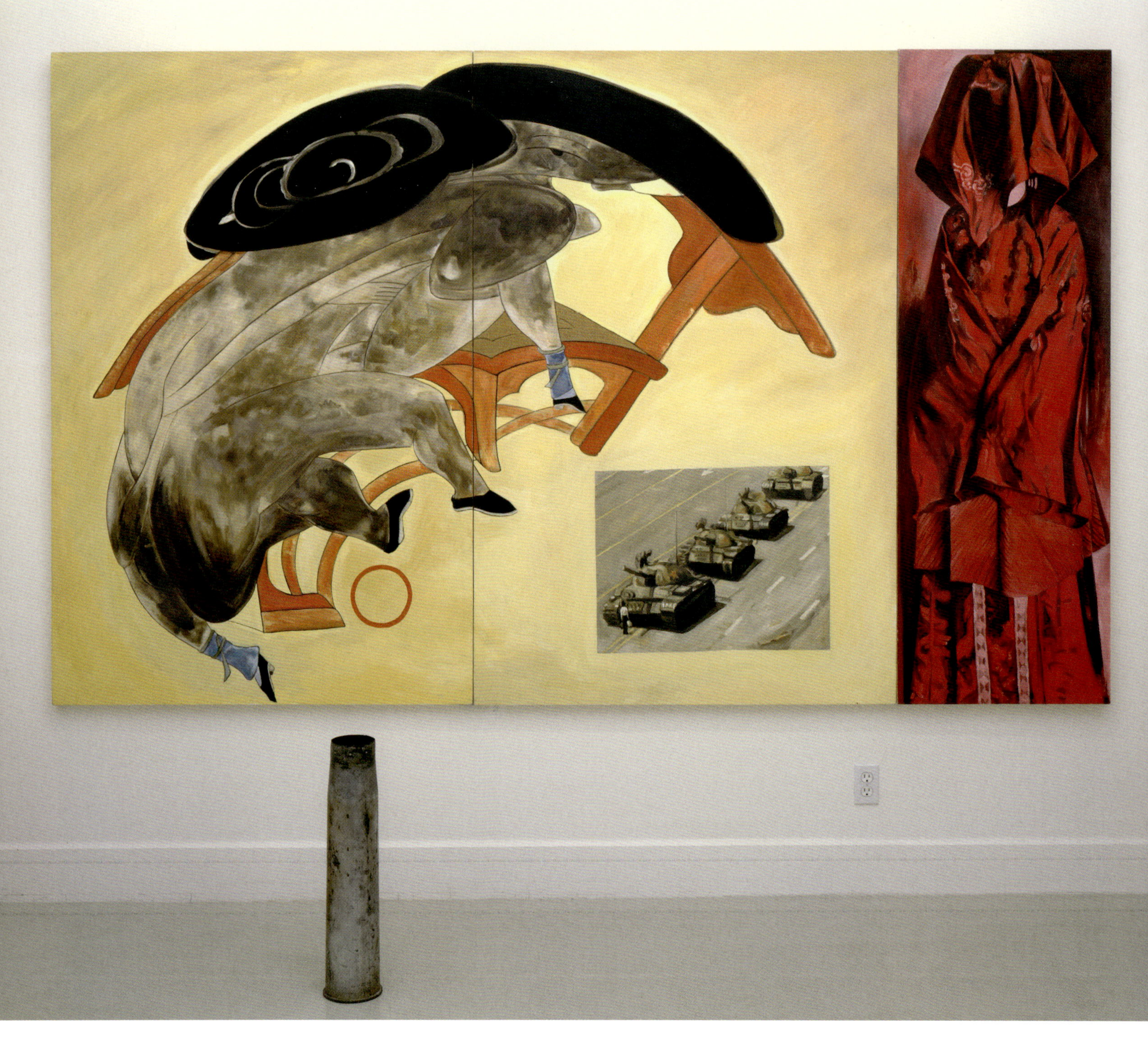

Fig. 11. Hung Liu
Peking Opera, 1989
Oil on canvas with cannon shell,
72 × 104 in. (182.9 × 264.2 cm)
Private collection

years. If Liu's work benefits from additional contextualization for audiences in the United States, it increasingly warrants a different but related kind of explication in China. Generations have been born and come of age in the decades since she left, and a hagiographic focus on the better parts of recent events means that the subjects she has explored and the history she has lived are not as widely known

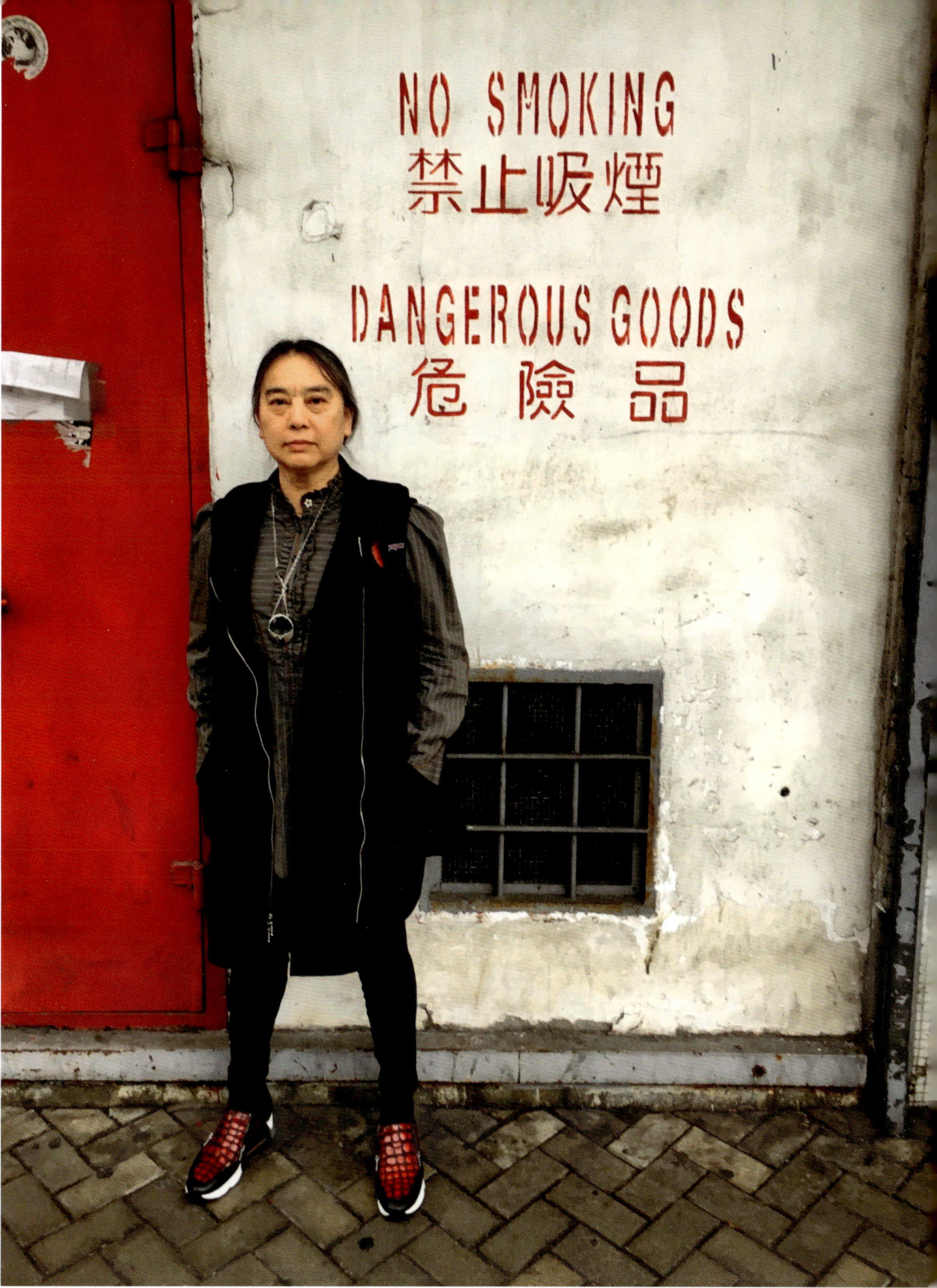

Fig. 12. Hung Liu in Hong Kong, 2016.

as one unfamiliar with the particulars of current Chinese ideology might expect.

The exhibition we planned at UCCA attempted a taxonomy of her ideas for a new audience in Beijing, looking at her art in relation to the notions of epic history, anonymous lives, mutable identity, diasporic narratives, and finally, American dreams. Unable to present this selection of works, we mourned the connections that went unmade, the stories that went untold, the faces that never got to enter the public visual memory of her spiritual hometown. She was deprived of a chance to come home to the family of artists who have, throughout her time away and their time together, pushed forward in languages related to her own. But perhaps more painfully, she was kept from testifying, from telling her story to her successors. Now, two years later, in a Washington that has since been the site of unprecedented corruption and dereliction, but also uprise and reassessment, she tries again.

Notes

1. See the catalogue for the exhibition: Britta Erickson, *Hung Liu: Prodigal Daughter* (Beijing: F2 Gallery, 2008).
2. See Amy Qin, "A Prominent Chinese-American Artist Is the Latest to Fall Afoul of China's Censors," *New York Times,* November 20, 2019.
3. William L. Fox and Liu Xiaodong, *Daughters of China* (Oakland, Calif.: Magnolia, 2007), 12.
4. John Yau, "Dual Citizen," in *Hung Liu: Daughter of China, Resident Alien,* ed. Jeff Kelley and John Yau (Washington, D.C.: American University Museum at the Katzen Arts Center, 2016), 17.
5. Peter Schjeldahl, "Irresistible: John Currin at the Whitney," *New Yorker,* December 15, 2003, 106.
6. See Hal Foster, "China Is Near," *Art in America* (March 1985): 126–32.

PLATES
Part II

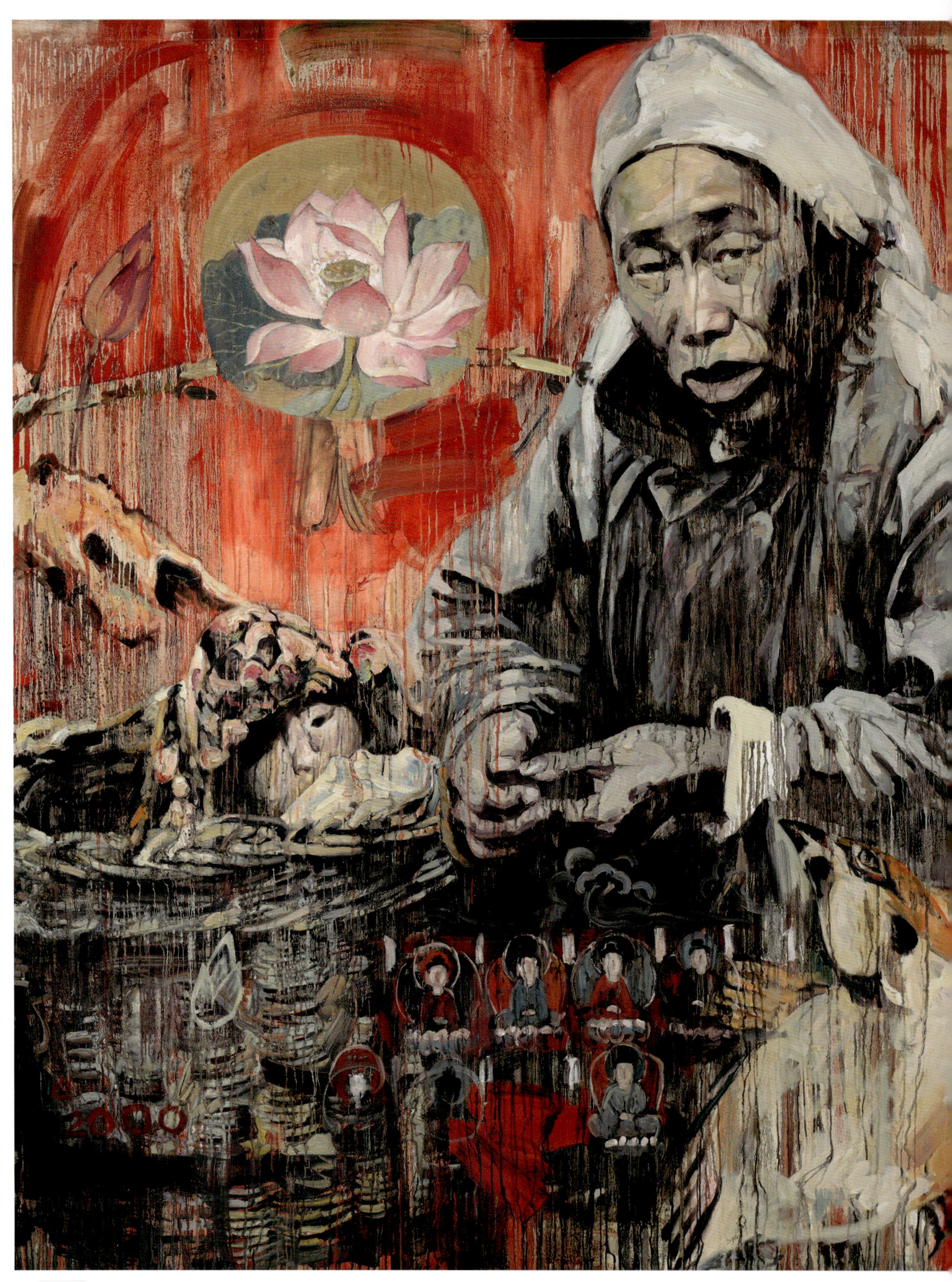

29. *Refugee: Woman and Children,* 2000
Oil on canvas
80 × 120 in. (203.2 × 304.8 cm)
Collection of Joan Mann, Oakland, Calif.

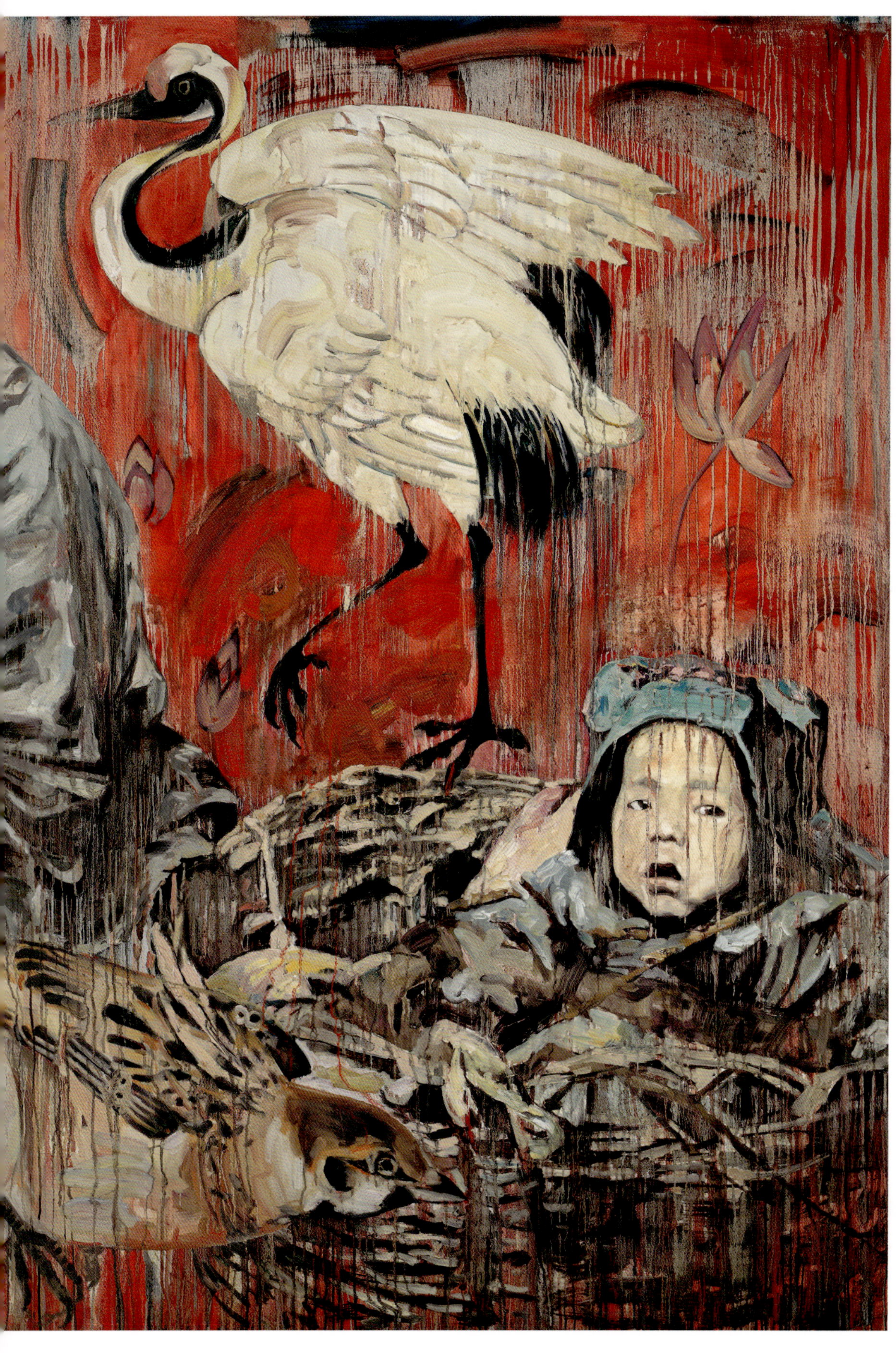

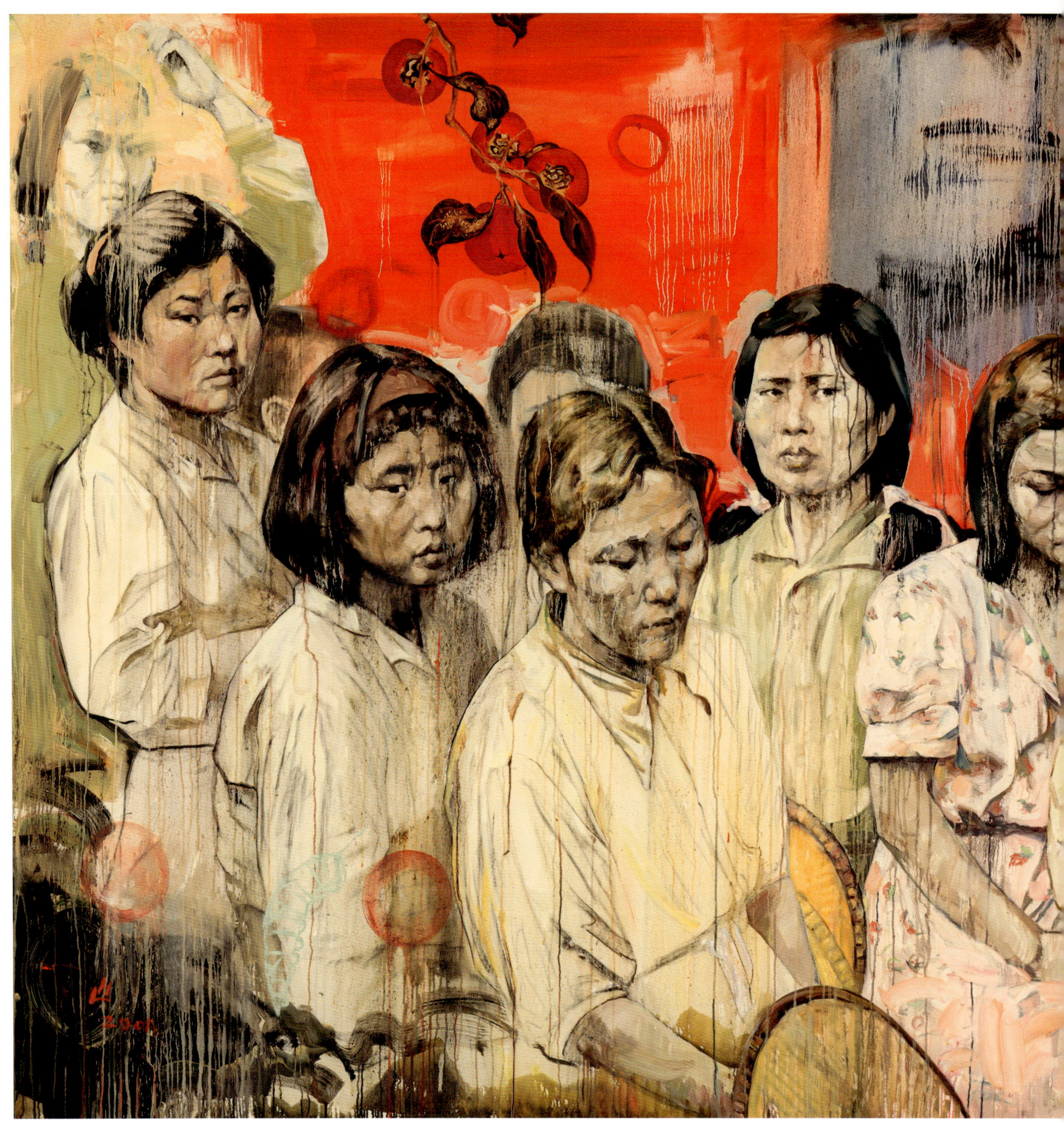

30. *Strange Fruit: Comfort Women,* 2001
Oil on canvas
80 × 160 in. (203.2 × 406.4 cm)
Karen and Robert Duncan Collection

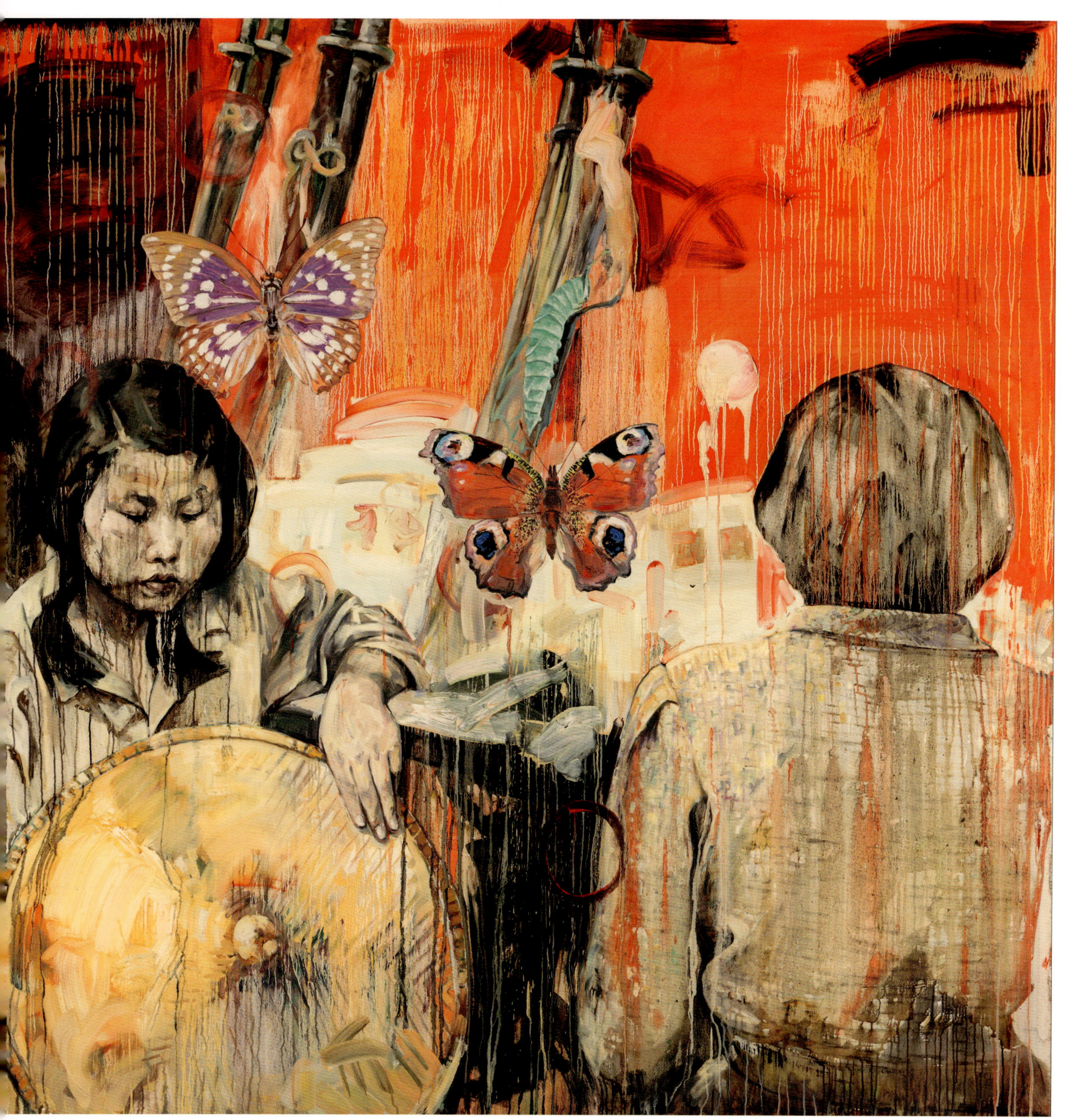

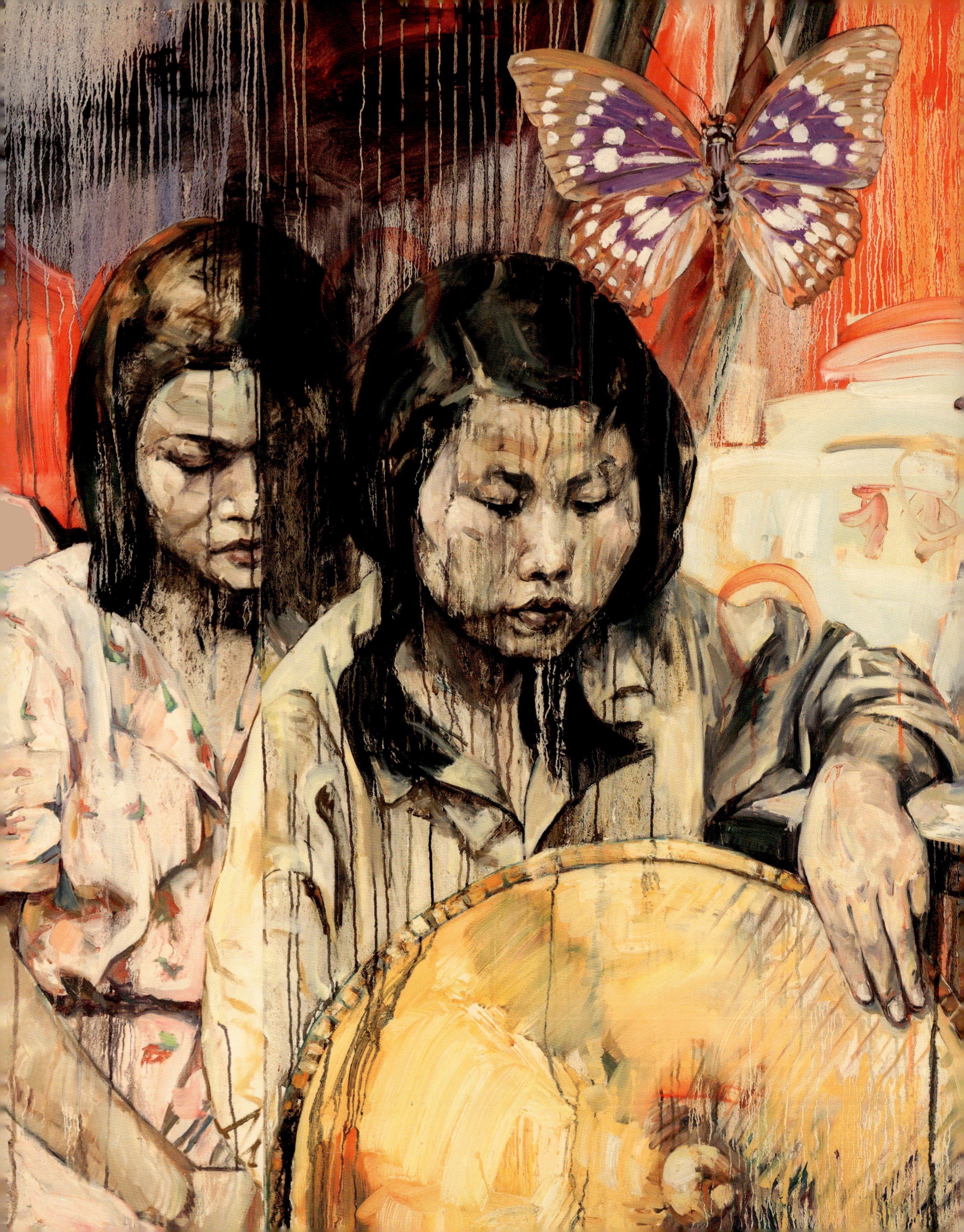

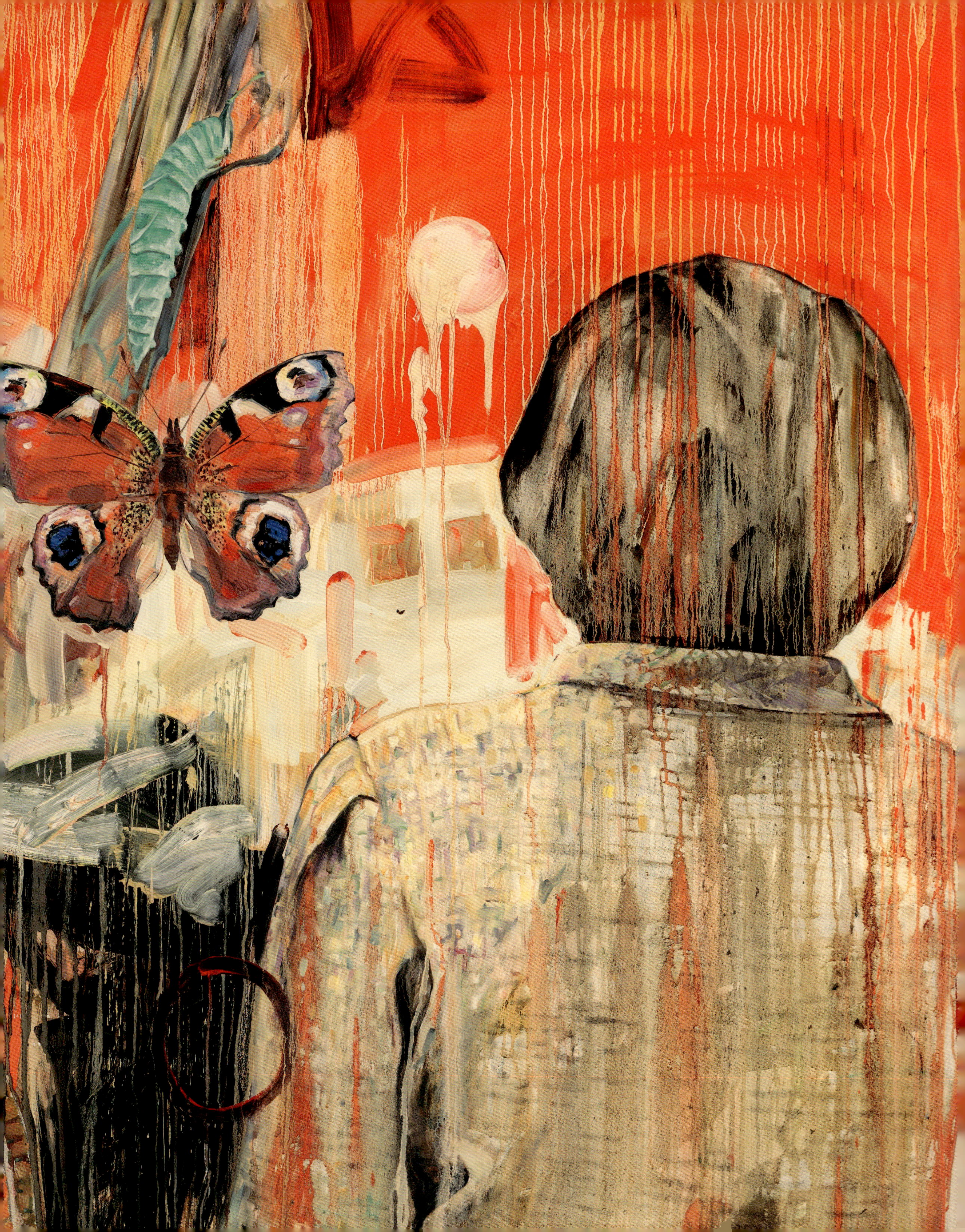

31. *Refugee: Opera,* 2001
Oil on canvas
114 × 78 in. (289.6 × 198.1 cm)
Collection of Peter and Dorothea Perrin

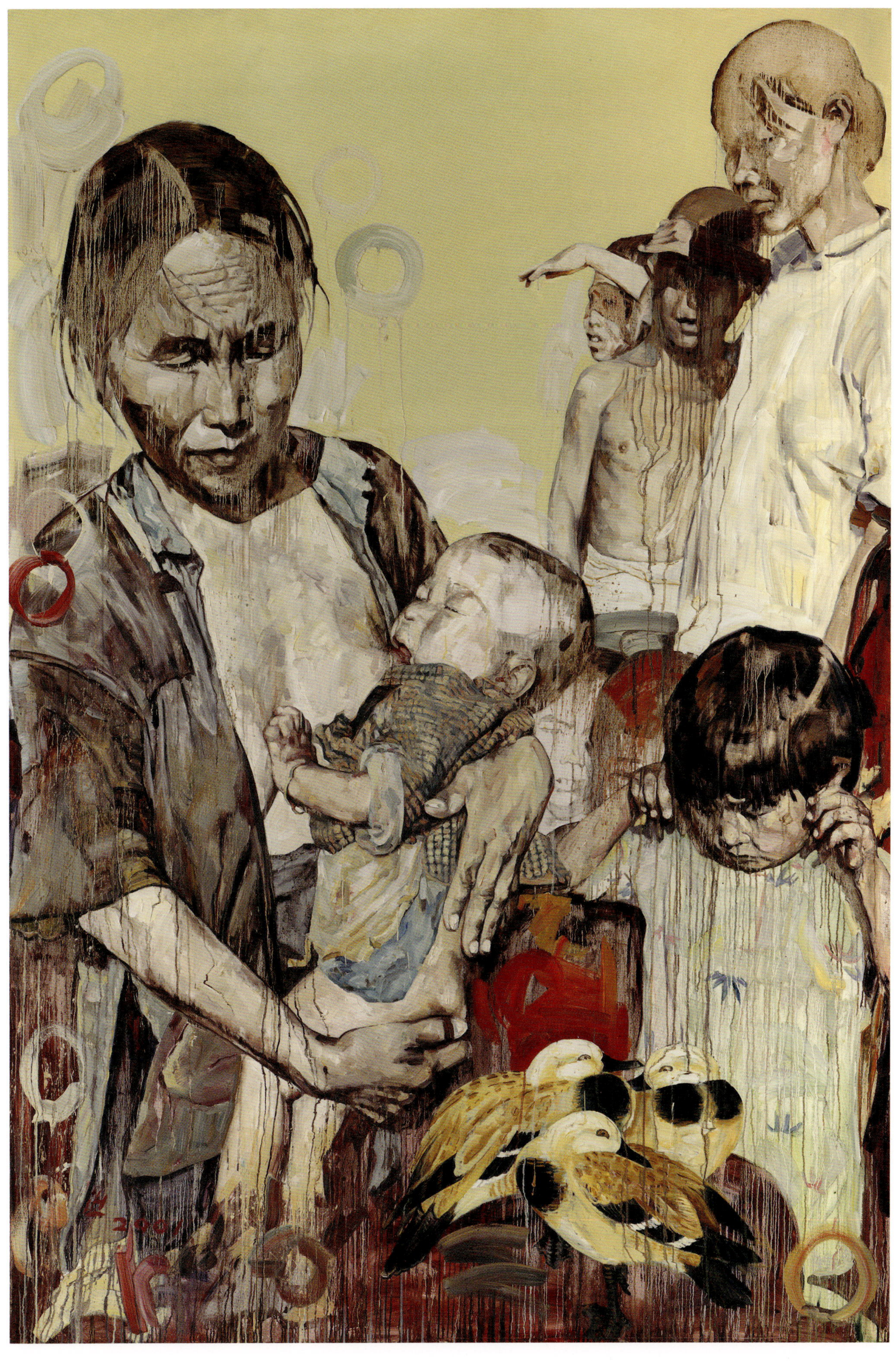

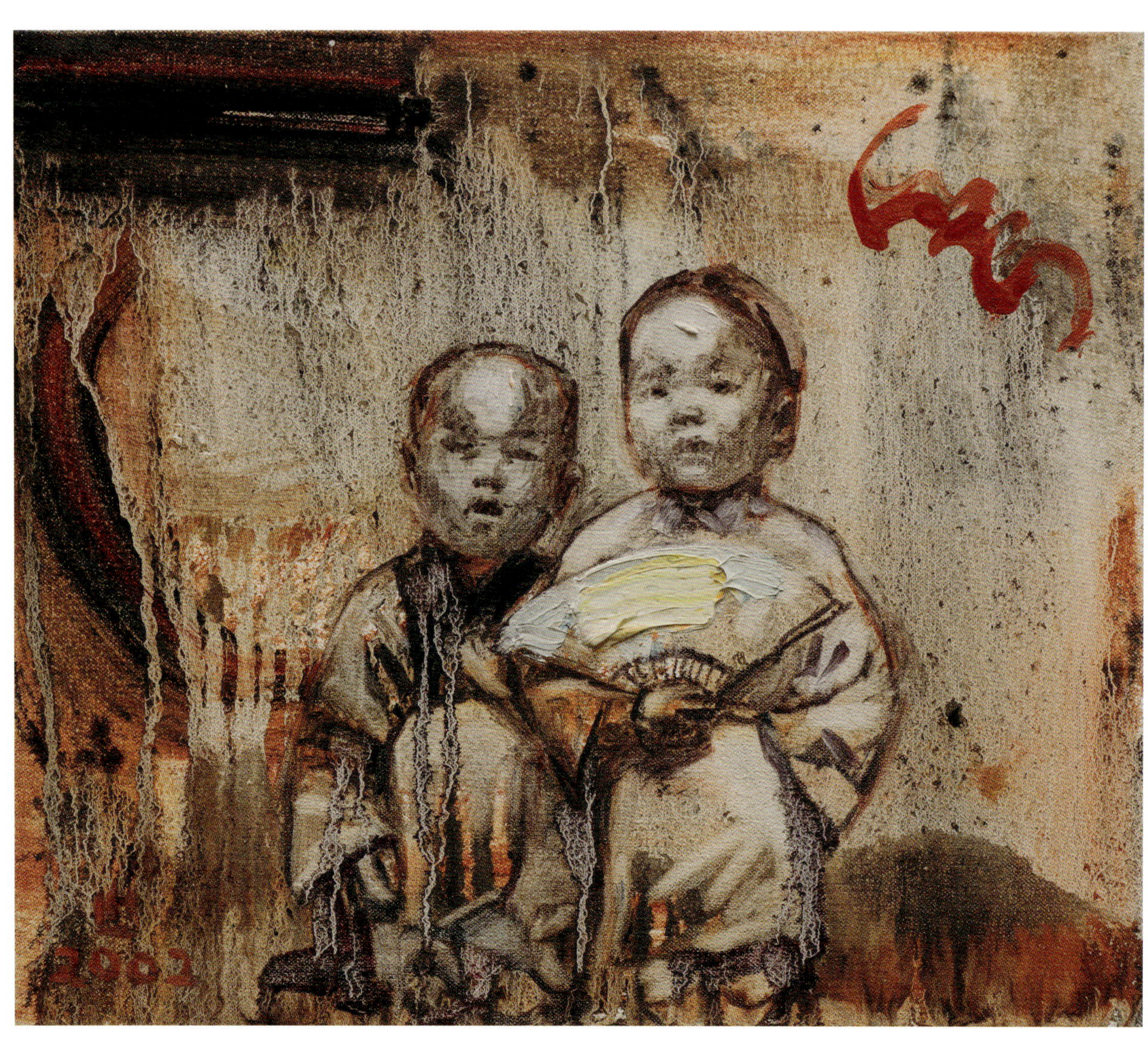

32. *Mission Girls 2,* 2002
Oil on canvas
12 × 14 in. (30.5 × 35.6 cm)
Castellano-Wood Family Collection

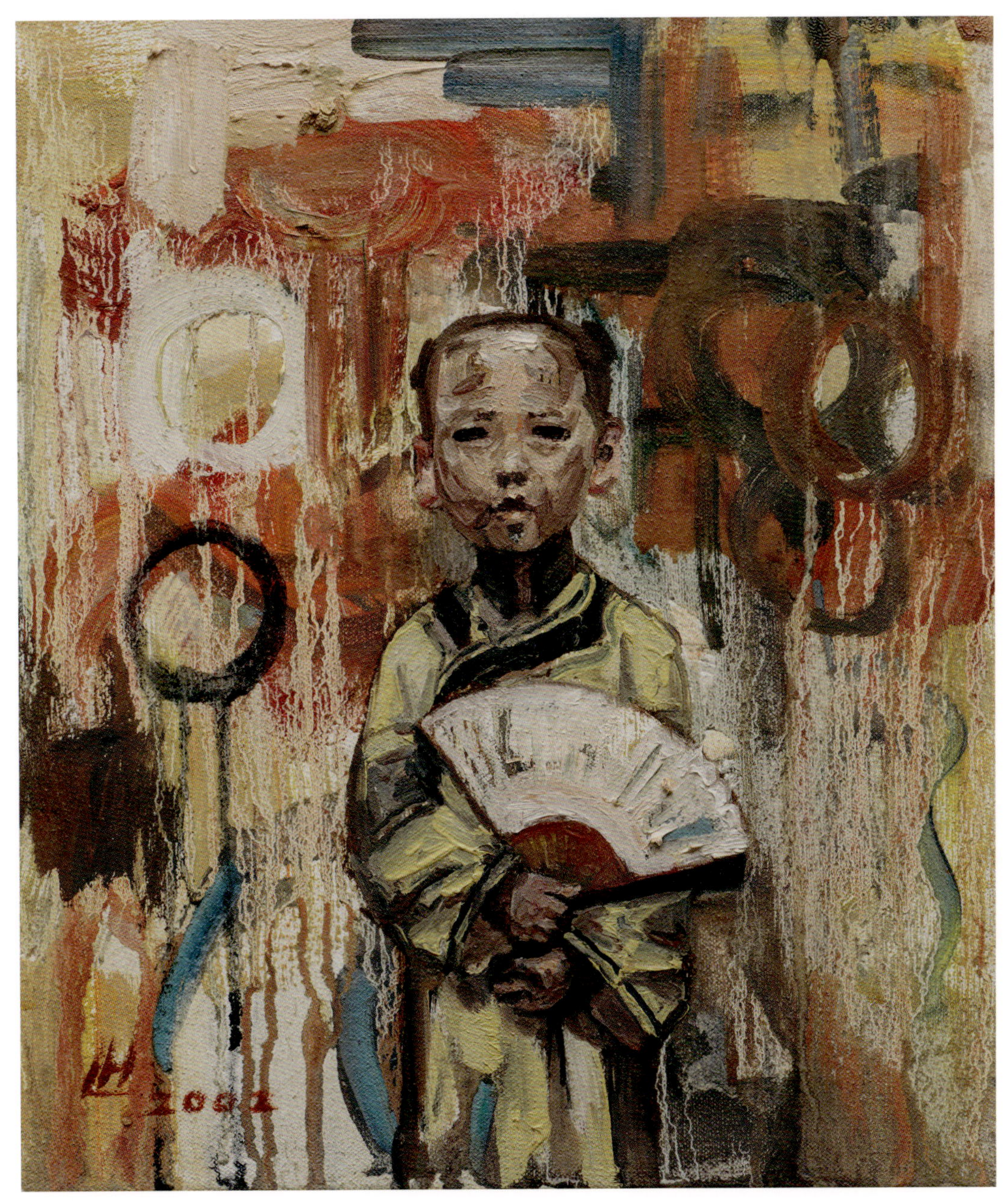

33. *Mission Girls 6,* 2002
Oil on canvas
14 × 12 in. (35.6 × 30.5 cm)
Castellano-Wood Family Collection

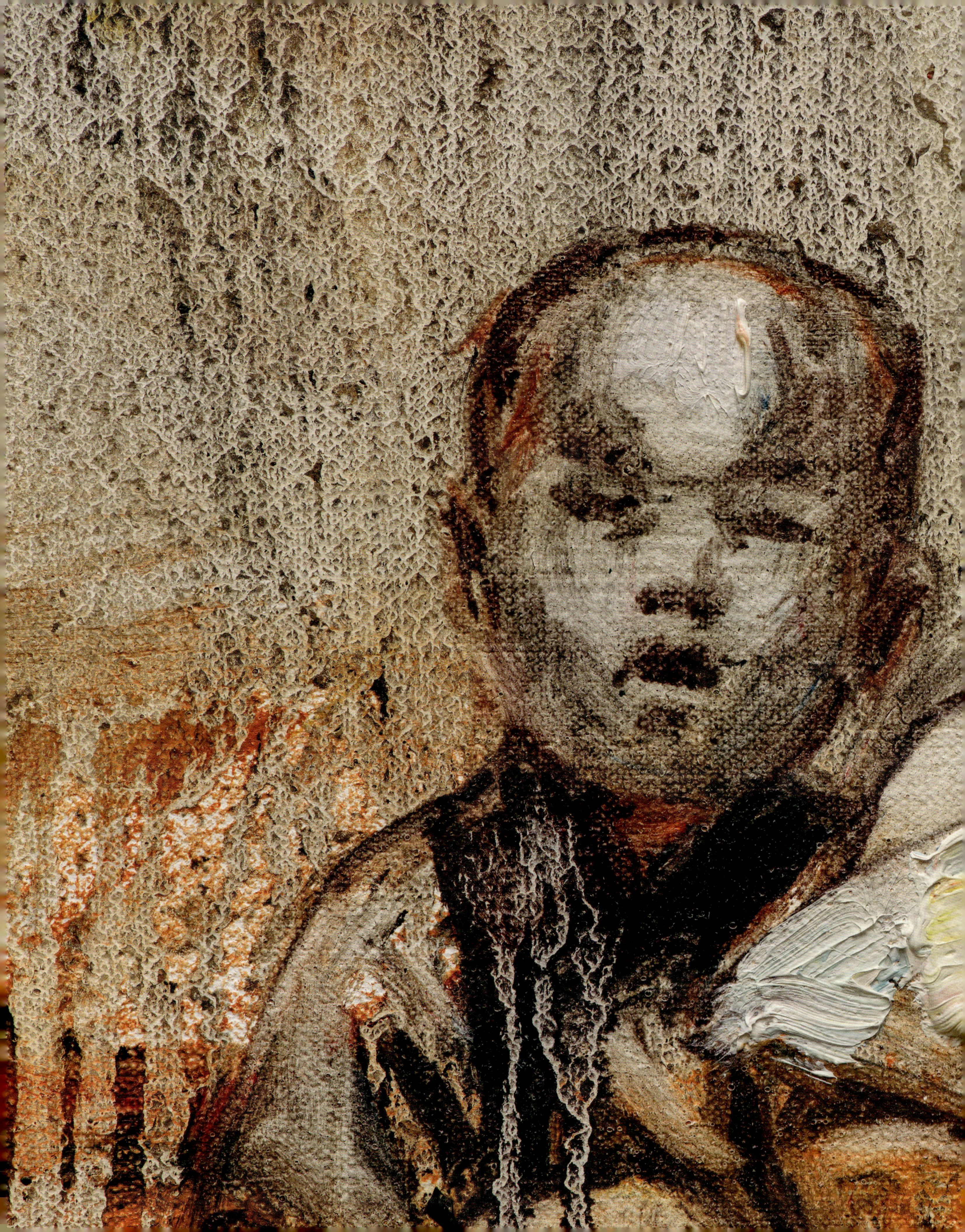

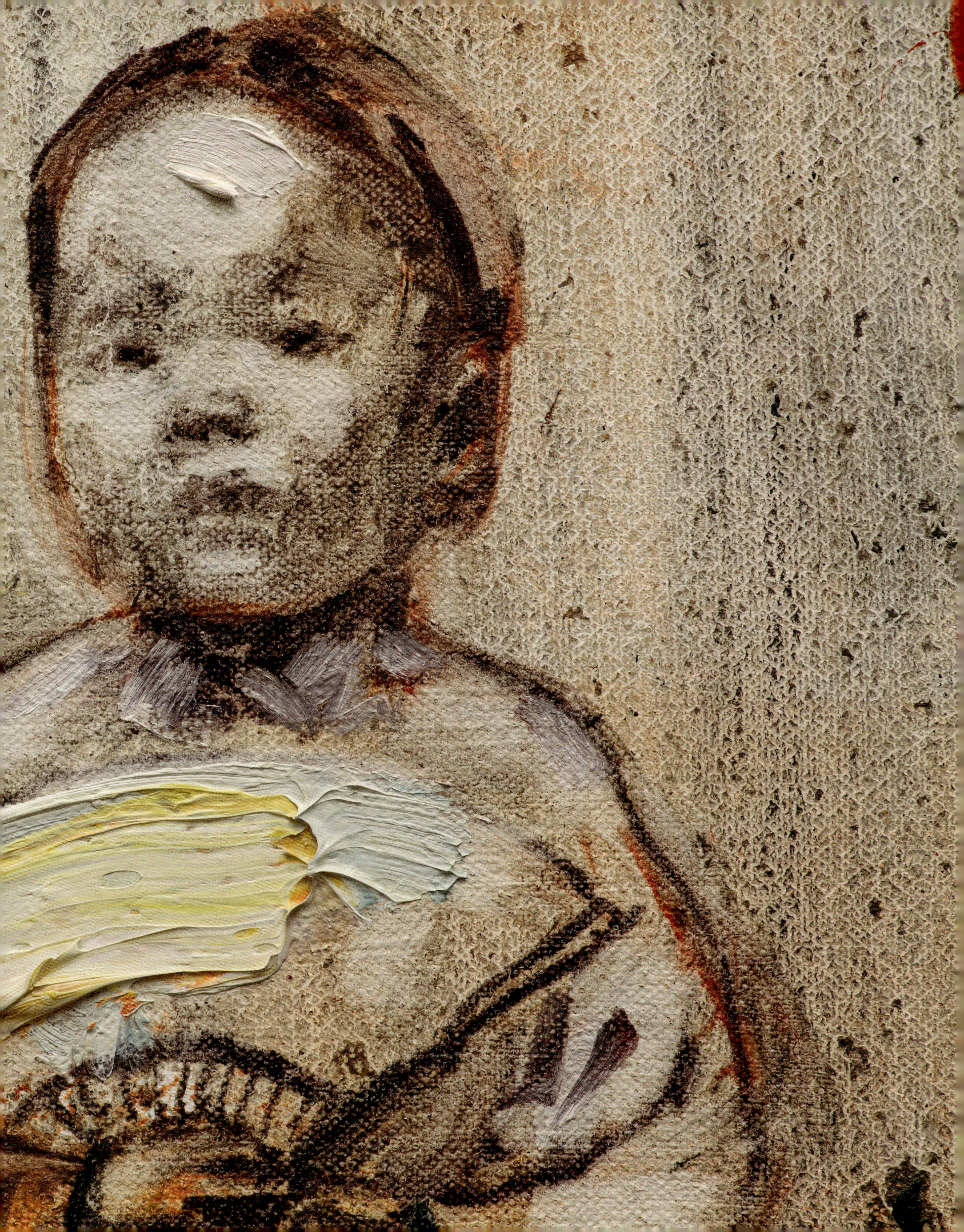

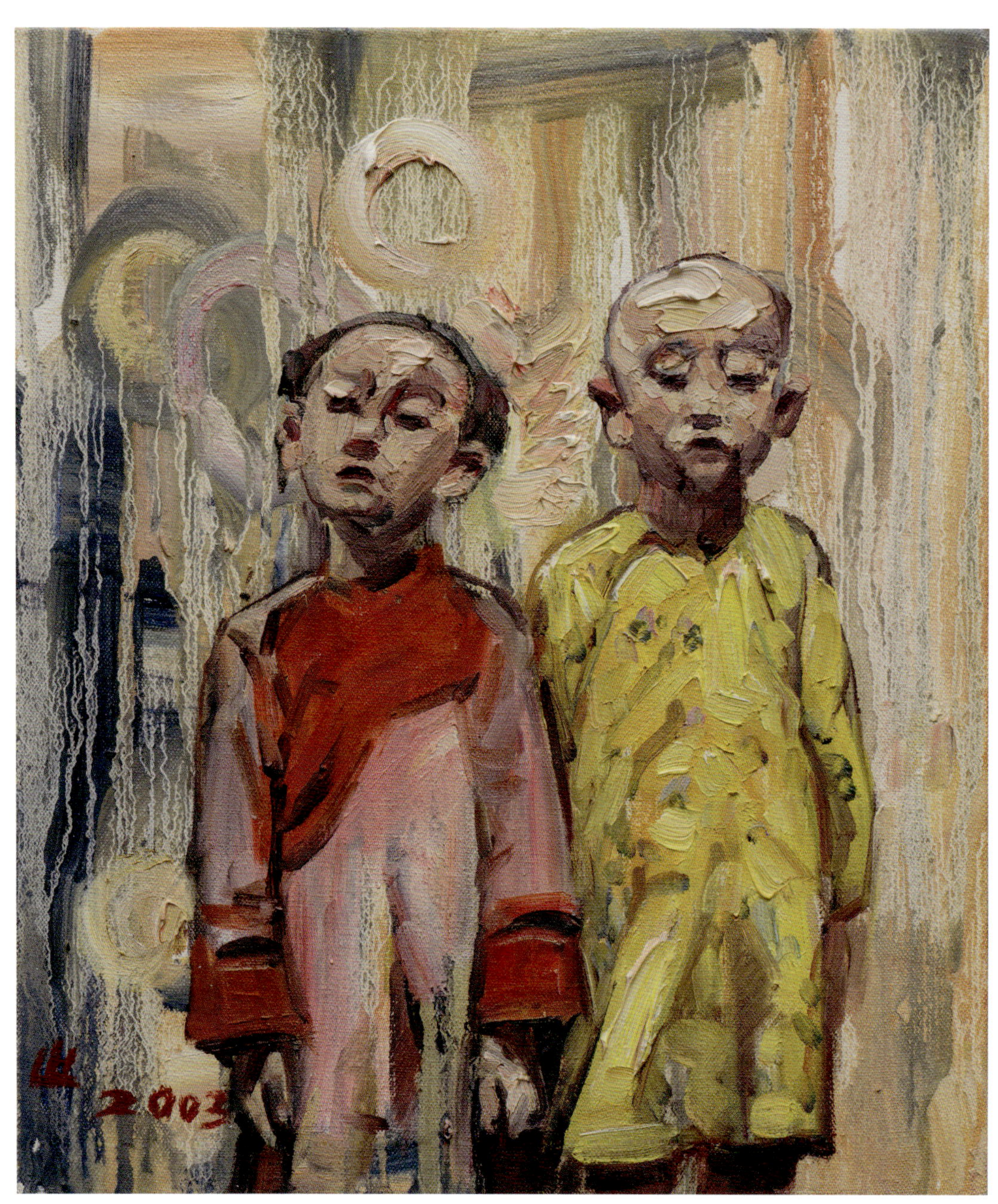

34. *Mission Girls 11,* 2003
Oil on canvas
14 × 12 in. (35.6 × 30.5 cm)
Castellano-Wood Family Collection

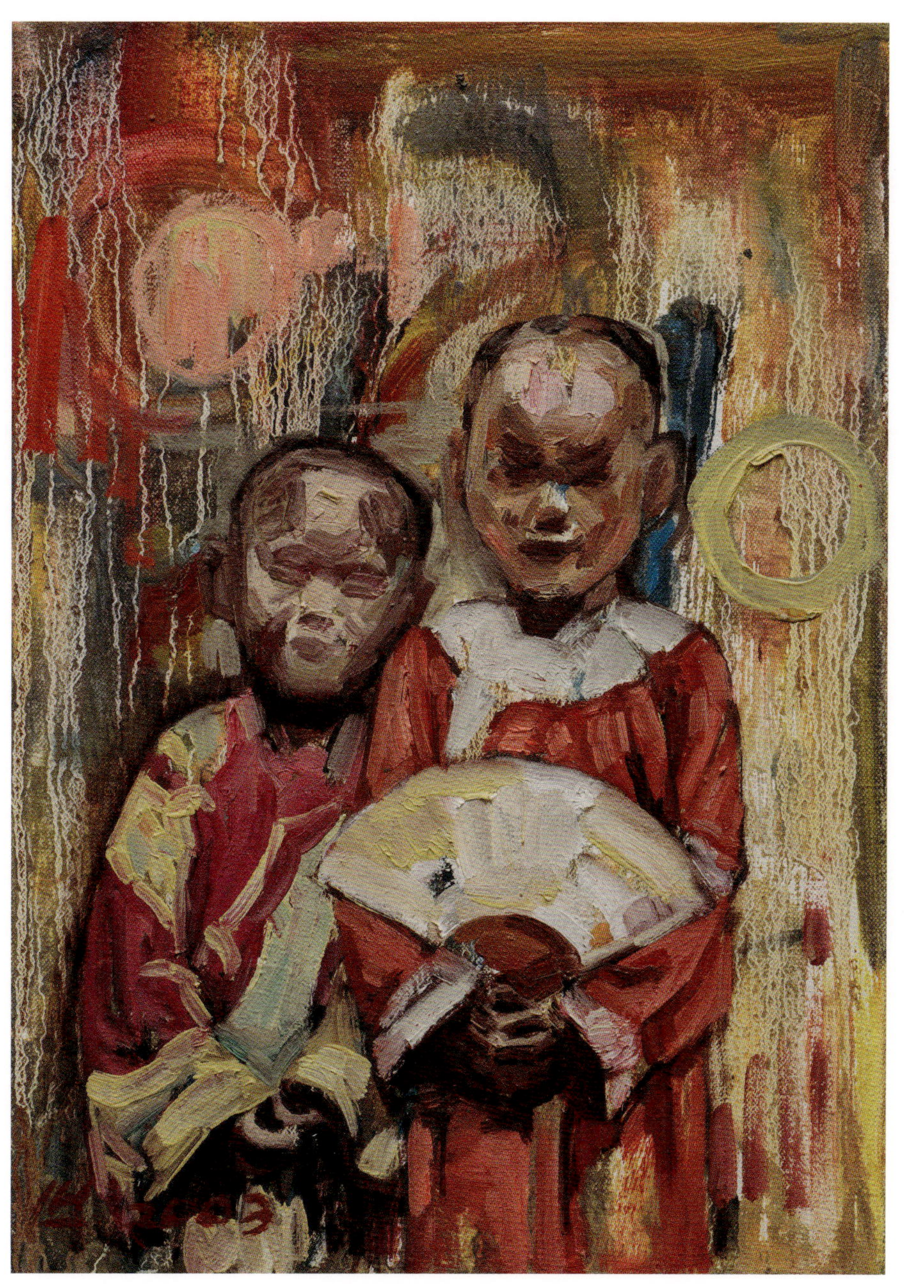

35. *Mission Girls 13,* 2003
Oil on canvas
14 × 10 in. (35.6 × 25.4 cm)
Castellano-Wood Family Collection

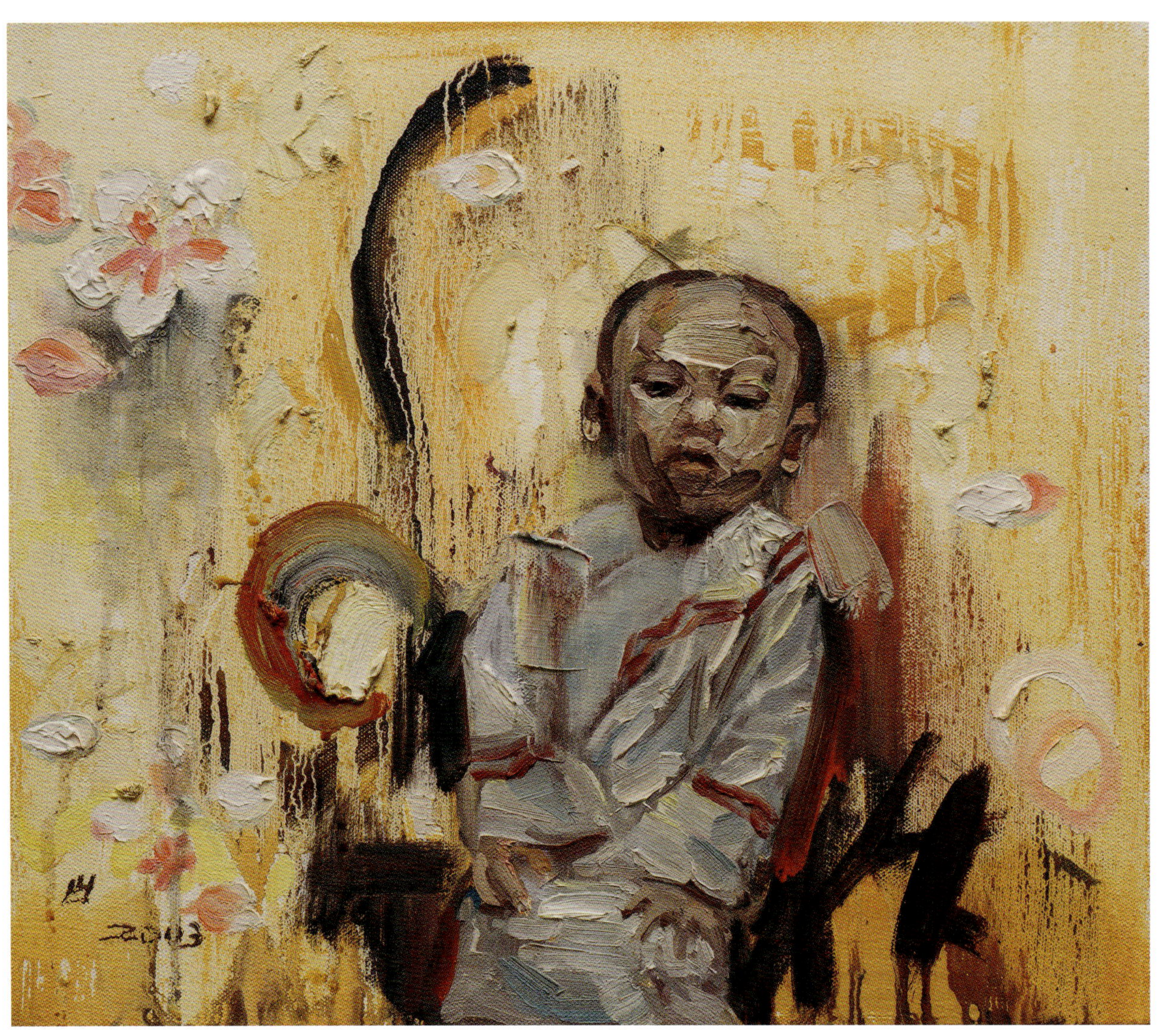

36. *Mission Girls 14,* 2003
Oil on canvas
12 × 14 in. (30.5 × 35.6 cm)
Castellano-Wood Family Collection

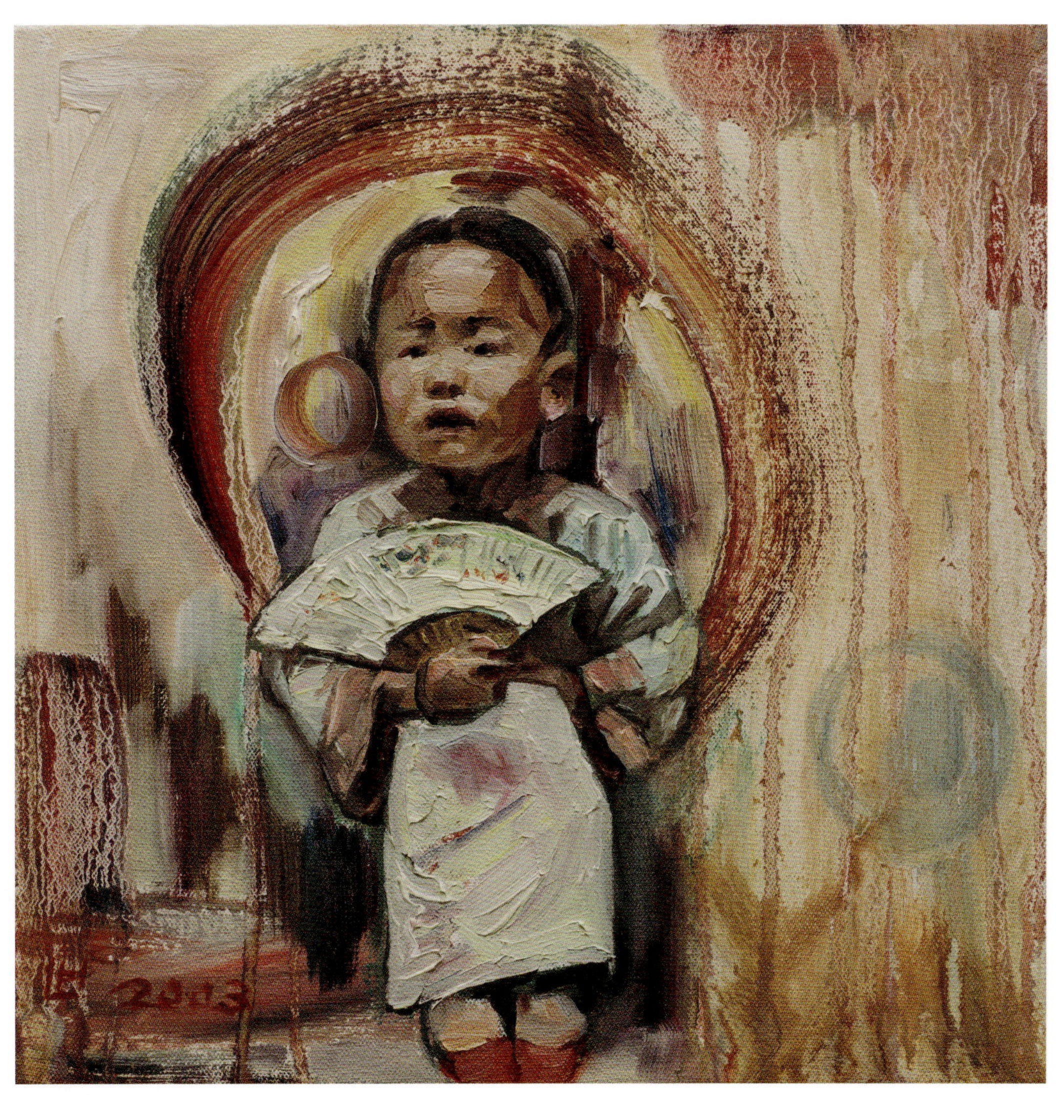

37. *Mission Girls 17,* 2003
Oil on canvas
12 × 12 in. (30.5 × 30.5 cm)
Castellano-Wood Family Collection

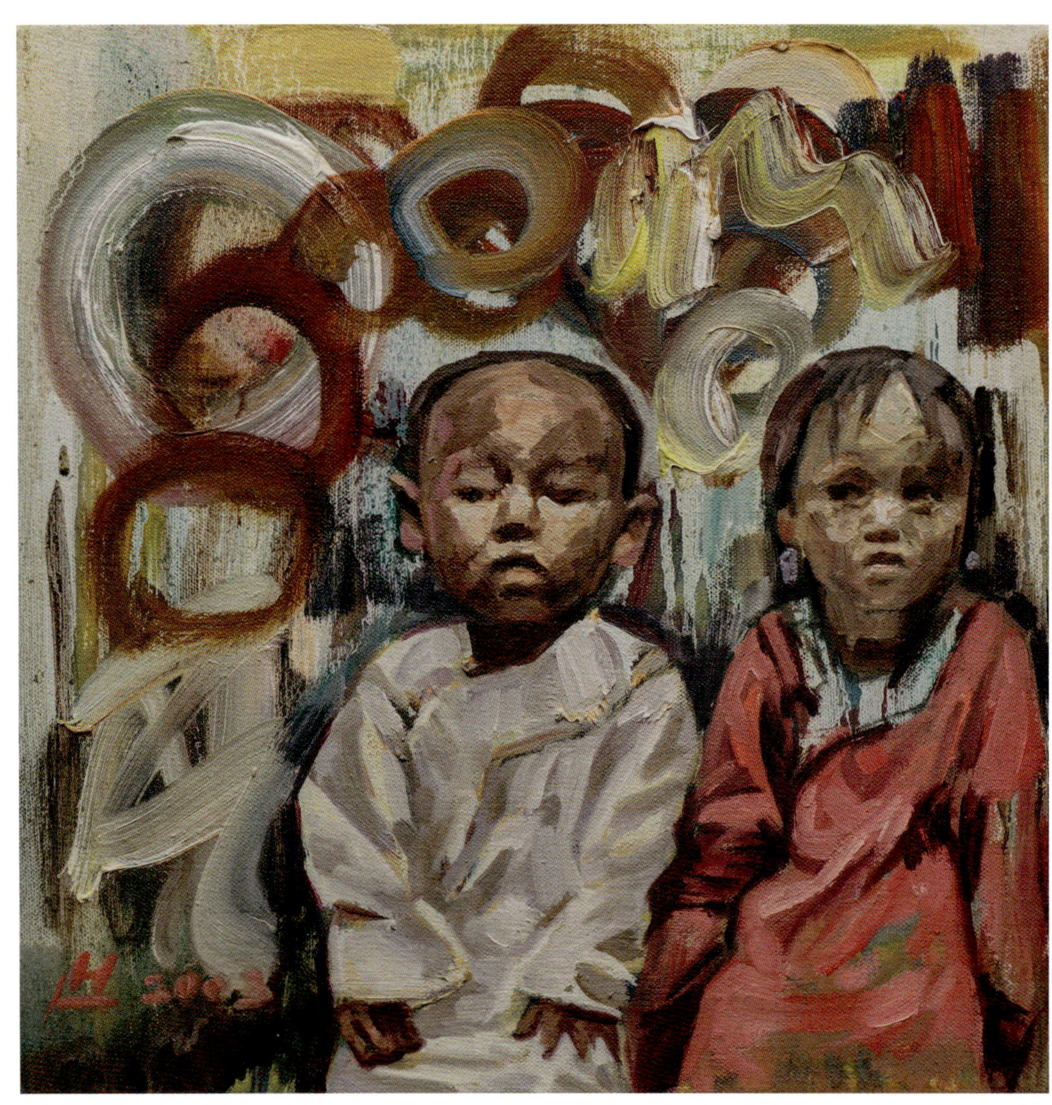

38. *Mission Girls 18,* 2003
Oil on canvas
12 × 12 in. (30.5 × 30.5 cm)
Castellano-Wood Family Collection

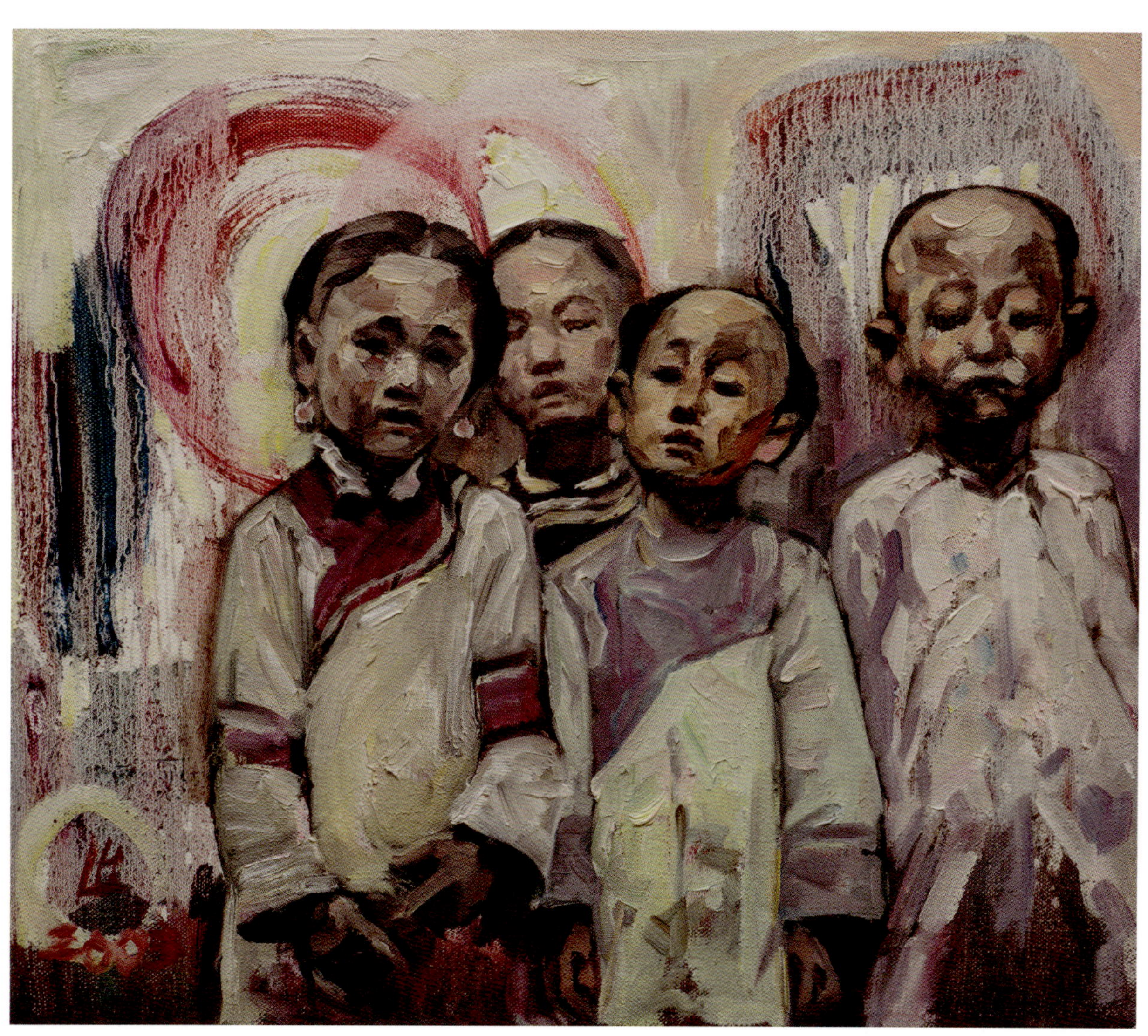

39. *Mission Girls 20,* 2003
Oil on canvas
12 × 14 in. (30.5 × 35.6 cm)
Castellano-Wood Family Collection

40. *Mission Girls 21,* 2003
Oil on canvas
12 × 12 in. (30.5 × 30.5 cm)
Castellano-Wood Family Collection

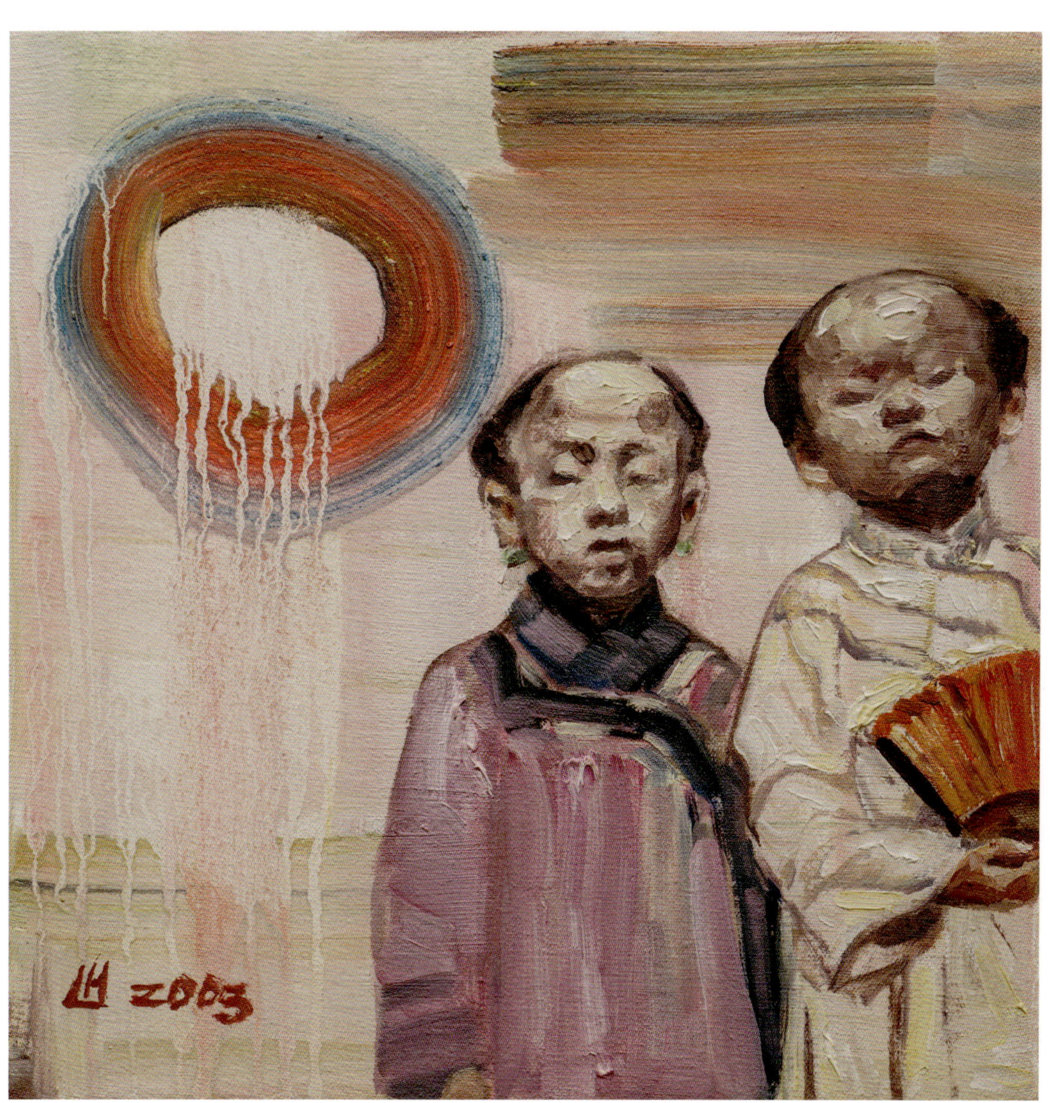

41. *Chinese in Idaho, Portrait II,* 2004
Oil on canvas
36 × 24 in. (91.4 × 61 cm)
Castellano-Wood Family Collection

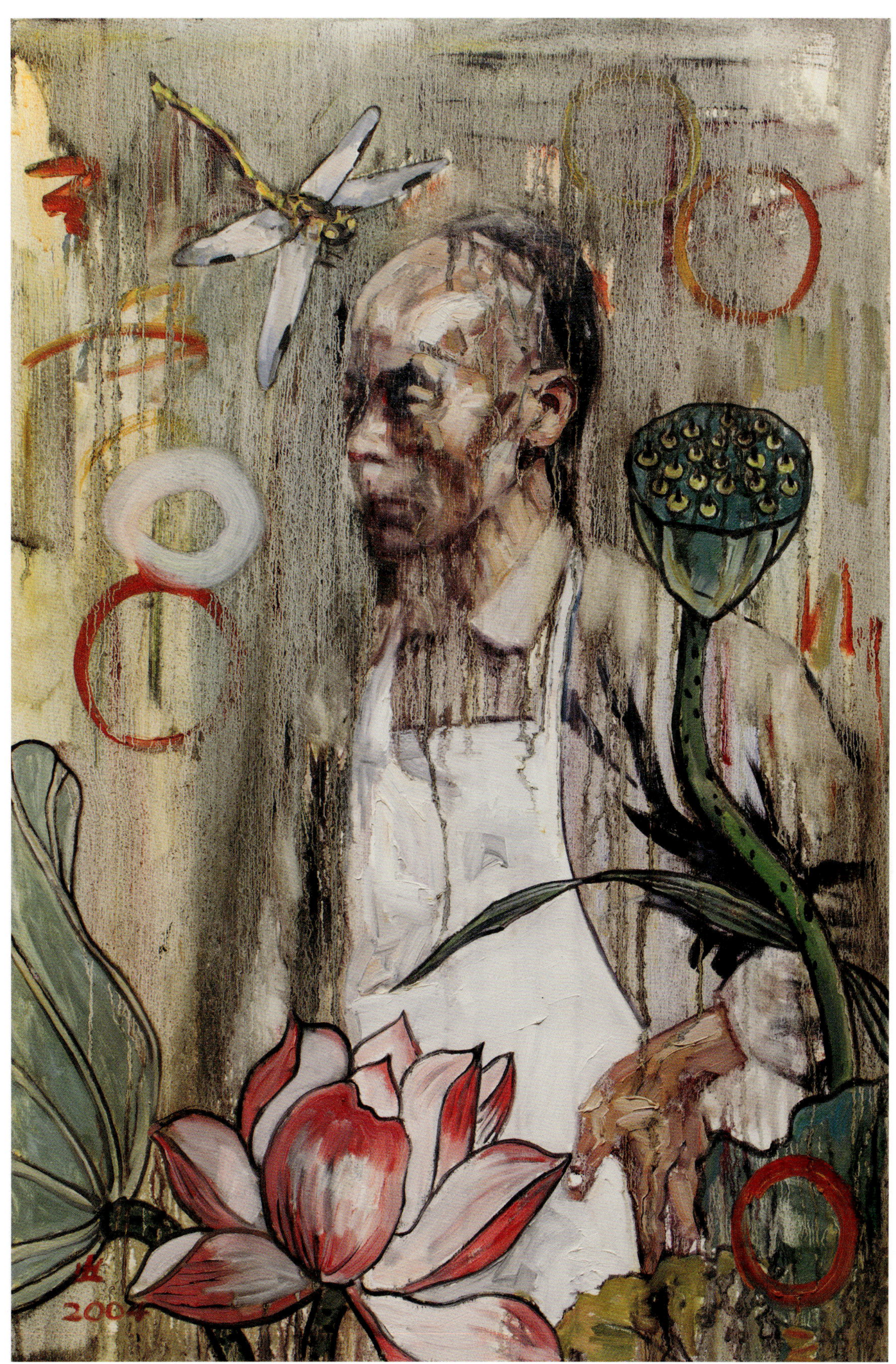

42. *Chinese in Idaho, Portrait IV,* 2004
Oil on canvas
36 × 24 in. (91.4 × 61 cm)
Castellano-Wood Family Collection

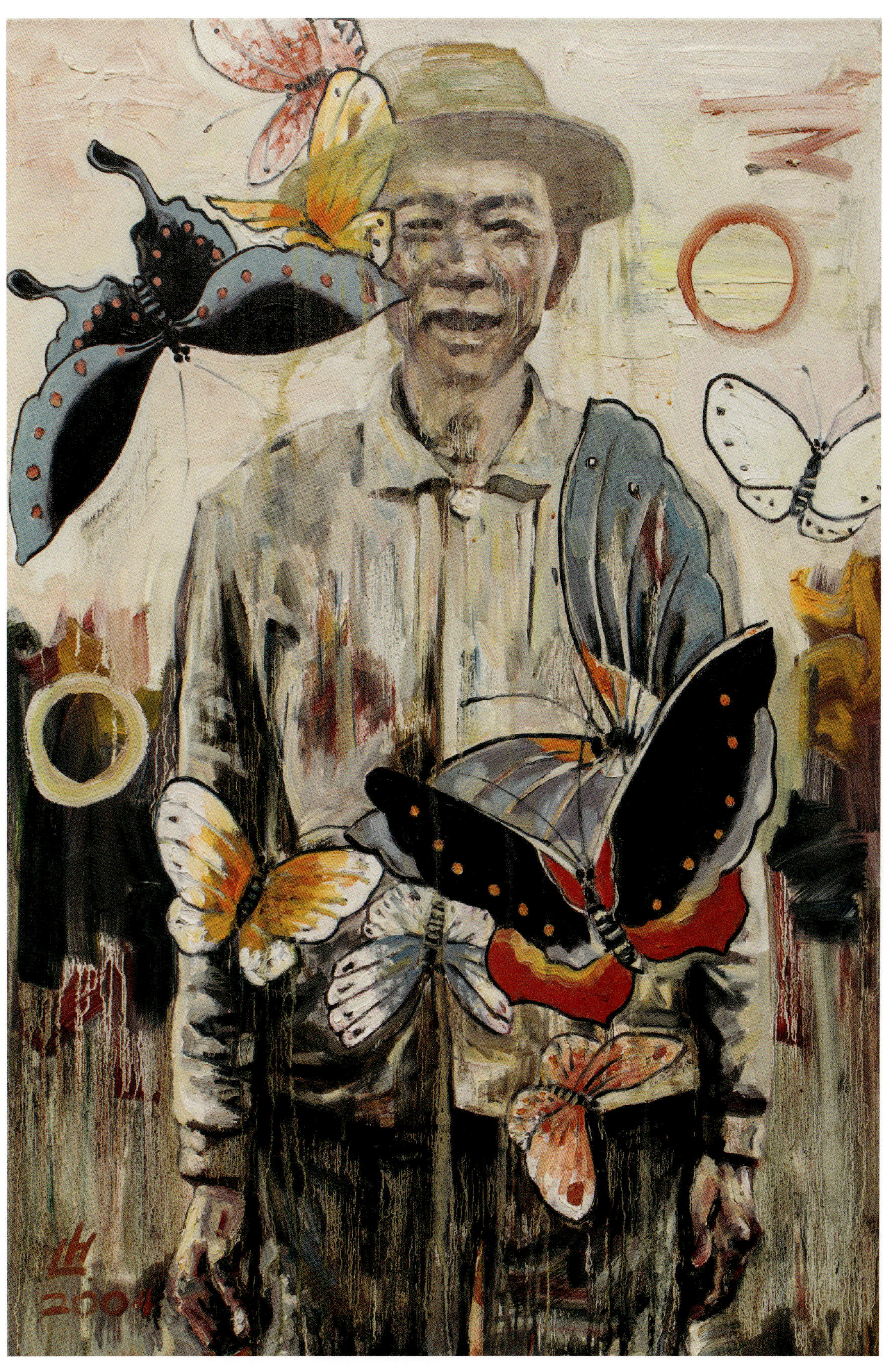

43. *Dangling,* 2005
Oil on canvas
80 × 80 in. (203.2 × 203.2 cm)
Castellano-Wood Family Collection

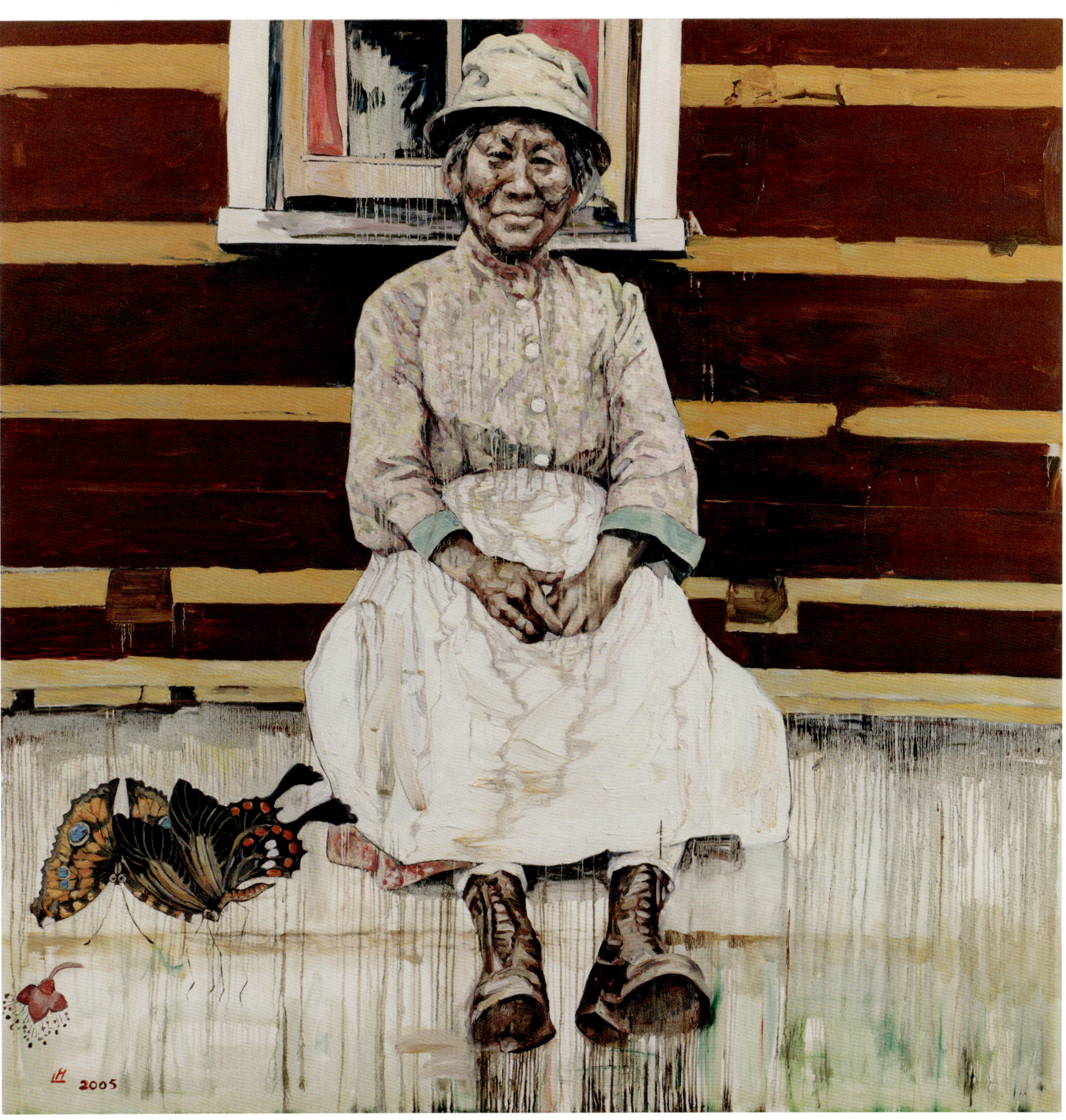

44. *The Botanist,* 2013
Oil on canvas
96 × 54 in. (243.8 × 137.2 cm)
San Francisco Museum of Modern Art. Gift of Lorrie and
Richard Greene and Accessions Committee Fund purchase

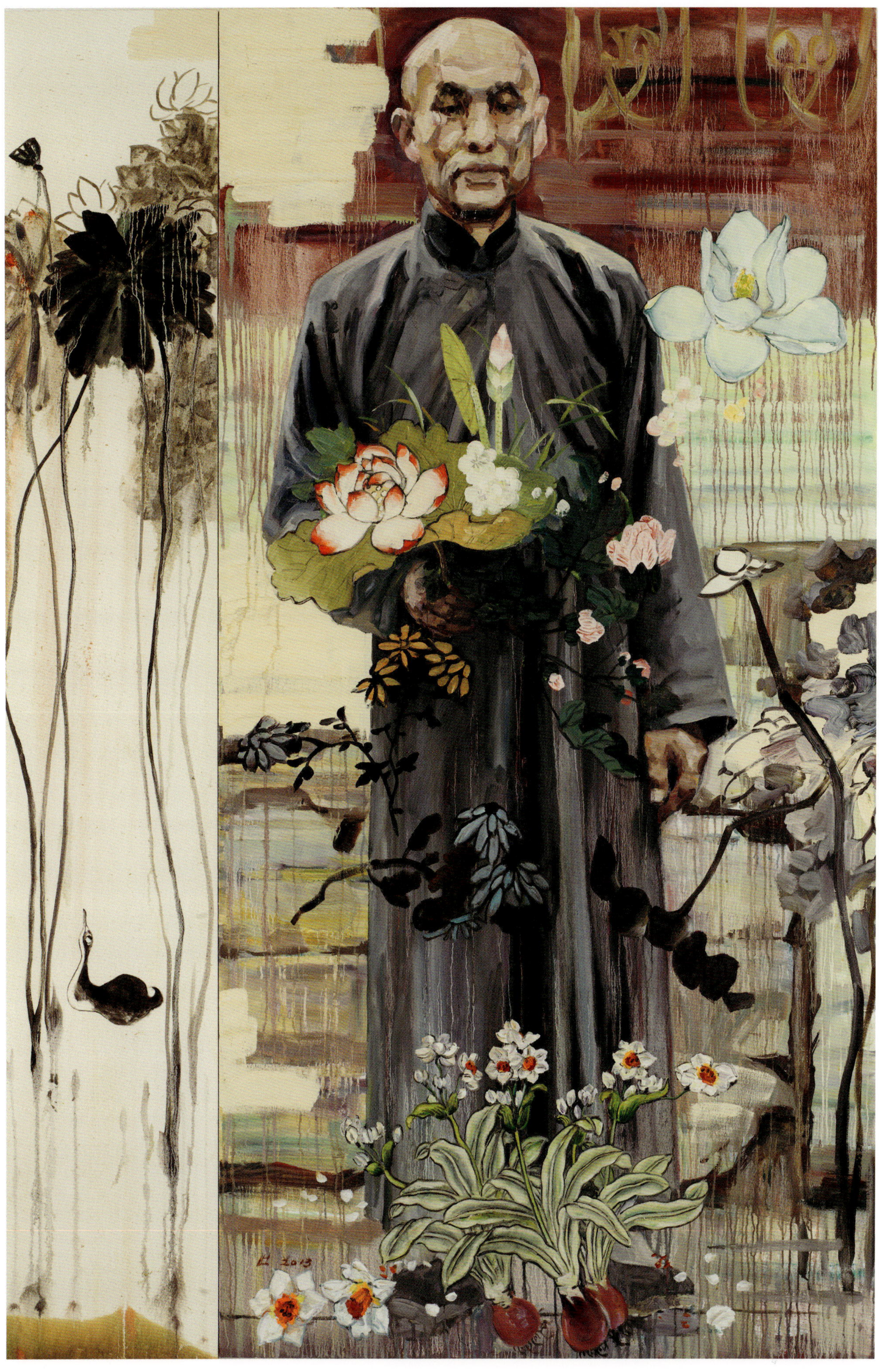

45. *Laborer: Farm Hand (Clarence Weems)*, 2016
Oil on canvas
36 × 36 in. (91.4 × 91.4 cm)
Collection of Josef Vascovitz and Lisa Goodman

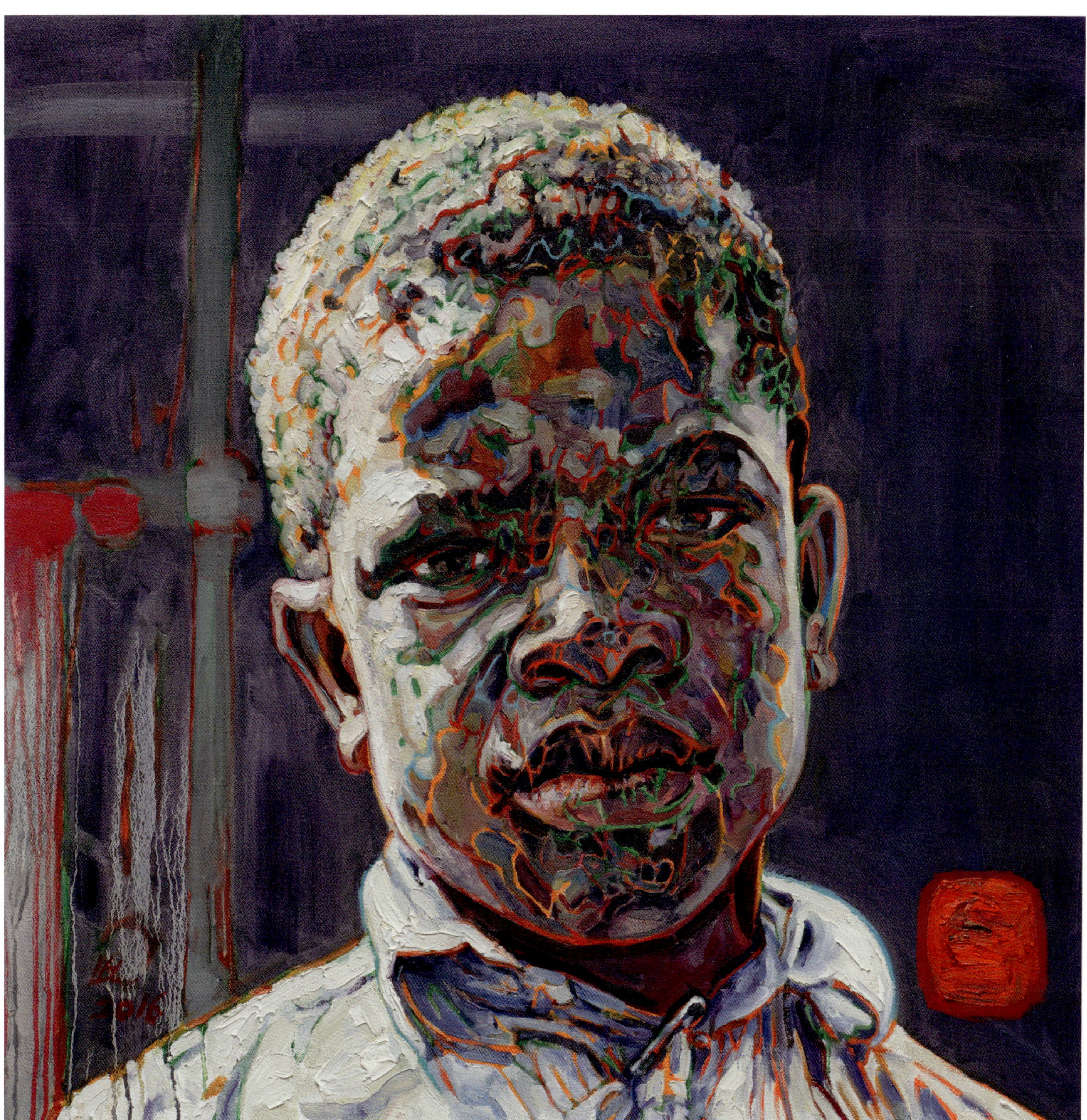

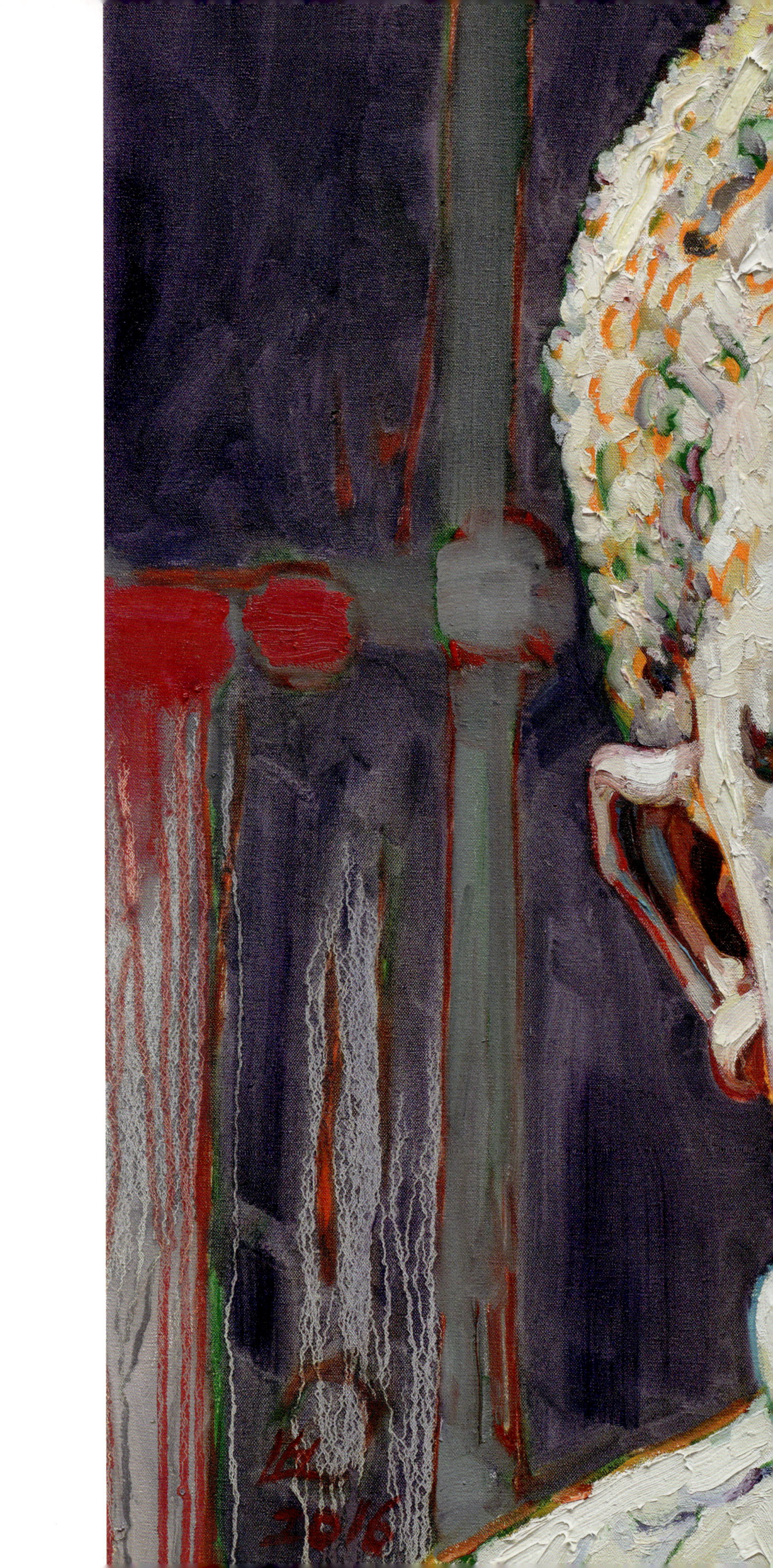

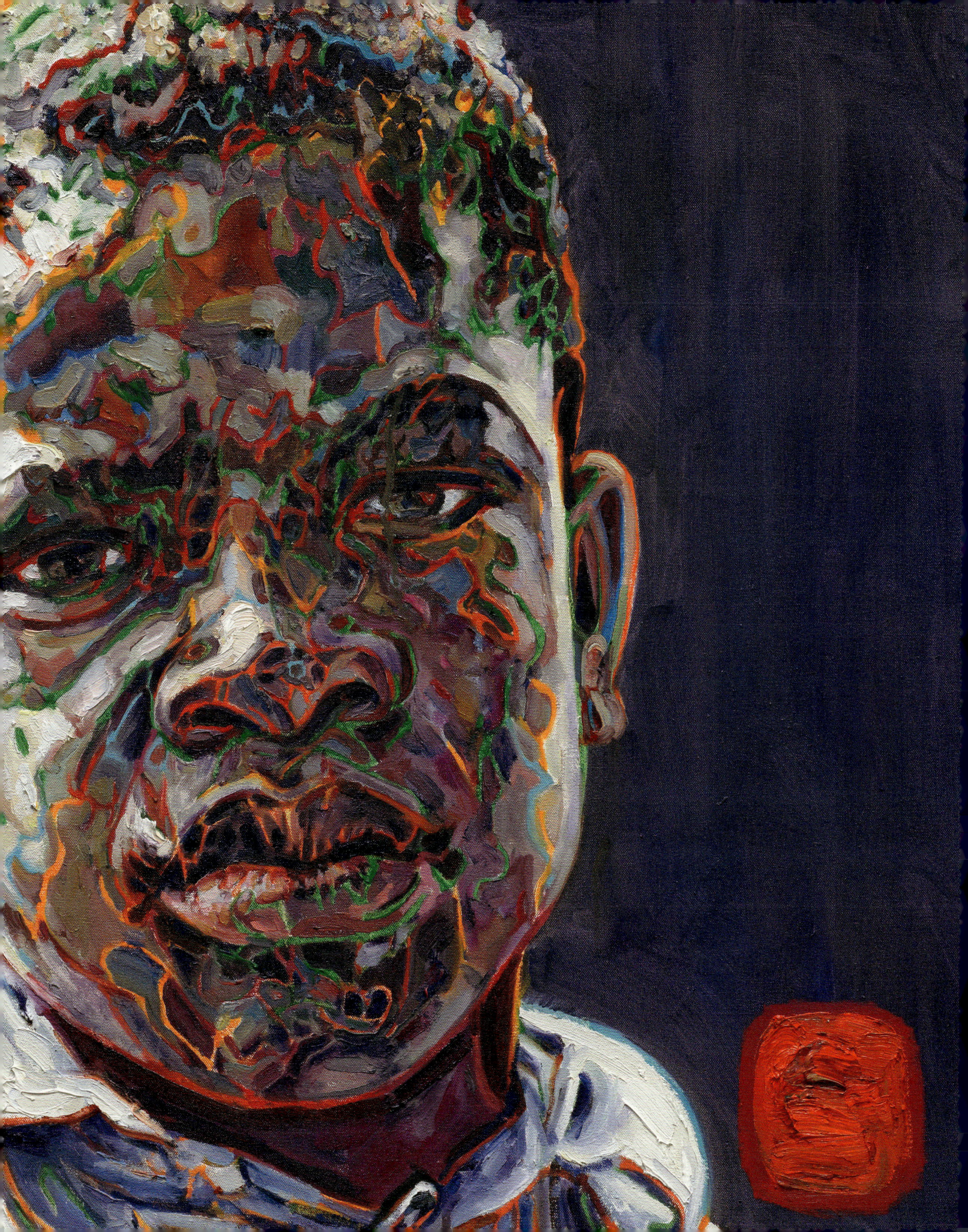

46. *Cotton Picker,* 2015
Oil on canvas
66 × 66 in. (167.6 × 167.6 cm)
Collection of Sig Anderman

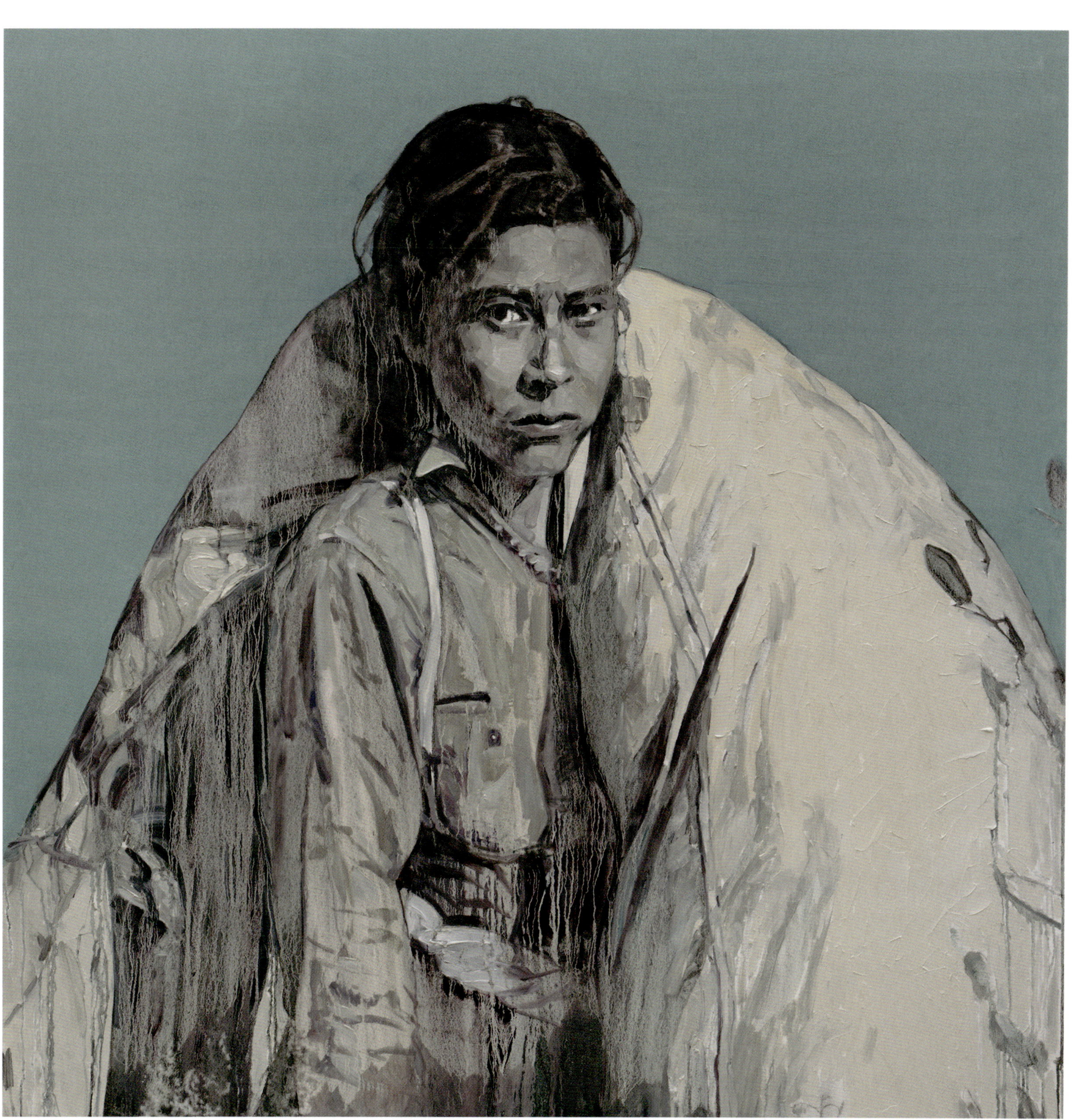

47. *Migrant Mother: Mealtime,* 2016
Oil on canvas
60 × 60 in. (152.4 × 152.4 cm)
Collection of Michael Klein

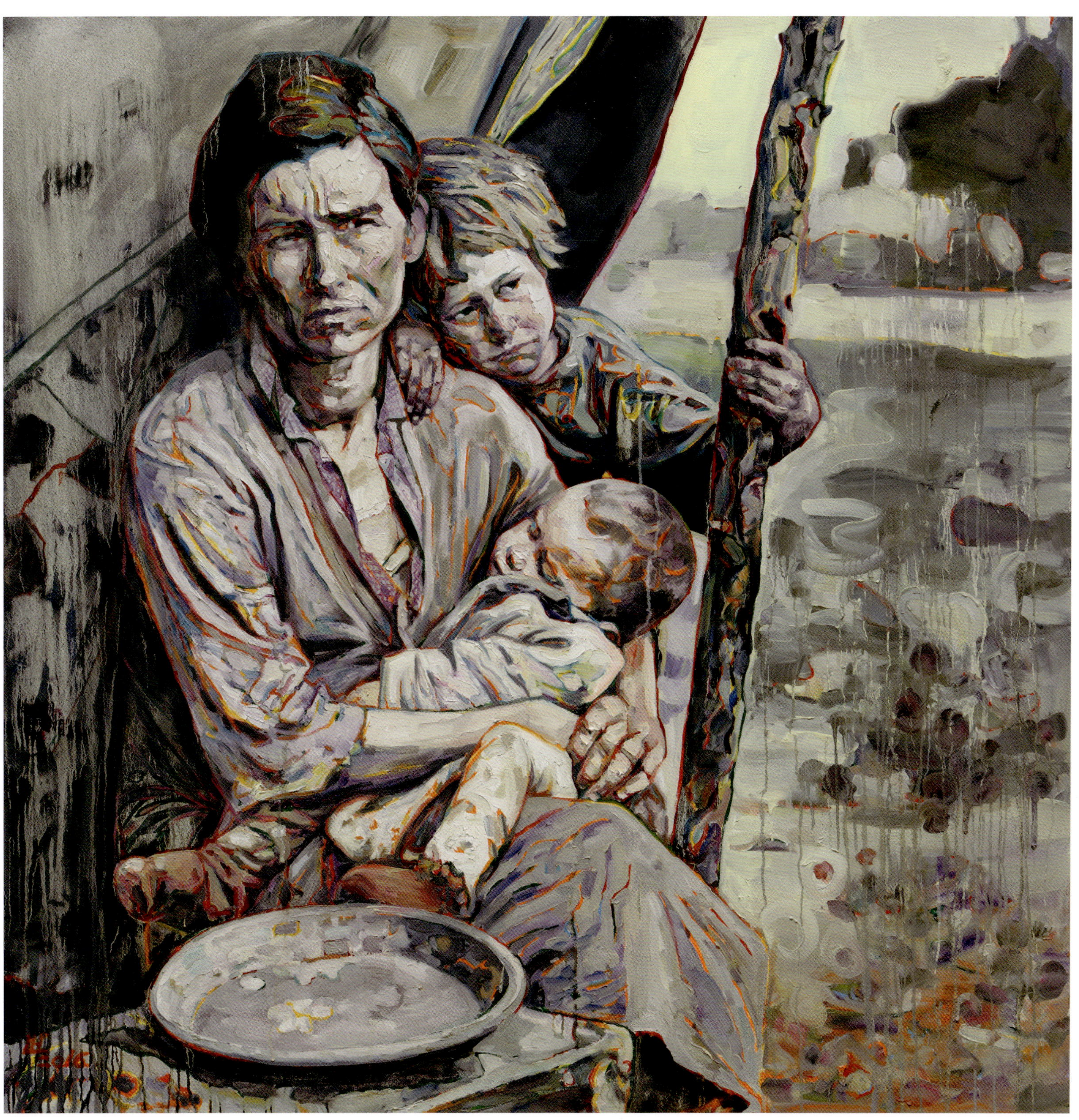

48. *August,* 2017
Oil on canvas
60 × 48 in. (152.4 × 121.9 cm)
Collection of David and Debbie Popper

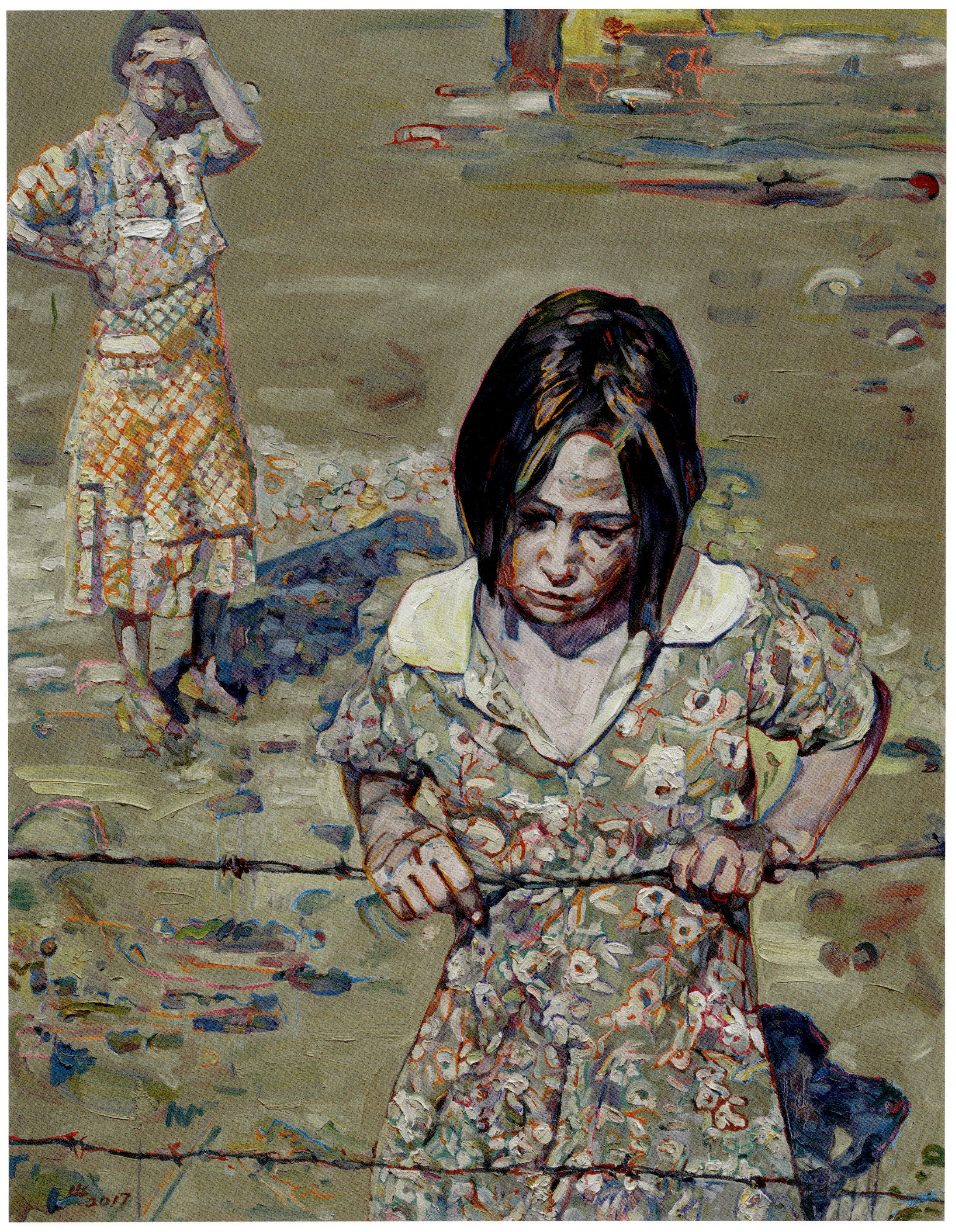

49. *South,* 2017
Oil on canvas
60 × 48 in. (152.4 × 121.9 cm)
Collection of Richard and Marcy Schwartz

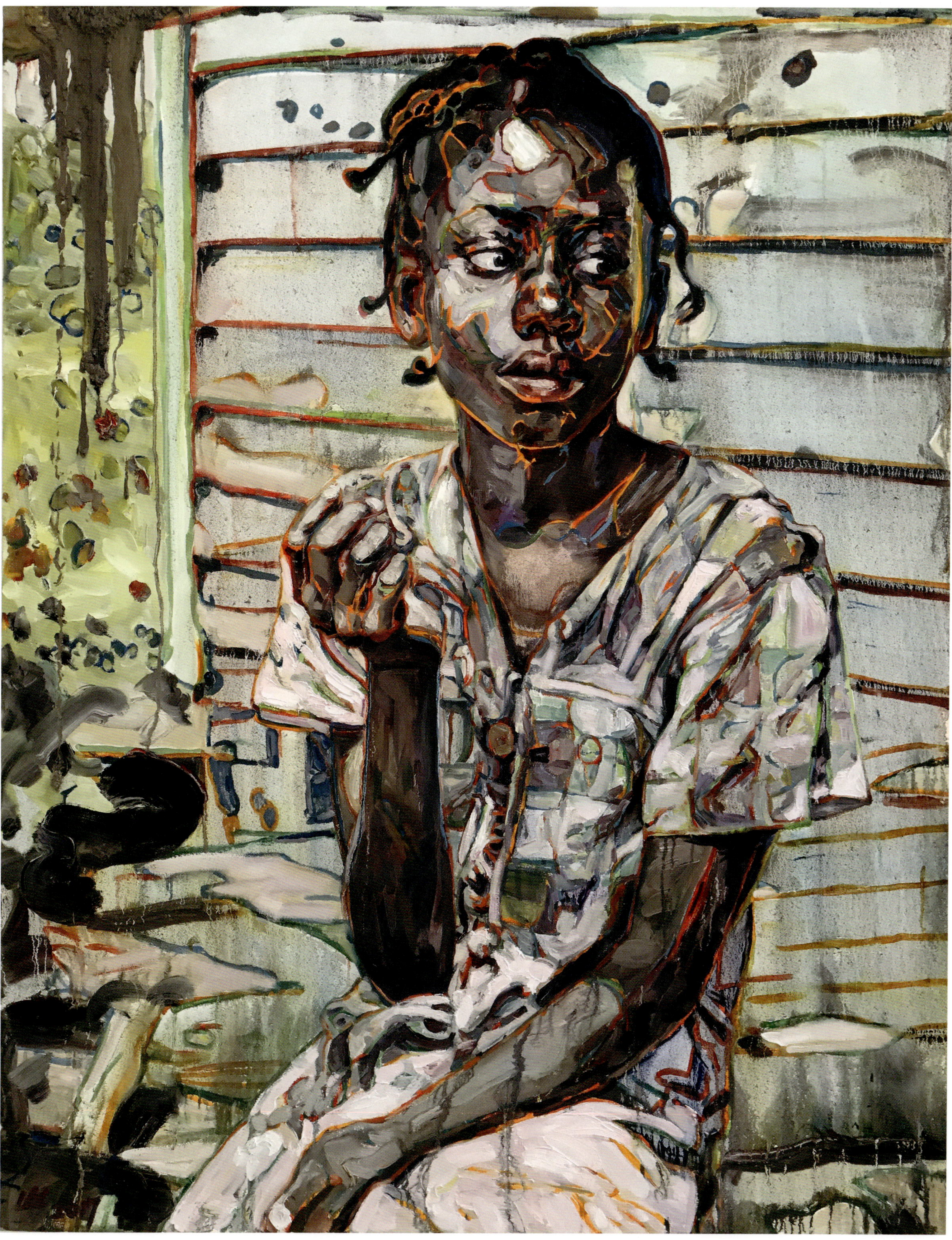

50. *Sanctuary,* 2019
Oil on canvas with gold leaf
80 × 72 in. (203.2 × 182.9 cm)
Courtesy of Nancy Hoffman Gallery, New York

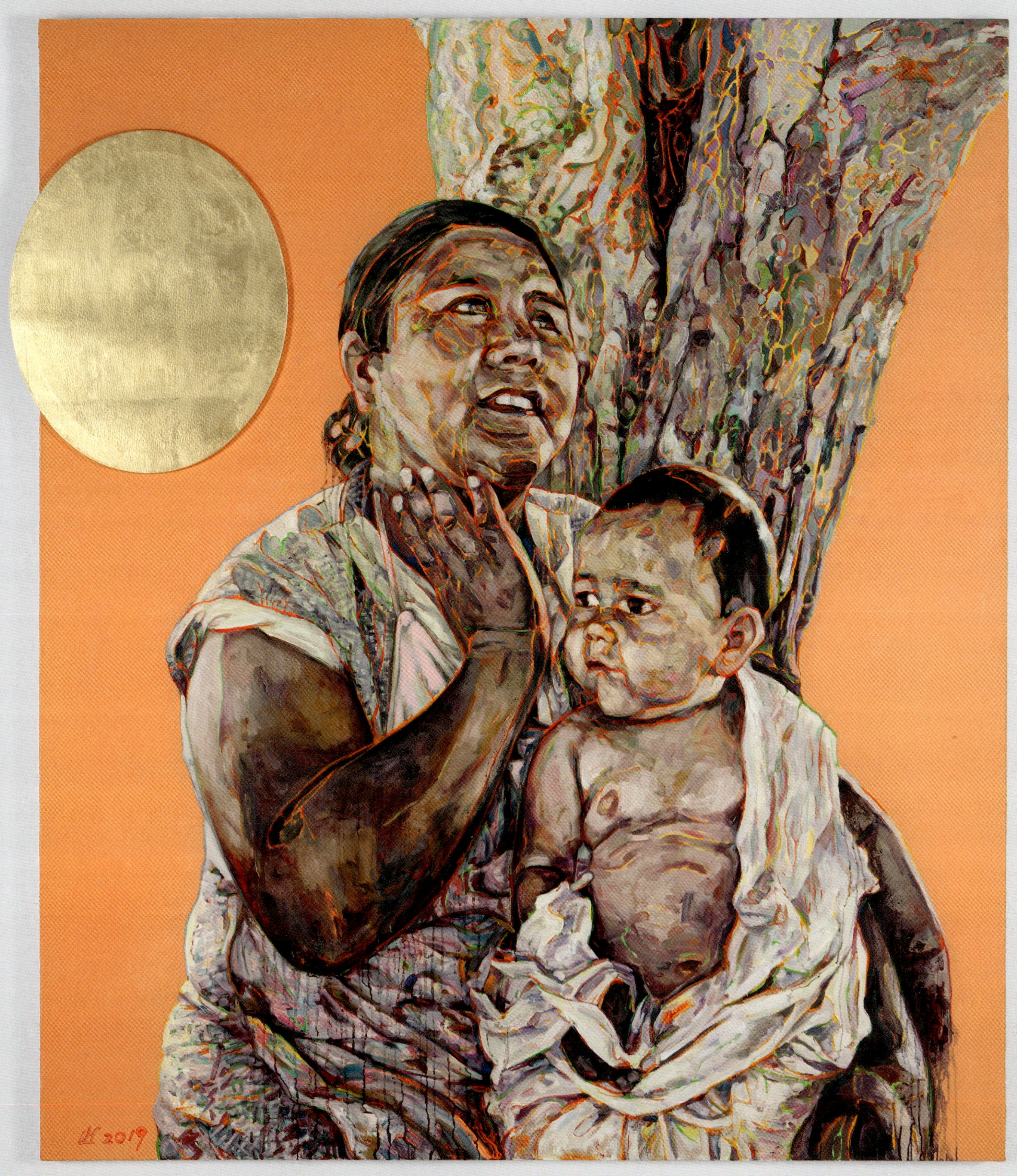

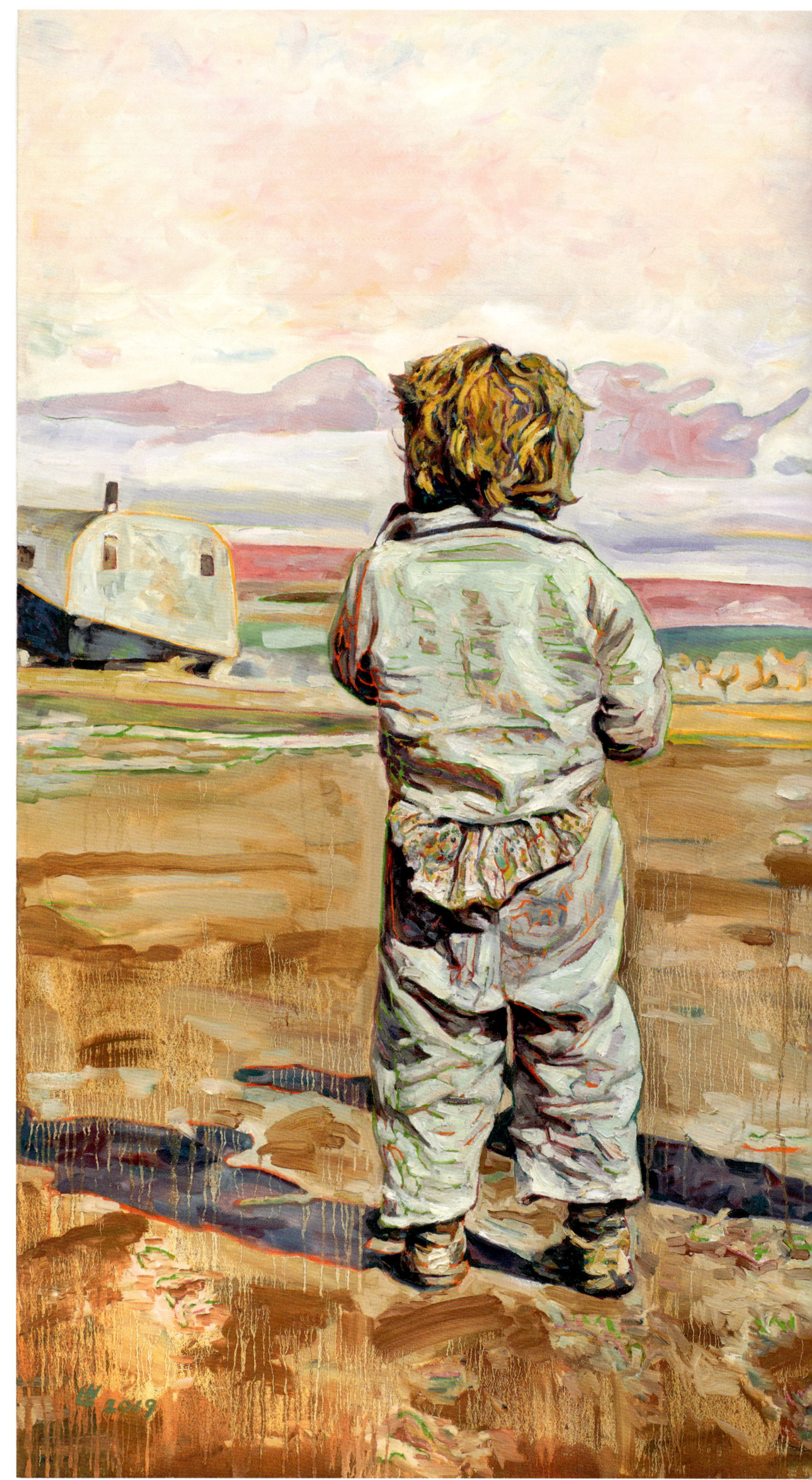

51. *Catchers,* 2019
Oil on canvas
70 × 80 in. (177.8 × 203.2 cm)
Collection of Tim and Donna Jones,
San Francisco

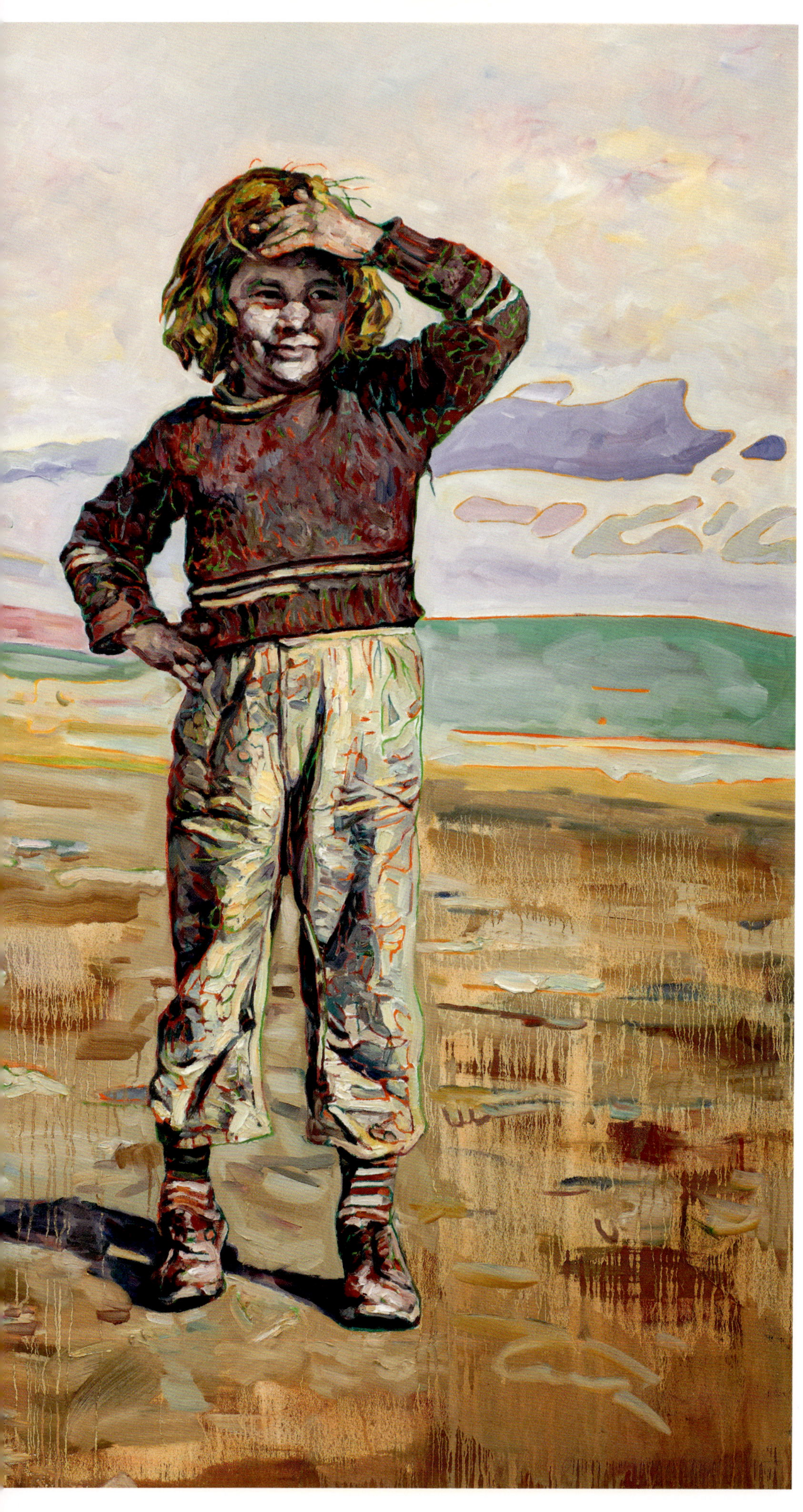

52. *Plowboy,* 2020
Oil on canvas
48 × 48 in. (121.9 × 121.9 cm)
Collection of Dr. Matthias Bolten and Mr. Matthias Brücklmeier
Courtesy of Nancy Hoffman Gallery

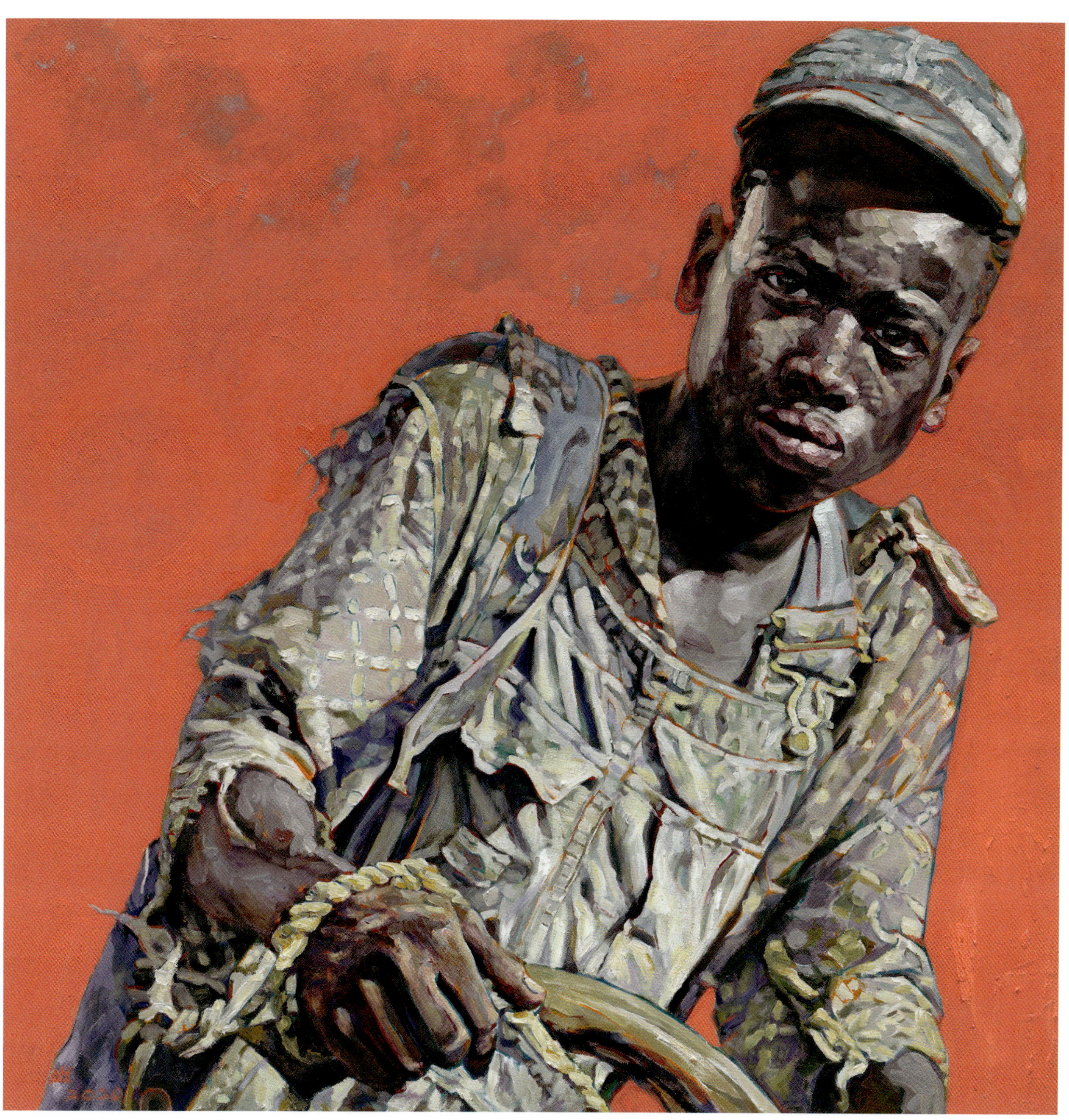

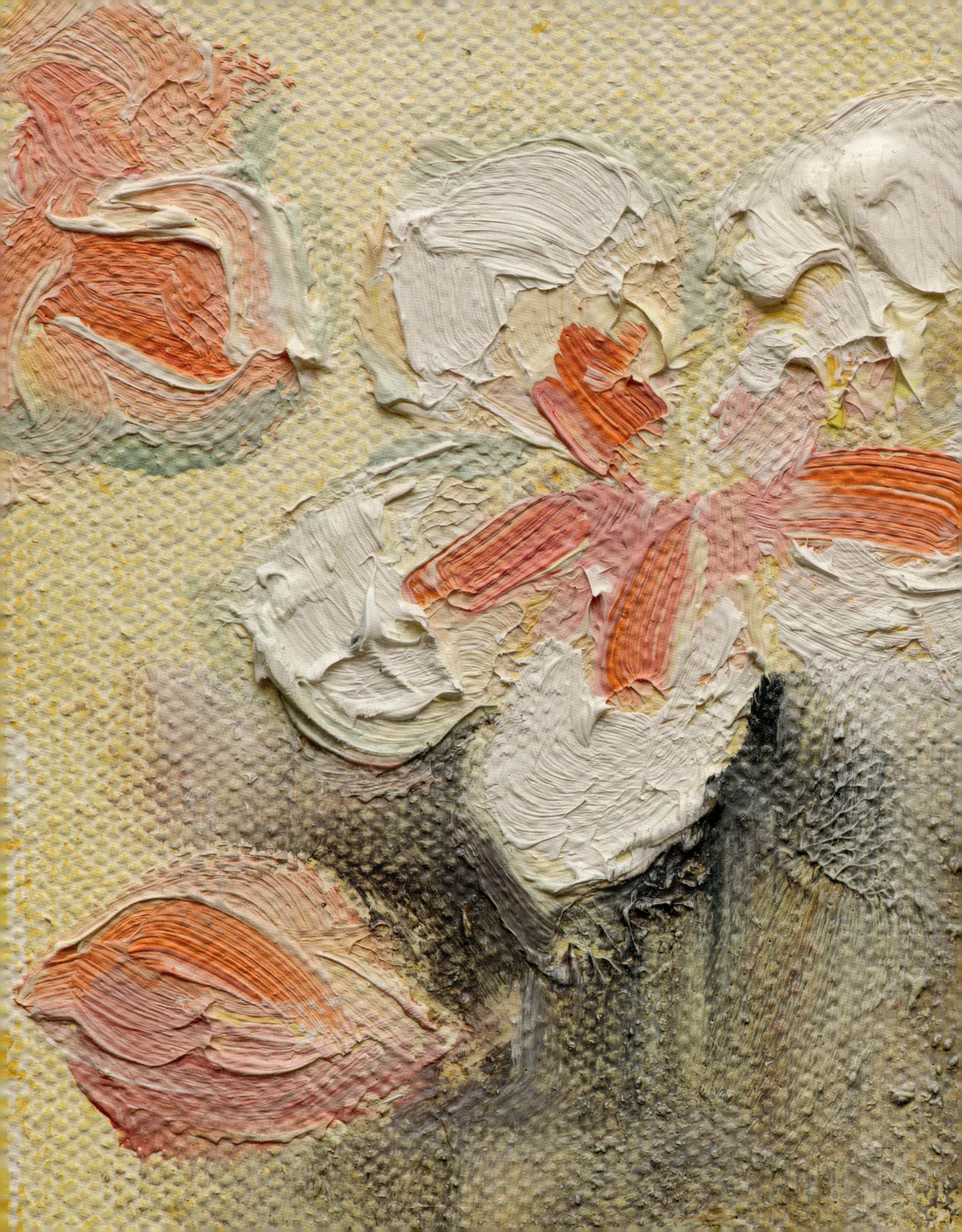

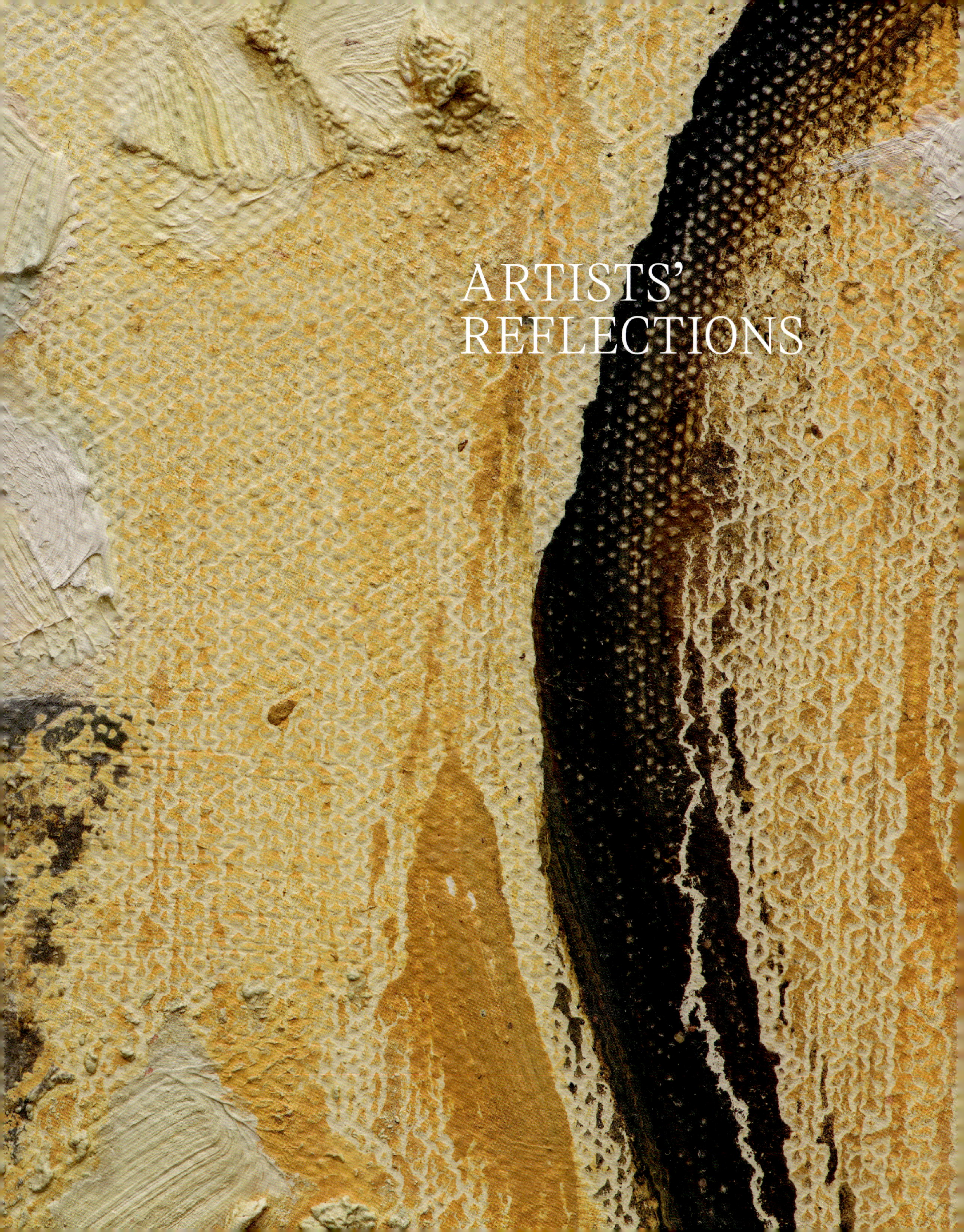
ARTISTS'
REFLECTIONS

ENRIQUE CHAGOYA

AMERICAN, B. MEXICO CITY, MEXICO, 1953;
LIVES IN SAN FRANCISCO, CALIFORNIA

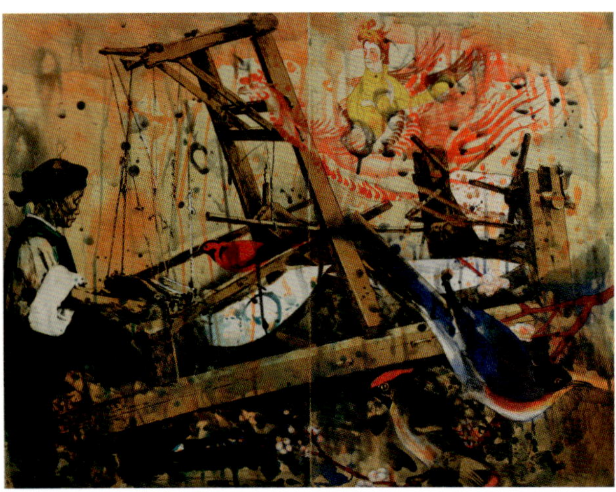

Hung Liu
Women Working: Loom, 1999
Etching, 40¾ × 50 in. (103.5 × 127 cm)

Hung Liu's artwork teaches us, without trying, that context makes art meaningful. The first time I saw a small painting she did while in a reeducation camp in China—when it was on view in her exhibition at the San Francisco Museum of Modern Art a few years ago—I was amazed at how such seemingly harmless landscapes were so subversive because they were made while hiding from the guards. In a different context, those paintings could be seen as skillful exercises in impressionism. However, once one thinks about the reason they were so small (to be hidden from the authorities), they take on a different meaning.

Since moving to the United States, Liu has been equally subversive—beginning with her humorous 1988 self-portrait painting of her resident alien card, which she signed, "Cookie, Fortune" (cat. 18). I myself had a similar card and had a good laugh the first time I saw the painting. Although now we are both naturalized citizens of this country, the original branding as aliens (as if from outer space) stays with us. Through my experiences of living in Mexico, the United States, and France, I have come to realize that immigration is not a change of passport but rather an inner change. We become all the places and cultures we move to and learn to love, with a whole new world of affections. I often feel like I belong to nowhere and to everywhere, a citizen of a borderless country, and I find that on many occasions, I run into other borderless country citizens like Liu, who is one of my dearest friends. A real borderless comrade in art.

In general, Liu's work is a critique of history that is pleasing on the surface, but upon closer exploration, her art exposes social inequalities. Her focus on women, workers, farmers, and even self-portraits go beyond identity politics. This can be seen in her most recent paintings, which reimagine Dorothea Lange's portrayals of American migrant families as they lived through the Great Depression (cats. 45–52).

At home, in our bedroom, we have one of her beautiful etchings from 1999, depicting a woman working on a loom surrounded by birds. I think of it as a visual poem. It's the first thing we see when we get up and is a great way to start the day, any day.

JUDY CHICAGO

AMERICAN, B. CHICAGO, ILLINOIS, 1939;
LIVES IN NEW MEXICO

Although I didn't know a lot about Hung Liu, I vividly remember seeing—and admiring—her installation *Going Away, Coming Home* (2006) whenever we flew into the Oakland airport. I thought it was one of the few pieces of airport art that really communicated any personal meaning and seemed so well suited to its environment. As I began to see more of her work, I repeatedly felt that I was seeing a truly authentic artist, one who was able to translate her unique personal history into images that reached out to a broad audience. When I finally met her in the summer of 2019, she seemed surprised when I told her how much of a fan I was. In addition to the excellence of her art, she struck me as a lovely human being, one whose work and persona transmitted a quiet wisdom as well as a formidable talent.

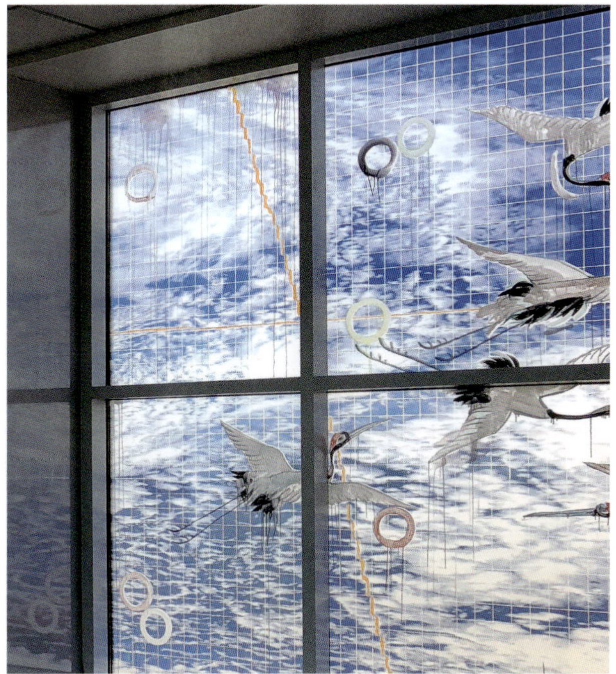

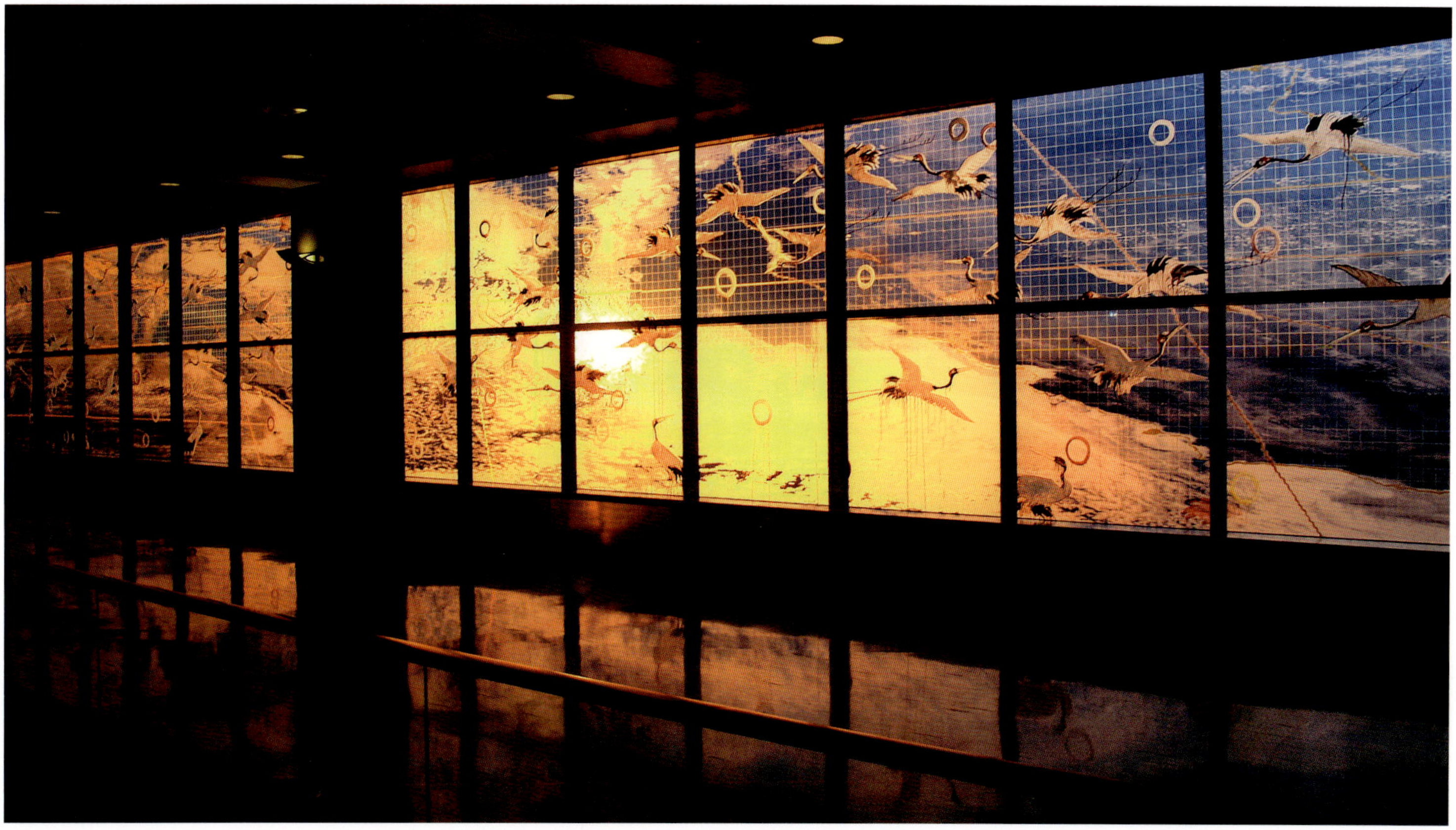

Hung Liu
Going Away, Coming Home, 2006
Paint on glass, 10 ft. × 160 ft. (3.1 × 48.8 m)
Commissioned by the Port of Oakland and installed at the
Oakland International Airport, Terminal 2

"

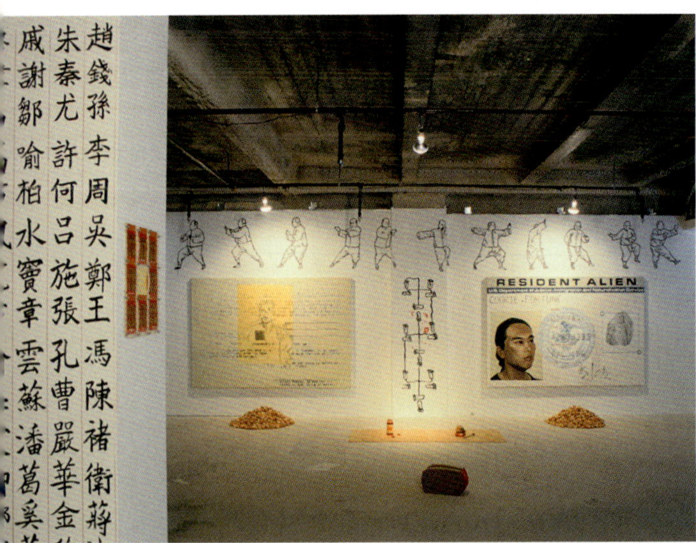

Installation view of Hung Liu's exhibition *Resident Alien* at Capp Street Project, San Francisco, 1988. Capp Street Project Archive at California College of the Arts Libraries, San Francisco, Calif.

MEL CHIN

AMERICAN, B. HOUSTON, TEXAS, 1951;
LIVES IN NEW YORK

As children of immigrants, we were warned that, if we didn't behave, the 绿衣 *lok yee* ("green clothes") would take us away. Born in the United States, the threat wasn't real for us, but for my grandfather, it was. The Chinese Exclusion Act was active from 1880 until 1943. It created "bachelor societies," made up of men without their wives and families, stranded in the Chinatowns across the United States.

Grandfather was called to leave his village and family in China in the 1920s because he could play an instrument, the *pipa,* that a deceased "bachelor" had played. The elders, stuck in the United States, needed him to fill lonely stretches between work hours that only a live musical ensemble could deliver. Fake papers were procured, and he landed in New York. He finally reunited with my grandmother in the 1960s, but died within a few years after their reunion. They had been apart for forty years.

I had a studio in New York for over twenty years, not far from Mott Street, where my grandfather once lived. I was deeply enmeshed in the contemporary art world, and that is where I first saw Hung Liu's work. When I encountered her *Resident Alien* (cat. 18), the work deeply resonated with me, bringing to mind all of my family's early trials in the United States. A painting of an ID card was laced with humor, with the name "Cookie, Fortune," and poignance. I saw a defiant portrait that reminded me of my mother. It captured her look when she tossed her U.S. naturalization workbook into the trash, proclaiming English to be an inadequate tongue.

Citizenship and its challenges were well known in the Chin home. My father came over the same way as my grandfather, with a paper name; but he broke the curse of the Chinese Exclusion Act by joining to fight as an American GI in World War II. After the war, as a citizen, he orchestrated waves of immigration for his mother, brother, and sister, and the many relatives we would meet as we grew up in Texas. He emphasized to us that citizenship was the highest virtue, over making money, over excellence in academics.

By the time I was invited to give a lecture at Mills College, where Liu presided, I was familiar with the prowess and messages of her paintings. I remember that when she introduced me, it was not as one of their many visiting artists, but simply as "Citizen Chin." She said it as if she had consulted with my father, and I was surprised and honored. I knew I had to reckon that Liu has the rare capacity to channel what is meaningful to another human being, and to us all, through her art.

YU HONG

CHINESE, B. XI'AN, CHINA, 1966;
LIVES IN BEIJING

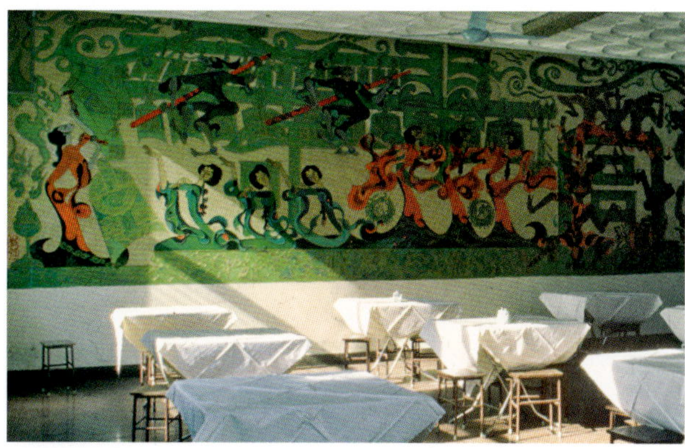

Hung Liu
Music of the Great Earth, 1981
Mural at the Central Academy of Fine Arts, Beijing
(no longer extant)

When I was studying at the Central Academy of Fine Arts in Beijing in 1984, the new students' dormitory had just sprung up. This landmark twelve-story building was a skyscraper in my eyes. The largest space on the first floor was the faculty dining hall, which featured a large-scale mural. Mysterious grayish-green hues; splendid gilded embossments; elegant, historical chime bells; and scenes of music—this full-fledged display of what was then a highly fashionable style of ethnic decoration was Hung Liu's mural *Music of the Great Earth.* In the early 1980s, China had just introduced the reforms and opening-up policies, and it became stylish to commission large murals for new buildings. Liu was granted this honor on the occasion of her graduation project, which demonstrated her artistic mastery.

Later on, Liu went to the United States to study. As a student of Allan Kaprow, she was directly involved in the avant-garde art practices of the 1980s and 1990s. In her highly experimental and widely recognized works, she addressed the identity and living conditions of Asian women born outside of the United States. As she grew older, her works reflected her larger accumulation of experiences as well as her ever-increasing control over the picture. Melancholy colors are eroded by unrestrained flows of turpentine oil; floating circles emerge between blurry figures that look like old photographs. These images take us back in time

and space to pursue the truth about historical events and to remember the lives left in the past.

In 1995, during a period of increasing urbanization in China, the Central Academy of Fine Arts left the city center and moved to Wangjing, outside the Fourth Ring Road. The "skyscraper" of my memory was razed to the ground. After years of ups and downs, Liu's mural, with its variegated colors, disappeared, taking with it not only a symbol of her youth but also the innocent student days of our generation. Today, China's pace is so fast that people cannot afford to spend the time or the money required to hold on to such memories. Even Liu herself has not kept many of the materials related to her mural. It may be a kind of fate that urges her constant rediscovery of the past and her mission to use her works, which are full of traces of time, preserving vanishing memories and transient lives.

Translation by Marco Betelli

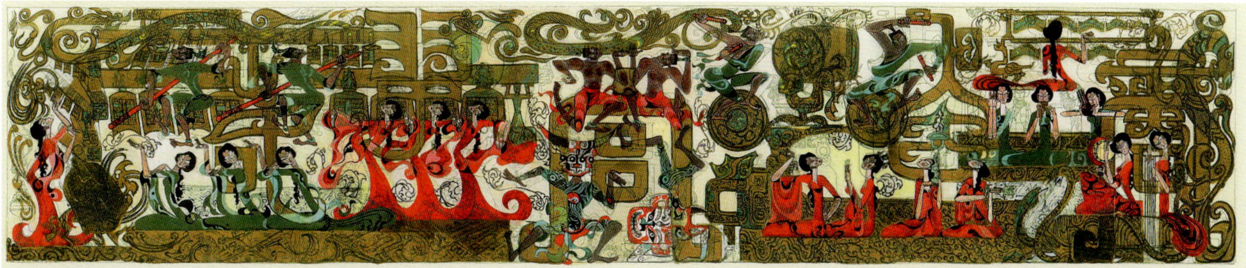

Hung Liu
Music of the Great Earth, Variation I, 2008
Ink on paper, 18 × 90 in. (45.5 × 225 cm)

MARTIN MULL

AMERICAN, B. CHICAGO, ILLINOIS, 1943;
LIVES IN LOS ANGELES, CALIFORNIA

As a fellow painter, I stand in awe of Hung Liu's competence and steadfast vision. Her sense of visual adventure never flinches, even when faced with the often-limiting constraints of portraiture—seamlessly sharing her respect for her subject and her romance with the paint that describes it.

AMY SHERALD

AMERICAN, B. COLUMBUS, GEORGIA, 1973;
LIVES IN JERSEY CITY, NEW JERSEY

I was introduced to Hung Liu's work as a young artist coming out of college in 1997. I was immediately captivated by her haunting images and the intersections of photography and painting in her work. Liu and I both recognize that the picture is just the beginning of a story. A moment frozen in time, waiting to be mined. By putting brush to canvas, she teases out new information and gives another life to the camera-captured picture. Painting beyond the moment of exposure is how she thinks of it, as she explores identity, history, gender, and representation. Photographs for Liu are not only a bridge from the past to the future, but a bridge from one world to another.

STEPHANIE SYJUCO

AMERICAN, B. 1974, MANILA, PHILIPPINES;
LIVES IN SAN FRANCISCO, CALIFORNIA

Identification cards, especially those issued by national governments, determine how one is recognized within a given society. Whether declaring one's citizenship, the right to travel, or one's ability to engage in an activity, such as driving, identification cards symbolize both freedom and limitations, depending on who is being granted what rights and privileges. Issued by the U.S. government, the permanent resident card, or "green card," as it became known due to its light-green color, held a particular contradiction in declaring the bearer as existing both inside *and* outside a system of belonging. Emblazoned with "Resident Alien" in bold letters across the top, it signaled that the cardholder was intrinsically foreign, and yet, *allowed* to be here. These two words conjure up both an otherworldly alien invasion as well as domestic tranquility, creating a frictional, contradictory reality for those who are issued such cards.

I first saw Hung Liu's self-portrait *Resident Alien* as a young art student in the 1990s, and although it was via a grainy slide image in a darkened classroom, it still hit me like a ton of bricks (cat. 18). As an immigrant from the Philippines who also had in my wallet the card that labeled me as both "of and not of," I identified with the anxiety of this work and chafed at the systematic way in which a single card could function to make me feel strange, foreign, and exempt. When asked to show my card, I was always embarrassed, as if the provisional nature of my status might result in my ejection at any moment. I knew I was supposed to feel grateful for having it, for being allowed to be here.

In particular, Asian immigrants—and by extension, Asian Americans—have always been seen as perpetual foreigners, no matter how long one's family may have resided in this country or how much one may have appeared to assimilate. Liu's painting was the first work I saw that explicitly mirrored my own situation, and its mere existence bolstered a sense of early confidence that I could make work that defies these conscriptions of meaning and forges an identity of resistance.

Resident Alien uses the language of the identification card to critique and defy governmental power structures. The satirical "Cookie, Fortune," an Asian woman who represents Liu, evokes the artist's status as a simplistic stereotype—one imposed upon American immigrants and "foreigners" across the spectrum. Liu's simple turn of enlarging this tiny object exposed the oversized influence of how this card functions to simultaneously grant access and alienate the person who must carry it.

Today, over three decades later, with the rising attacks on immigrants within the United States as well as the government's hostile efforts to restrict access further, the anxieties expressed in *Resident Alien* remain front and center. While contemporary "green cards" have retired the label "Resident Alien" (opting for the more humane moniker "Permanent Resident"), Liu's painting stands as both a literal translation of a historical "document" as well as a testament to the persistence of this nation's paradoxical past.

LAVA THOMAS

AMERICAN, B. LOS ANGELES, CALIFORNIA, 1958;
LIVES IN BERKELEY, CALIFORNIA

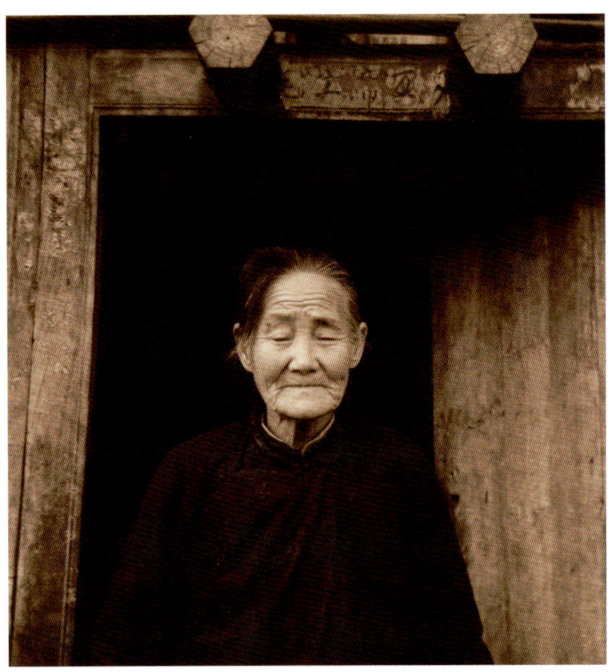

Hung Liu
Untitled from the series *Za Zhong* (*Bastard Paintings*), 2007
Resin on wood, 5 × 4½ in. (12.7 × 11.4 cm)

Not long ago, I received a gift from Hung Liu: a small portrait of an elderly Chinese woman from her *Za Zhong* (*Bastard Paintings*) series. The woman's eyes appear closed, and she stands in a doorway dressed in black. Her face, drawn with lines of age and years of labor, reveals toil and weariness. Standing straight-backed and cropped at the waist, her countenance conveys a strong, quiet dignity. The source photograph, *Village Photograph 5* (Peasant Grandma), was taken while Liu worked in the Beijing countryside during the Cultural Revolution (cat. 4). In the finished painting, the image has been transformed: transferred onto a wood support the size and heft of a child's large building block, it is gilded and covered with resin and shines like a gold ingot.

The portrait sits on my mantle. In the late afternoon, sunlight slices the room and slowly lowers itself to where the painting rests. When the beam of light reaches the painting, the room glows and the old woman's face is illuminated. As the early evening light moves across the portrait's surface, the sun's reflection grows so bright that the woman's face momentarily disappears; minutes later, when the sunlight passes, it appears again.

This jewel of a gift speaks to the exceptional generosity of Liu's spirit, which is reflected in her tireless production of paintings and prints; in her decades of teaching and mentoring young artists at Mills College; and in her willingness to extend herself to artists like me. It permeates her work, too: care and veneration are evident in Liu's use of paint to transform and elevate anonymous faces from historical photographs. Liu's paintings confer power upon the powerless, restoring and affirming the essential humanity of her subjects.

In Liu, I recognize a fellow agent of historical inquiry, perpetually interrogating and humanizing the photographic gaze. She remains an inspiring, galvanizing force: a reminder—both in her imagery and personal example—of women's limitless capacity to shape history.

CARRIE MAE WEEMS

AMERICAN, B. 1953, PORTLAND, OREGON;
LIVES IN SYRACUSE, NEW YORK

The art historian Simon Schama wrote, "Great art has dreadful manners. The hushed reverence of the gallery can fool you into believing masterpieces are polite things, visions that soothe, charm and beguile, but actually they are thugs. Merciless and wily, the greatest paintings grab you in a headlock, rough up your composure and then proceed in short order to rearrange your sense of reality" (*The Power of Art* [New York: Ecco, 2006]).

With exceptional skill, Hung Liu draws us into a world that informs, describes, and turns our notions of the world upside down. Through sheer grit, muscle, and determination, she deploys the wiles of sublime beauty to captivate, pull us in, and bid us look.

By making the unspeakable palatable, we come to know the troubled space of lived experience, of horror, loss, pain, struggle, work, and forced labor. Liu tells a tale rarely heard and seldom seen. Her paintings, breathtaking in their beauty, use unsurpassed skill to reveal the push of a people caught in the turmoil of upheaval, people trapped by oppressive systems meant to control. Whether exploring the conditions of women and children, the brutality of the Cultural Revolution, or the collapse of American feudalism, Liu's paintings humanize the lives of everyday people. She's remarkable.

The one thing I know for sure is that she did not come to play! She can paint, and had she been born a man—WOW—the doors that would have been opened for this extraordinary artist!

LIU XIAODONG

CHINESE, B. JINCHENG, CHINA, 1963;
LIVES IN BEIJING

In 1993, I went to New York, the super world filled with art legends that prompted me to wander through its galleries. The art center then was in SoHo, where there were art openings every Thursday evening. Danqing Chen took me around and, with limited time and my feet beginning to hurt, we visited some of the more reputable galleries. In front of the better galleries were usually masses of black; New Yorkers loved to wear black.

We pushed through the black mass, only to find the inside even more crowded. Danqing told me that this was a solo exhibition for Hung Liu, the only Chinese artist to enter the American mainstream art circle. On the wall was a self-portrait by Liu that measured about three meters tall. The outer frame of the canvas followed the outline of her scarf, instead of the traditional square-shaped canvas. The old-world colors and thin traces of linseed oil drips showed some faraway emotion. There was also a green cornfield that looked as if it was swaying in the rain. No rain was painted, but the canvas appeared moist. No one else can mix such a gray-green color or let it fall so naturally on the canvas like the greenness of a rainstorm, or the green-ness in deep layers of ice. Once I came to understand Liu's family history, I realized the meaning of that green: the kind of green embed-ded in the depth of one's heart when one is uncertain what to search for. Just from the field of green and her three-meter-tall self-portrait, I understood her former studies of realist painting in China. The realist style she deploys is a manifestation of the mysterious natural trickle within her inner heart: this dripping style in her later works became progressively more natural and more unstoppable.

Over the next several years, I made several trips to the United States. In many museums and on my strolls, I often found my thoughts interrupted by Liu's paintings. Sometimes the image was a monochro-matic episode in the life of an ancient Chinese woman. Sometimes it was of children playing. Sometimes it was flowers and birds, fish and insects. Up close, Liu's style looks natural, with earnest and flowing strokes; at some distance, the faded hues emanate a mysterious glow.

Later on, I collected many of her catalogues, which were always plain and very thin. When, by accident, I flipped through Jeff Kelley's book on Allan Kaprow, I saw pictures of Liu at the site of performance art pieces and learned that she was actually a student of Kaprow's, the father of the Happenings movement. When she first arrived in the United States in the early 1980s, she had also made many installation projects, including a pyramid of fortune cookies and a visa to protest the question of identity.

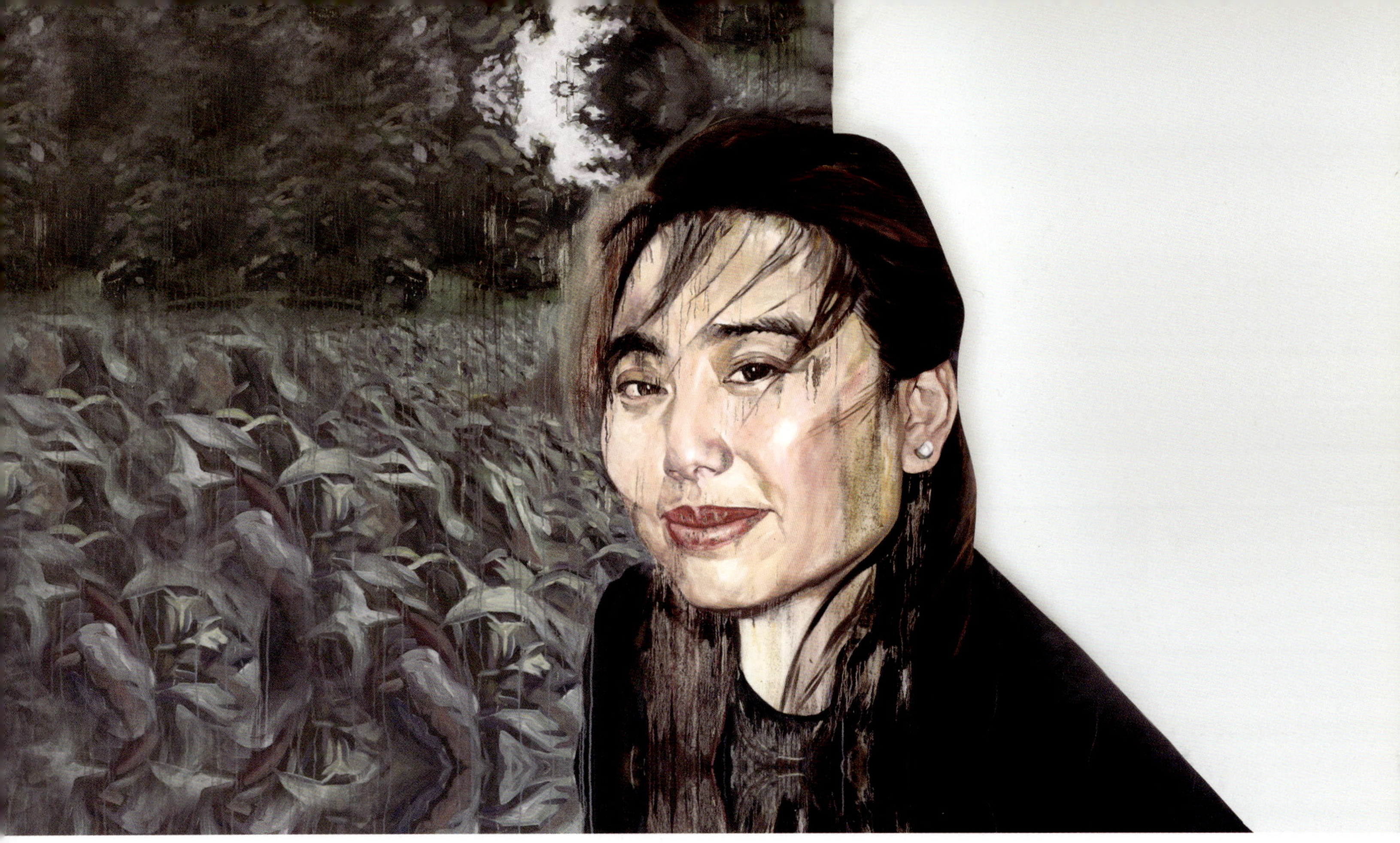

Hung Liu
Burial at Little Golden Village, 1993
Oil on shaped canvas, 74 × 96 in. (188 × 243.8 cm)
Collection of Rebecca Lee and Jeremy Steinbaum, MD

The old Central Academy of Fine Arts, due to China's urbanization and commercialization, has already been demolished. Within the debris lay the remnants of Liu's mural. This giant mural that once covered the cafeteria wall was one of her works from the early 1980s. That was her graduation piece. When I went to school in the mid-1980s, every morning was spent eating and playing in front of this mural. The now-vanished mural will always be a part of my memory.

In 2006, she invited me to be the guest speaker at her college in Oakland, California (Mills College). During a break, we painted each other's portraits. Usually her booming voice, spoken with Manchurian tones, brings me a great deal of laughter. But this time, while painting her wide, hearty face, I felt calm. I saw that her heavy eyebrows were knitted almost together, as if the mystery and sentiment of her work originated there.

Translation by Ling Chen Kelley (adapted from a 2006 reflection)

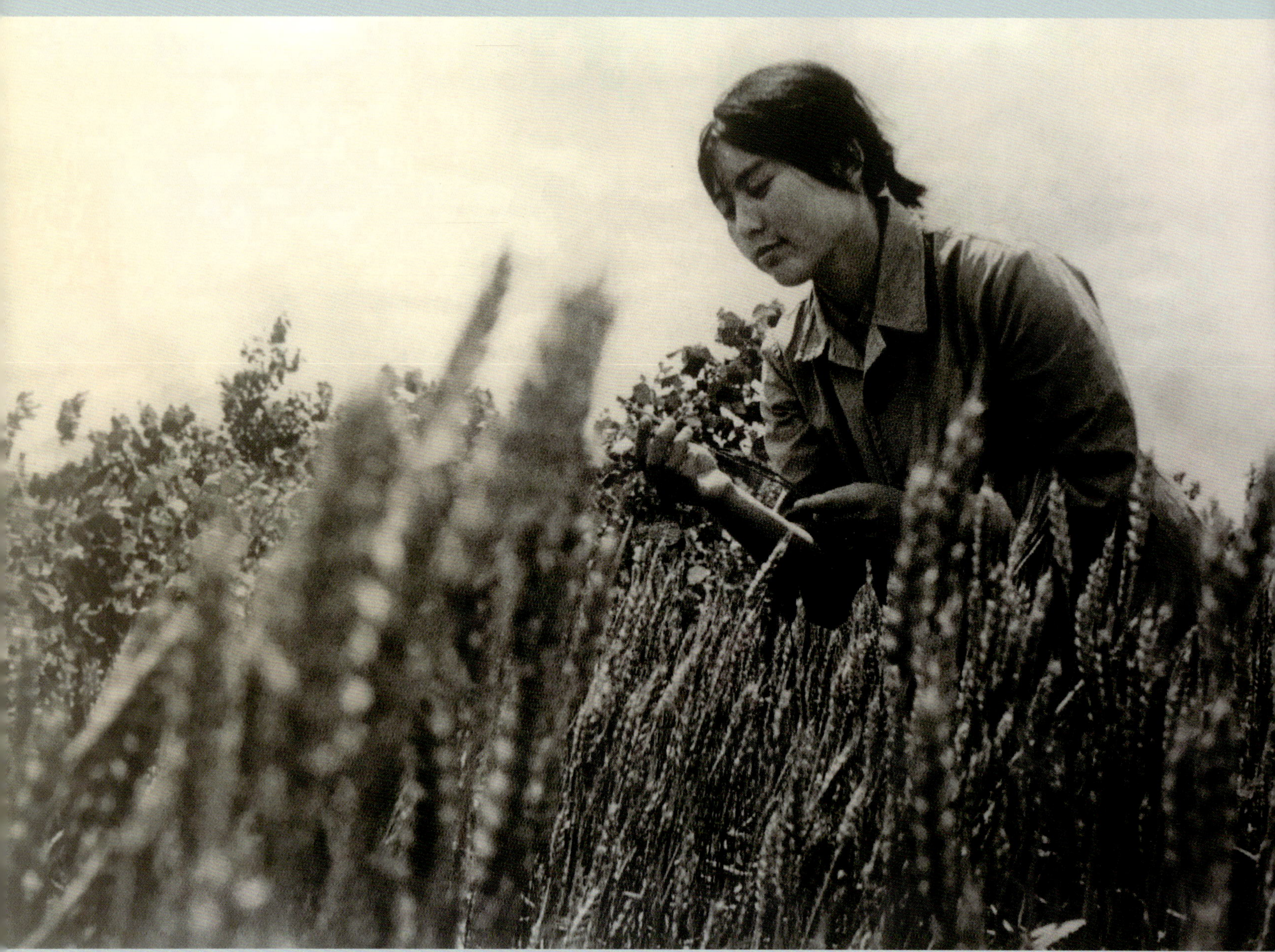

Hung Liu in a wheat field, c. 1971–72.

Chronology

1948

Hung Liu is born on February 17, 1948 (January 8 on the Chinese calendar, Year of the Rat), in Changchun, China.

Changchun, previously the capital city for the Japanese puppet dynasty of the exiled Emperor Puyi (1906–1967), is defended by the Nationalist Army (Kuomintang) of Chiang Kai-shek against the advance of Communist forces led by Lin Biao and Mao Zedong.

Liu's father, Xia Peng, is a captain in the Kuomintang army. The city is under siege for months, and starvation and panic ensue despite attempts by U.S. planes to drop food and supplies into Changchun.

In September, Liu's family flees the city looking for food, crossing over into Communist territory. Liu's father is detained by Communist troops at a checkpoint outside Changchun. She will not see him again until 1994.

Seeking refuge, Liu, her mother, aunt, uncle, and grandparents make their way to a village in the Manchurian countryside.

Changchun falls to the Communists in October. Soon after, Liu and her family return to Changchun, "the dead city."

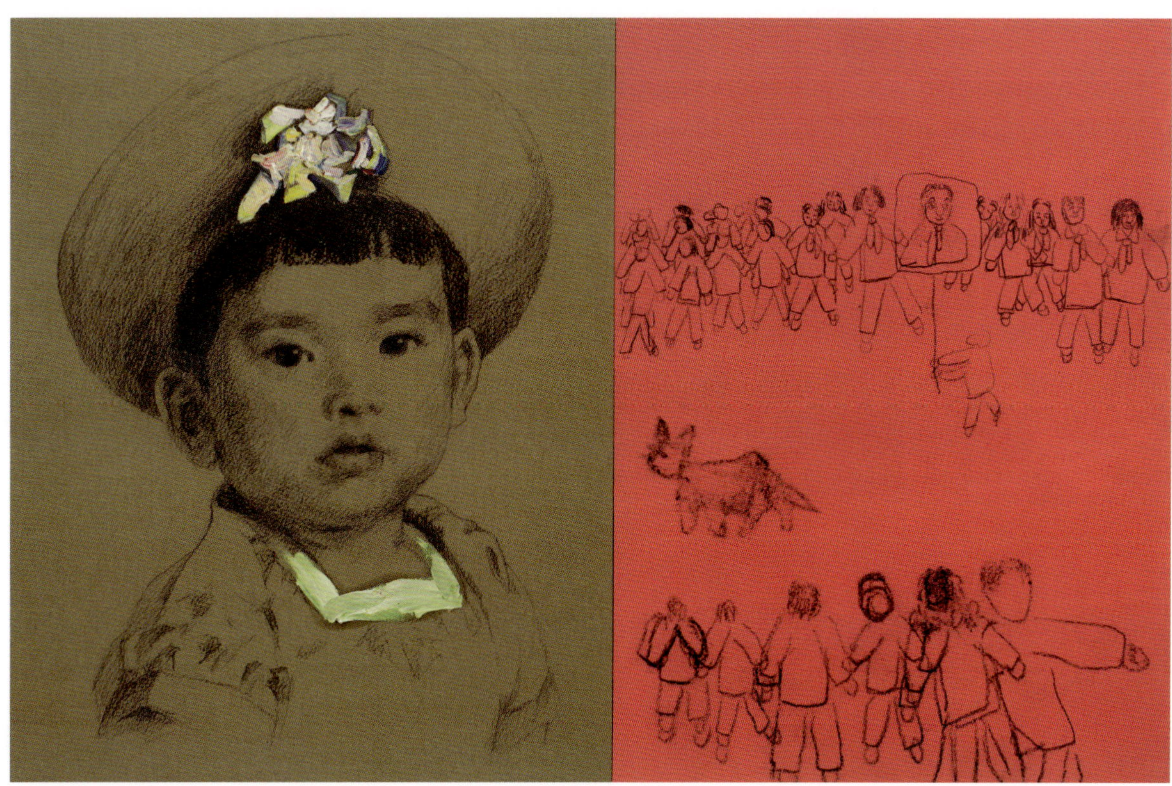

Hung Liu
Rat Year 1948, 2008
Oil on linen and mixed media on wood panel, 64 × 100 in. (162.6 × 254 cm)

1955

After completing kindergarten, Liu begins elementary school.

1957

Mao Zedong initiates the "Great Leap Forward," an attempt to catch up with the West in agricultural and industrial production.

1959

At age eleven, while standing with other family members at the Changchun train station, Liu begs her mother to allow her to accompany her aunt, Liu Zongyu, to her home in Beijing. Liu's mother allows her to go "with only the clothes on her back." The following year, Liu's grandparents and mother follow Liu, settling in with Zongyu in Beijing.

As a result of Mao's "Great Leap Forward," tens of millions of people in China die from starvation between 1959 and 1961.

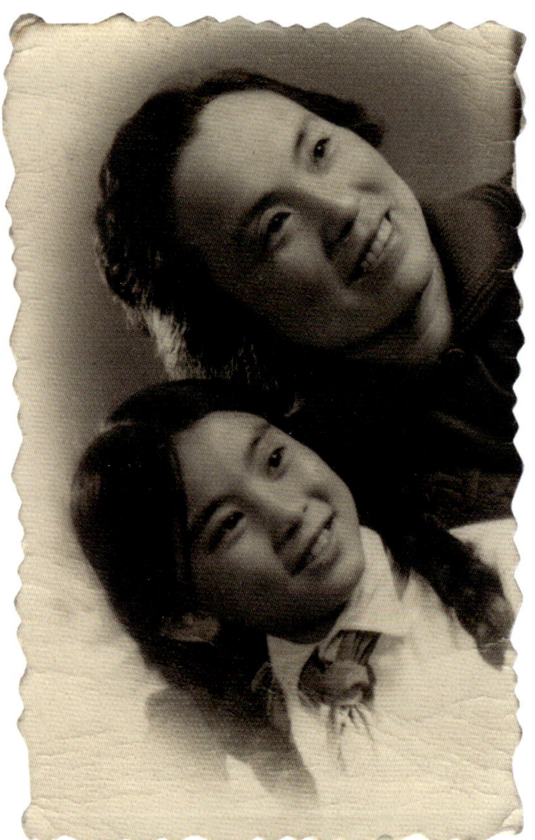

Hung Liu and her mother, c. 1955.

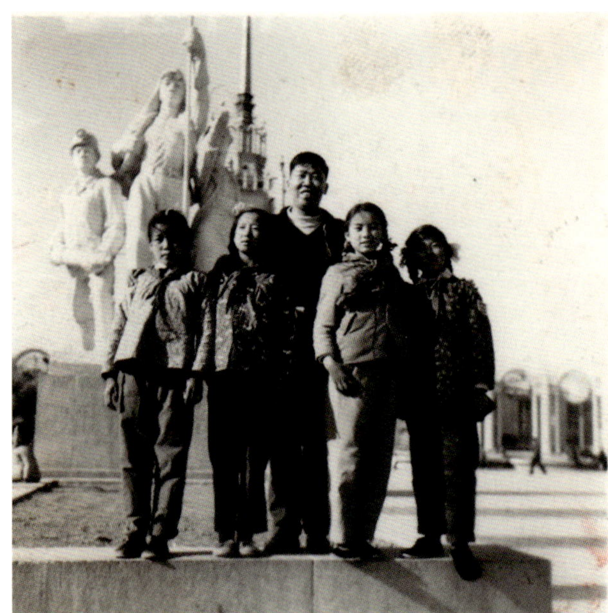

Hung Liu with her elementary school art teacher and classmates in Beijing, c. 1959.

1961

Liu gains admission to an elite boarding school, the Girls' Middle School attached to Beijing Normal University. She consistently performs at the top of her class, which includes children of top officials in the Communist Party.

1962

The famine finally begins to ebb in the cities.

Chinese-Soviet relations deteriorate.

Liu's grandfather, Liu Weihua, a scholar of the monasteries of Qianshan (Mount Qian) in Manchuria, dies (see cat. 44 and Moss essay, figs. 6, 12, 13).

1966

As Liu, age eighteen, prepares to graduate from the Girls' Middle School attached to Beijing Normal University, the Cultural Revolution begins. Mao unleashes millions of Red Guards in an effort to purge Chinese society of Western, "counterrevolutionary," influences.

Schools close across the country, and Liu is unable to receive her diploma.

Mao decrees free train travel for young people. Although not a Red Guard, Liu rides the trains throughout China—to Xinjiang, Guangzhou, Harbin, Dalian, Shanghai, and Tianjin.

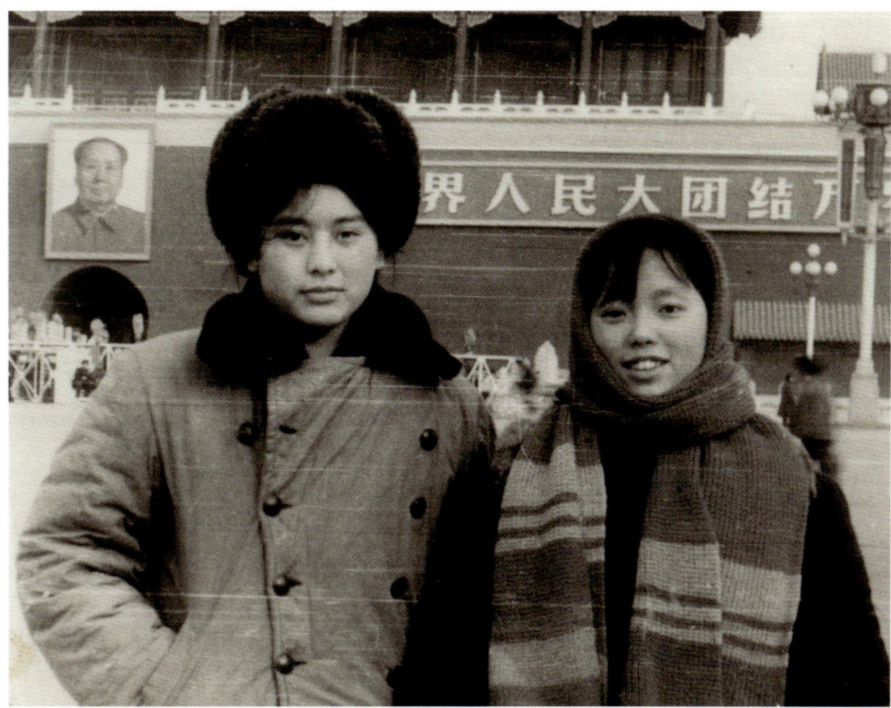

Hung Liu and her cousin Xiaofang in Tiananmen Square, 1966. The women switched their headwear for the photo. The artist wears a People's Liberation Army military hat, while her cousin wears the red scarf that Liu's mother knitted for her.

1968

Liu is sent for proletarian "reeducation" among the peasants in the countryside. While in Dadu Lianghe, she works in rice and wheat fields seven days a week for four years. During this time, she learns to use a camera and makes her first photographs (see cats. 1–4, and Lim essay, figs. 8–11).

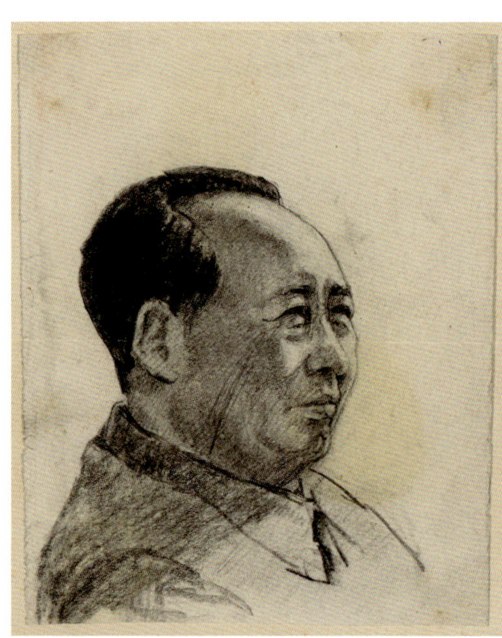

Hung Liu
Sketch of Mao Zedong, 1968–71
Graphite on paper, 5 × 3¾ in. (12.7 × 9.5 cm)

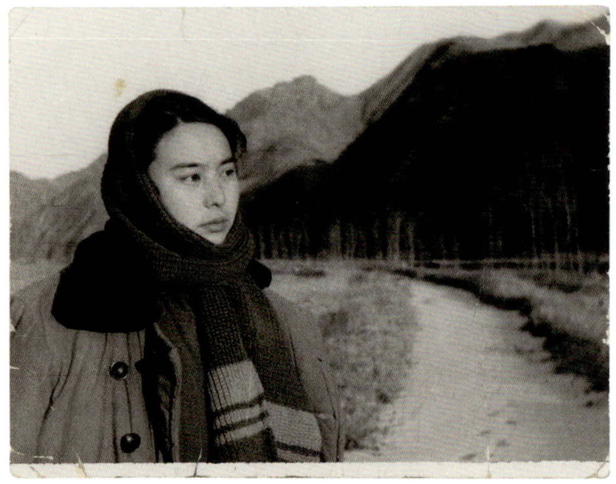

Hung Liu in the countryside, 1969–71.

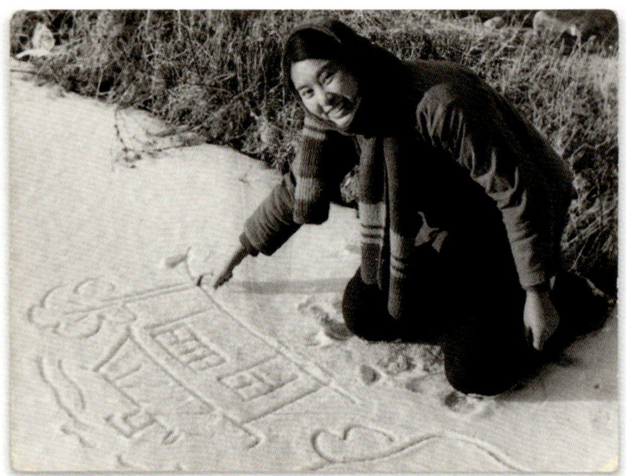

Hung Liu draws on a snow-covered field while in the countryside for reeducation, 1969–71.

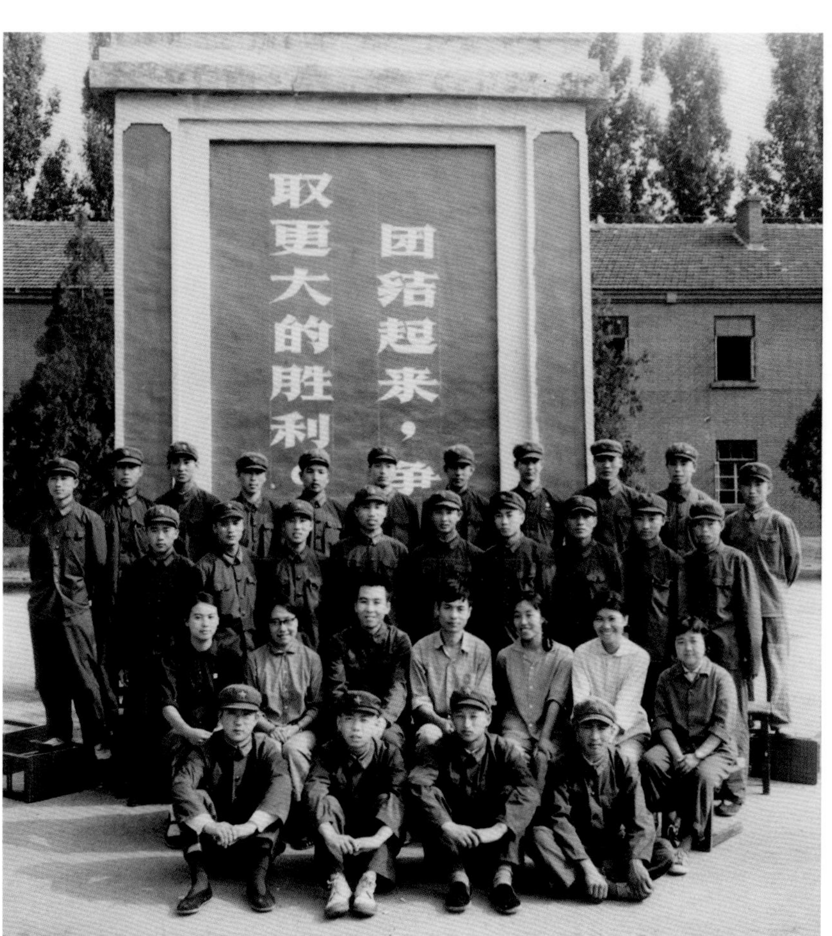

Hung Liu (second row, far left) during her military training at Beijing Teacher's College, 1973–74. She is in the company of People's Liberation Army soldiers and officers.

1972

U.S. President Richard Nixon arrives in China on February 21.

Schools begin to reopen. Liu enters the revolutionary entertainment department of Beijing Teacher's College to study art and art education. The Chinese Communist Party's policy insists that artists document (that is, idealize) the lives of farmers, soldiers, and workers, causing Liu to use creative means when creating and storing her paintings of Chinese daily life.

1975

Liu graduates from college and begins teaching art at the Jingshan School in Beijing.

Asked to teach children's art on national television, Liu gives weekly lessons from the studios of the Central China Television station. She attains unexpected fame, and her program, *How to Draw and Paint,* runs for several years.

1976

Chinese leader Zhou Enlai dies.

While traveling in northern China with a group of school art teachers, Liu experiences the Tang Shan earthquake, which kills an estimated one million people.

Mao Zedong dies. His body lies in state, and Liu is among the millions who pass by in procession.

The Gang of Four, including Mao's widow, Jiang Qing, is arrested.

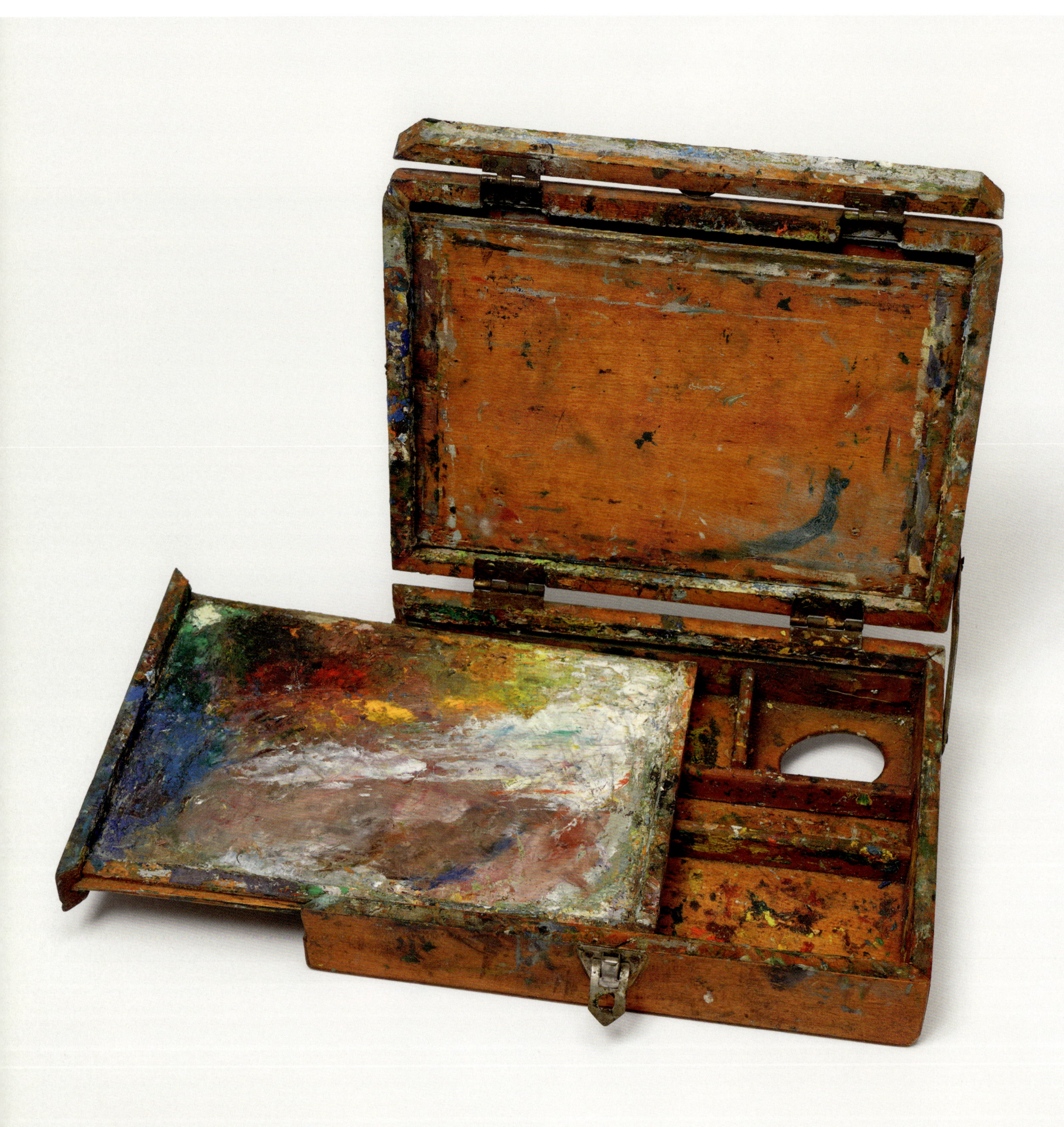

Hung Liu's paint box, which she used in the countryside in the early 1970s.

1977

At age twenty-nine, Liu marries an astronomer. They separate within a year.

1978

Liu gives birth to a son, Ling Chen (see Moss essay, fig. 16).

Deng Xiaoping emerges as the Paramount Leader of China.

The "Open Door Policy" toward the West is established.

Liu participates in a portraiture exhibition at the Winter Palace in Beijing.

1979

After taking China's national entrance exams, Liu is accepted by the country's two leading art schools: the Central Academy of Arts and Crafts and the Central Academy of Fine Arts (CAFA), both in Beijing. She decides to attend the latter, majoring in mural painting.

Liu travels to the famous Buddhist cave murals at Dunhuang, in the Gobi Desert along the Silk Road. During her stay, she meets artist Ai Weiwei and has a good experience until she becomes gravely ill, perhaps from drinking local water. She is transported back to Beijing and spends months recovering.

Liu's grandmother—Wang Jushou—dies.

1980

Liu returns to Dunhuang, where she spends forty days studying and copying the Buddhist cave murals. She also visits famous religious shrines throughout China.

Liu begins *Music of the Great Earth,* a graduation mural project designed for the Foreign Students' Dining Hall at CAFA (see p. 175).

She applies to the University of California, San Diego (UCSD), for admission to graduate school in the department of visual arts.

Liu finalizes the divorce with her first husband.

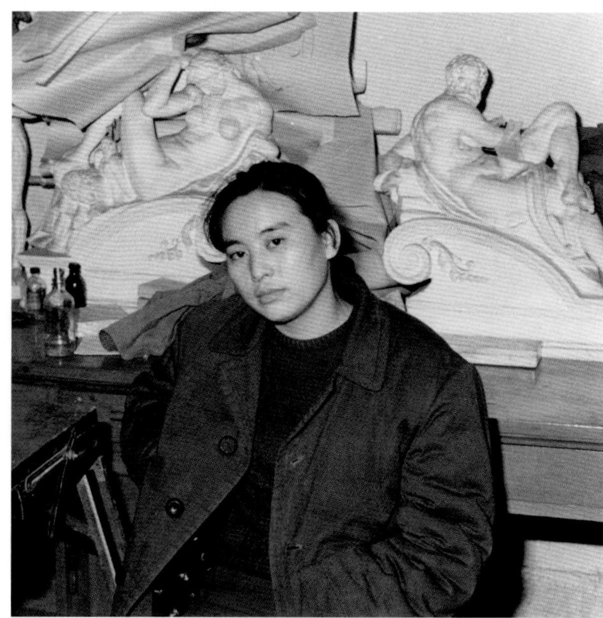

Hung Liu during her studies at the Central Academy of Fine Arts, Beijing, 1979–81. She is shown in her studio space with replicas of sculptures by Michelangelo.

1981

Liu completes *Music of the Great Earth* and begins teaching at CAFA.

She is accepted to UCSD, but the Chinese government refuses her bid for a passport.

1982

While teaching at CAFA, Liu studies traditional calligraphy and stamp-making with Niu Jun, an aging scholar and Peking Opera playwright. She works with him for three years.

1984

Liu obtains a limited passport for temporary travel to Hong Kong, hoping that it will be easier to travel from there to the United States. While in Hong Kong, she receives word from the Chinese Cultural Ministry that her request for a passport has been granted, and she returns to Beijing.

On October 26, Liu boards a China Air 747 in Beijing and departs for San Francisco. At the airport, she bids farewell to her mother, aunt, and son. It is the first time she has ever been on an airplane. She arrives at San Francisco International Airport with two suitcases and twenty dollars, spending one dollar to rent a luggage cart before flying on to San Diego.

Liu begins graduate studies at UCSD (see Moss essay, fig. 10). Her fellow graduate students include Lorna Simpson, Christine Tamblyn, and Jeff Kelley (her future husband).

1985

Allan Kaprow, known for his contributions to the Happenings of the 1960s, asks Liu's class to create art from the contents of a dumpster. The assignment leaves a strong impression on Liu, as it strays from her formal training in Beijing.

She participates in a residency at the Sun Valley Center for the Arts and Humanities in Idaho.

In November, she has her first one-person exhibition at the Sheppard Gallery, University of Nevada, Reno, where she uses the whole space for a mural installation based on the ancient grotto caves of Dunhuang.

1986

Liu visits New York and its museums, seeing important works of Western art for the first time, including paintings by Pablo Picasso, Joan Miró, Jackson Pollock, and Robert Rauschenberg.

In the spring, she marries Kelley at a friend's house in San Antonio, Texas. Her son, mother, and aunt travel from Beijing to join her and Kelley in San Diego.

At year's end, Liu presents her graduate exhibition before she and her family relocate to Arlington, Texas, where Kelley has accepted a teaching job at the University of Texas at Arlington.

1987

Liu teaches a Chinese art history course at the University of Texas at Arlington and works as an artist-in-residence for local public schools.

She shows her work in several Dallas/Fort Worth–area exhibitions.

Liu begins working as a security guard at the Kimbell Art Museum in Fort Worth. While there, she meets Emily Sano, who later becomes the director of the Asian Art Museum of San Francisco. They remain close friends.

Liu begins her series of drawings entitled *Where Is Mao?* (see cats. 8–17).

Liu's mother and aunt return to Beijing. Her son, Ling Chen, remains with her and Kelley.

1988

Liu spends the summer as a resident artist at the Capp Street Project in San Francisco. During that time, she produces a mural, *Reading Room,* for the community room of Chinese for Affirmative Action in Chinatown's historic Kuo Building. Her mixed-media installation, *Resident Alien,* is presented at Capp Street Project (in the Monadnock Building) as the culmination of her research into the history of Chinese immigration to California (see cat. 18).

1989

In the spring, students in Beijing begin assembling in Tiananmen Square, resulting, on June 4, in their violent removal by the People's Liberation Army.

The Tiananmen events serve as inspiration for Liu, who borrows an old, turn-of-the-century photograph of a Chinese woman whose feet were bound and paints *Goddess of Love, Goddess of Liberty* (see cat. 25).

In December, she presents the exhibition *Goddess of Love and Liberty* at Nahan Contemporary Gallery in New York.

She receives her first National Endowment for the Arts Painting Fellowship.

1990

In the spring, Liu accepts a teaching position at Mills College, in Oakland, California.

In June, before moving from Texas to California, she travels throughout Europe with Kelley, visiting the Venice Biennale, where Robert Rauschenberg signs his name on her Chinese passport, offering her "a passport to the art world."

1991

Liu receives her second National Endowment for the Arts Painting Fellowship and begins showing at Rena Bransten Gallery in San Francisco and at the Bernice Steinbaum Gallery in New York.

She returns to China for the first time since leaving in 1984. During her visit, she discovers photographs of Chinese prostitutes, taken at the turn of the century, which she later incorporates into paintings (see cats. 25, 26).

Liu and Ling Chen become U.S. citizens, taking the Oath of Allegiance in San Francisco.

1992

Liu intensifies the theatricality of her paintings by shaping the canvases, displaying kitsch and antique objects on lacquered shelves, and attaching fragments of traditional Chinese architecture (see cats. 19–22, 24).

1993

Liu participates in the *43rd Biennial Exhibition of Contemporary American Painting* at the Corcoran Gallery of Art in Washington, D.C.

She returns to China with her husband and son. They travel with Liu's mother to the family's small ancestral village near Shenyang, in northern China. While there, Liu obtains more archival photographs for incorporation into her art.

Drips start to appear as an erosive force in Liu's paintings, and she begins to create canvases that correspond to the outlines of her subjects.

Liu paints a number of "revolutionary" self-portraits (see cat. 20).

1994

Liu participates in *Asia/America: Identities in Contemporary Asian American Art* at the Asia Society in New York.

During the opening of *Year of the Dog,* an exhibition of Liu's work at the Steinbaum Krauss Gallery in New York, she meets the young Chinese artists Yu Hong and Liu Xiaodong (see pp. 175, 180–81).

Liu completes *Jiu Jin Shan* (Old Gold Mountain), an installation of two hundred thousand fortune cookies at the de Young Museum in San Francisco.

She learns that her father, whom she hasn't seen since she was an infant, has been living on a rural work farm for elderly inmates near Nanjing. She travels there, by coincidence, on Father's Day, to meet him, and learns that he has been imprisoned on and off since 1948 (see cat. 22).

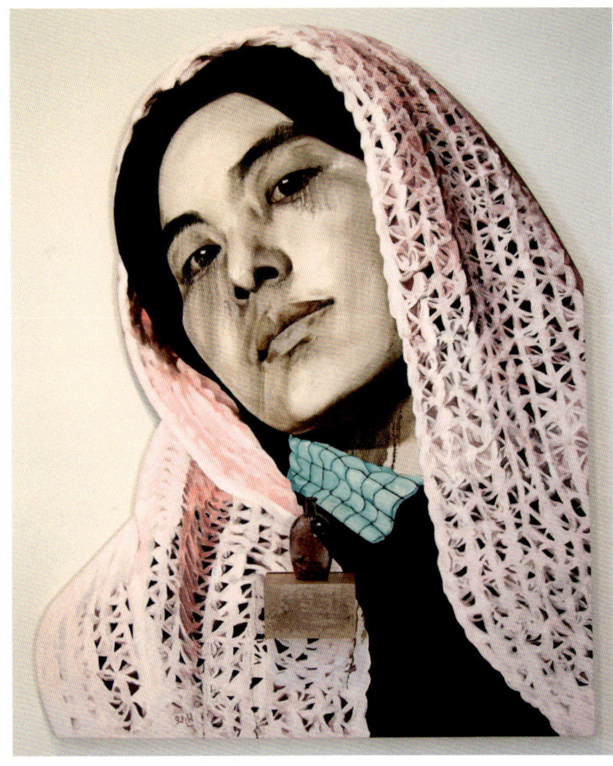

Hung Liu
Daughter of the Revolution, 1993
Oil on shaped canvas and wood, with antique bottle
78½ × 62 in. (199.4 × 157.5 cm)

1995

Inspired by Bernardo Bertolucci's film *The Last Emperor* (1988), Liu begins work on a series of paintings that draw inspiration from photographs of China's last imperial court, the Qing Dynasty (see cat. 27).

Liu receives tenure from Mills College.

1996

Liu participates in *American Kaleidoscope: Themes and Perspectives in Recent Art,* at the National Museum of American Art (now the Smithsonian American Art Museum) in Washington, D.C.

Meanwhile, in Japan, her work is included in *American Stories: Amidst Displacement and Transformation,* an exhibition organized by the Setagaya Art Museum and Asahi Shimbun that also includes art by Mike Kelley and Enrique Chagoya (see p. 172).

Liu's father—Xia Peng—dies.

Liu turns forty-eight in the "Year of the Rat," her year. In Chinese mythology, every twelve-year cycle brings a life-changing event, and at her celebration dinner, Liu reflects upon this truth: At twelve she moved to Beijing; at twenty-four, she left the countryside and went to college; at thirty-six, she immigrated to the United States; and at forty-eight, she experienced her father's death, her son's leaving home, her inclusion in a Tokyo exhibition as an "American" artist, and plans for a ten-year survey of her work.

1997

Hong Kong returns to Chinese rule.

Hung Liu: Unfolding Memory—Embodying History opens at the Center for Curatorial Studies, Bard College (where Ling Chen is a student).

Liu begins focusing on the theme of "women at work" in a number of her paintings.

1998

Liu's first retrospective exhibition, *Hung Liu: A Ten-Year Survey 1988–1998,* is presented at the College of Wooster Art Museum and travels to five additional U.S. museums.

Liu receives a Joan Mitchell Foundation grant.

Construction begins on the Great Firewall of China.

1999

Working on large canvases, Liu begins depicting women and children as refugees from war and social upheaval. She continues the series for the next few years (see cats. 29–31), aspiring to offer her subjects the solace of their own heritage by including motifs—birds and flowers, Buddhist iconography—from traditional Chinese painting.

Liu purchases a new studio in Oakland.

2000

Where is Mao? 2000 is exhibited at Chulalongkorn University, Bangkok, Thailand. During a discussion with students, Liu is asked what it feels like to be an American "after being Chinese." She replies: "China is my home-land. An American is something I'm always becoming—it's a verb."[1]

She participates in *Text and Subtext—Contemporary Art and Asian Women,* a show that travels over three years from Singapore to Sydney, Stockholm, Oslo, Copenhagen, Taipei, and Beijing.

In December, Liu makes her first trip to Russia, where her work is exhibited in a group exhibition. Outside Saint Petersburg, she sees the wintery, melancholy landscapes of Alexei Savrasov and the historical epics of Ilya Repin, painters she has studied since childhood.

2001

A U.S. spy plane collides with a Chinese fighter plane and makes an emergency landing in Hainan, China. The Chinese pilot is killed, and the U.S. crew is detained for ten days.

Liu's father-in-law, Don Kelley, dies in Las Vegas.

Liu awakens to a radio report that the World Trade Center towers in New York are on fire. In the aftermath of 9/11, she paints *September,* which depicts a traditionally rendered Song Dynasty duck crashing through the face of a young Chinese bride.

In the wake of 9/11, Liu explores the themes of annunciation and lamentation.

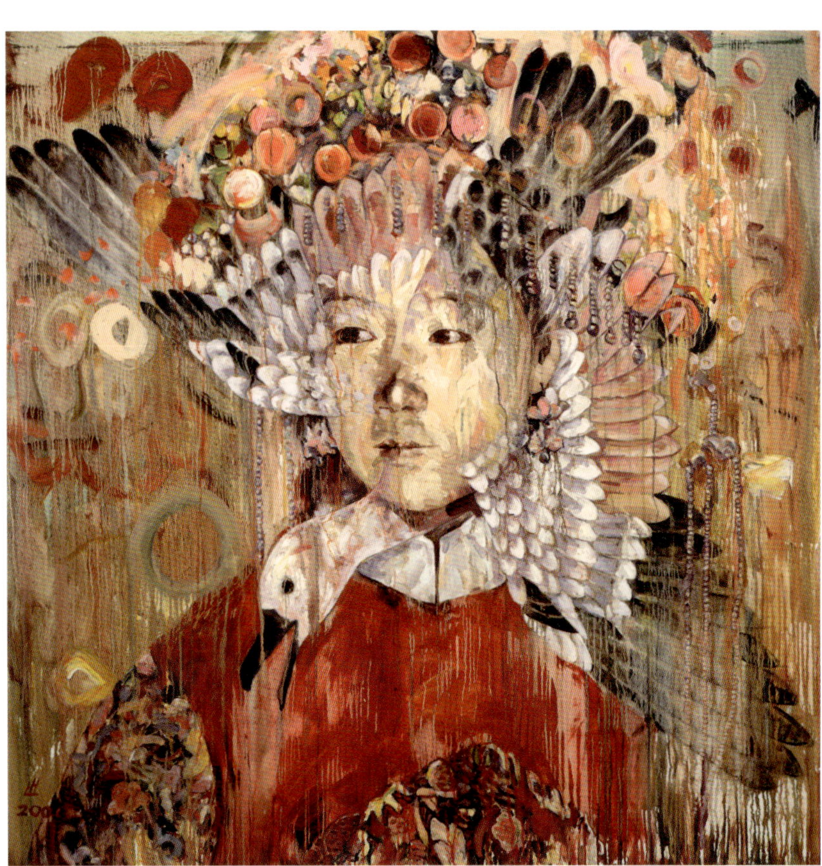

Hung Liu
September, 2001
Oil on canvas, 66 × 66 in. (167.6 × 167.6 cm)
Collection of Driek and Michael Zirinsky

2002

Strange Fruit: New Paintings by Hung Liu is organized by the Arizona State University Art Museum and the Boise Art Museum. The exhibition presents depictions of Korean "comfort women," famine victims, and prisoners of war (see cat. 30).

Liu exhibits in *Art/Women/California: Parallels and Intersections, 1950–2000,* at the San José Museum of Art.

Liu works with her mother to publish her grandfather's book (see Moss essay, figs. 12, 13).

2003

The United States invades Iraq.

Responding to the exhibition *Hung Liu: Towards Peng-Lai (Paradise)* at the Rena Bransten Gallery in San Francisco, critic Kenneth Baker writes: "Many modern artists have proclaimed painting a realm of freedom, but too little contemporary work makes us feel the truth of this view. . . . Hung Liu's new work at Bransten does."[2]

Liu paints *Mission Girls,* a series of twenty-nine small canvases based on an archival image (see cats. 32–40).

2004

Liu's beloved aunt—Liu Zongyu—dies in a senior care facility outside Beijing.

Liu exhibits in China for the first time since her departure in 1984. The exhibition, *Hung Liu: Lament,* is presented at Art Scene Warehouse in Shanghai.

2005

In response to a request from the Sun Valley Center for the Arts and Humanities, Liu paints a group of portraits based on archival photographs of Chinese immigrants who were living in Idaho during the nineteenth-century Gold Rush. The resulting exhibition, *The Vanishing: Re-presenting the Chinese in the American West,* features Polly Bemis as the primary subject (see cat. 43).

Liu accompanies Kelley and writer Bill Fox on a sojourn up the Yangtze River, where they meet up with Liu Xiaodong, who is at work on a group portrait of male peasant laborers.

Liu paints *Modern Time* (see Lippard essay, fig. 7), a pseudo-propaganda–style diptych that contrasts two dreams: the trance of the Marxist worker and an artist's reverie.

2006

Matriarchy: Hung Liu's New Work opens at Art Scene China Warehouse in Shanghai.

While in China, Liu travels with her mother and husband back to Qianshan. Known in English as "One Thousand Lotus Flower Peaks," the region features Buddhist and Taoist monasteries dating to ancient times.

Liu takes painting students from Mills College to Beijing, where they visit the studios of Ai Weiwei, Liu Xiaodong, Yu Hong, Sui Jianguo, Wang Gongxin, Lin Tianmiao, and other prominent Chinese artists.

Liu's *Going Away, Coming Home,* a 160-foot-long window mural, is installed in the new terminal of the Oakland International Airport (see p. 173). In designing the work, Liu combined the crane imagery from a twelfth-century Chinese silk painting (*Auspicious Cranes*) with digitized images from satellite weather maps of the U.S. West Coast and the Asia-Pacific region. The windows quickly become one of Liu's most popular works.

Liu invites Liu Xiaodong to speak at Mills College. During the visit, the two artists complete blind, simultaneous portraits of each other (they watch each other watching each other painting each other) and exchange the results.

2007

Liu turns to the Chinese propaganda film *Daughters of China* (1949) as she embarks on a new series. Each painting represents a single frame from the film, which tells the true story of a detachment of Chinese women soldiers who, in 1938, carried their dying and wounded into a river to drown as a way to keep them from surrendering to the Japanese (Lippard essay, fig. 12).

Daughters of China is exhibited at Rena Bransten Gallery in San Francisco.

Hung Liu: ZZ (Bastard Paintings) opens at Nancy Hoffman Gallery in New York. The show represents the most ambitious expression to date of Liu's mixed media and resin pieces created in collaboration with David Salgado of Trillium Graphics.

2008

On May 12, the day before Liu arrives in Beijing, a devastating earthquake strikes the Sichuan Province of China. Measuring a magnitude of 7.9, the Sichuan earthquake kills nearly ninety thousand people (according to the final official Chinese government assessment), including many children who were attending school in poorly constructed buildings.

Daughters of China travels to F2 Gallery in Beijing.

Liu presents *Tai Cang (Great Granary)* at the Xin Beijing Art Gallery. The exhibition centers around a reinvention of Liu's 1981 mural, *Music of the Great Earth* (now destroyed). Accompanied by a number of Liu's other paintings, the new mural hangs on a refurbished wall of the fourteenth-century Imperial Granary, while thirty-four antique wooden containers (*dou*), filled with grains and spices from every province in China, are deployed across the gallery floor.

Liu's mother, Liu Zongguang, completes *Rainbow over the Pacific,* a book on her daughter's life and art.

Liu's work is exhibited at the San Francisco Museum of Modern Art (SFMOMA) in *Half-Life of a Dream: Contemporary Chinese Art from the Logan Collection,* an exhibition curated by Jeff Kelley.

On August 8, the Beijing Summer Olympics open with a globally televised extravaganza that reminds Liu of political pageants from revolutionary China.

The Great Recession begins in the United States.

Rat Years is exhibited at the Walter Maciel Gallery in Los Angeles. A series of portraits depicting the artist at twelve-year intervals from infancy to sixty years of age, *Rat Years* contrasts each self-portrait with an image from a drawing or painting done by the artist in that same year.

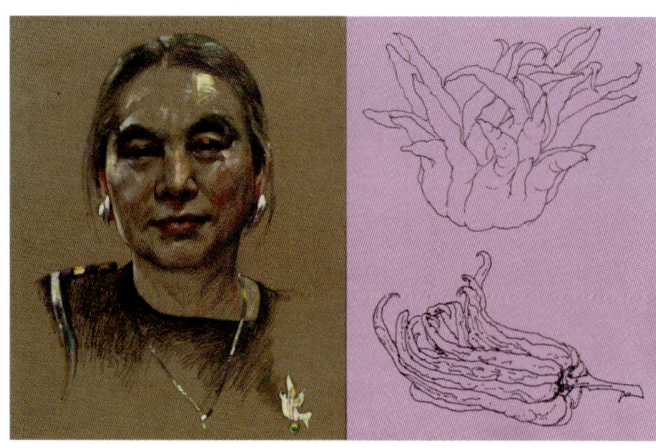

Hung Liu
Rat Year II 2008, 2008
Oil on linen and mixed media on wood panel, 60 × 100 in.
(152.4 × 254 cm)

2009

Liu and Kelley attend the presidential inauguration of Barack Obama in Washington, D.C.

Liu devotes herself to a series of paintings depicting people in the aftermath of the 2008 Sichuan earthquake. The subject of these paintings is less the disaster itself than the expressions of mythic emotions on the faces of the survivors: grief, shock, confusion, stunned silence, courage, and mourning.

Liu attends an art education conference in her hometown, Changchun. This is the first time she has returned to the "dead city" since her family fled the Communist forces in 1948.

Paintings from the *Daughters of China* series are exhibited at the 10 Chancery Lane Gallery in Hong Kong.

Liu donates her little painting box—the one she used in China before coming to the United States—to the Oakland Museum of California.

2010

Liu is awarded an honorary doctorate from the Laguna College of Art and Design.

While Liu is visiting with her mother in Beijing, her mother-in-law, Rosemary Kelley, dies in Maine.

As the year ends, Liu's mother falls ill in Beijing and enters Tongren Hospital.

2011

Liu Zongguang dies in Beijing on January 29, and her ashes are later scattered in the ocean off the coast of Kauai.

Liu is awarded the SGC International Lifetime Achievement Award for Printmaking.

First Spring Thunder opens at the Alexander Ochs Gallery in Beijing. Some of China's most prominent artists—including Fang Lijun, Liu Xiaodong, Yu Hong, Yang Shaobin, Lin Tianmiao, Wang Gongxin, and Zhan Wang—attend the opening.

(re)Pressed Memories, a mini-retrospective of Liu's prints, opens at the Tamarind Institute in Albuquerque.

Liu speaks at the International Conference on Chinese Women and Visual Representation held in Shanghai. It is the first feminist conference in China to openly welcome lesbians. The title of Liu's talk is "From Mulan to the Red Detachment of Women."

The Hung Liu Endowed Fellowship—an annual award for an outstanding graduate student of fine arts—is established at Mills College.

2012

One year after her mother's death, Liu completes a series of fifty-one small paintings over a mourning period that lasts forty-nine days (see Lippard essay, figs. 2–4).

Ling Chen marries Juan Yu, and Liu meets her Chinese daughter-in-law.

In a striking change, Liu begins a body of paintings that are based on the patriotic stories in Chinese picture books, or *xiaorenshu.*

Liu enters her final year of teaching at Mills College.

2013

On March 16, *Summoning Ghosts: The Art of Hung Liu* opens at the Oakland Museum of California. One of the most important exhibitions of Liu's career, it features more than sixty-five works. Large-scale paintings, photographs, sketchbooks, and informal painting studies are gathered from private and public collections around the world. The California governor attends the opening, and in a *Wall Street Journal* review of the show, the critic David Littlejohn deems Liu "the greatest Chinese painter in the U.S."[3]

On the heels of *Summoning Ghosts,* Liu creates a vast mural and installation for the San José Museum of Art: *Questions from the Sky: New Work by Hung Liu.* A very personal and poignant installation comprising several elegant video works and a sweeping (twenty-by-eighty-foot) wall mural, the work contemplates the cycles of life and death and the span of memory. Its title alludes to an ancient poem by Ch'ü Yüan.

During a residency at PV Studio in Puerto Vallarta, Mexico, Liu paints *Portraits of a Chinese Self,* a group of eight self-portraits that show her from age three to thirty-two.

She completes *Qianshan: Grandfather's Mountain* using photographs that Liu Weihua commissioned during his research trips to the mountainous region. The finished paintings incorporate the landscape, religious sites or shrines, the monks and nuns who lived there, and, very often, her grandfather.

2014

Following her retirement from Mills College, Liu acquires the status of professor emerita.

She meets civil rights icon and Congressman John Lewis at the Sun Valley Writers' Conference.

October 26 marks the thirtieth anniversary of Liu's arrival in the United States.

Summoning Ghosts opens at the Kemper Museum of Contemporary Art in Kansas City.

2015

Summoning Ghosts opens at the Palm Springs Art Museum.

The Asian Art Museum of San Francisco displays three of Liu's paintings from its collection.

Map No. 33, Liu's bold, multimedia artwork in the Esplanade Ballroom Lobby of the Moscone Center in San Francisco, is de-installed as the Moscone Center itself is soon to be demolished and rebuilt. Liu's larger-than-life re-creation of the first survey map of San Francisco, drawn in 1839 by Jean-Jacques Vioget, was originally installed in 1992, when the Moscone Center was new. The work's forty-one canvases, shaped to conform to the historic map's city blocks, charted the young port town of San Francisco when it was still a village, newly renamed from the original "Yerba Buena."

After spending time in the Dorothea Lange Archive at the Oakland Museum of California, Liu begins to make paintings based on Lange's photographs, shifting away from her decades-long focus on historical Chinese subjects.

2016

Liu and Kelley lead an art trip to China for members of the San José Museum of Art. They attend Art Basel in Hong Kong before traveling to Shanghai and Beijing to visit studios, galleries, and museums. They meet Uli Sigg, Urs Meile, and Arne Glimcher, among other collectors and gallerists, and visit artists Liu Xiaodong, Zhang Huan, Qiu Anxiong, Liu Jianhua, Li Songsong, Song Dong, Qiu Zhijie, Zhang Xiaogang, Wang Gongxin and Lin Tianmiao, Yang Shaobin, Fang Lijun, Yu Hong, Sui Jianguo, Yue Minjun, and Zhao.

She presents *Daughters of China* at the American University Museum at the Katzen Arts Center, in Washington, D.C. The presentation of two bodies of work, *Daughters of China* and *Jiu Jin Shan,* feels remarkably relevant given its proximity in time and place to the U.S. national election, which is focused on the politics of immigration and on the (heroic) possibility of a woman president.

On November 8, Donald J. Trump is elected president of the United States.

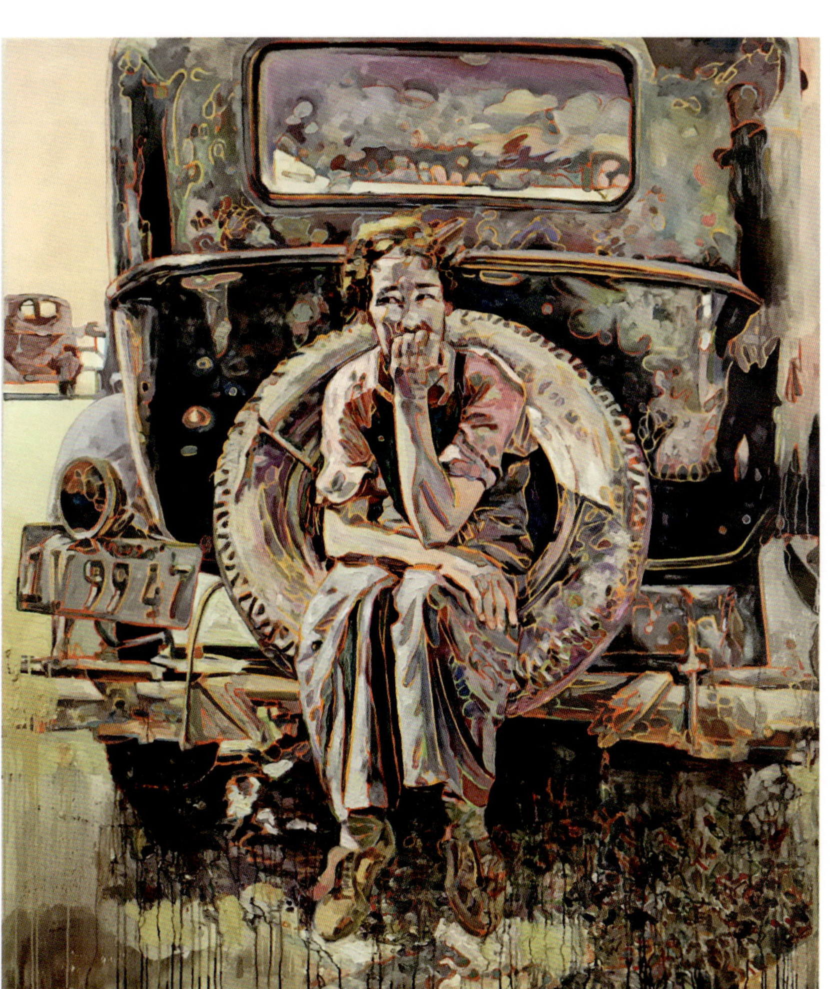

Hung Liu
Spare Tire, 2018
Oil on canvas, 80 × 70 in. (203.2 × 177.8 cm)
Collection of Lorna Meyer Calas and Dennis Calas

2017

Liu delivers a speech at the Women's March in San Francisco.

The exhibition *Hung Liu: Scales of History,* at the Fresno Art Museum, juxtaposes thirty-four of Liu's small-scale *My Secret Freedom* paintings, from the early 1970s, with a selection of her larger works, made after she immigrated to the United States.

Liu partially repaints *Reading Room,* her mural in the community room of the Kuo Building in San Francisco's Chinatown. Originally executed in 1988, the work is preserved and realigned to accommodate design changes in the building.

Liu and Kelley spend a week in residence at the Oxbow School in Napa, working with high school artists.

Liu exhibits a group of her Dorothea Lange–inspired paintings at Rena Bransten Gallery in San Francisco.

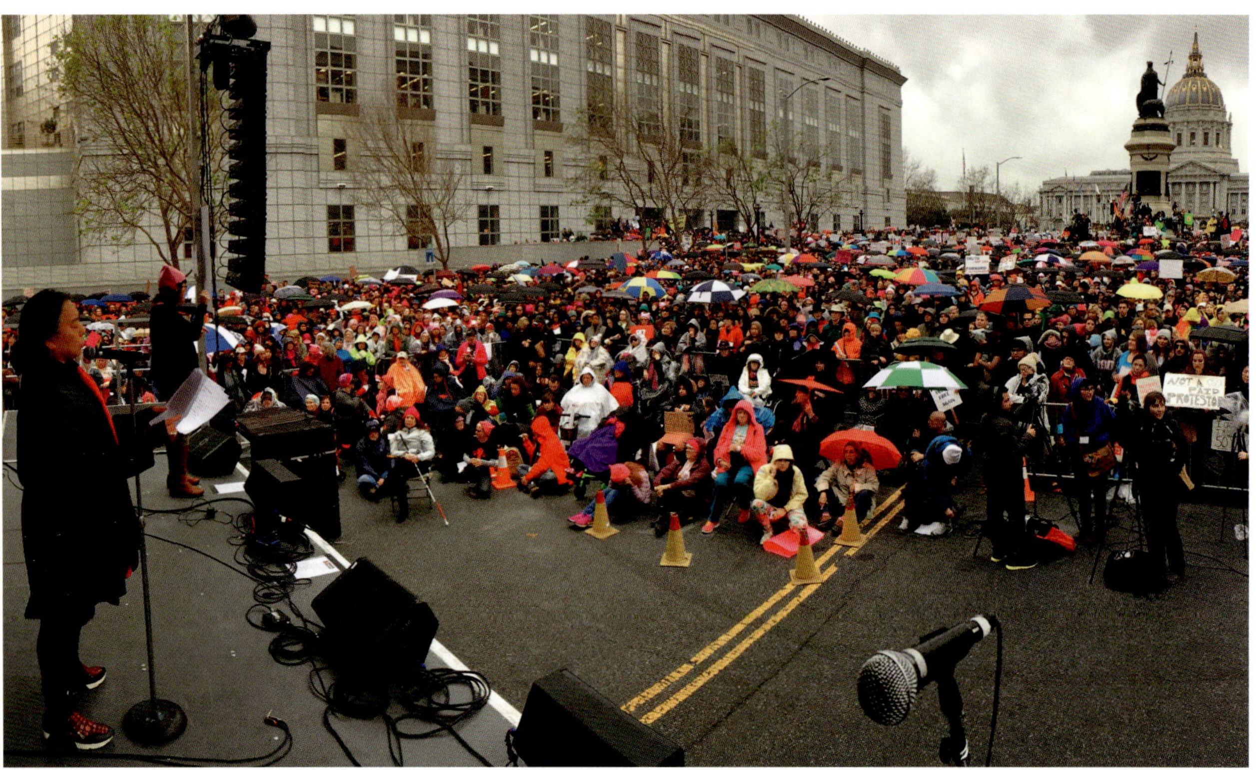

Hung Liu delivers a speech at the Women's March in San Francisco, January 21, 2017.

2018

Liu is invited to design an issue of *Zoetrope: All-Story,* the film director Francis Ford Coppola's quarterly literary magazine. Taking a cue from the process of writing itself, of shaping and extending a narrative, Liu decides to publish her most recent paintings, which are based on Dorothea Lange's documentary photographs.

Liu shows her *Secret Freedom* paintings at Walter Maciel Gallery in Los Angeles (see Lim essay, fig. 5, and Lippard essay, fig. 5).

Liu, in conjunction with David Salgado of Trillium Graphics, donates fifty-one resin paintings to the Jordan Schnitzer Museum of Art at the University of Oregon in Eugene. Working with Tonya Turner Carroll of Turner Carroll Gallery in Santa Fe, she also begins the process of funding an endowment at the university to reward innovative student artists.

Liu is formally invited by Kim Sajet, director of the Smithsonian's National Portrait Gallery in Washington, D.C., to have a one-woman show of her portrait-focused works at the museum in 2021.

For the first time at its annual gala, the San José Museum of Art honors an artist: Hung Liu.

Liu shows at SFMOMA in *Art and China after 1989: Theater of the World.* Organized by the Guggenheim Museum and having traveled to Bilbao before SFMOMA, the exhibition features *Avant-Garde* (cat. 20).

2019

As part of a lecture series at SFMOMA focusing on contemporary Chinese art, in association with *Theater of the World,* Liu discusses her experiences of having lived in China during the Cultural Revolution.

Philip Tinari, director of the UCCA Center for Contemporary Art in Beijing, invites Liu to exhibit there at the end of 2019.

Liu is appointed to the board of trustees at the San José Museum of Art.

At the Nevada Museum of Art, Liu joins artist Zhi Lin in a discussion on the sacrifices of Chinese railroad workers who raced to complete the U.S. rail lines in 1869. Following their remarks, a ceremonial gathering takes place at the exact time 150 years prior that the "golden spike" was hammered into the last rail at Promontory, Utah, by Leland Stanford. Liu and Zhi then recite the names of over eight hundred known Chinese railroad workers. This somber, contemplative recitation is accompanied by the playing of traditional Chinese instruments as the audience gazes westward at the vast Sierra Nevada through which the Chinese workers cut the tunnels of the Union Pacific.

Liu attends Judy Chicago's eightieth birthday celebration in Belen, New Mexico, where the artists meet for the first time. Chicago says, "You've made history," to which Liu replies, "I'm surprised you know who I am."

SFMOMA, with the guidance of Gary Garrels, senior curator of painting and sculpture, acquires all of Liu's *My Secret Freedom* paintings.

Liu continues her focus on Dorothea Lange's subjects as they migrate across the United States in the 1930s in search of work, dignity, and salvation. The title of her exhibition *This Land . . . ,* at the Nancy Hoffman Gallery in New York, invokes Woody Guthrie's anthem of 1940 but does not offer the ribbons of highway, the golden valleys, or the diamond deserts. Instead, Liu presents a landscape of broken-down cars, flattened tires, and stranded people.

In New York, Liu connects with fellow Chinese painter Li Songsong, who is presenting an exhibition at Pace Gallery.

On November 14, Liu's show *Hung Liu: Passer-by* is canceled by the Beijing municipal Bureau of Culture. Originally scheduled to open at UCCA on December 6, it is canceled when UCCA does not receive the necessary government approvals to import Liu's works from the United States to China. In essence, the Beijing government censors Liu's entire show. The reasons remain unclear, but it probably relates to the history of twentieth-century ideological struggle embodied in Liu's work.

The year ends with a "Cancellation Party" at the Piedmont home of Liu's dear friend Mary Ellen Herringer. Many friends show up: artists, curators and museum directors; dealers from San Francisco, Los Angeles, Santa Fe, and Ketchum; Phil Tinari from UCCA—all the way from China. The party takes place on the day Liu's Beijing show was scheduled to open. The art world press has covered the censorship, and major articles appear in the *New York Times, Artforum, Art News, The Art Newspaper, artnet News,* and more.

2020

Another Year of the Rat—Liu's year—dawns, and the hovering, prickly threat of the coronavirus is in the air. Liu has been to Wuhan, where the excavated bronze bells referred to in her 1981 CAFA mural are conserved and exhibited.

On March 4, California Governor Gavin Newsom declares a state of emergency, and a shelter-in-place order is issued for the Bay Area on March 17.

Liu is appointed to the board of trustees of SFMOMA.

She invents a new form of composing called "ensemble paintings," in which people and things from Lange's photographs are digitally plucked from their chemical grounds and printed on shaped wood, aluminum, and canvas. These images are then painted and reordered into new compositions, suggesting fresh narratives in the lives, belongings, and shelters of these Dust Bowl migrants.

She is offered an updated version of the canceled Beijing show at the de Young Museum in San Francisco, scheduled for 2021.

Hong Kong is essentially taken back by China.

A new "Rat" is born to Ling Chen Kelley and Juan Yu: Casimir ("Cas") Arthur Kelley. Hung Liu is a grandma.

She prepares for her major exhibition at the National Portrait Gallery in Washington, D.C.

Notes

1. Hung Liu quoted in *Summoning Ghosts: The Art of Hung Liu,* by René de Guzman et al. (Oakland, Calif.: Oakland Museum of California; Berkeley: University of California Press, 2013), 194.
2. Kenneth Baker, "Shedding Shackles of History and Style," *San Francisco Chronicle,* May 3, 2003.
3. David Littlejohn, "The Evils That Men Do," *Wall Street Journal,* June 6, 2013.

Following pages: *Rat Year 2020,* **2020**
Oil on linen and mixed media on wood panel, each: 64 × 100 in. (162.6 × 254 cm), diptych

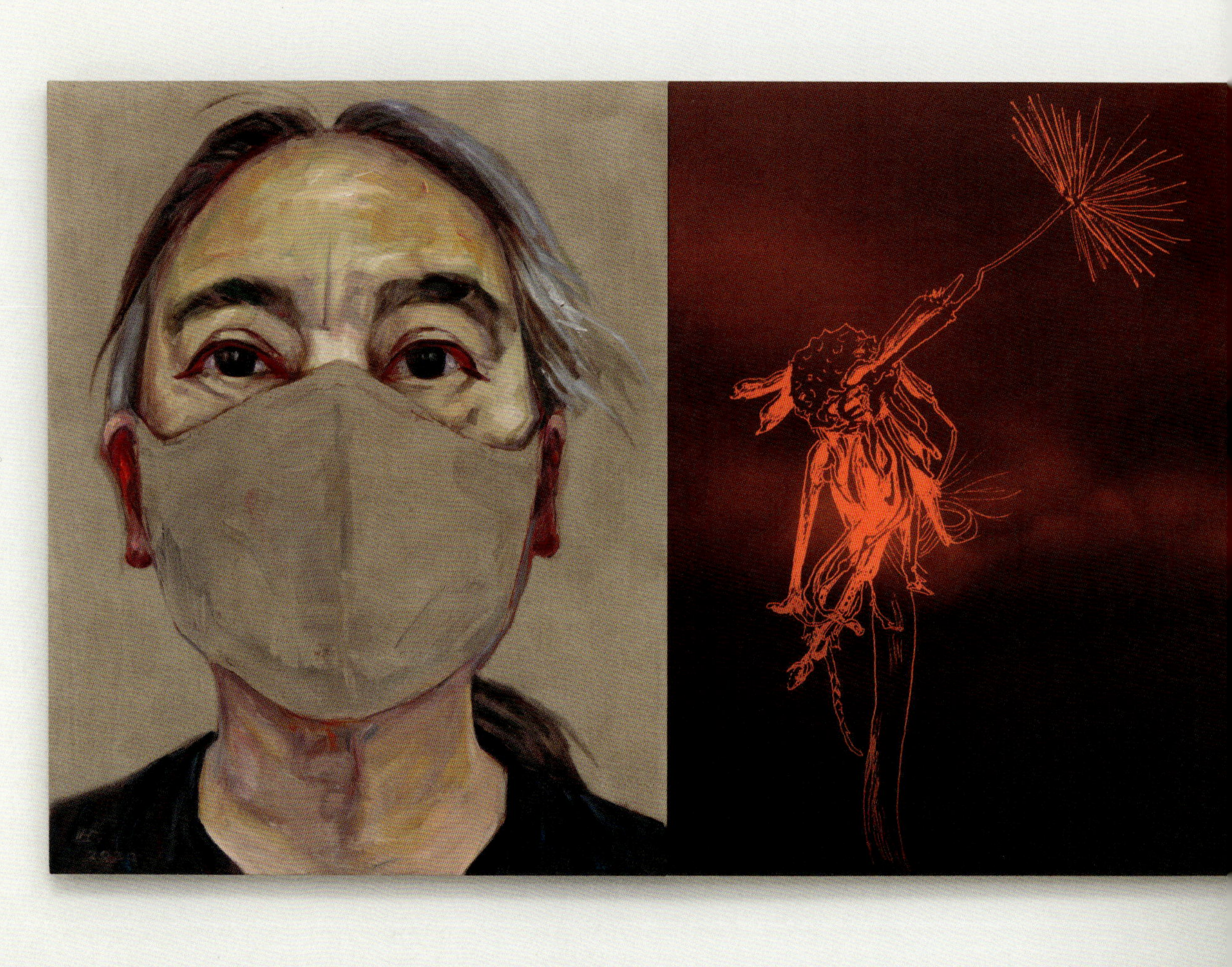

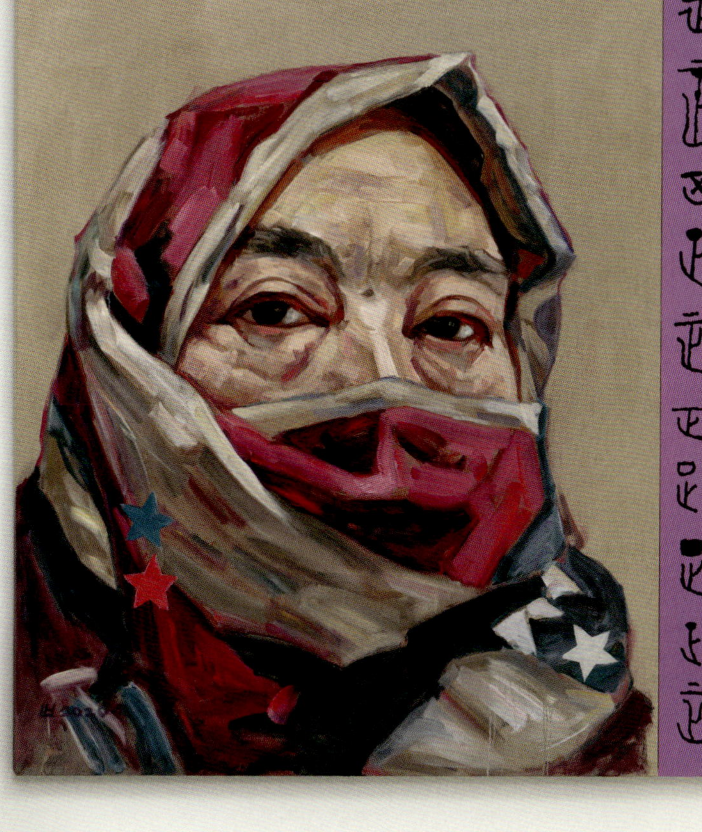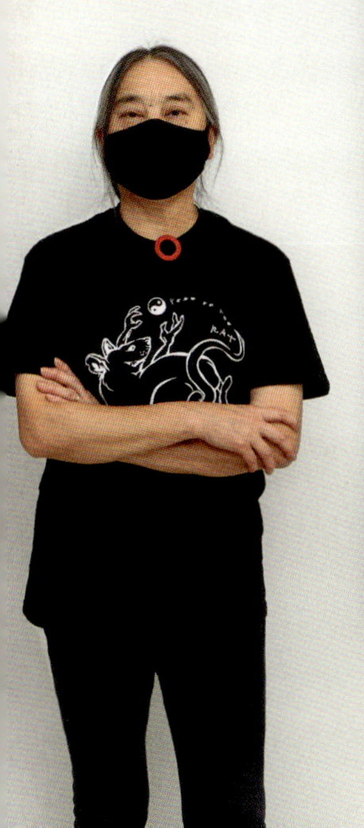

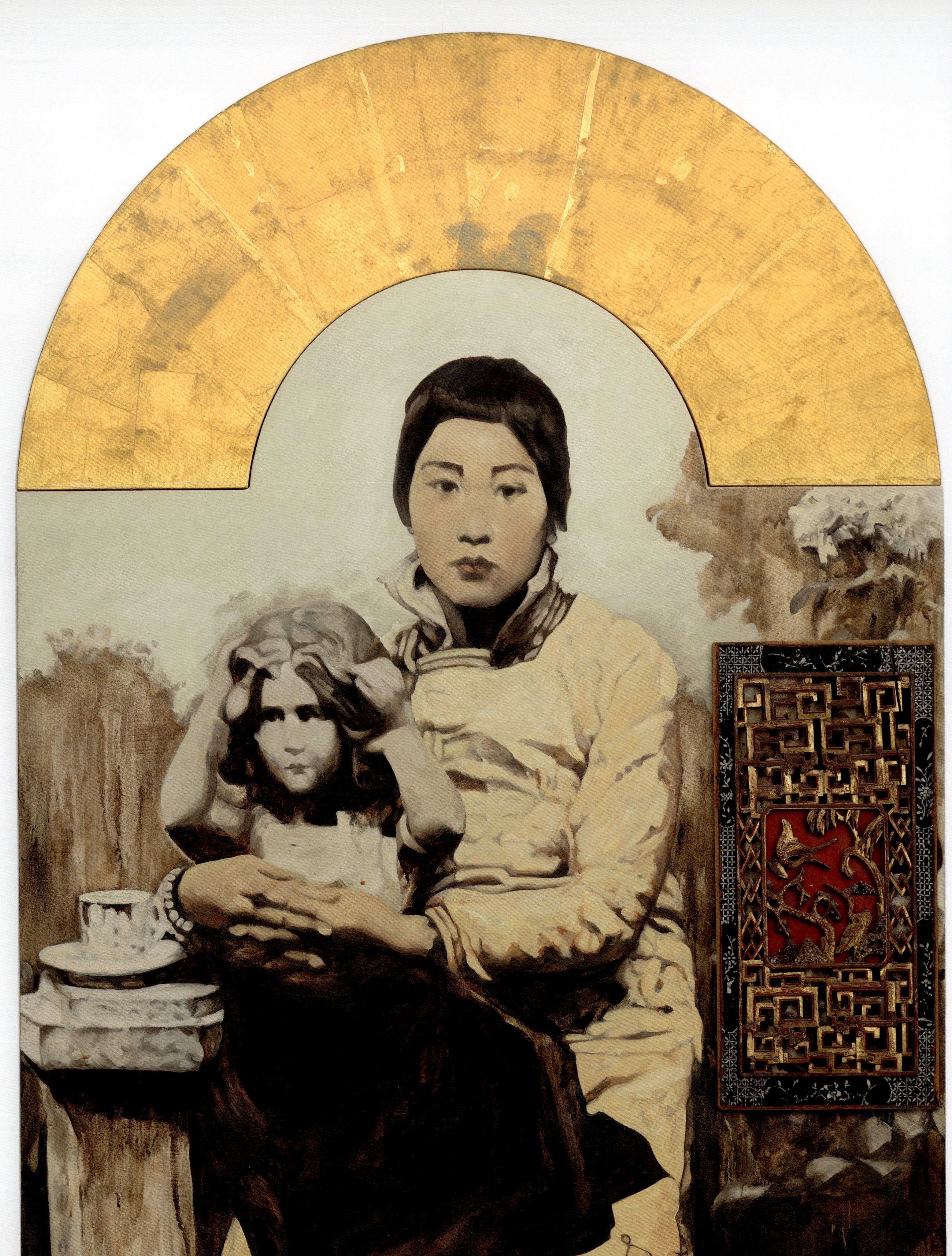

Selected References

Essays, Interviews, and Reviews

Arieff, Allison. "Cultural Collisions: Identity and History in the Work of Hung Liu." *Woman's Art Journal* 17, no. 1 (Spring/Summer 1996): 35–40. Also in *Reclaiming Female Agency: Feminist Art History after Postmodernism,* edited by Norma Broude and Mary D. Garrard, 435–45. Berkeley: University of California Press, 2005.

Baker, Kenneth. "Capp Street Wonders Go Public." *San Francisco Chronicle,* September 13, 1988.

Baker, Kenneth. "Hung Liu: Polly." *San Francisco Chronicle,* October 29, 2005.

Berkson, Bill. "Hung Liu: Action Painter." In *The Sweet Singer of Modernism and Other Art Writings 1985–2003,* 184–89. Jamestown, R.I.: Qua, 2003.

——. "Hung Liu: Capp Street Project." *Artforum* 27, no. 4 (December 1988): 129.

Brown, Glen R. "Beyond Names: Collaborative Works—Ron Nagle and Hung Liu." *Ceramics: Art and Perception,* no. 49 (September 2002): 88–92.

Cotter, Holland. "Art in Review, Hung Liu: *Apsaras.*" *New York Times,* October 23, 2009.

De Nigris, Ornella. "Traditional Imagery of Women as Seen through Female Visual Art: Hung Liu." *International Communication of Chinese Culture* 3, no. 1 (March 2016): 191–206.

Garchik, Leah. "Hung Liu: An Immigrant Takes on American History." *San Francisco Chronicle,* May 10, 2017.

Goodman, Jonathan. "Hung Liu." *Yishu: Journal of Contemporary Chinese Art* 9, no. 1 (January/February 2010): 62–71.

Hung, Wu. "Sixty Years on a Hard Journey for Art: A Conversation between Hung Liu and Wu Hung." In *Hung Liu: Great Granary,* edited by Wu Hung, 62–113. Hong Kong: Timezone 8, 2010.

Isbister, Dong Li. "Self as Diasporic Body: Hung Liu's Self-Portrait Resident Alien." *Intersections: Women's and Gender Studies in Review across Disciplines,* no. 7 (Fall 2009): 15–25.

Jennison, Rebecca. "Painting Life Back into History—Hung Liu's 'Hard-Won' Feminist Art." *Feminist Studies* 38, no. 1 (Spring 2012): 141–75.

Jones, Joyce. "American Art through a Prism." *Washington Post,* October 11, 1996.

Kelley, Jeff. "First-Generation Painting: A Conversation among Hung Liu, George J. Leonard, and Jeff Kelley." In *The Asian Pacific American Heritage: A Companion to Literature and Arts,* edited by George J. Leonard, 611–17. New York: Routledge, 1999.

Kim, Elaine H. "'Bad Women': Asian American Visual Artists Hanh Thi Pham, Hung Liu, and Yong Soon Min." *Feminist Studies* 22, no. 3 (Autumn 1996): 573–602.

Li, Xiarong. "Painting the Pain: An Interview with Hung Liu." *Human Rights Tribune* 3, no. 1 (Spring 1992): 10–12.

Liu, Hung. Oral history interview, April 25–29, 2010. By Joann Moser. Archives of American Art, Smithsonian Institution, Washington, D.C.

Moser, Joann. "A Conversation with Hung Liu." *American Art* 25, no. 2 (Summer 2011): 76–103.

Muchnic, Suzanne. "Beauty in Service to the Truth." *Los Angeles Times,* September 24, 2006.

Ollman, Leah. "Paintings, Text Speak of the 'Trauma' in China's Body Politic." *Los Angeles Times,* September 15, 1989.

Pleasant, Amy. "Contemporary Painter, Hung Liu: 'I Felt the Weight of History.'" Huffington Post, January 2, 2017, https://www.huffpost.com/entry /contemporary-painter-hung-liu-i-felt-the-weight _b_586a93aee4b014e7c72ee2fa.

Pollock, Griselda. "Hung Liu: Odalisque." In *Fresh Talk/ Daring Gazes: Conversations on Asian American Art,* edited by Elaine H. Kim, Margo Machida, and Sharon Mizota, 119–22. Berkeley: University of California Press, 2003.

Qin, Amy. "A Prominent Chinese-American Artist Is the
 Latest to Fall Afoul of China's Censors." *New York
 Times,* November 20, 2019.
Roth, David M., and Nick Stone. "Hung Liu: 'Daughters
 of China' at Kala and Interview!" Squarecylinder:
 Northern California Art, December 22, 2017,
 https://www.squarecylinder.com/2017/12/hung
 -liu-daughters-of-china-kala-interview/.
Selz, Peter. "Hung Liu at Rena Bransten." *Art in America*
 (June/July 2008): 204.
Tamblyn, Christine. "Hung Liu: 'Reading Room,' 'Resident
 Alien.'" *High Performance* 44 (Winter 1988): 81.
Tanner, Marcia. "A Must-See: Hung Liu's Women
 Warriors, *Daughters of China* at Kala." Berkeleyside,
 November 30, 2017, https://www.berkeleyside.com
 /2017/11/30/must-see-hung-lius-women-warriors
 -daughters-china-kala.
Tinari, Philip. "Hung Liu: Towards Panglai." *LEAP* (June
 2011): 146–56.
Whiting, Sam. "China Yanks Oakland Artist Hung Liu's
 Big Beijing Show." *San Francisco Chronicle,*
 November 21, 2019.
———. "Hung Liu's Color Only Adds to Starkness of
 Dorothea Lange Images." SFGate, April 26, 2017,
 https://www.sfgate.com/art/article/Hung-Liu-s
 -color-only-adds-to-starkness-of-11100765.php.
Wyrick, Mary. "Feminist Semiotics in the Art of Hung Liu
 and Carolee Schneemann." In *Semiotics and Visual
 Culture: Sights, Signs, and Significance,* edited
 by Deborah Lee Smith-Shank, 80–85. Reston, Va.:
 National Art Education Association, 2004.

Exhibition Catalogues and Brochures

Atkins, Robert. *Hung Liu: The Year of the Dog, 1994 = Liu
 Hung, I chiu chiu erh.* New York: Steinbaum Krauss
 Gallery, 1994.
Atkinson, Alan. *Hung Liu: Now and Then.* Norman:
 University of Oklahoma, Fred R. Jones Jr. Museum
 of Art, 2008.
Berkson, Bill. *Hung Liu: Chinese Types.* San Francisco:
 Rena Bransten Gallery, 1998.
Corrin, Lisa G. "In Search of Miss Sallie Chu: Hung Liu's
 Can-ton." *The Baltimore Series.* Brochure. Baltimore:
 The Contemporary, 1995.
de Guzman, René, Wu Hung, Yiyun Li, Karen Smith, Bill
 Berkson, and Stephanie Hanor. *Summoning Ghosts:
 The Art of Hung Liu.* Oakland, Calif.: Oakland
 Museum of Art; Berkeley: University of California
 Press, 2013.
Edwards, Jim. *Precarious Links: Emily Jennings, Hung Liu,
 and Celia Munoz.* San Antonio, Tex.: San Antonio
 Museum Association, 1990.
Erickson, Britta. *Hung Liu: Prodigal Daughter.* Beijing:
 F2 Gallery, 2008.
Harthorn, Sandy, and Heather Sealy Lineberry. *Hung Liu:
 Strange Fruit.* San Francisco: Rena Bransten
 Gallery, 2001.
Hung Liu: Questions from the Sky. San Jose, Calif.:
 San José Museum of Art; San Francisco: Hardy
 Marks, 2015.
Hung, Wu, ed. *Hung Liu: Great Granary.* Hong Kong:
 Timezone 8, 2010.
Kelley, Jeff. *Hung Liu: Apsaras.* New York: Nancy Hoffman
 Gallery, 2009.
———. *Hung Liu: Scales of History.* Fresno, Calif.: Fresno
 Art Museum, 2016.

Kelley, Jeff, and John Yau, eds. *Hung Liu: Daughter of China, Resident Alien.* Washington, D.C: American University Museum at the Katzen Arts Center, 2016.

Kuspit, Donald B. *Hung Liu.* San Francisco: Rena Bransten Gallery, 1993.

Moldenhauer, Susan. "Hung Liu: The Chinese Wyoming Portraits." Brochure. Laramie: University of Wyoming Art Museum, 2006.

Nash, Steven A. "Hung Liu and Jiu Jin Shan (Old Gold Mountain)." Brochure. San Francisco: Fine Arts Museums of San Francisco, 1994.

Poole, Kristin. *The Vanishing: Re-presenting the Chinese in the American West.* Sun Valley, Idaho: Sun Valley Center for the Arts, 2004.

Porges, Maria. *Hung Liu: Promised Land.* San Francisco: Rena Bransten Gallery, 2017.

Reichert, Rachelle. *Hung Liu: Qianshan, Grandfather's Mountain.* New York: Nancy Hoffman Gallery, 2013.

Reichert, Rachelle, Lori Fogarty, Drew Johnson, and David Pagel. *Hung Liu: American Exodus.* New York: Nancy Hoffman Gallery, 2016.

Tom, Chip. "The Other Side: Chinese and Mexican Immigration to America." Brochure for exhibition featuring the work of Hung Liu and Andrea Bowers, Margarita Cabrera, Tony de los Reyes, Blane De St. Croix, and Zhi Lin. Houston: Asia Society, 2015.

Tromble, Meredith, Glen Helfand, and David Salgado. *Hung Liu: ZZ (Bastard Paintings).* New York: Nancy Hoffman Gallery, 2007.

Zurko, Kathleen McManus, ed. *Hung Liu: A Ten-Year Survey, 1988-1998.* Wooster, Ohio: College of Wooster Art Museum, 1998.

Further Reading

Chiu, Melissa, ed. *Breakout: Chinese Art outside China.* Milan: Charta, 2006.

Duc, Marie. *Dissidence: The Rise of Chinese Contemporary Art in the West.* Cambridge, Mass.: MIT Press, 2018.

Higa, Karin. "What Is an Asian American Woman Artist?" In *Art/Women/California 1950-2000: Parallels and Intersections,* edited by Diana Burgess Fuller and Daniela Salvioni, 81–94. Berkeley: University of California Press; San Jose: San José Museum of Art, 2002.

Hung, Wu, ed. *Zooming In: Histories of Photography in China.* London: Reaktion, 2016.

Hung, Wu, ed., with Peggy Wang. *Contemporary Chinese Art: Primary Documents.* New York: Museum of Modern Art, 2010.

Lippard, Lucy R. *Mixed Blessings: New Art in a Multicultural America.* New York: Pantheon, 1990.

Machida, Margo. *Unsettled Visions: Contemporary Asian American Artists and the Social Imaginary.* Durham, N.C.: Duke University Press, 2009.

Munroe, Alexandra, with Philip Tinari and Hou Hanru. *Art and China after 1989: Theater of the World.* New York: Guggenheim Museum, 2017.

Partridge, Elizabeth. *Dorothea Lange: Grab a Hunk of Lightning.* San Francisco: Chronicle, 2013.

Yang, Alice. *Why Asia? Contemporary Asian and Asian American Art.* Edited by Jonathan Hay and Mimi Young. New York: New York University Press, 1998.

Acknowledgments

I met Hung Liu when she was serving as a juror for the National Portrait Gallery's 2013 Outwin Boochever Portrait Competition. We were reviewing the entries when she relayed advice that she had frequently shared with her students: "In order to make a good portrait, you must paint something you believe in." I was struck by Liu's commitment to her practice, her brilliant mind, her quick wit, and her deeply generous spirit. Our intellectual and creative bond formed quickly. I soon found myself in her sunny studio in Oakland, absorbed in her work, for hours, while listening to stories of her extraordinary life's journey. As I studied the artist's layered, textured, and colorful canvases and learned about how her life experiences relate to her subject choices, I felt an urgency that the National Portrait Gallery must organize a retrospective on her searing and transformative portraiture.

Liu brings those who have been on the margins of history to the center of the narrative by creating monumental portrayals that testify to the resilience of the human spirit. Her brushstrokes are imbued with vivid memories of her childhood in China, evoking both the strength and tenderness of her family members in the face of war and displacement. Above all, her art channels the courage, persistence, and hope that is within her and that draws her to her portrait subjects. The stories of struggle, told through a feminist lens, offer new perspectives on history and convey universal truths. At this moment of healing and rebuilding, on so many levels, her work provides a path forward for so many of us who have suffered loss. I lost my own father during the pandemic,

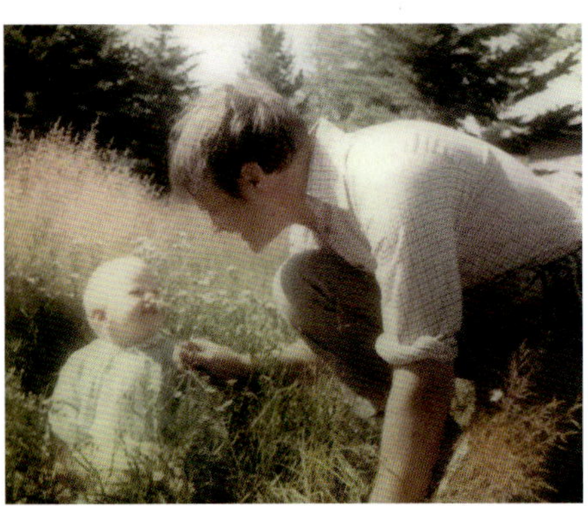

The author with her father at Jackson Lake, Wyoming, 1972

and I looked to Liu and her work to guide me in his last days. I shared with her a photograph, from 1972, of my father holding a field flower as a gift for me while I adoringly smiled at him. I told her I imagined what she might have been doing at that moment, in her student days in the countryside. Our worlds were very different then, but the bonds we shared with our families, especially our fathers, would one day unite us.

Wildflowers and dandelions appear in her work as symbols of new beginnings and regeneration. I dedicate this book to Hung Liu's father, Xia Peng, and to my father, Robert L. W. Moss. Their spirits travel with us in all we do.

Hung Liu's husband, Jeff Kelley, is an arts writer and curator who provided immeasurable insight. He penned the valuable Chronology in this volume and helped coordinate the Artists' Reflections. Those reflections attest to Hung Liu's generosity in the field, as do the essays by Nancy Lim, Lucy R. Lippard, Elizabeth Partridge, and Philip Tinari. Having the chance to discuss Liu's work with each of these remarkable individuals has been a gift. Our conversations have surely brought us closer to ensuring that *Hung Liu: Portraits of Promised Lands* reflects the artist's humanistic vision and groundbreaking contributions to portraiture.

We had the good fortune to partner with Yale University Press, and this book is the product of an inspired collaboration with their team. In particular, I wish to thank Amy Canonico, Heidi Downey, and Mary Mayer for their invaluable insight and unwavering commitment to the project. We are also grateful to Raychel Rapazza, Laura Hensley, Robin Charney, and Enid Zafran for their conscientious editorial work. Book designers Miko McGinty and Rita Jules possess astonishing skill and imagination; it has been a privilege working with them. At the museum, Rhys Conlon, head of publications, served as our brilliant, insightful, and dedicated editor, whose keen artistic eye is also very much part of each page of the book. She was joined by the museum's editor, Sarah McGavran, whose comments further strengthened the manuscript. All of these individuals made my role joyful and rewarding.

I am deeply grateful for the visionary leadership of the National Portrait Gallery's director, Kim Sajet, with whom Hung Liu and I have shared many conversations and dinners over the years, both in the Bay Area and in Washington, D.C. I also feel fortunate to have had the generous support of Gwendolyn DuBois Shaw and the steadfast guidance of Brandon Brame Fortune. My kind and inspiring colleagues in the curatorial department kept me focused whenever obstacles emerged. I extend deepest thanks to my excellent interns and researchers who have made contributions to the exhibition over time:

Libby Fischer, Elizabeth Ho-Sing-Loy, Moselle Kleiner, Jiete Li, Katie O'Hara, Samantha Page, Isabel Ruiz, and Sara Sims Wilbanks.

Claire Kelly, head of exhibitions, and Allison Keilman, exhibition program specialist, coordinated the moving parts and countless logistics of the project with grace, professionalism, and collegiality. I am grateful to Todd Gardner, Laura Hovenac, Dale Hunt, Wayne Long, Marissa Olivas, and Jennifer Wodzianski, all in the office of the registrar, for their dedication in bringing the show to fruition. In the office of design and production, Michael Baltzer, Peter Crellin, Tibor Waldner, and Caroline Wooden developed an elegant setting for audiences to experience the power of Liu's art. I also wish to thank Alex Cooper, Mark Gulezian, and Grant Lazer, in the office of exhibition technology, and Deb Sisum, in the office of new media, for their invaluable contributions to both the in-person and online versions of the presentation. While caring for the objects and their frames, conservators Im Chan, Christina Finlayson, and Lou Molnar provided invaluable expertise. The exhibition could not have happened without them.

Once an exhibition opens, its success depends largely on the work of the museum's audience engagement team. Rebecca Kasemeyer, who directs the department, along with Kaia Black, Caitlin Blake, Ashleigh Coren, Beth Evans, Vanessa Jones, Jocelyn Kho, Geri Provost Lyons, Irina Rubenstein, and Briana Zavadil White, have ensured that the exhibition reaches countless visitors in sensitive and innovative ways. Concetta Duncan, head of communications, along with Brendan Kelly, Gaby Sama, and Karen Vidángos, managed the demands of today's fast-paced media outlets with the National Portrait Gallery's signature warmth and professionalism. In the office of advancement, I thank Megan Beck, Raven Bradburn, Lindsay Gabryszak, Sydney Golden, Matthew Gray, Sarah Mazzoleni, Jen Moran, Hannah Pfaltzgraff, Brandon Pinzini, and Kristy Snaman.

The National Portrait Gallery's staff worked closely with colleagues in other sectors of the Smithsonian Institution. I extend my thanks to Alejandro Gutierrez in the office of contracting, who oversaw many agreements and contracts as we developed the book. I am also deeply grateful to the leadership team of Smithsonian American Women's History Initiative and to Lisa Sasaki at the Smithsonian Asian Pacific American Center for providing generous financial support to make the exhibition possible. And I extend heartfelt thanks to Smithsonian Secretary Lonnie Bunch III for leading with grace and compassion. Secretary Bunch's leadership made it possible to move forward with the planning and implementation of a major loan exhibition even as the Smithsonian faced myriad challenges of closure during the pandemic.

This exhibition would not have been possible without the generosity of the individuals and institutions who allowed their works by Hung Liu to travel to the National Portrait Gallery. We thank the following lenders: Allen Memorial Art Museum, Oberlin College; Dallas Museum of Art; Denver Art Museum; San Francisco Museum of Modern Art; San José Museum of Art; Sig Anderman; Dr. Matthias Bolten and Mr. Matthias Brücklmeier; the Castellano-Wood Family; Karen and Robert Duncan; Bill and Christy Gautreaux; Nancy and Peter Gennet; Janet L. Holmgren; Tim and Donna Jones; Michael Klein; Joan and Roger Mann; Peter and Dorothea Perrin; David and Debbie Popper; Richard and Marcy Schwartz, Entrust for Ariel Steinbaum; Josef Vascovitz and Lisa Goodman; the Estate for Esther S. Weissman; and those collectors who prefer to remain anonymous. I owe my deepest thanks to Hung Liu's gallerists, particularly Rena Bransten, Tonya Turner Carroll, Nancy Hoffman, Walter Maciel, and Gail Severn, for their dedication to the exhibition and their commitment to ensuring Hung Liu's well-deserved place in the history of art.

As Hung Liu reminds us, "Things of the spirit stay with us much longer than things of the flesh." Indeed, Liu's generous spirit will be felt by all who encounter her work on these pages and in this exhibition. For this monumental gift to us all, I thank Hung Liu.

Dorothy Moss
Curator of Painting and Sculpture
Coordinating Curator, Smithsonian American Women's History Initiative
National Portrait Gallery

Index

Numbers in bold indicate catalogue entries from the unfolioed plates sections; page numbers in italics indicate figures.

A

action paintings, 71, 79, *80*
Ai Weiwei, 119, 189, 195
Americanization and American dreams, 72, 121
anonymous subjects, 15, 22, 76, 89, 103, 121
Antin, Eleanor and David, 13
Auspicious Cranes (12th-century Chinese silk painting), 195
avant-garde movement, 116–17, 175

B

Baker, Kenneth, 195
"Ballad of Mulan," 14
Barthes, Roland, 16
Beijing: Central Academy of Fine Arts, 12, 13, 75, 101, 118, 119, 175, 181, 189; Children's Palace of Culture, 27; Girls' Middle School, 91, 185; Jingshan School, 100, 187; Normal University, 91, 93, 185; Teacher's College, 10, *11,* 100, 187, *187*
Bemis, Polly, 80–81, *81,* 195
Bey, Dawoud, 18
bound feet, 14, 75, 76, 80, 81, 83, **cat. 25**
Boxer Rebellion, 83

C

calligraphy, 81, 101, 190
Capp Street Project (San Francisco), 72, *72,* 86n1, *114, 174,* 191
cave drawings (Dunhuang), 75, 119, 189, 190

Central Academy of Fine Arts (Beijing), 12, 13, 75, 101, 118, 119, 175, 181, 189
Chagoya, Enrique, 172, 193
Changchun, China, 20, 22n2, 90–91, 183, 197
Chen, Danqing, 180
Chicago, Judy, 173, 201
childhood, 10, *17, 19,* 20, *26,* 27, 28, 98–105, 194
Chin, Mel, 174
Chinese avant-garde art, 115–18
Chinese Exclusion Act, 174
circle motif. *See* ring symbol, use of
citizens, 18, 172, 173
citizenship, 73, 116, 174, 177, 191
collage, 15, 80, 81
colors, meaning of, 15–16, *17,* 28, 29, 175, 180
copying, 13, 189, 23n19
countryside, 10, 16, 20, 25, 29, 93, 94, 95, 96, 100, 112, 178, 183, 186, 188, 193
communist (and communism), 6, 7, 25, 27, 28, 31, 34, 74, 90, 91, 93, 100, 101, 183
"Cookie, Fortune," 82, *114,* 115, 172, 174, 177, **cat. 18**
Cotter, Holland, 18
cranes, imagery of, 81, 104–5
Cultural Revolution (1966–76), 5, 10, 20, 25–36, 74, 82, 93, 110, 178, 185, 201, **cat. 17**
Currin, John, 116

D

Dadu Lianghe, 25, 26, 28, 30–31, *94,* 95, 186
Daughters of China (film), 83, 196
death, 5, 6, 14, 73, 81, 93, 174, 193, 198
Dixon, Maynard, 96, 97
drips and dripping paint, 8, 9–10, 16, 82, 85, 116, 180, 192

E

ecological crises, 79
'85 New Wave, 116–17
empathy, 8, 9, 17, 71, 105–6
Engels, Friedrich, 77, *77*
Evans, Walker, 99

F

faces in portraiture, 7, 8, 9, 14, 16, 78, 89, 178
family of Hung Liu. *See* Juan Yu (daughter-in-law); Kelley, Casimir ("Cas") Arthur (grandson); Kelley, Jeff (husband); Kelley, Ling Chen (son); Liu Weihua (grandfather); Liu Zongguang (mother); Liu Zongshi (aunt); Liu Zongtian (uncle); Liu Zongyu (aunt); Wang Jushou (grandmother); Xia Peng (father)
family depicted in paintings by Liu, 10, **cats. 19, 21–23, 44**
family portraits of Liu family, 5–23, *6–7;* destruction of, 2, 5, 36; father, **cat. 22;** grandfather, *7, 10,* 13–14, *15,* 16; grandmother, *7,* 14, **cat. 21;** Hung Liu as child, *6–7,* 16, *17;* Hung Liu's identity based on, 18; Hung Liu with her cousin, *185;* Hung Liu with her father, 18, *18,* **cat. 22;** Hung Liu with her mother, *7, 7, 184;* mother, 16, *21,* 22, *73,* **cat. 19;** preservation of, 6, 15; son, 16, *19,* 19–20, *19–20,* **cat. 23;** studio photographs, 6, 15, 16; women's prominence in, 6
Fang Lijun, 197, 199
Farber, Manny, 13
Farm Security Administration (FSA), 91, 97, 100, 107n1
feminism, 14, 83, 197
Fischer, Hal, 13
the forgotten and invisible, 9, 14, 22, 76, 83, 89, 102, 103–4
Foster, Hal: *Art in America,* 116
Fox, William L., 116, 195

G

gaze, 78, 80. *See also* faces in
portraiture
gender: changes in gender roles, 83,
85; equality/inequality, 14, 83,
172, 180; International
Conference on Chinese Women
and Visual Representation (2011),
197; women as family historians
and caretakers, 73; women at
work as theme, *172*, 193
Geng Jianyi: *Form and Certificate (Can
Be Confessed)*, 115, *115*
Goddess of Democracy, 75
Gold Rush, 80, 103, 192, 195; Gold
Mountain, 103, 192
Great Depression, 20, 89, 95–100, 112,
172
Great Leap Forward, 28, 91, 184
green card, 110, 177

H

Happenings movement (1960s), 13,
102, 180, 190
Herringer, Mary Ellen, 202
Hiroshima and Nagasaki, 104–5
history, recording of, 3, 121–22;
Liu as agent of historical inquiry,
178; "summoning ghosts," 16;
truth about past events and
remembrance of past lives, 175.
See also family portraits of Liu
family; Lange, Dorothea; memo-
ries; photographs
Hong, Yu, 119, 175, 195, 197, 199
Hong Kong, 101, 112, 121, 190, 193, 197,
199, 203
How to Draw and Paint (Central China
Television show), 118, 187
Hutcheon, Linda, 2

I

identity and identity politics, 8, 82, 83,
121, 172, 177, 180
immigration and immigrant status, 13,
73, 86, 101, 110, 115, 121, 172, 174,
190, 199. *See also* green card; Liu,
Hung, artwork by: *Resident Alien;*
refugees, images of
impressionism, 172
internment. *See* Japanese American
internment during World War II

J

Japanese American internment during
World War II, *104,* 104–5
Japanese occupation of China, 83, 95
Juan Yu (daughter-in-law), 197

K

Kaprow, Allan, 13, *13,* 18, 76, 102, 175,
180, 190
Kelley, Casimir ("Cas") Arthur (grand-
son), 203
Kelley, Jeff (husband), 13, *13,* 72, 82,
102, 180, 190, 195, 196, 197,
199, 200
Kelley, Mike, 193
Kentridge, William: *Felix in Exile,*
116, *117*
Kim, Elaine, 16
Kimbell Art Museum (Fort Worth), 191
Kirby, Peter, 13, *13*
Kollwitz, Käthe, 2–3
Korean comfort women, 195, **cat. 30**
Kuomintang (Nationalist Army), 6, 7,
22n2, 90–91, 93, 183
Kuspit, Donald, 80

L

laborers, photographs of, 2–3, *90, 94,
98, 99. See also* villagers in Dadu
Lianghe
landscapes, 27, 30, 35, *74,* 75
Lange, Dorothea, 89–90, 95–100, *97;*
Liu's paintings inspired by, 17, 20,
78–79, 91, 103–6, *105,* 112, 172, 198,
200–201, 202, 203, **cats. 45–52;**
works by: "All races serve the
crops in California," 97, *98;* An
*American Exodus: A Record of
Human Erosion* (with Paul
Schuster Taylor), *106; Coachella
Housing, Coachella Valley,
California, 97;* "Mexican Labor,
Imperial Valley, Calif.," *90;*
"Mexican mother in California,"
99, *99;* "Migrant agricultural
worker's family," 91, *92;* "Migrant
children. Merrill, Klamath County,
Oregon," *95; Migrant Mother*
series, 79, 91, *91–92; Mississippi
Delta Negro Children, 99, 100;*
Mochida family awaiting evacua-
tion bus in Hayward, California,
104, *104; White Angel Bread Line,
San Francisco, 96,* 96–97; *Young
Cotton Picker, San Joaquin Valley,*
99, *99*
large-scale paintings, 8, 16, 18, 193, 198
layers/layering in paintings, 8, 15, 22,
80, 81, 119
Lenin, Vladimir, 77, *77*
Li Singsong, 202
Ligon, Glenn, 15, 22n12
Lim, Nancy, essay by, 25–36
Lin Tianmiao, 195, 197, 199
Ling Chen Kelley (son), *19,* 19–20, 73,
74, 100–101, 102, 181, 189–91, 197
Lippard, Lucy R., 15; essay by, 71–87
Littlejohn, David, 198
Liu, Hung: as art teacher in Beijing,
100, 187, 190; awards and honors
given to, 191, 197, 201; birth of,
183; chronology of, 183–203;
compared to Lange, 89–90;
critical reception of, 110, 195, 198;
Cultural Revolution, rural resettlement during, 5, 10, 20, 25,
35–36, 74, 93–95, 110, 178, 186,
201; on disappointment of canceled 2019 exhibition in China,
112; early work of, 25–36; early
years of, 90–91, 183; education of,
10, 13, 30, 75, 91, 100, 101, 185;
family move to Beijing, 91, 184;
first exhibition in China since

departure (2004), 195; first marriage, 100–101, 189; first retrospective exhibition (1998), 193; first solo show in China (2008), 83, 109, *110;* first solo show in United States (1985), 190; immigration to United States, 13, 73, 101, 110, 190; learning English in school in China, 27, 91; at Mills College as art professor, 13, 111, 119, 178, 191, 193, 197; Oakland studio of, 119, *121,* 193; overview of life and career of, 112, 119–21, 183–203; paint box of, 101, *188,* 197, **cat. 1;** photographs of, *7, 11–13, 17, 19, 24, 72, 94, 121, 184–87, 189, 200;* return visits to China, 73–74, 119, 191, 192, 195, 196, 197, 199; reuniting with father, 18, 73–74, 183, 192; second marriage to Jeff Kelley, 72, 102, 190; self-portraits of, *27, 28,* 82, 172, 180, 192, 198, **cat. 18, cat. 20;** as UCSD student, 13, 20, 74, 76, 101–2, 189–90; at University of Texas at Arlington (1987), 191; U.S. citizenship of, 73, 191
Liu, Hung, artwork by
August, 172, **cat. 48**
Avant-Garde, 11, 192, 201, **cat. 20**
Blue Boy, 84–85, 85
The Botanist, 8, *10,* **cat. 44**
Boy with Hat in Winter (sketch), 75, **cat. 7**
Burial at Little Golden Village, 181
By the Rivers of Babylon, 102–3, 103
Catchers, 95, 172, **cat. 51**
Chinese in Idaho series, 80–81
Chinese in Idaho, Portrait I, 81
Chinese in Idaho, Portrait II, 80–81, **cat. 41**
Chinese in Idaho, Portrait IV, 80–81, **cat. 42**
Chinese patriotic stories series, 197
Chinese Pieta (from installation *Trauma),* 75, *75*
Chinese Profile II, **cat. 28**
Corn Carrier, 79, *80*

Cotton Picker, 99, 172, **cat. 46**
Dangling, 80–81, 195, **cat. 43**
Daughter of the Revolution, 192
Daughters of China series, 196, 197
drawing by Hung Liu, graded by her grandfather Liu Weihua, 13, *14*
ensemble paintings, 203
Father's Day, 18, 18–19, 74, 192, **cat. 22**
Goddess of Love, Goddess of Liberty, 14, 85, 191, **cat. 25**
Going Away, Coming Home, 173, 173, 195
Grandma, 14, 192, **cat. 21**
Hi Ho, 82
Imperial Consort, 193, **cat. 27**
Internees, 104, *105*
Laborer: Farm Hand (Clarence Weems), 172, **cat. 45**
Little Artist, 19, **cat. 23**
Ma, 192, **cat. 19**
Madonna, 85, 191, **cat. 26**
Man with Coat and Hat (sketch), 75, 95, **cat. 5**
Mao Zedong (sketch), *186*
Map No. 33, 198
Migrant Mother: Mealtime, 17, 91, 172, **cat. 47**
Mission Girls series, 20, 78, *78,* 195, **cats. 32–40**
Mission Girls 2, 78, **cat. 32**
Mission Girls 6, 78, **cat. 33**
Mission Girls 11, 78, **cat. 34**
Mission Girls 13, 78, **cat. 35**
Mission Girls 14, 78, **cat. 36**
Mission Girls 17, 78, **cat. 37**
Mission Girls 18, 78, **cat. 38**
Mission Girls 20, 78, **cat. 39**
Mission Girls 21, 78, **cat. 40**
Miss Y, 77–78, 192, **cat. 24**
Modern Time, 76–77, 77, 195
Mu Nu (Mother and Daughter), 83, *83*
Music of the Great Earth (Central Academy of Fine Arts canteen mural), 118, 175, *175,* 181, 189–90, 196
My Little Swan, 36, 36, 186
My Secret Freedom series, 200, 201

My Secret Freedom 1, 74, 75
My Secret Freedom 19, 30, *30*
Peeking Opera, 119, *120*
Plowboy, 172, **cat. 52**
Portraits of a Chinese Self, 82, 198
Qianshan: Grandfather's Mountain, 198
Rat Year diptychs, 82, *183,* 196, *196, 204–5*
Reading Room (mural), 191, 200
Red Flag Flowing, 82
Refugee: Mother and Son, 87n10
Refugee: Opera, 17, 91, 193, **cat. 31**
Refugee: Woman and Children, 193, **cat. 29**
Resident Alien, 82, 113–16, *114,* 172, 174, *174,* 177, 191, **cat. 18**
The River's Awakening, 35, *35,* 186
Sanctuary, 86, 99, 172, **cat. 50**
Self-Portrait, 27, *28*
September, 194, *194*
Sichuan earthquake series, 197
Sister Hoods (also known as *Sisters in Arms),* 78, *79*
Soldier, 34, *34*
South, 86, 72, **cat. 49**
Spare Tire, 199
Strange Fruit: Comfort Women, 193, **cat. 30**
Tis the Final Conflict series, *82,* 83
To Live 23: Slippers, January 17, 2012, 73, *73,* 197
To Live 26: Telephone, January 20, 2012, 73, *73,* 197
To Live 33: Bed, January 27, 2012, 73, *73,* 197
Village Photograph 4 (Paint Box), 95, **cat. 1**
Village Photograph 5 (Peasant Grandma), 35, 95, 178, *178,* 186,
Village Photograph 8 (Her Village), 95, 186, **cat. 3**
Village Photograph 10 (Water Children), 95, **cat. 2**
Village Photograph (Peasant Family Dinner), 34, *34,* 186
villagers in Dadu Lianghe (sketches), *26,* 27–28, 30–31, *31,* 95

Where Is Mao? 86n6, 112, *112,* 191, 194, **cats. 8–17**
Women Working: Loom, 172
Young Woman (sketch), 75, 95, **cat. 6**
Za Zhong series (*Bastard Paintings*), 178
Liu, Hung, exhibitions of
Alexander Ochs Gallery, Beijing (2011): *First Spring Thunder,* 197
American University Museum, Katzen Arts Center (2016): *Daughters of China,* 199
Arizona State University Art Museum and Boise Art Museum (2002): *Strange Fruit: New Paintings by Hung Liu,* 195
Art Scene Warehouse, Shanghai (2004): *Hung Liu: Lament,* 195
Art Scene Warehouse, Shanghai (2006): *Matriarchy: Hung Liu's New Work,* 195
Asian Art Museum, San Francisco (2015), 198
Asia Society, New York (1994): *Asia/America: Identities in Contemporary Asian American Art,* 192
Bard College (1997): *Hung Liu: Unfolding Memory—Embodying History,* 193
Beijing (2008): *Prodigal Daughter,* 83, 109, *110–11*
Capp Street Project, San Francisco (1988), 191
Chulalongkorn University, Bangkok, Thailand (2000): *Where is Mao? 2000,* 194
College of Wooster Art Museum (1998): *Hung Liu: A Ten-Year Survey 1988–1998,* 193
Corcoran Gallery of Art, Washington, D.C. (1993): *43rd Biennial Exhibition of Contemporary American Painting,* 192
Dallas/Fort Worth (1987), 191

de Young Museum, San Francisco (1994): *Jiu Jin Shan* installation, 192
de Young Museum, San Francisco (2021), 203
Fresno Art Museum (2017): *Hung Liu: Scales of History,* 200
F2 Gallery, Beijing (2008): *Daughters of China,* 196
Kemper Museum of Contemporary Art, Kansas City (2014): *Summoning Ghosts: The Art of Hung Liu,* 198
Nahan Contemporary Gallery, New York (1989): *Goddess of Love and Liberty,* 191
Nancy Hoffman Gallery, New York (2007): *Hung Liu: ZZ (Bastard Paintings),* 196
Nancy Hoffman Gallery, New York (2019): *This Land . . . ,* 202
National Portrait Gallery, Smithsonian Institution (2021): *Hung Liu: Portraits of Promised Lands,* 201
Oakland Museum of California (2013): *Summoning Ghosts: The Art of Hung Liu,* 198
Palm Springs Art Museum (2015): *Summoning Ghosts: The Art of Hung Liu,* 198
Rena Bransten Gallery, San Francisco (2003): *Hung Liu: Towards Peng-Lai,* 195
Rena Bransten Gallery, San Francisco (2007): *Daughters of China,* 196
Rena Bransten Gallery, San Francisco (2017): Lange-inspired paintings, 200
Russia, group exhibition (2000), 194
San Francisco Museum of Modern Art (2008): *Half-Life of a Dream: Contemporary Chinese Art from the Logan Collection,* 172, 196
San Francisco Museum of Modern Art (2018): *Art and China after 1989: Theater of the World,* 201

San José Museum of Art (2002): *Art/Women/California: Parallels and Intersections, 1950–2000,* 195
San José Museum of Art (2013): *Questions from the Sky: New Work by Hung Liu,* 198
Setagaya Art Museum and Asahi Shimbun, Japan (1996): *American Stories: Amidst Displacement and Transformation,* 193
Sheppard Gallery, University of Nevada, Reno (1985), 190
Smithsonian American Art Museum (1996): *American Kaleidoscope: Themes and Perspectives in Recent Art,* 193
Steinbaum Krauss Gallery, New York (1994): *Year of the Dog,* 192
Sun Valley Center for the Arts and Humanities (2005): *The Vanishing: Re-presenting the Chinese in the American West,* 195
Tamarind Institute, Albuquerque (2011): *(re)Pressed Memories,* 197
10 Chancery Lane Gallery, Hong Kong (2009): *Daughters of China,* 197
traveling show, global (2000): *Text and Subtext—Contemporary Art and Asian Women,* 194
UCCA Center for Contemporary Art: *Hung Liu: Passer-by* (canceled 2019), 110–12, 121–22, 202
Walter Maciel Gallery, Los Angeles (2008): *Rat Years,* 196
Walter Maciel Gallery, Los Angeles (2018): *My Secret Freedom* series, 201
Xin Beijing Art Gallery (2008): *Tai Cang (Great Granary),* 196
Liu Weihua (grandfather), 5–7, *7, 10,* 13–14, *14–15,* 90, 184, 185, 198; book by, 14, *15,* 195, **cat. 44**
Liu Xiaodong, 109, 119, 180, 195, 196, 199

Liu Zongguang (mother), 5–6, *7,* 13, 16, 20, *21,* 73, 90, 109, 119, 184, 190–92, 195, 196, 197; clothes made for Hung Liu by, 16, *17;* clothes made for Hung Liu's son by, 19; *Rainbow over the Pacific* (book on Hung Liu's life), 109, 196
Liu Zongshi (aunt), 7
Liu Zongtian (uncle), 7
Liu Zongyu (aunt), 7, *7,* 184, 190–91, 195
Lu Xun, 85

M

Machida, Margo, 78
Madonna figure, *65, 75,* 85
Mao Zedong, 16, 25, 34, 36, 80, 86n6, 91, 93, 101, 112–13, *112–13,* 183, 185, *186,* 187, **cats. 8–17**
Marshall, Kerry James, 8; *Better Homes, Better Gardens,* 9
Marx, Karl, 77, *77*
Marxism, 16, 195
meditation, repetition and copying, 23n19
Mei Lanfang, *84–85,* 85
memories, 2, 6, 9–10, 13, 15–16, 86, 175. *See also* family portraits of Liu family
migrant children, images of, 18, 20, 91, *95,* 104–5, *104–5,* **cat. 29.** *See also* childhood
Migrant Mother, 91, *92. See also* Lange, Dorothea
military labor/training, *11,* 33, 95, 185, *187*
Mills College, 13, 111, 119, 174, 181, 191, 193, 197
Mochida family, 104–5, *104–5*
Moss, Dorothy, essay by, 4–23
mourning, 73, 83, 105, 197. *See also* death
Mull, Martin, 176
multiculturalism, 2, 17, 20, 72, 73, 115
murals, 13, 18, 75, 100–102, 118, *175,* 181, 189, 195, 196, 198

N

Nationalist Army. *See* Kuomintang
Native American children, 78
nature, 81, 193
Nevada Museum of Art, 201
New Era of China, 110, 118
Niu Jun, 190
Nixon, Richard M., 112, *112,* 187, **cat. 16**
Nochlin, Linda, 3
"No U-Turn" poster (1989), 117, *118*

O

Oakland International Airport, 173, *173,* 195
Oakland Museum of California, 89, 105, 107n1, 197
Occidentalism, 86
Olympic Games (2008), 109, 119, 196
Orientalism, 78, 86

P

palimpsest, 81
Parks, Gordon, 97
Partridge, Elizabeth, essay by, 89–107
Party-approved motifs, Hung Liu's rejection of, 30–31, 80
Peking Opera, 85, *120*
People's Daily photo of Mao and Nixon (February 22, 1972), *112*
People's Liberation Army Navy, 7
photographs: architecture as compositional aid in, 34, 192; camera, as rarity in China, 33, 96; as documentation of China's revolutionary progress, 33; as gifts to villagers, 35–36; from grandfather's research trips, *10,* 14, *15,* 198; historical photographs, 5, 36, 76, 89, 103, 192; Hung Liu's first use of camera, 33–36, 95, 186; painterly nature of, 35; as source for paintings, 7, 13, 14, 17, 22, *78,* 103, 116, 176; veracity of, 2. *See*

also family portraits of Liu family; Lange, Dorothea
politics: artwork as propaganda, 101, 102, 104, 195; political upheaval and, 75, 90, 179. *See also* socialist realism
Pollock, Griselda, 78
portraiture: faces in, 7, 8, 9, 14, 16, 78, 89, 178; of marginalized people, 9, 14, 22, 71, 76, 83, 89, 102, 103–4; old photographs in Hung Liu's work, 71, 76, 89; use of term, 71. *See also* family portraits of Liu family; Lange, Dorothea; photographs
post-Orientalism, 86
"preserve and dissolve" technique. *See* drips and dripping paint
prostitutes, images of, 14, 18, 76, 78, 81, 85, 102, 191
pseudo-realism, 29

Q

Qianshan, China, 6, *10,* 13–14, 15, 185, 195, 198

R

railroad workers from China in United States, 201
Rauschenberg, Robert, 190, 191
realism. *See* socialist realism
Red Guards, 5, 6, 93, 185
Red Lantern Girls, 83
Reform era and Opening of China, 110, 112, 189
refugees, images of, 18–19, 20, 91, 97, 102–3, 193, **cat. 29, cat. 31**
reverse mirroring, 78
ring symbol, use of, 81–82, 175
Rolland, Romain, 20
Roosevelt, Franklin Delano, 97, 100
Roth, Moira, 13, 77

S

Sajet, Kim, 201, foreword by, 2–3
Salgado, David, 196, 201
San Francisco: Capp Street Project, 72, *72,* 86n1, *114, 174,* 191; Moscone Center, 198; Museum of Modern Art (SFMOMA), 172, 196, 198, 201, 203; Women's March (2017), 20, 200, *200*
San José Museum of Art, 195, 198, 201
Sano, Emily, 191
Schama, Simon, 179
Schjeldahl, Peter, 116
seal carving, 101
semiotics, 16, 117
Shan Lianxiao: *I Want to Live Like Her (Carry on the Revolution to the End),* 27–28, *29*
shape of canvas, 4–5, 18, 77, 85, 180, 192, 198, 203, 81, 84–85, 192, **cats. 19–22, cat. 25**
Sherald, Amy, 176
Simpson, Lorna, 13, 190
social inequities, 172
socialist realism, 13, 29, 80, 82, 101, 116, 180
socialist surrealism, 29
social realism, 82, 116
South African Apartheid, 116
Stalin, Joseph, 77, *77*
subversiveness, 172
"supreme leader" portraiture, 2. *See also* Mao Zedong
Syjuco, Stephanie, 177

T

Tamblyn, Christine, 13, 190
Taylor, Paul Schuster, 97, *106*
tears, 10, 80, 116
Thomas, Lava, 15, *22*n12, 178
Thompson, Florence Owens, 91
Thomson, John, 77
Tiananmen Square massacre (1989), *75,* 75, 110, *120,* 191

time: depiction of, 10, 77; temporal layering effect, 15, 22. *See also* history, recording of
Tinari, Philip, 201, 202; essay by, 109–22
truth, 22, 93, 104, 175, 193, 195
Turner Carroll, Tonya, 201

U

universality of faces, 8, 14, 16
University of California, San Diego (UCSD), 13, 20, 74, 76, 101–2, 189–90
University of Oregon, Eugene, 201
University of Texas at Arlington, 190, 191

V

Van Gogh, Vincent, *76,* 77
villagers in Dadu Lianghe (sketches), *26,* 27–28, 30–31, *31,* 95

W

Wang Gongxin, 195, 197, 199
Wang Guangyi, 112; *Mao Zedong: Red Grid No. 2, 113*
Wang Jushou (grandmother), 7, *7,* 14, 20, 184, 189
Wang Youshen: "No U-Turn," 117, *118*
Warhol, Andy, 116
warrior women, 83
Weems, Carrie Mae, 8, *8,* 13, 18, 179; *From Here I Saw What Happened and I Cried* series, *8*
"Western" style developed by Hung Liu, 76–77
Wolcott, Marion Post, 97
women. *See* feminism; gender
Women's March (2017), 20, 200, *200*

X

Xia Peng (father), 6, 9, *18,* 18–19, 73–74, 183, 192, 193, **cat. 22**
Xiaodong, Liu, 109, 119, 180, 195, 196, 199

Y

Yau, John, 116
Young Pioneers of the Soviet Union, 16
Yu Hong, 119, 175, 195, 197, 199

Z

Zhang Dali: *Second History 85: Chengzhuang Agriculture Labour School, 32,* 33
Zhi Lin, 201
Zifeng Ling, 83
Zoetrope: All-Story, 201

Illustration Credits

Unless otherwise noted, all images reproduced in this book are courtesy of and/or © Hung Liu.

Artists' Copyrights
p. 8: © Carrie Mae Weems and courtesy of the artist and Jack Shainman Gallery, New York.
p. 9: © Kerry James Marshall.
p. 113: © Wang Guangyi.
p. 115: © Geng Jianyi.
p. 117: © William Kentridge.

Photographic Credits
FIGURES
pp. 4, 5: Daniella Mia.
pp. 6, 7, 10 (fig. 6), 11, 15, 17, 26, 28, 31, 94, 185–86: digital images by John Janca.
pp. 8, 96, 106: digital images © The Museum of Modern Art/ Licensed by SCALA/Art Resource, NY.
pp. 9, 112: courtesy of the Denver Art Museum.
pp. 10 (fig. 7), 108–9: courtesy of the San Francisco Museum of Modern Art.
p. 29: courtesy of the Chrysler Museum of Art.
p. 32: courtesy of the artist and Eli Klein Gallery.
pp. 70–71: Photo by Colin Doyle.
pp. 72, 114, 174: from the Capp Street Project Archive at California College of the Arts Libraries, San Francisco, California.
pp. 79, 81, 82, 103: courtesy of Rena Bransten Gallery.
p. 83: courtesy of the Kemper Museum of Contemporary Art. Photo: Gamma One Conversions.
pp. 84–85: Adam Reich.
pp. 88–89, 105: courtesy of Nancy Hoffman Gallery.
pp. 90, 97 (fig. 7), 99 (fig. 10): © The Dorothea Lange Collection, the Oakland Museum of California.
pp. 91, 92: courtesy of the Prints and Photographs Division, Library of Congress, Washington, D.C.

pp. 95, 97 (fig. 8), 98, 99 (fig. 11), 100: Prints and Photographs Division, Library of Congress, Washington, D.C.
p. 104: courtesy of the National Archives and Records Administration, Records of the War Relocation Authority.
p. 113: courtesy of M+Sigg Collection, Hong Kong.
p. 115: courtesy of ShanghART Gallery.
p. 117: The Solomon R. Guggenheim Foundation / Art Resource, NY.
p. 118: courtesy of Wang Youshen and Asia Art Archive.
p. 121: James McManus.
p. 172: © San José Museum of Art. Photograph by Douglas Sandberg.
p. 178: courtesy of the artist and Trillium Graphics.
pp. 188, 204–5: John Janca.
p. 210: Marguerite McKee Moss

CATALOGUE ENTRIES
cats. 5–7, 21, 27, 29, 45, 47, 48, 52: John Janca.
cats. 8–17: courtesy of the Denver Art Museum.
cats. 18, 28: © San José Museum of Art. Photograph by Douglas Sandberg.
cat. 19: courtesy of the Allen Memorial Art Museum.
cats. 20, 44: courtesy of the San Francisco Museum of Modern Art.
cat. 22: Daniella Mia.
cat. 24: Seymour & McIntosh Photography.
cat. 25: courtesy of the Dallas Museum of Art.
cat. 26: Mark Gulezian.
cat. 30 (cover): photo by Bill Ganzel, Ganzel Group Communications, Lincoln, NE.
cats. 32–43: photos by Colin Doyle.
cats. 46 (back cover), 50: courtesy of Nancy Hoffman Gallery.
cats. 49, 51: courtesy of Turner Carroll Gallery.